Documenting Movements, Identity, and Popular Culture in Latin America

Papers of the Forty-Fourth Annual Meeting of the
SEMINAR ON THE ACQUISITION OF
LATIN AMERICAN LIBRARY MATERIALS

Nashville, Tennessee
May 30 – June 3, 1999

Richard F. Phillips
Editor

SALALM Secretariat
Benson Latin American Collection
The General Libraries
The University of Texas at Austin

ISBN: 0-917617-63-0

Documenting Movements, Identity, and
Popular Culture in Latin America

SALALM Secretariat
Benson Latin American Collection
The General Libraries
The University of Texas at Austin

Contents

III. Women and Identity

IV. Society

Preface

As I look back on my Peace Corps service days in Brazil in 1971–1972, I recall being profoundly struck with an eager interest in all things *sertanejo,* an expression of the truly essential character of the hearty folks of the rugged interior of Pernambuco. In my mind it is no great leap to see where the inspiration for the theme of the 1999 meeting of the Seminar on the Acquisition of Latin American Library Materials (SALALM) came from. One draws from experience.

Indeed, I have always drawn upon my experiences. I grew up in a diverse community in eastern New York and count among my friends many Shinnecock Indians from the nearby reservation. I also shared many good times during my youth with migrant workers in the area. To me, living in Pernambuco was in some ways like living in that community.

But, of course, Latin America is not the same as it was in the 1970s. Ensuing years have been marked by an opening of the cultural and political channels of Latin American societies to marginalized groups. Voiceless groups are suddenly organizing, sharing experiences, clamoring for opportunity, and generating documentation of their goals, dreams, and objectives.

Faced with new flows of information in formats and vehicles previously little known and often undervalued, libraries, librarians, and *libreros* have had to look for new ways to identify, collect, and organize such materials. Nontraditional publishing presents many challenges for both collector and dealer.

I want to thank many people who helped organize the SALALM meeting. Paula Covington, local arrangements chair, provided vision and "savvy." Her staff and assistants were extremely valuable in many ways. I am also very grateful to Vanderbilt University for its commitment to making our meeting a success.

Thanks also go to the panel organizers and participants. Their ideas formed the SALALM XLIV program. I want to express my gratitude to the SALALM Secretariat as well for its efficiency and helpfulness. Let me also acknowledge Dale Canelas, Sam Gowan, John Ingram, and Mary Gallant at the University of Florida Libraries for their support. Carole Bird, Justino Llanque-Chana, Irmi Feldman, and Paul Losch also merit my profound thanks.

Last, family and friends too numerous to mention are in my prayers and thoughts. These are special people. These are special times.

I. Challenges for Librarianship

1. Considerations for Outsourcing Cataloging

Claire-Lise Bénaud

Outsourcing is the transfer of an internal function to an outside vendor. In its most basic form, it is a fancy term for paying someone else to do your work. It implies that the "someone else" will provide the product cheaper than can be achieved in-house. The growth of outsourcing in cataloging departments in the 1990s can be attributed to budgetary shortages and advances in technology. The practice is perhaps reinforced by cataloging's lack of visibility in the library. The cataloging community has been vocal about outsourcing: the main concern for catalogers remains the accuracy of the bibliographic record and the integrity of the online catalog, while the main concerns for library administrators are cost and productivity. The recipient of the bibliographic record—the library user—is often not consulted.[1]

General Considerations

Most academic libraries today are not receiving substantial funding increases. If new acquisitions have to be made, if library hours have to be maintained, if reference desks have to be staffed, the funds to support these services must come from the library's budget. Cataloging is invisible to patrons and administrators, whereas reference services, teaching, and computer terminals for Internet access are visible to all. The high cost associated with processing every book and serial and the perception that cataloging can be done more cheaply by a vendor make cataloging an obvious target for budget cuts. Cataloging is also a good target because, unlike other library departments, it is a production department: it is easy to quantify output and to specify the number of records that can be purchased from a vendor. Outsourcing also allows administrators to budget a predictable amount of money for cataloging. In contrast, hiring staff does not guarantee that a certain number of books will be cataloged. When a library finds itself in the opposite situation, that is, when it receives extra funds, these typically go toward acquisitions. There is usually no corresponding funding increase for processing, and administrators are more willing to spend money on outsourcing than to hire more staff.

Although the motivation to outsource is based on the need to save money, technology is making outsourcing of cataloging a viable option. For example, records can be loaded into databases quickly and effortlessly and optical scanning technology is readily available, making it easy to add table of contents, for example. Vendors are taking full advantage of these technological developments. While libraries may purchase cataloging records from various vendors, they may also purchase a full package of products from a single vendor: the book itself, the matching catalog records (bibliographic, authority, and/or item), and physical processing for the book.

The position of the OPAC relative to other databases also affects how cataloging is perceived. Web-based products are playing a more prominent role and many no longer see the OPAC as the library's central database. For example, at the University of New Mexico (UNM) General Library, access to the electronic journal holdings is more efficient through a specialized Web page than through the OPAC. The OPAC is simply one of many databases available to library users. Vendor-produced indexes and full-text databases such as First-Search, Lexis/Nexis, and EBSCO are commonplace. Other libraries may follow the same logic for their OPAC, that is, they may have it produced and maintained by a commercial vendor rather than by the library's cataloging department. It is conceivable that libraries can build an OPAC without a cataloging department.

Outsourcing: An Evolving Concept

The concept of outsourcing has evolved during the last three decades. The business literature reveals that in the 1970s outsourcing simply involved a supplier providing a service to a company by managing and performing a function formerly done in-house. During the 1980s there evolved closer collaboration between the vendor and the company, while in the 1990s the trend is toward fuller partnerships. Consider the following definition: "Outsourcing really means finding *new suppliers* and *new ways* to secure the delivery of raw materials, goods, components and services."[2]

Similarly, outsourcing cataloging was at first limited to selective, well-defined processes (retrospective conversion, authority control processing for an initial load of bibliographic records into the OPAC, or government documents). Today it encompasses all of these processes and can also include purchasing bibliographic and authority records for books received on approval plans, books received on firm order, and, in certain cases, all the books purchased by a library. Vendors can also offer value-added services, functions not routinely performed by catalogers, such as adding table of contents. A shift is taking place from selective outsourcing to total outsourcing.

What to Outsource

As a rule, companies outsource nonessential activities and retain in-house essential functions, referred to as core competencies. These activities are essential to the identity of the organization and if taken away would eliminate the need for the company to be in business. Core competencies, also called "key," "critical," or "fundamental," are not easy to define. They are a set of skills rather than specific tasks. Organizations cannot function only by performing core competencies. A host of peripheral operations which provide the infrastructure are also needed. Thus, a car manufacturer, a software company, and a library all need personnel departments, janitorial services, and security services. These functions enable them to operate but do not define their business. Outsourcing such peripheral operations allows the company to pay more attention to its core competencies. Defining what the core competencies are is a subject of debate and has far-reaching consequences for the labor force.

Whether to outsource cataloging depends upon whether cataloging is considered a core competency: is it mission-critical? If so, to what degree can it be outsourced? Until recently, cataloging was considered central to a library's mission. The very coreness of cataloging is now under scrutiny. How can a function defined as "core" become less "core"? Part of the explanation lies in the fact that the model has changed. Advances in automation and cooperative cataloging make it possible for large amounts of cataloging data to be produced, shared, and distributed to a virtually unlimited number of libraries. Along these lines, Arnold Hirshon argues that while the product of cataloging is a core function, its creation is not.[3]

Selective outsourcing, an increasingly common practice, does not fully answer the question of "coreness." The level of editing performed may define what is a core cataloging activity for a particular library. On the one hand, some may argue that original cataloging is core but copy is not. Others may say that if substantial copy editing is performed, then cataloging is core. On the other hand, total outsourcing, a rare practice, clearly means that cataloging is no longer considered a core competency and no longer represents a basic professional activity. Even though what is core and what is not is not completely answered, a set of circumstances leads every library to evaluate its in-house cataloging operation. Usually these circumstances involve the continued erosion of the budget, reductions in staff, the existence of backlogs, the perceived high cost of cataloging, a reemphasis on public services, or inefficient cataloging departments.

Why Outsource?

Economic Gains

Cost savings.—Cataloging costs libraries money, whether outsourced or performed in-house. The question is: will outsourcing cost less or more than in-house cataloging for a similar level of quality? Outsourcing cataloging reduces staff salaries, overhead costs, database searching and telecommunications charges, hardware and software costs, and the need for training and evaluation. Vendors can provide catalog records more cheaply. Rather than cataloging the same book hundreds of times, vendors benefit from an economy of scale, selling the same record to many libraries. Savings occur when libraries outsource mainstream materials. For example, a vendor may resell the cataloging for mainstream publications over and over but may not be able to do so for esoteric materials held by a handful of libraries. Similarly, for older or foreign language materials, it is unlikely that the vendor can find acceptable copy or it may have to perform original cataloging. In that case, vendors do not realize economies of scale and pass on the cost to libraries, requiring them to pay a premium for this type of cataloging.[4]

Greater Efficiency.—While a basic motivation of outsourcing is to cut costs, the business literature claims that almost all outsourcing arrangements are vulnerable to failure if the organization is concerned only with cost savings. In the view of these observers, the vendor's function is not only to save money for the organization but also to help the organization become more competitive.[5] In cataloging, this translates into greater efficiency, more timely cataloging, increased productivity, and value-added services.

In academic libraries, a cataloger is a librarian first, and a cataloger second. Studies show that original catalogers spend only 40 percent of their time cataloging.[6] Another survey shows that professional catalogers spend 22.1 hours per week cataloging in ARL libraries (and 20.6 hours per week in non-ARL libraries) and that paraprofessional catalogers spend 30.1 hours per week cataloging in ARL libraries (and 28.9 hours per week in non-ARL libraries).[7] The rest of the time is devoted to management, meetings, professional activities, and research. In-house catalogers, under the pressure of other responsibilities, can put cataloging work aside. In contrast, because catalogers working for vendors devote less time to nonproduction activities, vendors can be more productive than libraries. Libraries outsource their cataloging operations because they are unable to increase in-house productivity.

Vendors may provide a shorter turnaround time. When outsourcing with a materials jobber, the vendor typically delivers the cataloging record at the time the book is selected for the library. If the library sends the book to the vendor, the book is returned and cataloged, usually within a month. This prevents backlogs from accumulating.

Libraries expect greater productivity from a vendor. Psychologically, when the library buys cataloging from a vendor, a time factor enters the equation. It is not acceptable for the vendor to backlog cataloging, but the culture of academic libraries tolerates backlogs. Indeed, reports from the field support this assertion. For example, outsourcing cataloging at Loyola University of Chicago resulted in a 50 percent increase in productivity over the previous year and 151 percent over the previous five years. The library's backlog was significantly reduced and books were cataloged, processed, and placed on the shelves within ten days.[8]

The question of value-added services adds another dimension to the debate. Each time an in-house cataloger or a vendor handles a record, what further value do they add to it? In his study, James E. Rush writes that "most local cataloging contributes nothing to the value of the bibliographic record." In his opinion, repetitive cataloging is leading to unacceptably high costs, "especially when considered in light of the lack of added value the repetitive cataloging provides." He sees outsourcing as a way to eliminate wasteful duplication of effort.[9]

Access to Experts.—Lack of in-house expertise is invariably cited as a reason for outsourcing. Employers are looking at outside labor resources because they do not have people with the necessary skills in-house. Outsourcing to acquire expertise is frequent when the cataloging department lacks personnel with language or format expertise. For example, at the UNM General Library, we would like to outsource the cataloging of approximately 270 Sanskrit monographs. It certainly would be cheaper to buy these records from a vendor than to catalog in-house but there is no extra money in the budget right now to do this. Buying expertise is not a panacea. Because the department lacks the expertise in the first place, it will be unable to verify the accuracy of the vendor records.

Ideological Motives

Reasons for outsourcing can also be ideological. Many believe that the private sector is inherently more efficient and can provide services more economically than the public sector.[10] At UNM, some support outsourcing just because it is trendy. The whys and hows and pros and cons have not been adequately explored. There is a sense, however, that outsourcing is inevitable and that catalogers should no longer spend a great deal of time cataloging and should instead participate in the library's new paradigm. This new paradigm is not yet well defined but outsourcing seems to fit into its definition. Catalogers feel like the craftsmen who still work at perfecting the horse buggy when the automobile is just around the corner.

Political Motives

Outsourcing can also be used as a political tool to eliminate poor performers, to deal with difficult personnel problems, or to reduce the power of internal troublemakers.

Drawbacks to Outsourcing Cataloging

There are many potential problems associated with outsourcing: loss of intellectual capital, loss of institutional memory, deterioration of staff morale, loss of flexibility, diminished quality of records, loss of spirit of national cooperation, and lack of fairness. I will elaborate on a few of these.

Loss of Control

Loss of control over the content of the database is a major concern for catalogers. Cataloging is about bibliographic control. The cataloging apparatus consists of sets of national and local rules, hair-splitting rule interpretations, and subtleties that few can appreciate. While vendors focus on fulfilling their contractual obligations, they may not be concerned with the intellectual framework that undergirds cataloging. When difficulties occur with a vendor, the library has no mechanism to correct the problem promptly. A good contract is the only tool that gives the library leverage over its vendors. Libraries that have extensive experience working with materials vendors know that it can often take several months to resolve a problem.

Loss of Expertise

A common apprehension regarding outsourcing is that once an operation is contracted out, expertise leaves the company. A certain level of internal expertise is needed to manage the outsourcing arrangement and to negotiate present and future contracts. In cataloging, gaining or losing expertise is a matter of degree and depends on whether the library engages in selective or total outsourcing. It is clear that the library loses expertise when it outsources some of its cataloging. Catalogers do not catalog out of context. They are not cataloging just to describe specific items. The broader aim of cataloging is to provide access to a particular library's collections for particular library users.

Quality of Records

Outsourcing generates quality-control issues, a prime concern for catalogers.[11] From the cataloger's point of view, the downside of increased efficiency is a decrease in quality because libraries are forced to accept somebody else's cataloging without revision. One title at a time, in-house catalogers review and edit records found in national databases to assure quality. Libraries are often disappointed with the quality of the product they receive from vendors. Libraries get what they pay for and should not expect quality records for a low price.

The Cookie Cutter Approach

In-house departments can respond to the special needs of public services. Catalogers work closely with the reference staff, and many reference librarians consult with catalogers about how to find items or have them recataloged to improve access. For example, UNM catalogers routinely alter classifications to help patrons browse the reference collections, improve access to New Mexicana by adding contents notes, and add statements to gift books to recognize library benefactors. Vendors are less capable of providing customized cataloging and are often unwilling to do so. If they do perform this additional function, the price goes up, making it too expensive for libraries to request this type of service on a regular basis.

Losing the Spirit of Cooperation

One benefit of the current system, where thousands of academic, research, public, and special libraries contribute cataloging to cooperative union catalogs, is breadth and depth of cataloging.[12] In the last quarter century, catalogers have built huge bibliographic and authority databases. Both endeavors are labor-intensive and costly, but they have greatly benefited the cataloging community. The number of cooperative programs has increased since the development of the online union catalog. In order to maintain an acceptable level of quality in these databases, the library profession, with leadership from the Library of Congress, is addressing the issue of quality. The Program for Cooperative Cataloging (PCC) is raising the standard by training librarians across the country. It is hoped that this initiative will result in better and more usable records, thus eliminating the need for local libraries to enhance or change those records. OCLC's Enhance and Upgrade capabilities enable member institutions to make permanent corrections or additions to bibliographic records in the OCLC database. All these measures are designed to improve the quality of the database and of the records. These cooperative efforts cannot be duplicated by vendors since the primary goal of a commercial operation is profit rather than benefit to the cataloging community. Over the years, catalogers have participated in countless meetings to make those agreements workable. Catalogers feel responsible for the quality of national databases and question how the outsourcing of cataloging will affect that quality.

The Reality

Libraries view outsourcing of cataloging in different ways: some see it as a means to increase productivity, some as a way to reduce costs, while others want it all and expect top-quality records for the lowest price. For a couple of dollars, a vendor will provide a generic record. If the library wants additional editing, authority control, table of contents, and physical processing, the price goes up accordingly. Outsourcing can be used to support contradictory objectives. Routine cataloging can be outsourced in order to enable experienced in-house catalogers to do complex cataloging. Complex and original cataloging can be outsourced to supplement the library's expertise. At UNM, we purchase records for federal documents. The bibliographic records—created by GPO—are adequate, but there are problems with authority records (some are duplicates, others are not provided) and with items records (the generic location does not allow codes for branch and reference locations). The Government Information Department is continuously fixing these problems.

A survey of academic cataloging departments conducted in the fall of 1996 shows that outsourcing of cataloging is on the rise. Sixty-three percent of respondents indicated that they engage in some form of cataloging outsourcing:

44 percent use Marcive; 25 percent use TECHPRO; 21 percent use other cataloging vendors; 8 percent use PromptCat; and 1 percent use Diogenes. Regarding the types of records acquired, 45 percent of libraries buy bibliographic records for federal documents; 14 percent buy records for unique collections; 11 percent buy records for unique languages such as CJK, Judaic languages, and Arabic; 11 percent acquire Library of Congress bibliographic records; and 15 percent report buying other types of records. The survey revealed that libraries purchase a remarkable variety of records for a remarkable variety of materials: for all monographs received through approval plans; all monographic cataloging; original cataloging only; member input records only; English-language materials only; foreign-language materials only; original cataloging of Latin American collection materials; scores, sound recordings, special collections materials only; children's literature only; generic backlog material; HTML processing of texts; item records; upgrading of CIP records; and videos. The scope of outsourcing is also broad. One library reports that it outsources all its cataloging, 45,000 records a year, while another library indicates outsourcing no more than 35 records a month. As a rule, ARL libraries outsource cataloging more than non-ARL libraries (71 percent of ARL libraries outsource some cataloging compared with 56 percent of non-ARL libraries).

Conclusion

In the early 1990s libraries could select from a number of vendors if they purchased mainstream materials and if they had few needs for customization, such as classification, subject headings, or notes. It was more difficult to find a vendor who could supply cataloging for non-English materials or for specialized classification systems and there was a heavy reliance on bibliographic utilities for source records. But this picture is changing, though incrementally. Outsourcing is evolving as vendors gain experience meeting the needs of cataloging departments and introduce new services and improvements. Today vendors hire catalogers, offer original cataloging and authority control, and work directly with bibliographic utilities to provide better services.

Vendors often advertise services that promise quick and accurate cataloging of materials for a price which cataloging departments cannot possibly match. Nonetheless, both sides describe the value they can add to bibliographic records. In-house catalogers add value by customizing records for local needs, by performing extensive quality control, and by participating in various national programs. Vendors provide services such as table of contents and physical processing. In all cases, the result is a better product, and in all cases a price is associated with the added value. It takes in-house catalogers more time to enhance or upgrade a record than to simply produce and download an existing record. Similarly, vendors charge a premium for adding table of contents to bibliographic records or to physically process the books.

Evidently, outsourcing cataloging reduces the number of catalogers in a library. This situation raises the following questions. Will catalogers go the way of full-time bibliographers? Will only the largest academic libraries retain their catalogers, while small to medium-sized libraries will turn to vendors to manage their cataloging activities? Outsourcing is typically advocated by administrators, not by rank-and-file catalogers. To ensure that they will have a voice in the future of their profession, catalogers need to be aware of all the implications of outsourcing and take an active role in determining its shape and content. Otherwise, vendors and administrators will make the decisions for them and they may not like the results.

NOTES

1. For detailed discussion of these issues, see Claire-Lise Bénaud and Sever Bordeianu, *Outsourcing Library Operations in Academic Libraries: An Overview of Issues and Outcomes* (Englewood, CO: Libraries Unlimited, 1998).

2. Brian Rothery and Ian Robertson, *The Truth about Outsourcing* (Hampshire, England: Gower, 1995), p. 4.

3. Arnold Hirshon, "The Lobster Quadrille: The Future of Technical Services in a Re-engineering World," in *The Future Is Now: The Changing Face of Technical Services; Proceedings of the OCLC Symposium ALA Midwinter Conference, February 4, 1994* (Dublin, OH: OCLC Online Computer Library Center, 1994), p. 16.

4. Colleen F. Hyslop, "PromptCat Prototype: Accelerating Progress in Technical Services," in *The Future Is Now: The Changing Face of Technical Services; Proceedings of the OCLC Symposium, ALA Midwinter Conference, February 4, 1994* (Dublin, OH: OCLC Online Computer Library Center, 1994), p. 35.

5. Dennis Livingston, "Outsourcing: Look Beyond the Price Tag," *Datamation* (November 15, 1992), 93.

6. Nancy J. Gibbs, "ALCTS/Role of the Professional in Academic Research Technical Services Departments Discussion Group," ALA Midwinter 1994 Conference Reports, p. 322.

7. Claire-Lise Bénaud, Sever Bordeianu, and Mary Ellen Hanson, "Cataloging Production Standards in Academic Libraries," *Technical Services Quarterly* 16:3 (1960), 50.

8. Ellen J. Waite, "Reinvent Catalogers! Reply to M. Gorman," *Library Journal* 120 (November 1, 1995), 37.

9. James E. Rush, "A Case for Eliminating Cataloging in the Individual Library," in *The Future Is Now: The Changing Face of Technical Services; Proceedings of the OCLC Symposium, ALA Midwinter Conference, February 4, 1994* (Dublin, OH: OCLC Online Computer Library Center, 1994), pp. 9–10.

10. Murray S. Martin, "Outsourcing," *The Bottom Line* 8:3 (1995), 28.

11. Glen E. Holt, "Catalog Outsourcing: No Clear-Cut Choice," *Library Journal* 120 (September 15, 1995), 34.

12. Daniel CannCasciato, "Tepid Water for Everyone? The Future OLUC, Catalogers, and Outsourcing," *OCLC Systems & Services* 10 (Spring 1994), 7.

2. Documenting Cultural Heritage: The Oral History Collections at The University of the West Indies

Margaret D. Rouse-Jones
Enid Brown

It has become increasingly evident that oral history, "the recollections and reminiscences of living people about their past," has a valid role in the education process in that it provides an approach and opportunity for reflection and data gathering on cultural issues. Consequently, there has been increased use of oral history as a means of capturing popular historical memory, particularly in societies that have a multicultural base.[1]

This paper examines the development of oral history collections at the St. Augustine and Mona campuses of The University of the West Indies (hereafter U.W.I.). The two societies discussed, Trinidad and Tobago and Jamaica, can be considered fertile ground for the flourishing of oral history programs, given their cultural diversity occasioned by historical experience—Amerindian settlement, European colonization, slavery, indentureship, and migration. The consequent cross-fertilization of peoples is a gold mine for the oral history student. The University of the West Indies with its three campuses—Mona, Jamaica; St. Augustine, Trinidad and Tobago; and Cave Hill, Barbados—is considered one of the truly regional institutions and the primary university serving the English-speaking Caribbean. In the fifty years[2] of its existence, the faculties and departments, including the libraries, have assiduously attempted to keep abreast of contemporary trends in all aspects of teaching, learning, and information provision. This is the backdrop against which oral history collections have been developed at U.W.I.

Rationale and Organization of Programs

One main difference between the establishment of the oral history collections at the two campuses is that at U.W.I., St. Augustine, the library has the main responsibility for all aspects of the collection. Willa Baum, writing about the librarian's role in oral history, sees the major steps as "creating," "curating," "consuming," and "counseling" (the four Cs). Although the creation of oral history archives is not essentially a library function, many oral history projects do emanate from libraries.[3] The perception of the role of the librarian in collecting oral history seemingly prompted the establishment of the oral history project at The University of the West Indies, St. Augustine campus (hereafter U.W.I., St. Augustine) in April 1981. According to the then campus librarian, the project "grew out of the perceived need to enhance historical research resources for the study of Trinidad and Tobago by drawing mainly on available human resources in the society which were then largely untapped."[4] A group of interested persons, mainly academics, responded to an invitation from the campus librarian to attend an informal meeting to discuss the possibility of a project to collect oral and pictorial records. From these tentative beginnings in 1981, the project was renamed a continuing program in 1983, the Oral and Pictorial Records Programme *(sic)*—hereafter OPReP.

The program is managed by an executive board[5] and has the following objectives:

1. To gather historical data on Trinidad and Tobago through interviews with persons who have created history or witnessed important events.
2. To identify other repositories/researchers in the field of oral history and other sources of pictorial research.
3. To photograph notable old buildings, monuments, and sites and to collect photographs, sketches, and other illustrative material of historical interest.
4. To lodge all material gathered, organize it, and make it accessible in order to facilitate research into the history and culture of Trinidad and Tobago.

It is understandable that in the process of gathering historical material, popular culture will also be documented as part of the historical record. This has indeed been the OPReP experience.

In order to accomplish its main objective, at the start of the program a number of themes were identified as areas in which the oral record could fill the gaps in historical knowledge. These included topics that were historical/political in nature, for example, the 1937 labor disturbances; the Second World War; the history of the university; and others that seem to fall into what might be called culture—the development of the Calypso, steel band, and other art forms. At the same time, certain elderly persons who had played an important part at various levels of the society were also identified as persons to be interviewed. Individuals such as C. L. R. James, Owen Mathurin, Lulworth Punch, J. D. Elder, all prominent citizens of Trinidad and Tobago in different spheres of activity, were included in this category.

As the program continues, other names and themes are added. For example, one of the senior lecturers in the Faculty of Natural Sciences, who is also a cricket enthusiast, suggested that we conduct a series of interviews with some of the retired cricketers. Similarly, when the library and personal papers of the late Dr. Eric Williams, former prime minister, were deposited at U.W.I., St. Augustine Library, a decision was made to conduct a series of interviews with people who knew Dr. Williams to supplement the collection.

OPReP's second major thrust is to keep abreast of all work being done in the area of oral history in Trinidad and Tobago and to serve as a repository for materials being collected. As a result, the collection includes work by other researchers who have deposited copies of their tapes with OPReP. Students doing final-year undergraduate Caribbean Studies Projects as well as those reading for a master's degree in history are urged to explore themes using the oral history method under the supervision of members of the OPReP executive. These students and other researchers both of U.W.I. and overseas universities who conduct oral history interviews as part of their research are encouraged to lodge copies of their taped material with the collection. OPReP has also been able to acquire copies of work done by researchers who pioneered anthropological material in Trinidad and Tobago.

The pictorial side of the program is subsumed in the library's general policy regarding the collection of West Indian materials. OPReP's role has tended to focus on locating sources of historical photographs and encouraging the acquisition of maps, prints, postcards, and other types of pictorial material that may be of historical interest, and bringing them to the attention of readers and users (by means of displays and the like). One set of photographs, commissioned by the program in 1982, captured the architecture of St. Joseph, Trinidad's oldest town. These photographs, which reflect the cultural history of the peoples of the island, have become invaluable because some of the buildings no longer exist or are too dilapidated to be studied in detail.[6]

The library at The University of the West Indies, Mona campus (hereafter U.W.I., Mona) does not attempt to collect and document oral material in the same manner as its sister campus library at St. Augustine. It also has not taken responsibility for the housing and organizing of such collections where they exist on the campus. The U.W.I., Mona Library has a very small collection of audiocassettes and videocassettes which document Jamaica's cultural heritage. These include recordings of Jamaican folk singers, recordings that trace the story of Jamaican music, and a conversation with C. L. R. James.

However, other departments at U.W.I., Mona have been active in collecting and documenting various aspects of the cultural heritage of Jamaican society. The university is currently showing great interest in cultural studies. It intends to upgrade staffing, introduce graduate studies in the area of culture, establish a nonprint archive of cultural material, and support significant library development in the area.

Foremost among the oral history collections on the Mona campus is the Social History Project, based in the department of history of the Faculty of Arts and Education, as it is now known. This project can be considered the counterpart of the OPReP collection at St. Augustine. The Social History Project, the brainchild of Professor Barry Higman,[7] was established in 1979. It later became incorporated within the Institute of Caribbean Studies, which was established by the same faculty member. Since its inception the project has been administered by a director who is assisted by a committee comprising members of the staff of the history department; later, postgraduate input was added.

The Social History Project differs from its St. Augustine counterpart in that it "was established with a view to guiding and supporting postgraduate research in the Department of History." Consequently, there was more systematic involvement of students at all levels in the life of the program. "Its focus was . . . confined essentially to the study of Jamaican social history in the post emancipation period,"[8] and one of its main objectives is the collection and preservation of oral history data.

The project received some measure of separate institutional support through grants from the Board of Postgraduate Studies and the Research and Publications Committee of the University. Tape recorders were also acquired for loan to students interested in conducting research in oral history or who were involved in projects that required the use of oral testimonies. Students reading for the master's by coursework carried out systematic interviews with persons working in certain occupations, in particular dressmakers and tailors. The project acquired the completed tapes and transcripts from the final-year and postgraduate students, covering a wide variety of subjects.

Popular Culture Content

It is interesting to note that the all-embracing nature of the program, in terms of the informants interviewed, has resulted in the collection of information on a variety of cultural themes. For the most part, OPReP has concentrated on interviewing elderly persons; our oldest informant, Anne Murray (popularly known as "Teacher Thynie"), was born in 1886 and was 102 years old at the time of the interview.[9] Many others (for example, C. L. R. James, Ivan Rouse, Lulworth Punch) were born in the first two decades of the twentieth century, and thus were able to give a firsthand account of many of the social and economic conditions in Trinidad and Tobago at that time. Because informants also came from different parts of the island and from various socioeconomic backgrounds, the result is a rich and varied picture of life in several communities of Trinidad and Tobago. Indeed, a substantial portion of the content deals with aspects of the popular culture of Trinidad and Tobago: East Indian immigration, economic diversification in the post-emancipation period, cultural continuities of the different ethnic groups, social and economic movements toward independence, and social life and art forms in the Caribbean, to mention a few.

Among the interviews commissioned by OPReP are several that document the history and development of distinctive communities in Trinidad and Tobago: Belmont, Chaguanas, Charlotteville, Tunapuna, Arouca, and Princes

Town. For example, one informant, talking about the popular Port of Spain suburb of Belmont, describes a small savanna, known as "Chinese Savanna" which
no longer exists. The details about this savanna are not popularly known, but
they shed light on the complexities of race relations at the time. China was
among the countries that supplied labor to Trinidad in the years after 1840.
Anne Murray, on the other hand, describes in vivid detail the visit of the governor to Tunapuna in 1894—she was about eight years old at the time—and
remembers the request, made to the governor, for basic amenities such as a
school, a market, and piped water.

Scattered throughout the interviews is information on agricultural practices on estates, which provides insight into economic diversification in the
post-emancipation era. James Barratt examined the economic life of Chaguanas which he describes as a "factory village," served by two estates, cocoa and
cane. He also describes the farming activities of the sugarcane laborers who
were also independent small farmers. In contrast, J. D. Elder's interview sheds
light on estate life in Charlotteville, a rural area on the sister island of Tobago
whose historical experience differed somewhat from that of Trinidad, but
where land was given over to pasture and a variety of crops, in addition to
cocoa production.

With regard to the everyday social life of specific social and ethnic
groups, there is considerable documentation of the two major ethnic groups in
the society. Three sets of interviews, one dealing with the Bhojpuri-speaking
Indians, another with East Indian family life, and a third with the experiences
of indentured laborers and their descendants, give a clear picture of many
aspects of social life among East Indians. Interviews with J. D. Elder and other
Tobagonian informants and with Andrew Beddeau (an Orisha priest, African
drummer, and masquerader) examine African elements in the society. Because
of the migration of persons within the region, interviews may also shed light on
conditions of life in other islands. For example, Andrew Beddeau, in talking
about oral traditions handed down to him by his parents, gives information on
Saraka feasts and celebrations in Grenada as well as in Trinidad.

The interviews on cricket (an important aspect of the culture of the
English-speaking Caribbean) deal not only with the technicalities of the game
but also with the childhood experiences of those who became professionals.
The narratives relate to the broader themes of social life, recreation, and the use
of free time. In Rouse's interview, which includes details of many of his
extracurricular activities, much can be learned about the literary and debating
societies of the 1930s and 1940s. This material is also supported by evidence
from an interview with another informant, Max Ifill.

The 1930s was a period of great social unrest throughout the region and
culminated in the rise of nationalist movements. Sir Philip Sherlock, a
Jamaican who served as the first campus principal of the St. Augustine campus
of U.W.I., gives some insight into the development of national and regional

identities. He describes the bad economic conditions and deprivation that were building up in Jamaica and the English-speaking colonies, the low wages and unemployment, and poor living conditions, all of which spawned an anger that was expressed in violence and unrest. Sherlock describes the impact of this period on his own thinking and how it engendered in him a "move to a Jamaican outlook." In the wake of this turmoil he became secretary of a group of Jamaicans and English who were agitating for a University of Jamaica and was later named to a committee sent out from the United Kingdom to the Caribbean to plan for higher education in the region. His involvement in this effort, and the fledgling University College of the West Indies, caused him to move from a Jamaica-centered outlook to a West Indian one.[10] This set of interviews is a key element in the documentation of the development of West Indian identity.

In considering the historical experience of Trinidad and Tobago, in particular the use of indentured labor, mention was made above of the fact that Trinidad experimented with other sources of labor before the use of East Indians was agreed upon. In the years after emancipation and apprenticeship, some Portuguese labor was brought in for use on the plantations.[11] Portuguese descendants form an ethnic minority in Trinidad, and OPReP has been instrumental in uncovering oral and other data about this group. A descendant of one of these families recorded interviews with grandparents and other elderly members of the Portuguese community. All of them had at least one Madeiran-born parent and two of them were born in Madeira and migrated to Trinidad and Tobago in the 1930s.[12] The research indicated that a few Portuguese had come to Trinidad in 1834 to work on the sugarcane plantations but they all died or returned to Fayal in the Azores. The descendants of the modern-day Portuguese came from Madeira beginning in 1846. They came in two waves—one group fleeing from severe economic disaster and the other from extreme religious persecution. The economic refugees came to several territories of the West Indies and in particular to Trinidad and Guyana as indentured laborers. They did not remain long on the plantation, however, and soon became shopkeepers. The religious refugees who arrived later were converted Protestants who had fled increasing hostility in Roman Catholic Madeira. Generally these were educated urban dwellers who began as owners of dry goods stores and as market gardeners.

One of the more noteworthy interviews conducted by OPReP was that with Sir Ellis Clarke while he was president of Trinidad and Tobago. From fairly humble beginnings in Belmont, Clarke trained as a lawyer in England and served in many areas of public office and the diplomatic service over his long career before becoming a resident of the republic. The interview gives much insight into significant political events in the history and political/cultural heritage of the twin-island state. Clarke discusses the events leading up to the aborted Federation of the West Indies and subsequent independence of Trinidad and Tobago. He also goes into considerable detail about his thinking on the Federation, relationships between and among the other Caribbean leaders at the time (Grantley Adams, Norman Manley, Robert Bradshaw), and the drafting of the independence constitution of Trinidad and Tobago. He also deals at length with the events surrounding the death of Prime Minister Williams and the naming of the new head of government, an issue over which there were many conflicting reports.

The Social History Project mirrors the St. Augustine program in its focus on the events of 1938.[13] These interviews are derived from field assignments given to students reading for a degree in the then Faculty of Arts over a three-year period (1986–1988) who had registered for a history course titled "Techniques of Historical Investigation." The students were required to do an oral history exercise, which sought to build a database of interviews of individuals who had taken part in the 1938 labor disturbances in Jamaica. More than 140 eyewitness accounts were collected including testimonies from journalists, lawyers, political activists, and port workers at the time. This labor struggle contributed significantly to the development of Jamaican national consciousness in the pre-independence period.

The interviews conducted by the three research fellows focused on Oracabessa, a once bubbling seaport town on the north coast of Jamaica from which bananas were exported; The University of the West Indies, Mona; individuals in the banking industry; women in the banana industry; and women employed as nursemaids.

Other topics covered in this oral history collection are the history of lifestyles, culture, festivals and celebrations, domestic architecture, internal migration (country to Kingston), ethnic groups, minorities (the Chinese and Lebanese) and their distinctive cultures, folklore (duppy or ghost stories), crafts, and customs (for example, faith healing, urban and rural death rituals, herbal medicine, rural birth rituals, tea meetings, and morning sport which is community cooperation for building purposes). Interviews also cover the first election, held in 1944, after the granting of universal adult suffrage in Jamaica, the Salvation Army School for the Blind, and the development of Ports in Jamaica. Mento yard (an exposition of Jamaica's traditional music and folk songs, dance, food, arts and crafts, and a popular feature of Jamaica's national heritage celebrations held annually) is also captured on tape in an interview.

Issues of Collection, Access, and Retrieval

The OPReP at U.W.I., St. Augustine has received no separate budget or funding but has been considered part of the collection development activity of the West Indiana and Special Collections Division (hereafter WISCD) of the Main Library. At present (May 1999) the collection consists of more than 380 audiocassettes and a small number of videocassettes and reel-to-reel tapes.

Despite the modest nature of the program, it maintains a regular schedule of interviews.

Once the program became formally established, the legal issues of copyright and ownership of the literary property rights of the material collected had to be addressed. This was also necessary because it was thought that it would be advantageous to encourage informants to disclose information they might consider "sensitive" by offering them an option to keep it closed for a specific period of time. A questionnaire explains the policies regarding literary property rights, access to the material, copying, and dissemination. Informants are asked to state whether they wish to place any restrictions on the material. An agreement is then entered into by both parties with the interviewer representing the university library. So far very few interviewees have placed restrictions on the material.[14] In practice, however, some informants prefer to make the decision after seeing the transcript rather than at the time that the interview is conducted.

The material constitutes one of the special collections of the WISCD, the Library's closed access postgraduate/research collection. The material does not appear in the library's online public access catalog. Details about material collected are also available in a separate database. The database is updated as material is added to the collection and therefore represents the entire holdings of OPReP. The database is available for searching in the WISCD. There is a published guide to the material in the collection as of December 1997.[15] Ideally the tapes are transcribed and the transcript is generally the document that is used for historical research. The process from "tape to type" is a lengthy one and the program has a backlog in this area.

The Social History Project at Mona has approximately two hundred tapes, some of which have been transcribed. Focus has been on occupations. The project owns the copyright to the material and use is restricted to the university community. Transcripts and tapes are cataloged and stored as a resource available to the research community.[16]

The tapes are identified by the name of the interviewer and then filed alphabetically in cabinets according to subject. Although the room where they are housed is air-conditioned, the air-conditioning is turned on only when the room is in use. This fluctuating temperature could affect the shelf-life of the tapes and result in the loss of very valuable information.

Owing largely to a lack of funding, the Social History Project has not been as active in oral data collection as was originally anticipated. The inability to employ a staff of research fellows on a consistent basis has hampered data collection, but the project also needs staffing in just about every aspect of its operations.

Cullom Davis, a visiting Fulbright professor at the Mona campus of the university during the winter of 1987–1988, on special assignment as oral history specialist in the Social History Project, commented as follows on the development of oral history in Jamaica:

> The combination of strong raison d'être, highly qualified and eager practitioners, and impressive beginnings ought to have produced a rich harvest of Jamaican oral histories by this time. Regrettably, the record to date falls somewhat short of that promise. . . . The problems familiar to oral historians everywhere but perhaps unusually acute in Jamaica, have been the twin perils of under-staffing and under-funding.[17]

In a recent report, the director of the Social History Project states that one of the goals of the project for 1998–1999 is to conduct an island-wide study of alternative or folklore medicinal practices and that funding is being sought for this initiative. He expresses concern at the underutilization of the facilities and makes a special appeal for use of the available research material. An effort is being made to make the material more accessible.[18]

Publications

Since March 1988 OPReP has published the *OPReP Newsletter*. It appears every quarter and has in a sense served as fillip to the program, in that the need to report on activities has often been the driving force to sustain the schedule of interviews. Each issue of the newsletter carries a feature article, excerpts of the transcript of an interview, one or two photographs, and other miscellaneous items. In one issue, for example, an article discusses the importance of photographs in preserving the historical record for tracing African cultural continuities in Trinidad. The feature article in the same issue, titled "Oral Tradition in Caribbean Research: Case Studies from Jamaica, Trinidad and Guyana," argues for the use of oral evidence in Caribbean social history and makes the point that "historical, oral and anthropological evidence suggests . . . dynamic processes of creolisation . . . in colour-class stratified societies, and of culture building in response and resistance to colonialism, slavery, plantations and the capitalist world system."[19]

The Social History Project has also published the *Social History Project Newsletter* since June 1980. It outlines the work of the project, reports on research in progress, and covers news on the work of related bodies. Information relating to oral history is very often highlighted.

One issue of the newsletter reports on a local symposium that marked the tenth anniversary of the project. The symposium included a panel discussion on oral history research in Jamaica. Presentations included "Jamaican Family Histories," by Charles Carnegie of the African-Caribbean Institute of Jamaica; "Oral Histories of the 1938 Labour Unrest in Jamaica," by Karl Watson; "Occupations in Oracabessa in the Early 20th Century," by Erna Brodber, the project's first research fellow; and "Testimonies by Women of the Jamaica Federation," by Linnette Vassell.[20]

In addition to the Social History Project, the Mona campus is also the repository for other oral history collections: the Folklore Studies Project; the Social Welfare Training Centre Tape Project of the sociology department of the Faculty of the Social Sciences; the Library of the Spoken Word; and the Cultural Studies Initiative Visual Library.

Folklore Studies Project.—This project, which sought to encourage folklore studies as a legitimate area of research, was established in 1982 by an interdisciplinary committee to direct research in such areas as music and dance, language, folk festivals, proverbs, religion, and ring games. It "is largely concerned with the documentation of our 'verbal art'—the expressive behavior of the folk: how Caribbean people view their world; their religious based folk beliefs of the natural and spiritual world and the unique expression of wisdom."[21] During the period of its activity, the Folklore Studies Project received funding and the interviews concentrated on folk medicine. Several interviews were conducted between doctors and their patients and with spiritual mothers and bush doctors. Professor Mervyn Alleyne holds approximately fifty of these tapes on folk medicine.[22] The Folklore Studies Unit also has housed within the department of language, linguistics and philosophy hundreds of reel-to-reel tapes donated by Professor Frederic Gomes Cassidy which contain interviews conducted throughout the Caribbean during his "Linguistic Survey of the West Indies." Though the aim of this survey was to understand the languages of the peoples of the Caribbean, several tapes document Caribbean traditions, customs, life experiences, family connections, occupations, folktales, and songs.

Social Welfare Training Centre Tape Project.—A study designed to meet some of the needs of social work training at the U.W.I., Mona resulted in many available oral accounts documenting cultural heritage, identity, and popular culture in Jamaica. In their interviews, students have identified the characteristics and cultural patterns of "yards" and "yard-life."[23]

The tapes record the life experiences of mainly octogenarians and cover the following themes: fashion and social life; color and class; customs relating to the Nana or local midwife; the newly born and the burial of the dead; courting styles and marriage customs; church and religious life; family life and children's upbringing; childbearing as therapy; "taking children" (the informal adoption of children); medicinal cures and balm-yard healers; and sex role differentiation especially in agricultural occupations.[24]

Funds were allocated for field study and for transcription of the tapes by the Institute of Social and Economic Research. The tapes and transcripts are now housed in the Documentation Centre of the Institute of Social and Economic Research on the Mona campus.

Library of the Spoken Word.—Also located on the Mona campus, the Library of the Spoken Word falls under the administration of the Cultural Studies Initiative Office of the Vice Chancellor. It is an exclusively nonprint repository of university and regional history and is a research facility serving not only the U.W.I. community but other tertiary- and secondary-level educational bodies, as well as local and overseas researchers. The collection goes beyond what is traditionally accepted as oral history. In addition to 5,000 recordings of interviews, it includes conferences, lectures, seminars, and drama of an educational or historical nature. Dating from the early 1950s and collected over more than a forty-year period by the Radio Education Unit of the University, the recordings cover a wide range of subjects. Included among the vast collection is material relating to Caribbean culture—life, music, languages, sociology, and social studies. The collection consists largely of edited recordings of lectures and talks given on the campus, rather than taped interviews. These are usually final productions of the university's Radio Education Unit. Many of these items document our heritage.

The subject matter includes Rastafarianism, its philosophy and music; Jamaican dancehall styles and substyles; lectures from the "Reasonings in Culture" and "Arts and Cultural Studies" series; Jamaican rhythms; and national identity and attitudes to race and color.

A few of the recorded productions of the Philip Sherlock Centre of the Creative Arts are also housed in this library, but only if the recording was produced by the Radio Education Unit. A rough catalog and the physical arrangement of materials make them easily accessible. The Philip Sherlock Centre, a division of the Office of Outreach and Institutional Relations of the university, is an active cultural body which coordinates both entertainment and intellectual activities. Other recorded material is held in the center itself.

Although there is no parallel collection to the Library of the Spoken Word at U.W.I., St. Augustine, OPReP also has among its holdings tapes of three major conferences held on campus: "The African Past and the African Diaspora"; "Slavery, Emancipation and the Shaping of Caribbean Society"; and "Challenge and Change: The Indian Diaspora in Its Historical and Contemporary Contexts." As the titles suggest, these conferences deal with various aspects of the cultural heritage—race relations, music, language, kinship and family, role of religion—of the two major ethnic groups in the islands.

Other fringe collections of videocassette recordings at both campuses should be mentioned because of their relevance to the musical and literary heritage of the region. The U.W.I., St. Augustine Library holds, as a part of its audiovisual collection, the Calypso Showcase Series produced originally for television viewing. It consists of more than 120 interviews with snippets of performances of the calypsonians and constitutes important documentation of the calypso as well as other aspects of Trinidad and Tobago's literary and musical heritage.

Cultural Studies Initiative Visual Library.—This collection at U.W.I., Mona, administered by the Library of the Spoken Word, houses about fifty videocassettes. Coverage includes interviews with and documentaries of the lives of famous West Indians, for example Louise Bennett, noted Jamaican dialect author and dialect performer and one of Jamaica's precious national treasures. The documents include cultural studies, lectures and conferences, recordings of the first Research Day at the Mona campus, and medical and health material of the Diabetes Outreach Project of the Faculty of Medical Sciences.

In order to expand the collection, donations are solicited and the administrator of the library has recently made arrangements to collect and house the tapes of the annual festivals of the Jamaica Festival Commission. However, unless substantial funding can be identified, the ability to purchase blank tapes and to reproduce and convert master tapes, which are loaned for the purpose of building the collection, will be severely limited.

Technology and the Changing Face of Oral History

It may be argued that because the narrators are not being interviewed, some of the material held in the Library of the Spoken Word, by OPReP (lectures, conferences, and discussions), and by the Cultural Studies Initiative Visual Library should not be considered oral history. These collections are described here because they document identity and popular culture of particular societies. However, they also raise issues related to technology and the changing face of oral history.

The use of the videocamera is yet another means of supporting and enhancing the preservation of history for our descendants. There are many small privately owned videocassette oral history collections on the campus, but their owners will have to be persuaded to donate the material to the main collections in order to make them more accessible. These videocassettes capture on tape much of our cultural heritage and form a visual complement to the oral history documents.

Oral history, as defined by Martha Zachert, is

> . . . a record of recall. The record is authored by an individual who participated in, or observed at close range, events whose documentation will aid future researchers in understanding some facet of twentieth-century life. The oral author is aided in his recall by an interviewer versed both in the segment of life to be recorded and in appropriate techniques for creating this unique record. To this extent oral history is a collaboration: the oral author is the contributor of substance, the interviewer is the contributor of recording skill. . . . For accuracy the record is tape recorded; for convenience it is usually transcribed.[25]

Clive Cochrane discusses the changing nature of oral history. He argues that local news programs, magazine programs, studio discussions, and phone-ins all reflect current trends, issues, and developments in a community and would provide an invaluable resource for the future. He states:

Oral historians look both at history in the more conventional sense and at contemporary history. Local radio is an important creator and source of information . . . there is admittedly a huge difference between a well-researched interview with a carefully selected informant and a short radio interview which may have been edited for a variety of reasons before being broadcast. It cannot be denied, however, that archival collections of oral history in the conventional sense and broadcast material each in their own way contribute to our understanding of society. . . . Nevertheless, bearing in mind the advantages and disadvantages of each, the oral historian's collection of the recorded sound has a vital role to play in supplementing documentary evidence and providing rich source material for the local historian. . . . Oral history is becoming an audiovisual technique rather than one using only sound. . . . The idea that oral history is primarily concerned with past events is being questioned as the concept of contemporary history receives greater attention.[26]

Chris Baggs talks about the increasing trend toward using videotape when interviewing rather than audiotape.[27] Cochrane notes, "[the fact that] local radio archives have found their way into a number of libraries . . . together with other developments such as the use of video and the growing interest in contemporary history, is challenging the commonly accepted definition of oral history."[28]

The University of the West Indies through its oral history program has been successful in documenting various aspects of the popular culture of two of the larger nations in the English-speaking Caribbean.

Although the programs are similar, one of the major differences, as noted, is that the U.W.I., St. Augustine oral history program is library-based, whereas at the Mona campus the collections reside in various faculties and centers. Also, the collection at Mona is broader in scope.

As researchers become more aware of the significant role of oral history in the education process—providing an opportunity for reflection and data gathering on cultural issues—the issue of access to the collections becomes critical. Although some attempt has been made to provide access to both collections, this effort needs to be pursued more vigorously.

It is evident that some thought is being given to new technologies, insofar as they allow multimedia access and dissemination of popular culture. This would suggest a broadening in the definition of the oral history method and process and a challenge for future researchers to document this convergence.

NOTES

1. D. Kyvig and M. Marty, *Nearby History: Exploring the Past Around You* (Nashville, TN: American Association for State and Local History, 1982).

2. The first campus of The University of the West Indies was established at Mona, Jamaica, in 1948.

3. Willa Baum, "The Expanding Role of the Librarian in Oral History," in David K. Dunaway and Willa K. Baum, eds., *Oral History: An Interdisciplinary Anthology* (Nashville, TN: American Association for State and Local History, 1984), pp. 387–406. When this article was written, Baum was director of the Regional Oral History Office at the University of California, Berkeley, a position she had held since 1954.

4. Alma Jordan, "Introductory Message," *OPReP Newsletter* 1 (March 1988), 1.

5. An executive of five persons—two librarians, one historian, one sociologist, and one creative artist—currently manages the program. The composition of the executive changes according to the responsibilities of the non-library members and the particular thrust of the interview program at any given time.

6. These photographs were the subject matter for a B.A. Undergraduate Final-Year Caribbean Study Project. See Shurla A. Henry, "Trinidad Architecture: A Study of Some of the Different Forms of Architecture in St. Joseph with Reference to the History of the Area," Caribbean Studies Project, University of the West Indies, 1989.

7. Professor Barry Higman was the former head of the department of history of the then Faculty of Arts (now Faculty of Arts and Education) on the campus.

8. Brian L. Moore, "The Social History Project: Ten Years and After," *Social History Project Newsletter* 21 (December 1990), 5.

9. She died in 1990.

10. Given the failure of the West Indies Federation and the uncertain success of other attempts to unify the region, a popularly held view is that the sport cricket and The University of the West Indies are two of the main institutions that hold the former British Caribbean together.

11. See Bridget Brereton, "The Experience of Indentureship: 1845–1917," in John La Guerre, ed., *Calcutta to Caroni: The East Indians of Trinidad,* 2d rev. ed. (St Augustine, Trinidad and Tobago: University of the West Indies, Extra-Mural Unit, 1985), p. 21.

12. Jo-Anne Sharon Ferreira, "Some Aspects of Portuguese Immigration into Trinidad and Tobago: An Investigation Based on Oral History," *OPReP Newsletter* 8 (December 1989), 3–5. While conducting her oral history research, Ferreira also unearthed some privately published materials about the Portuguese community in Trinidad. Photocopies of these have been added to the West Indian collection. Her study began as an undergraduate Caribbean Studies Project and was expanded and subsequently published under the title *The Portuguese of Trinidad and Tobago: Portrait of an Ethnic Minority* (St. Augustine: Institute of Social and Economic Research, University of the West Indies, 1994.)

13. Although this paper does not focus on the oral history collections at the Cave Hill campus, Barbados, it is useful to note that an Oral History Project was started at U.W.I., Cave Hill, in 1974–1975, through the initiative of Professor Woodville Marshall, Dr. Tony Phillips, and a few graduate students of the history department, all of whom were interested in the labor movement, the politics of the 1930s, and the evolution of villages in Barbados. Unfortunately, the project was inactive for many years and has only been recently being revived. The Barbados National Library Service also has a modest Oral History Project which was started in 1987 as a spin-off from an exhibition to commemorate the 1937 disturbance. The collection includes 83 audiotape and 20 videotape interviews that document social life, personalities, crafts, festivals, folklore, customs, and folk medicine in Barbados. We are grateful to Dr. Aviston Downes of the Cave Hill campus and Mrs. Evonda Callender of the Barbados National Library Service for supplying this information.

14. In one OPReP interview done in 1984, the informant requested that the material be closed until the year 1991 or until his death whichever was later. He died in 1992.

15. Margaret Rouse-Jones and Kathleen Helenese-Paul, *Spoken History: A Guide to the Material Collected by the Oral and Pictorial Records Programme* (St. Augustine: The Main Library, University of the West Indies, 1997).

16. Lesley Lim, "Dr. Erna Brodber's Report on Her Term of Appointment as the Social History Fellow," *Social History Project Newsletter* 21 (December 1999), 17.

17. Cullom Davis, "Oral History in Jamaica," *Social History Project Newsletter* 17 (May 1988), 5–6.

18. "From the Director," *Social History Project Newsletter* 31 (December 1998), 2.

19. See items by Kwaku Senah and Jean Besson in *OPReP Newsletter* 18 (June 1992).

20. Moore, p. 4.

21. Erna Brodber, "The Second Generation of Freemen in Jamaica, 1907–1944," Ph.D. dissertation, University of the West Indies, Mona, 1984.

22. As a result of the work of this project, the university approved a graduate program in folklore studies and there has been one M. Phil. graduate in this area.

23. Erna Brodber's *Life in Jamaica in the Early Twentieth Century, a Presentation of Ninety Oral Accounts: Some Notes on Its Purpose and Contents* (Kingston, Jamaica: Institute of Social and Economic Research, 1980) is a product of these oral studies. These ninety oral narratives of Jamaicans born around 1900 and their life experiences up to 1944 form the basis of Erna Brodber's dissertation (see note 21). It gives an interesting account of the process of documenting oral history for social workers. It also lists and annotates the documents collected during this project. The language used in these narratives (Creole dialects) has also been analyzed by Velma Pollard in "Past Time Expression in Jamaican Creole: Implications for Teaching English," Ph.D. dissertation, University of the West Indies, Mona, 1987.

24. Regardless of the main interviewing topic, the interviewees frequently mention the 1938 labor disturbances in Jamaica.

25. Martha Jane K. Zachert, "The Implications of Oral History for Librarians," *College and Research Libraries* 29:2 (March 1968), 101. When this article was written Zachert was an assistant professor at the Library School, Florida State University.

26. Clive Cochrane, "Public Libraries and the Changing Nature of Oral History," *Audiovisual Librarian* 11:4 (Autumn 1985), 204–206. When this article was written Cochrane was on the faculty of the Department of Library and Information Studies, Queen's University of Belfast.

27. Chris Baggs, "Video and Local Studies Librarianship—A Slight Return: Report on a Weekend School on 'Video History,'" *Audiovisual Librarian* 11:1 (Winter 1985), 47–49.

28. Cochrane, "Public Libraries," p. 206.

3. La importancia de la información en la construcción de la identidad cultural

Saray Córdoba G.

La información es un producto del trabajo intelectual que procede del procesamiento, interpretación y organización de los datos, producidos a su vez por la investigación; esto es, por el conocimiento que se genera. Por ello es que la información adquiere valor de uso, pues es uno de los objetos que contienen y permiten la transmisión del conocimiento en presencia de un sujeto: el usuario.

En la sociedad de la información ese valor se ha traducido en poder, pues al reforzarse la relación del ser humano con el conocimiento, ese objeto, que es su soporte tangible, se torna valioso como mercancía al ocupar el lugar que anteriormente ocupó la máquina y aún más atrás, la naturaleza. Por ello Robert Vitro ha afirmado que el sector información es el medio a través del cual una sociedad se expresa cultural, educativa y científicamente (Vitro 1989:2).

Esto ha provocado que de la información como bien social, pasemos a otro concepto: la información como mercancía y consecuentemente, a la división entre países pobres y países ricos en información. Nunca antes el conocimiento había sido tan determinante para las leyes del mercado y nunca como ahora han surgido tantas compañías transnacionales dedicadas a monopolizar, comercializar y consecuentemente, controlar las bases de datos a nivel mundial. Un estudio realizado en 1984 detectó que en 1980 existían 86 empresas transnacionales que controlaban la producción de más del 75% de los bienes y servicios de información del mundo.

Esa división entre países info-ricos e info-pobres (Morales 1996) es otra consecuencia de la concentración de la riqueza que en nuestro caso está dada por la tenencia y control de la infraestructura informativa; esto es, la tecnología de la información, a lo cual se suma la ausencia de una cultura de información (Menou 1996:298), aspecto casi inexistente en los países de la subregión centroamericana.

No obstante, al igual que sucedió en otras épocas, contamos con la materia prima, pues generamos nuestra propia información, lo cual nos da una cuota de poder que no siempre sabemos explotar, al no tener conciencia de ella. No obstante, en la red de relaciones mundiales, la costumbre y las relaciones del mercado nos llevan a consumir el conocimiento que se produce y difunde en los países del norte. Por ello es que cada vez nos parecen más familiares las bases de datos como Dialog, First Search, BRS, GPO, que aunque haya que pagar un alto costo por ellas, creemos que es lo único que existe en el mundo, sin cuestionarnos si son las fuentes más adecuadas que justifiquen su inversión.

Así, nos convertimos en meros consumidores de tecnología importada, que no siempre llena nuestras expectativas, pues en ellas no se refleja la producción intelectual de nuestros países pobres, sobre todo en los campos de las humanidades y ciencias sociales.

Esta situación nos ha permitido "ignorar" nuestra realidad, evadir la riqueza que tenemos encubierta y lamentablemente podríamos correr el riesgo de repetir la historia de nuestros antepasados: cambiamos el oro (la información) por cuentas de vidrio (los productos tecnológicos).

Ese oro que poseemos es el conocimiento de nuestra realidad, es la infodiversidad—como la llama Morales (1996)—que contiene la realidad variopinta, diversa y compleja que nos caracteriza. Nuestra identidad cultural es parte de esa realidad y por ello es determinante que en estos momentos en que la globalización pretende absorbernos para uniformarnos, encontremos los mecanismos que coadyuven a dar respuesta a la pregunta ¿cómo somos?

La tarea de rescatar la infodiversidad pluricultural y pluriétnica de nuestros países, para agregarle valor y no ofrecerla como simple materia prima, es una urgencia que no podemos seguir soslayando; ésta será una manera de favorecer el conocimiento de la realidad social, económica y política para lograr una visión prospectiva, que promueva el desarrollo de la ciencia autóctona y contribuir así al mejoramiento de la calidad de vida.

Tal como lo afirma Páez (1992:111) "el problema de los países menos avanzados económicamente no es que carezcan de información (o estén subinformados), sino en que no generan su propia inteligencia o no inteligencian la incorporación de más y mejores niveles de conocimiento en los bienes y servicios que generan". Esto se debe precisamente a la ausencia de más y mejores instrumentos que faciliten el acceso a la información autóctona, a la falta de una cultura de información que aumente su uso y además, a la necesidad de un reconocimiento acerca de la importancia que tiene el aprovechamiento y explotación de nuestras oportunidades. Pero sobre todos estos factores, se encuentra la ausencia de una política nacional y regional de información que podría promover la formación y desarrollo de estas bases de datos que inteligencien el conocimiento y la convergencia de ellas en redes especializadas que faciliten su acceso.

La información se vende a precio de oro en los países del norte, porque ellos no solo tienen conciencia de su valor, sino que tienen el poder que les da la tecnología para lograr su manejo eficiente. En el caso de la región centroamericana sin embargo, la información debidamente organizada y sistematizada coadyuvaría a integrar comunidades regionales, mostrando puntos de encuentro que identifiquen esas características que nos rigen, nos ayuden a tomar las decisiones precisas para fortalecer el "cómo somos" y promuevan el desarrollo de un imaginario colectivo que, tal como lo plantea el venezolano Andrés Serbin, construya una identidad inclusiva y no exclusiva, que comparta valores, objetivos comunes y los mecanismos para fortalecerla.

El Centro de Información y Referencia sobre Centroamérica y el Caribe

Ante este contexto deseo destacar la experiencia que el Centro de Información y Referencia sobre Centroamérica y el Caribe (CIRCA) ha venido desarrollando durante seis años. En su afán por responder a la dispersión de datos en la subregión, a la fragmentación informativa y a la subinformación, este Centro ha desarrollado varias herramientas que facilitan la obtención de diversos productos y la oferta de actividades y servicios variados. Pero además, se ha empeñado en generar nuevo conocimiento a partir de encuentros de especialistas de diversas áreas y de facilitar el intercambio por medio de su *Boletín CIRCA*.

Su ámbito temático es pluridisciplinario, pero gira alrededor de un eje aglutinador: la cultura y la identidad en la región Centroamericana y del Caribe. Su crecimiento a la sombra del Centro de Investigación en Identidad y Cultura Latinoamericanas (CIICLA) de la Universidad de Costa Rica, ha permitido que se conjuguen diversas actividades que alimentan los instrumentos de trabajo con que cuenta, lo cual a su vez facilita la ampliación de la oferta de servicios, según vemos a continuación.

Instrumentos de trabajo

El CIRCA cuenta con tres bases de datos públicas que favorecen el acceso a la información que no solo se almacena en su acervo bibliográfico, sino que se encuentra ubicada en otras unidades dentro del país. Éstas son:

1. CIRCA: Es una base que contiene cerca de 4,500 registros, los cuales componen su acervo básico. Éste se ha construido con base en donaciones y el canje que mantiene con diversos centros de investigación homólogos, ubicados tanto dentro como fuera de la región.
2. CANJE: Contiene alrededor de 600 direcciones de personas, instituciones u organizaciones afines, interesadas en el campo de la cultura y la identidad centroamericanas y latinoamericanas. Ella nos permite mantener relaciones de intercambio para la investigación, publicaciones, organización de eventos e información en general, contribuyendo a formar una especie de colegio invisible para diversos fines.
3. BIBLIO: Es la base para la elaboración de uno de nuestros productos: los Módulos Bibliográficos, cuyas características se exponen más adelante. Esta base contiene actualmente 500 registros de documentos

existentes en el país sobre identidad latinoamericana. Sin embargo, su contenido puede variar de acuerdo con el módulo que se esté preparando y además, puede trasladarse a otra computadora para que el investigador interesado prepare en su oficina el módulo que desee publicar.

Servicios, productos y actividades

A partir de los instrumentos supracitados, el CIRCA ofrece varios servicios y actividades que se sintetizan en los siguientes:

1. Documentales: Incluye los servicios típicos de una biblioteca, tales como préstamo de documentos, búsquedas bibliográficas, diseminación selectiva de información y alerta. Varios de estos servicios son restringidos a sus investigadores, pero también se ofrecen a estudiantes y usuarios extranjeros utilizando el correo electrónico, a quienes estén interesados en su temática, tanto dentro como fuera del país.

2. *Boletín CIRCA*: Constituye el medio de comunicación más importante con que cuenta el CIRCA y pretende coadyuvar a la comunicación interregional para dar a conocer las actividades docentes, de investigación y divulgación que se desarrollan tanto dentro como fuera del área. Su publicación es semestral y supone la realización de un trabajo colectivo interinstitucional e interdisciplinario que permita enriquecer y retroalimentar las actividades que se realizan.

3. Módulos bibliográficos: Consisten en trabajos bibliográficos de diversa temática que facilitan la divulgación del conocimiento que genera el CIICLA. Incluyen tanto bibliografías sobre un tema, como estudios biobibliográficos e historiográficos sobre autores, obras o temas más generales. Aunque su publicación es irregular, la preparación es constante y se lleva a cabo por parte de los especialistas que colaboran con el CIICLA.

4. Encuentros de especialistas: Son eventos que se realizan alrededor de un tema determinado, cuyo propósito fundamental es favorecer la confluencia de ideas que se estén generando dentro o fuera de la región centroamericana, pero relacionada con su eje aglutinador primordial. Estos encuentros han permitido realizar contactos con numerosas personas, de manera que podamos ampliar la red de relaciones con especialistas afines.

Como puede observarse, las actividades, servicios y productos que ofrecemos se convierten a la vez en la entrada de datos que alimentan la investigación, lo cual lo vemos ilustrado en el siguiente gráfico.

CIRCA: Organización y gestión

Qué	**Cómo**	**A Quiénes**

Recuperación de Información → Organización y Funcionamiento → Sectores Meta

De esta manera, el *Boletín CIRCA,* como uno de sus ejemplos, deja de ser un producto para convertirse en el insumo que genera nueva investigación sobre un tema determinado. Esta doble condición hace que la información sea el enlace obligado de los componentes de un ciclo que facilita la generación, divulgación y organización del conocimiento.

Textos Documentos Personas Instituciones → Bases de Datos Encuentros de Especialistas → Productos Varios Boletín Módulos Bibliográficos Publicaciones

Por lo anterior, la misión del CIRCA trasciende las tareas simplemente documentales para facilitar la transferencia del conocimiento que genera el CIICLA hacia los usuarios y otros centros de investigación afines. La tecnología con que cuenta—aunque limitada—constituye una herramienta más para facilitar este trabajo; lo más importante es el recurso humano y la comprensión de cómo llevar a la práctica este cometido, que desde 1992, ha ido evolucionando de acuerdo con las necesidades de los usuarios, los programas de posgrado afines y los especialistas sobre la región centroamericana que colaboran con el Centro. No obstante, el uso de la tecnología de información ha ampliado infinitamente esa gama, abriendo las puertas a multiplicidad de personas que estudian el tema de la cultura y la identidad latinoamericanas alrededor del mundo.

La apertura de una página Web (http://cariari.ucr.ac.cr/~filo/ciicla/index.html) para el CIICLA, ha generado numerosas consultas y nuevas relaciones, facilitando también el envío y la comunicación con esos nuevos usuarios, distribuidos alrededor del mundo. Recientemente también se ofrece como servicio el *Boletín CIRCA* en su versión electrónica, lo cual facilitará aún más la recuperación de las reacciones de sus usuarios y ampliará la diseminación del conocimiento que se produce en el CIICLA.

No obstante la limitación de recursos que enfrenta el CIRCA, el trabajo que se realiza es satisfactorio, por cuanto ha permitido elaborar un modelo para la Universidad de Costa Rica, cuyos centros e institutos de investigación, en su mayoría, carecen de un instrumento tan útil como es el CIRCA para el Centro de Investigación en Identidad y Cultura Latinoamericanas. Así nos lo han hecho saber nuestros usuarios en las evaluaciones realizadas.

Queda pendiente organizar una red de investigación e información sobre cultura centroamericana. Sólo así se podrá cumplir con el cometido que dio origen al CIRCA pues ella reforzaría el nexo entre las organizaciones colaboradoras y que de por sí, ya forman una red informal en este campo.

El campo de la identidad y la cultura latinoamericanas es un terreno fértil para cultivar el conocimiento y agregarle valor. Centroamérica es una región políticamente dividida pero unida por características comunes: desigualdades económicas y sociales; costumbres arraigadas, a veces, pero en peligro de ser arrebatadas, en otros casos; recursos naturales todavía florecientes e información concentrada en escasas manos y en manos de pocas personas.

Conocer nuestra realidad es vital para actuar en ella y solo facilitando la recuperación de la información existente es posible llegar al conocimiento que se encuentra encubierto. Descifrar el "cómo somos" es imposible sin información y sin conocernos, es probable que el fenómeno globalizador nos absorba para igualarnos al resto del mundo y así quedar sumergidos en él.

BIBLIOGRAFÍA

Córdoba González, Saray. 1996. "Estudiando las necesidades del usuario a partir de su práctica". *Revista AIBDA* 17 (2), 149–161.

_____. 1997. "La relación, información y desarrollo en el contexto de América Latina". *Ciencias de la Información* (Cuba) 28 (4), 234–240.

Menou, Michel J. 1996. "Cultura, informação e educação de profissionais de informação nos países em desemvolvimento". *Ciência de Informação* 25 (3), 298–304.

Morales, Estela. 1996. "Infodiversidad y cooperación regional". *Revista Interamericana de Bibliotecología* 19:2 (julio–diciembre), 47–60.

Páez Urdaneta, Iraset. 1992. *Gestión de la inteligencia, aprendizaje tecnológico y modernización del trabajo informacional: retos y oportunidades.* Caracas: Instituto de Estudios del Conocimiento de la Universidad Simón Bolívar y Consejo Nacional de Investigaciones Científicas y Tecnológicas.

Programa de las Naciones Unidas para el Desarrollo. 1999. *Informe sobre desarrollo humano 1998.* Madrid: Ed. Mundi – Prensa.

Smith, Jack T. 1996. "Meta-Analysis: The Librarian as a Member of an Interdisciplinary Research Team". *Library Trends* 45 (2), 265–279.

Vitro, Robert A. 1989. "Prospects: Knowledge-Based Development as an Incentive for Educational Innovation". United Nations Educational, Scientific and Cultural Organization Congress, "Education and Informatics: Strengthening International Cooperation" (Paris).

4. Selecting for Storage: Local Problems, Local Responses, and an Emerging Common Challenge

Dan Hazen

Off-site storage has become increasingly common as academic libraries run out of space and the political and financial costs of central campus construction soar out of reach. Storage, as it splits collections and denies browsability, is commonly regarded as a necessary evil for which there are no obvious alternatives. How we select what we store is therefore central in ensuring results that disrupt students, scholars, and collections as little as possible. Grappling with storage as a local phenomenon can also highlight some of the challenges it shares with cooperative programs to create shared or distributed collections. More imaginative ways to describe and manage all of our holdings may emerge as a result.

This essay, after reviewing the purposes of off-site storage, considers the conditions necessary for viable storage arrangements and suggests how these basic conditions have evolved over time. It then explores criteria that can be employed in selecting materials for storage as well as the interplay between these criteria, the mechanics of storage operations, and the pressures associated with storage goals. The paper closes by suggesting some of the larger challenges for which our struggles with storage may provide useful models.

Why Store?

First and foremost, we store our books when the library runs out of space. Lack of space is a condition normally determined as much by economics and politics as by absolute physical limitations. Building new libraries is far more expensive than warehousing little-used materials in remote storage: some projections put off-site construction costs at about 10 percent of those for central facilities. Unoccupied space that could accommodate enlarged libraries, or any other new construction, is often at a premium in campus centers. Promises of eventual empty space as digital collections replace print holdings have not yet borne fruit. In the meantime, remote storage provides a compelling solution.

While space constraints are the most common cause for storage, other considerations can also enter into the mix. One such element is the need to rationalize the physical distribution of library collections. Two scenarios are particularly common. Space constraints have often resulted in collections in which topically related materials are split between different sections of the stacks. In some older libraries, the scatter is even worse as a result of multiple classification schemes. (Many of these libraries developed idiosyncratic local classifications in their early years, eventually switching over to the Library of Congress system but without then recataloging their older holdings.) Full shelves make it difficult to shift books around, so users are expected to do the moving instead. A second problem emerges when the evolution of research interests, book collections, and library buildings leaves high-use materials far from entry points to the stacks, with little-used collections more readily at hand. The efficiencies possible by moving heavily used books close to library patrons can, once again, be difficult to achieve when the stacks are full.

Preservation is another consideration in storage decisions, since off-site housing can provide secure and environmentally favorable conditions for materials that would be at risk in open stacks. Deteriorated items, books or newspapers with inherently fragile paper, and materials susceptible to vandalism or theft can thus be relocated to remote facilities from which they can be recalled for controlled use. Storage facilities can normally accommodate a broad range of at-risk holdings.

Finally, remote storage can provide a lever for certain kinds of cooperative programs. Two examples may suggest both the possibilities and their limitations. The Center for Research Libraries (CRL) has appointed a "Foreign Official Gazettes Task Force" to formalize its effort to absorb hardcopy backfiles of foreign official gazettes, heretofore collected extensively by perhaps a half dozen North American libraries, in order to create master sets.[1] These publications are voluminous, normally printed on poor quality paper, and used only occasionally. They are also essential research resources for which a single, well-managed collection of record may suffice. Cooperative reliance on remote storage at CRL's Chicago headquarters will at once ensure the availability of the materials, rationalize access, produce savings for participating institutions, and strengthen CRL's institutional presence.

Other attempts to make the leap from a cooperative storage facility to common collections policies have proven more problematic. Some consortial storage facilities, for instance, have insisted that they will accept but one copy of any work.[2] Should a second copy be submitted, the duplicate will either be returned or discarded. The effects can be difficult, and not just because participants' volume counts may suffer. Local collection integrity is challenged by this kind of approach. Scarce or unusual materials sent to storage for security reasons, or materials acquired by gift or donation, can all be important to retain regardless of whether the title is already held within a certain group of libraries. Insisting that a storage facility can only house non-duplicative materials of last resort can, paradoxically, undermine the potential of remote storage as a tool for cooperation.

Making Off-Site Storage Work

Whatever the reasons for remote storage, its success depends heavily on how well its proponents address several philosophical, psychological, and operational concerns. Technological change has permitted ever more satisfactory arrangements over time, though our solutions are still far from ideal. The areas requiring attention include bibliographic control, inventory control and physical access, political and financial support, and the adequacy of the storage facility itself.

Bibliographic Control

The possibilities of bibliographic control, and also user expectations concerning bibliographic access, have expanded with time. Early storage facilities, for instance the Midwest Inter-Library Center (the predecessor of The Center for Research Libraries) or the New England Deposit Library, were created in an era of catalog cards and manual files. Book catalogs, printed lists, and general statements of collecting policy—proclamations of CRL's commitment to foreign dissertations, for instance—were the only available access tools. The limitations of this approach, in turn, affected the nature of storage decisions. It proved more satisfactory to relocate categories of materials or entire classification segments (some newspaper backfiles and certain classification segments from Harvard's holdings to the New England Deposit Library, for instance) than to move a scatter of unrelated pieces.

Online catalogs, and more recently the gradual implementation of meaningful serial holdings statements, have transformed both possibilities and expectations. Storage decisions by now almost invariably focus on materials with complete online records. Processing and retrieval efficiencies are thus possible for the library, while users have a better chance of identifying the materials that they need. Fully adequate bibliographic access remains a weak point in remote storage operations, but the improvements have nonetheless been dramatic.

Inventory Control and User Access

Early storage facilities in many ways simply replicated the central libraries that they supplemented. Whether the stacks were open or restricted, materials were shelved in call number order because that was the only way to arrange and then retrieve them. Bar codes and computer-assisted methods for inventory control have since enabled more efficient arrangements. Current storage is built around bar-coded materials that are packed in cartons sized for books of specific dimensions and then housed in efficient, quasi-industrial structures. These systems save space and facilitate retrieval. Physical browsing, however, has become impossible.

Libraries, as they have coped with limited space, have typically adhered to a fairly predictable sequence of palliatives. Parts of the central collections may in the first place be hived off to form independent units. Holdings in music or fine arts, for instance, may thus be relocated to separate quarters, usually amid proclamations of increased efficiency for both specialized users and the mass of library patrons who work with the general collections. Compact shelving, to house more efficiently parts of the library's classified collections, is often the next step. Frazzled users and damaged books are more common than we like to admit, though at least the materials remain on-site.

The next tier of decisions often focuses on relocating little-used materials off-site. Some library systems have constructed what amounts to a branch library for these resources, which are maintained in open-stack, staffed facilities in locations where costs are cheaper than on the central campus.[3] Remote, closed-stack, classified collections are another possibility, though most such arrangements appear to have been implemented when sophisticated methods for inventory control (bar codes and the like) were not available. Some storage facilities have provided reading rooms as well. Size-based shelving in book warehouses completely dissociates book locations from users, leaving computer-based tracking systems as the only means to reestablish the connection.

The best bibliographic control and the most sophisticated storage arrangements mean little unless users can readily get hold of the materials they want. Efficient delivery services are therefore essential. Most libraries with storage facilities now promise deliveries within one working day. Some are considering more frequent runs, as well as the use of Ariel or other document delivery software to service requests for specific articles and other "small" pieces.

Requirements concerning delivery locations can raise additional complications. Most online catalogs allow users to request stored materials without coming to a circulation desk. But the books typically need to be retrieved on-site.[4] In multiunit library systems, each unit will often retain formal rights of ownership and control over the materials it has deposited. This may mean that users can pick up or use the materials only at the library itself. Users may thus face a continued profusion of service points, even though the items they request are all coming from a single location.

Political and Administrative Support

Users particularly resist off-site storage because it limits browsability. Librarians typically counter that our collections are already fragmented and incomplete, with the holdings split among shelving locations that include the main stacks, the reference room, the current periodicals area, and with an invisible portion of materials checked out, on reserve, in preservation queues, or otherwise not on the shelves. Such correct but not necessarily helpful clarifications aside, access and browsability clearly become more difficult when materials are moved off-site. The degradation is especially palpable in libraries whose strength and appeal include extensive holdings of little-used materials.

Careful politicking, as well as effective financial and operational support, is essential. Service and deliveries must be quick and reliable, and both the storage facility and the units that prepare books and bibliographic records for transfer must be fully staffed. Service guarantees must typically come from the highest levels of the university administration, as well as the library. Even when remote storage is a fiscal and operational imperative, implementation will only work when the tradeoffs are openly acknowledged and when there is a clear-cut, ongoing institutional commitment for support.

The Storage Facility Itself

Arrangements for remote housing have evolved from makeshift shelves in unappealing and environmentally inappropriate basements or attics, to rented warehouse space, and most recently to specially constructed modular structures featuring state-of-the-art security systems and environmental controls. Here, as in other areas associated with remote storage, standards and expectations have risen together. Quarters that might once have passed muster are no longer acceptable.

Criteria for Selecting for Storage

Once off-site storage has been embraced (or mandated), both the political process to secure user acceptance and the logistics of relocation require decisions concerning general selection criteria and specific transfer procedures. Users must be convinced that the decisions will be as sensible as possible. They must likewise know that mistakes can be corrected. Librarians of course share these goals, even as they are more likely to feel the pressure of their overflowing shelves. The way that the process typically plays out suggests a number of general observations:

1. Libraries usually begin to move materials only when their buildings are full. "Full" in some cases implies a comfortable shelving load with as much as 15 percent free space to accommodate collection growth, minor stack shifts, and open shelves for users to spread out books. More often, and dramatically, it can reflect an emergency situation in which books are piled on windowsills, floors, and in special staging areas. Such conditions can be compelling in presenting the case for storage to reluctant library users.

2. Starting to store when the library is full implies that one volume must be relocated for every volume added to the stacks. This usually leads to arrangements to divide current receipts between materials for the stacks and for storage. Selectors typically make the decisions, though some libraries also display all incoming materials so that users can identify any items that they find particularly important. New receipts are "unknown" to the existing collection, and choices made upon receipt allow these items to be directed off-site through a single decision and

processing sequence. Storing many current materials may not, however, be an optimal approach in terms of research priorities and needs.

The criteria for relocating materials that are already in the stacks tend to
be more contentious, and the processes more complex. Priorities for this
process usually include the following considerations.

Easy Decisions

Storage decisions reflect the relationship between transfer candidates and
bibliographic control, at times with unintended consequences. Contemporary
library systems and practice mandate automated bibliographic records for all
stored items. New receipts are ordinarily processed entirely online, so they are
easy candidates. Research libraries that have fully converted their card catalogs
can freely draw from retrospective holdings as well, since all these materials
are also represented online. But some libraries have made only piecemeal
progress with RECON. Their automated records may thus reflect specific projects to improve access to particularly important parts of the collection. Virtually all libraries by now rely on automated circulation, so items charged out
without full online records are normally processed fully upon their return.
Under these circumstances, records for older materials that are considered
important, plus those for items that have actually been used, will be the first to
appear in automated form. Storage decisions in these repositories are thus limited to a universe comprised of recent receipts, high-profile holdings, and high-
use parts of the collection. The dusty volumes that no one wants are likely to
remain untouched. The rhetoric of storage typically speaks of moving research
materials that exhibit low use. In collections not yet fully converted, this "use"
criterion can easily be turned upside down.

Shelf space and decision-making time are typically the commodities in
shortest supply as transfer processes are put into place. Serials, multivolume
sets, and fat books are especially attractive candidates for storage: one decision
can free lots of shelf space; it is easier to change a single record to reflect a new
location than to adjust many; the impact in the stacks is visible and dramatic.
The unintended consequence, however, can be an in-house collection increasingly biased toward thin books and pamphlets. Moving long runs of unindexed
serials can be particularly grave in terms of diminished user access.

The simplest sort of storage decision is simply to move an entire classification segment or category of materials. As research agendas become broader
and the supporting resources more encompassing, this kind of "clear cutting"
is less and less likely to work. When it does, it can be extremely effective.

A Hassle-Free Process

Goodwill and efficiency are alike served by storage decisions that are easily borne by both users and the library staff. Certain faculty constituencies may
in some cases want to review carefully all storage recommendations. Other

groups may remain more comfortable with decisions made within the library. A balanced approach is essential in order to demonstrate that no collections are exempt from storage. But it is also important to minimize antagonism and disruption.

A Reversible Process

Users require general assurances, and also concrete procedures, to bring back permanently materials that have been transferred off-site. Repeatedly retrieving materials from storage incurs real costs, so many libraries also utilize "automatic" procedures to identify heavy-use off-site items that might be returned to the stacks. Circulation counters, for instance, can generate reports of materials reaching a predetermined circulation threshold. (Some rare or vulnerable items, of course, may deliberately remain off-site, regardless of their level of use.)

A Cost-Effective Process

Storage decisions should privilege materials that are easy to identify and process, and that will generate significant free space. Such categories as duplicates of little-used materials, superseded editions, some translations into some foreign languages, and other libraries' accession lists may represent some of these areas. Considerations of cost-effectiveness should inform the entire storage cycle, both in overall terms and for specific operations including selection, processing, and storage and retrieval.

Collection Integrity

Research libraries have built their collections through expensive, carefully planned efforts that have extended over decades and in some cases centuries. Their holdings are deliberate creations of mutually reinforcing materials, not just haphazard accumulations of books and journals. The depth that distinguishes these research collections is reflected most immediately, albeit imperfectly, by the materials in the stacks. Multiple classification systems, separate shelving locations, materials not on the shelf at a given moment, and other "imperfections" of course limit how much of any collection can actually be apprehended at any one time. Removing materials for remote storage substantially exacerbates the problem. When criteria of costs and benefits prevail exclusively, little-used items are those most likely to be relocated. The process thus tends to remove precisely the sorts of materials that give research library collections their character. Off-site storage can easily result in on-site holdings that offer only minimally more than the core collections in much smaller libraries.

Possible solutions include measures to leave some distinctive materials in the stacks, even if they have not been used. For some literature collections, for instance, at least one work by every author might be retained. A few narrow topical segments might likewise be left intact, as well as occasional (non-circulating) examples of rare or classic works that students, in particular, might otherwise never encounter. New approaches to bibliographic control, as described below, may allow more imaginative solutions.

Security and Preservation

Contemporary storage facilities are secure. They also provide near-ideal environments for books. They therefore enable libraries to preserve materials at risk due to high value, susceptibility to theft or vandalism, scarcity, or poor physical condition. Most repositories own materials that should not be shelved in open stacks, and off-site storage provides an obvious solution.

Practical Approaches to Selecting for Storage

Politics, Communication, Consensus

Off-site storage is often a difficult prospect for both librarians and library users. Reduced access to library holdings is always unsettling, even discounting users' sometimes romanticized visions of current arrangements.[5] The mechanics of moving materials can leave everyone suspicious that his or her areas of interest are being unfairly targeted. Communication, collaboration, and consensus-building are crucial.

Off-site storage has to be sold on two levels. The university and library administration need to explain and justify the general concept of remote storage, usually by demonstrating the hard facts of exhausted library space and limited capital budgets. But explaining storage as an unavoidable though abstract solution is only a first step. Focused meetings with individual departments and faculty members are also essential in order to build consensus around the specific criteria that will inform transfer decisions. The choices will normally be based on local patterns of use and on research trends within each discipline and field. They must also reflect the concrete research interests of specific professors and students. Agreements can sometimes be reached through discussion alone. In other cases it may be useful to share and evaluate sample lists of transfer candidates. And sometimes it is most productive to walk the stacks with one or two faculty members, discussing specific items and categories of materials while they are immediately at hand. Whatever the approach, faculty involvement is essential.

Decision-Making on the Ground

The simplest storage decisions are based on entire categories of materials. Hardcopy newspaper backfiles, materials housed on-site in limited access "cages" (semi-rare materials, items susceptible to vandalism or theft, etc.), children's books, folio volumes, and the like are among the possibilities. Very few classified collection segments can be relocated in their entirety, no matter how esoteric they seem or how little they are used. Sooner or later, item-level selection almost always becomes essential. In some cases "intermediate" decisions may also be possible. When a library owns long runs of several news magazines from a particular country, for instance, it may be possible to keep one set in the stacks and to move other backfiles to storage, often with a cut-off date to keep all issues from the past five or ten years on the shelves. Users seeking to compare accounts of a particular process or event can orient themselves by consulting the title remaining in the stacks, and then recall complementary volumes as needed. When good indexes are available, some scholarly journals can also be considered for storage. Some materials that have been reformatted in microform editions or as digital products may likewise be plausible transfer candidates, though usability, demand, and functionality must all be weighed.

Item-level selection for storage is typically a two-stage process. Potential transfer candidates are first identified through a mechanical procedure, and the tentative choices are then ratified by bibliographers and/or users. The initial phase often consists of a broad sweep through some part of the collection to identify materials that have received little use. The threshold will vary between institutions, partly as a function of local decisions about the amount of space to be cleared. In Harvard's case, the automated circulation system can generate lists of all items that have not been charged out since its inception in the late 1970s. Libraries without good online circulation information may need to assess use by consulting the "date due" stamps in the back of each book. Specific approaches will also be informed by the feasibility of generating and working from lists of holdings, or sending teams of students or paraprofessionals into the stacks to flyer or otherwise mark physical volumes.

Variants are possible as well, for example more sophisticated computer algorithms that go beyond the single criterion of past circulation to weigh differential use patterns among separate classification segments (a surrogate for academic fields), and such additional features as whether a particular work is a translation or an additional edition, and its language and publication date. At least in theory, the result is a weighted, rank-order list that predicts whether a given book is likely to circulate in the future. Such models can be costly to devise and validate, and the lists themselves tend to be more expensive to prepare than straightforward tallies of past circulation.

No matter how the candidates for transfer are initially identified, a successful process requires subsequent review by a bibliographer and perhaps by faculty members as well. Apart from possible errors from coding mistakes, machine-generated lists may include non-circulating reference-like works that have been housed in the stacks. Bare-bones lists of items that have not circulated also fail to convey the broader context of the surrounding collection, which will typically inform transfer decisions as well. When low-circulation items have been flyered or otherwise marked in the stacks (one common technique is to apply pressure-sensitive colored dots to the spines of transfer candidates), both librarians and users can be invited to remove the markers from materials that they want to keep on-site. Even in list-based storage selection exercises, decisions are usually most effective when the materials are also inspected in the stacks. Stack reviews also can reveal other storage candidates—for instance materials needing preservation attention, duplicates that are no longer in demand, superseded editions, and the like—that may not emerge from circulation lists alone.

The most common approach to storage decisions begins with preselection based on circulation. Uncritically accepting use as the primary criterion for storage, however, can easily compromise collection integrity. Some of the most difficult professional judgments concerning transfers come in attempting to represent a collection's richness and depth without subverting the economistic logic that underlies our whole concept of off-site storage.

A final check on storage decisions typically comes from the staff members who process the transfers. Selection anomalies, for instance when a single volume in a multivolume set has been marked for relocation, can be returned for reconsideration. Processing staff can also keep track of items not found on the shelves in order to enable tracing activities and the possible determination that particular pieces need to be replaced or declared "lost."

Remote Storage Writ Large: Problems, Palliatives, and the Link to Distributed Collections

More and more research libraries are grappling with storage. Off-site facilities nonetheless remain a decidedly second-best alternative to the classified, inclusive, open-stack collections whose successful expansion has made them necessary. The two major disadvantages of off-site storage respectively center on bibliographic and on physical access.

Bibliographic Access

Today's storage facilities house closed collections in arrangements that facilitate inventory control and minimize costs at the expense of browsing. In a non-browsing environment, books and journals can only be identified through the bibliographic records in local OPACs. Both the descriptions and the retrieval tools therefore need to be as good as we can make them. Four aspects merit particular emphasis:

1. Catalog records for materials housed off-site need to be as complete as possible. "Minimal-level cataloging" and other abbreviated records are problematic as the sole means of access to physically remote materials. Full records are essential.
2. Complete MARC catalog records include a wealth of coded and free-text information. Our on-line catalogs are only slowly becoming able to manipulate all these data. Constructing sophisticated searches too often remains difficult. Our catalogs should allow users to take quick and effective advantage of all the information built into full catalog records.

3. Serials are at once attractive and problematic candidates for storage. Moving a serial can save lots of space, but effective access can then be almost impossible. In many fields, journals are the principal outlet for current research. Articles, not monographs, are the basic units in scholarly exchange. In many parts of the world, the economics of publishing also puts a premium on journals, which are produced more cheaply and easily than monographs. Serials are critical for scholarship, but their effective utilization requires access to their contents.

We can by now represent detailed serial holdings in our online records. With appropriate initial processing, users should thus be able to verify a library's precise holdings of an off-site serial. Knowing what is inside these volumes and issues, however, can be far more difficult. Printed indexes are an obvious resource, and many serials periodically produce cumulative indexes to their contents. External indexing services may also cover a specific journal, though it is important to confirm both time frame and completeness.

Digital technologies may also have a role to play. Perhaps the simplest approach is to scan page images of tables of contents for users to consult online, through a product somewhat analogous to the notebooks of photocopied tables of contents available in some institutions.[6] Creating searchable text files of tables of contents, which could support queries based on author name, keywords, and the like, might be a (more expensive) next step. Full indexing, finally, could enable users to receive automatic bibliographic updates alerting them to articles falling within personalized subject profiles.

4. Digital representations of serial tables of contents may suggest other ways to exploit electronic technology in improving access to stored library materials. Browsing often consists of quick riffles through a group of books. Most users can quickly assess the potential utility of a work by glancing at its table of contents, gauging the level and nature of the prose, noting the presence of footnotes and the type font, etc. The title page, the table of contents, and the introduction are perhaps the most revealing pages. Scanning a very few "key" pages from monographs destined for storage, and then linking those digital images to catalog records, might provide a partial surrogate for browsing. Users could at least get a peek at potentially useful materials, and on that basis decide whether to recall them from storage.

Physical Access

Physical access can also be problematic for materials housed off-site. Stored books and journals need to be recalled through a process that involves both a time delay and occasional requirements to retrieve or consult the piece in a specific library unit. Users may eventually have to contend with a proliferation of service points, reading rooms, and access hoops. Document delivery capabilities, for instance Ariel and fax transmission of journal articles, can minimize some of the inconvenience. Additional enhancements need to be worked out as well.

Conclusion

More and more libraries are running out of space and turning to off-site storage. These libraries face a multitude of political, philosophical, and practical challenges in selling the concept, selecting materials to move, and implementing their storage decisions. Browsability, bibliographic access, and physical access to collections all become problematic when materials are no longer at hand in the stacks.

These same challenges also arise for materials held (off-site) by other libraries. Here, even more emphatically than with local storage facilities, users must rely on bibliographic records and on-line catalogs to evaluate materials of potential interest. Physical access is mediated through interlibrary loan and document delivery. The solutions we devise for off-site storage are therefore pertinent to many of our misgivings about cooperative collection development and distributed research collections.

Both off-site storage and distributed collections are likely to be only grudgingly accepted until the issues of enhanced bibliographic records and systems, limited digitization of book contents as a partial surrogate for on-site browsing, and streamlined mechanisms for physical access are more directly confronted. When the issue of access to remote materials is cast in terms of our national and international library system, rather than as a purely local matter of storage and retrieval, the need to improve access to *all* of our holdings also comes into sharper relief. Off-site storage, which affects us one library at a time, requires rigorous local responses. The very similar problems of remote resources pose a challenge for us all.

NOTES

1. See http://www.crl.uchicago.edu under "Special Projects Currently Underway."

2. For instance, see the general statement of "Material Eligible and Not Eligible for Deposit" in the "Statement of Operating Principles" for California's Northern Regional Library Facility (http://www.lib.berkeley.edu/nrlf). Special collections materials are exempted from NRLF's non-duplication mandate.

3. As reported during SALALM's 1999 conference, Vanderbilt University maintains this kind of facility in downtown Nashville.

4. Harvard's experiments with direct drop-offs at faculty offices suggest extremely high costs.

5. See, for example, Grace Palladino's opinion piece, "Out of Sight, Out of Mind: Shelving by Height at the Library of Congress," *The Chronicle of Higher Education*, June 11, 1999, p. B6. Palladino's essay reacts to proposals to reshelve the books within LC's central stacks.

6. Harvard's "Digital Contents Pilot Project" (DCPP), for scholarly journals being relocated to storage, is exploring this kind of approach. See http://hul.harvard.edu/ldi/html/dcpp.html.

5. Centros de documentación y bases de datos sobre asuntos de la mujer y género en América Latina

J. Félix Martínez Barrientos

La información juega un papel trascendente en la perspectiva de los cambios y modificaciones de las relaciones entre los géneros y en la creación de instancias específicas para abordar la problemática de los géneros como temas de estudio. Así mismo se dice que estos cambios y modificaciones, este forcejeo y esta aspiración legítima en la lucha por la igualdad entre los géneros constituyen un asunto profundamente político. Si así se manifiesta la problemática entre los géneros, la utilidad de la información y su impacto en la conformación de nuevas relaciones intergenéricas, resulta o se constituye en un recurso estratégico fundamental.

El trabajo que aquí se presenta es apenas un acercamiento preliminar a las condiciones y desarrollo de los centros de documentación y bibliotecas en el tema de la mujer y género en América Latina y las bases de datos que cada centro genera. En trabajos posteriores se deberá realizar un censo más completo y detallado a fin de cubrir las carencias que presenta este trabajo.

Para la elaboración del tema se han utilizado las siguientes fuentes: el documento de Isis Internacional, Chile, *Centros de información, documentación y bibliotecas en el tema de la mujer en América Latina y el Caribe: análisis y catastro;* el servicio de información en línea sobre mujeres denominado "Mapping the World of Women's Information Services" elaborado por el Centro Internacional de Información y Archivos para el Movimiento de la Mujer con sede en Amsterdam, Holanda; la información proporcionada por una de mis jefas, la Mtra. Lorenia Parada-Ampudia, del cuestionario aplicado a los centros y programas de instituciones de educación superior en México en el área de género y la respuesta a un cuestionario enviado a Latinoamérica que algunas/os colegas han tenido a bien contestarme.

El estudio contiene dos partes: la primera consiste en una reflexión sobre la relación entre feminismo y documentación y en segundo término una descripción y análisis de las condiciones y desarrollo de los centros y bibliotecas sobre la mujer y género en Latinoamérica.

Feminismo y documentación

La aparición del feminismo en el ámbito internacional se da alrededor de los años sesenta y setenta. Este hecho va acompañado del auge y del estallamiento de la crisis del denominado estado del bienestar y del surgimiento de un amplio movimiento social que incluye al movimiento obrero. Estas manifestaciones sociales ya no se inscriben dentro del tradicional esquema planteado por los principios y programas de las organizaciones sindicales y políticas, pues se reconoce que la dualidad capital-trabajo no constituye el único marco de acción de los movimientos sociales.

De esta manera la presencia de movimientos de carácter sectorial como los de estudiantes y jóvenes, los de mujeres y los de la comunidad homosexual, entre otras, exige reconocimiento y legitimidad a su existencia como tales y la satisfacción a sus necesidades específicas. De este modo el análisis se orienta ya no en función de la visión dicotómica de la lucha social, sino a partir del reconocimiento de otros actores sociales que reclaman un nuevo orden social sin modelos preestablecidos, visión dicotómica que sustrae el reconocimiento a lo diverso como condición básica de existencia de las sociedades modernas (Molina 1996:4).

En este contexto la condición opresiva de la mujer y la voluntad de construir nuevas condiciones de existencia, pasa por la necesidad de reconocerse como nuevo sujeto, independiente, que obliga a la mujer a documentar su historia, su movimiento y a generar las bases para la construcción de un nuevo conocimiento. Se crean así, las condiciones para la aparición del trabajo documental y la conformación de centros de documentación que en algunos casos han tenido su inicio en el trabajo de compilación bibliográfica individual que varias mujeres han realizado con objeto de documentar la historia y lucha de las mujeres.

Los centros de documentación son parte y fruto del propio movimiento feminista y a su vez lo recrean constantemente, ya que son cuerpo y sustento de la reflexión y del análisis de la condición y actividad de las mujeres. Actualmente su ámbito de acción se ha extendido aún más a los sectores universitarios y académicos, y al uso de la información con el objetivo de instrumentar el diseño y aplicación de las políticas públicas.

En la declaración del primer taller sobre organización y funcionamiento de centros de información y documentación en el tema de la mujer en América Latina, se dice lo siguiente:

> . . . nuestros centros de documentación se constituyen en las únicas fuentes de suministro de información sobre la vida de las mujeres. Son espacios fundamentales que registran día con día el protagonismo de las mujeres: su actividad en el barrio, su presencia en las fábricas, en el gabinete de trabajo en las universidades o en la soledad del trabajo creador.[1]

Para América Latina la década de los setenta pero sobre todo la de los ochenta constituye el espacio de aparición y desarrollo del movimiento feminista, pues en los noventa de la misma manera que en otras partes del mundo se observa un fuerte proceso de institucionalización del movimiento, que a la vez que amplia los espacios de acción de las mujeres suscita diversas interrogantes y cuestionamientos.

La conferencia de Beijin significó el punto culminante de este proceso pues por primera vez una parte significativa del movimiento se adentró en los espacios oficiales, nacionales e internacionales y, como sociedad civil, negoció intensamente sus propuestas desde adentro y desde afuera, desde códigos diferentes y extraños y desde lógicas que no eran las del movimiento.[2]

Así los espacios documentales e informativos están sujetos a este tipo de circunstancias y asumen características propias según cada situación que se presenta.

En el Cuadro 1, hemos agrupado los centros y/o bibliotecas por década de fundación y por tipo de organización, toda vez que se busca con ello, establecer una relación entre la periodización natural del movimiento feminista y el año o década de fundación de los centros de documentación, y el tipo de organización a la que cada centro pertenece.

En el citado cuadro hemos registrado 2 centros o bibliotecas cuya fecha de fundación se encuentra en la década de los cincuenta. Uno es el Centro de Documentación e Información "Carmen Lyra" de la Alianza de Mujeres Costarricenses que es un Centro Popular de Asesoría Legal, con sede en la ciudad de San José de Costa Rica el cual tiene como fecha de fundación el año de 1952, es decir varias décadas antes del auge del movimiento feminista latinoamericano de la década de los ochenta. La explicación de su larga existencia puede deberse a que esta nación centroamericana siempre se ha

Cuadro 1. Número de centros y/o bibliotecas y tipo
de organización por década

Década	ONGs	Académico	Gobierno	Organización Internacional	Otro	Totales
1950	1			1		2
1960	4	1				5
1970	13	1		3		17
1980	39	3	4			46
1990	18	12	2		1	33
S/año	5	3	2			10
Totales	80	20	8	4	1	113

Fuente: Elaboración propia con datos de catastro e información de cuestionarios y textos de "Mapping the World".

caracterizado por la tradición de ya más de 100 años del ejercicio de la democracia electoral, de la supresión de su ejército en favor de otros programas de carácter social, sin que por ello se pueda hablar aún de una sociedad igualitaria.

El otro centro de documentación—más bien biblioteca—es FLACSO-Chile fundada el año de 1957, a la que propiamente no puede considerarse como resultado del movimiento feminista, toda vez que sus objetivos corresponden a otras estrategias de desarrollo como organismo internacional. No obstante eso no quiere decir que su trabajo informativo no repercuta favorablemente en el desarrollo del movimiento feminista o de las mujeres en general.

Otros aspectos a destacar son la correspondencia entre el auge del movimiento feminista y el mayor número de centros fundados en la década de los ochenta con 39; el incremento de los centros de documentación vinculados a las universidades, con la posibilidad de seguir creciendo a consecuencia de la cada vez mayor institucionalización y formalización de los estudios de género y mujer en las universidades latinoamericanas en la década de los noventa; y, por último, la persistencia mayoritaria de los centros vinculados a las ONGs, que dan fe todavía de la importancia de la autonomía y de su vínculo estrecho con el movimiento feminista.

De manera general el trabajo documental y la creación de centros específicos para el desarrollo de esta actividad al interior del movimiento feminista y de las mujeres, constituyen una expresión o una extensión del propio movimiento y la disciplina de estudios que de él deriva, pues los objetivos y la actividad de cada centro se encuentran inscritos dentro de la actividad general de cada organización del movimiento.

Conviene destacar este vínculo, ya que si bien en cada organización o institución académica que cuenta con una biblioteca o centro, éstos forman parte orgánica de aquella, al igual que de sus objetivos y metas, en modo alguno pueden compararse con el carácter militante que tipifica a los centros o bibliotecas vinculados al movimiento feminista y/o de las mujeres.

Según Virginia Vargas, el movimiento feminista es una expresión del movimiento de mujeres que hace del conocimiento y la eliminación de las jerarquías sexuales su objetivo fundamental (Vargas 1987:83–90). Así, la situación de pertenencia al movimiento de los diferentes centros de información y/o documentación hacen suyo este planteamiento y de diversas formas plasman como su objetivo más general la demanda de la igualdad y la equidad entre los géneros.[3]

Se podría decir entonces, que el vínculo de la actividad documental con el movimiento feminista o con la lucha de las mujeres en general se expresa de manera tal que posibilita:

- Documentar la actividad del movimiento, tanto en su acepción de proveedor de información, que busca sustentar la práctica política feminista, como la de compilador de información cuyo objetivo consiste en resguardar la memoria histórica del movimiento.

- Hacer visible las aportaciones de las mujeres en los distintos ámbitos del trabajo cultural y científico, y el de la propia vida cotidiana.
- Crear condiciones para el acceso al conocimiento sobre el papel de la mujer en la sociedad y la oportunidad para cambiar patrones o roles que permitan la reinserción de la mujer bajo una nueva perspectiva de acción social.
- Informar para empoderar a la mujer, que ha sido el clásico "slogan" de las metas que se persiguen en los servicios de información orientados hacia la mujer, sólo que con el sentido del uso del poder no en términos de autoridad sino como la posibilidad de *poder* hacer.
- Vincular el trabajo documental con los objetivos de equidad e igualdad entre los géneros.

Por otra parte la evolución del movimiento de las mujeres y del feminismo en particular, ha repercutido de manera diversa en los centros de documentación. En primer lugar me interesa destacar aquí, la relación existente entre las demandas del movimiento con la amplitud y flujos temáticos de la información que se observan en el trabajo cotidiano de cada centro de documentación.

En este sentido se puede decir que las demandas y la problemática económico-social de las mujeres constituyen los delimitadores de los contenidos y los flujos temáticos de la información. Considérese por ejemplo cómo cambió el espectro temático una vez que el movimiento de las mujeres y del feminismo en particular, asumieron su identidad de género, propiciando que temas como la sexualidad, las relaciones de pareja, o la violencia masculina pasaran a formar parte de las demandas del movimiento de las mujeres. Anteriormente el feminismo se caracterizaba por hacer la defensa de las mujeres y la de sus condiciones de vida, es decir avanzar en la comprensión de la situación de la mujer, pero no en la suya propia, sino la de las "otras" (Vargas 1998).

Otros factores relacionados con la amplitud de los contenidos temáticos de la información son: la incorporación del concepto de género que permitió una creciente apertura a nuevos temas y nuevos sectores sociales tales como el asedio sexual en los lugares de trabajo, la nueva masculinidad y el estudio de las homosexualidades (1998:11). El otro es la gestión gubernamental hacia las mujeres que ha detonado interesantes procesos de reflexión y debate público, mismos que han permitido visibilizar una serie de temáticas, como derechos reproductivos, feminización de la pobreza, exclusión política y otros que menciona en su texto, Natacha Molina (Molina 1996:5).

En segundo lugar llamo la atención sobre las repercusiones de tres fenómenos que se suscitan al interior del movimiento de las mujeres: la institucionalización, la creciente apertura (con todo y los diferentes problemas que tienen para su creación) de centros o programas de estudio en el área de género en las universidades latinas, y la incorporación de la perspectiva de género en el diseño de políticas públicas. Todos ellos generan presiones constantes sobre los centros debido al incremento de la demanda informativa, lo cual plantea diferentes retos a resolver en el entorno latinoamericano.

Así entonces la perspectiva de género en el trabajo documental reside en la posibilidad real de que en cada centro o biblioteca, la organización de la información, así como la oferta de sus servicios, contemplen las diferencias de sexo con objeto de incidir en el proceso de generación de nuevo conocimiento, de nuevos saberes que equilibren las diferencias de equidad y favorezcan el empoderamiento de la mujer, de lo que se trata es de hacer visible lo invisible y datar las condiciones de vida de la mujer para ofrecer alternativas de cambio e incrementar el acceso a la información de parte de las mujeres.

Condiciones y desarrollo de los centros de información, documentación y bibliotecas de América Latina

Según el Cuadro 2 existen alrededor de 113 centros de información, documentación o bibliotecas en el tema de la mujer y género en América Latina. De este gran total y de 23 países de la región, Argentina, Brasil, Chile, Colombia, Costa Rica, México, Nicaragua, Perú y República Dominicana, se destacan con el mayor número, pero aún cuando no se encuentran censados la totalidad de los centros de información existentes en cada país, el dato es muy importante. México concentra el mayor número de centros pero esto se debe al mayor acceso que se tuvo de la información requerida.

En relación con las áreas de especialización de cada centro (véase Cuadro 3), cada una de ellas muestra en cierto sentido, las diferentes problemáticas sociales de la mujer y en algunos casos, en los que se agrupan mayoritariamente alrededor de algunos temas, una parte de los grandes problemas de nuestra región. Me refiero por ejemplo a los 44 centros que manejan información especializada sobre el tema de la violencia contra la mujer y los 32 relacionados con el asunto de la salud; en algunos otros como identidad de la mujer (41 frecuencias) o como el tema de economía y trabajo (15 frecuencias), que constituyen temas clásicos de la investigación feminista.

Si bien es cierto que este cuadro de especializaciones muestra la preferencia o el compromiso de las organizaciones con ciertas áreas de trabajo, en realidad la mayor parte de los centros agrupa su información haciendo uso de la lista de descriptores que contiene 30 categorías generales a partir de las cuales se controla el flujo de información y en este sentido ofrecer una información más diversificada.

En el Cuadro 4 se pueden observar las categorías de personas a las que están destinados los servicios de información. Es curioso pero resulta ser que no son los sectores populares los que mayoritariamente hacen uso de los servicios de información, sino más bien los sectores vinculados con los medios educativos y universitarios los que gozan de este privilegio. Es contradictoria esta situación en la medida que siendo mayoritarios los centros vinculados a ONGs no se pueda decir lo mismo de los usuarios de estos. Por otra parte es

Cuadro 2. Centros de información, documentación y bibliotecas en el tema de la mujer y género en América Latina

País	Número de Centros
Argentina	9
Bahamas	1
Barbados	1
Belice	1
Bolivia	4
Brasil	11
Chile	10
Colombia	7
Costa Rica	7
Ecuador	7
Guatemala	1
Guyana	1
Honduras	1
México	20
Nicaragua	5
Panamá	1
Paraguay	3
Perú	6
Puerto Rico	2
República Dominicana	8
Trinidad y Tobago	1
Uruguay	4
Venezuela	2
Total	113

Fuente: Elaboración propia con datos de catastro e información de cuestionarios y textos de "Mapping the World".

interesante el fenómeno por las expectativas que abre en términos de la reproducción del pensamiento o de los estudios sobre la mujer y el género; luego de acuerdo con el orden de frecuencia se sitúan las usuarias/os de ONGs y el sector de mujeres y mujeres populares urbanas.

Vista como un todo (véase Cuadro 5) la cantidad de registros de las distintas bases de datos por país da un total de 239,096, procedente de 15 países con 89 bases de datos y de 48 instituciones involucradas. De acuerdo con esta cifra la cantidad de recursos informativos disponibles plantea una serie de posibilidades de trabajo que sin duda alguna fortalecen el acceso a la información de parte de las mujeres y la de las/os estudiosas/os del género.

Descartando los registros repetidos, estas bases de datos más las que no alcanzaron a registrarse, conforman un poderoso instrumento de consulta de

Cuadro 3. Areas de especialización de los centros

Temas de Especialización	Número de Centros o Bibliotecas
Agricultura y desarrollo rural	3
Bibliografías, directorios	3
Bisexualidad	1
Ciclos de vida	1
Comunicación e información	4
Cooperación para el desarrollo	5
Cultura	16
Demografía	11
Democracia	2
Derecho y legislación	33
Derechos de las mujeres	1
Derechos humanos	4
Desarrollo científico y nuevas tecnologías	1
Economía y trabajo	15
Educación y capacitación	19
Escritoras de América	1
Familia y pareja	4
Feminismo	1
Género	10
Historia del feminismo	1
Identidad de la mujer	41
Ideologías	4
Indígenas	3
Investigación y desarrollo científico	1
Jóvenes	1
Lesbianismo	2
Literatura	1
Masculinidad	4
Medio ambiente y urbanismo	11
Metodología feminista	1
Movimiento lésbico	1
Movimientos sociales	1
Mujer	4
Niñas	1
Organización social y actores sociales	4
Política, sistemas y procesos	7
Religión	1
Salud	32
Salud reproductiva	17
Sexualidad	11
Teoría y análisis	37
Violencia en contra de la mujer	44
Violencia intrafamiliar	2
Violencia sexual	1

Fuente: Elaboración propia con datos de catastro e información de cuestionarios y textos de "Mapping the World".

Cuadro 4. Usuarios y sectores o estratos de procedencia

Sectores o Estratos de Procedencia	Número de Centros de Ocurrencia	%
Agentes sociales	5	2.6
Comunidad lésbico/gay	4	2.0
Docentes, universitarias/os, profesionales (sector educativo)	76	39.6
Funcionarios y miembros de la propia institución	8	4.2
Jóvenes	3	1.6
Medios de comunicación	9	4.7
Mujeres rurales	11	5.7
Mujeres y mujeres populares urbanas	25	13.0
ONGs	29	15.1
Organismos internacionales	3	1.6
Público en general	4	2.0
Reclusas/os	1	0.5
Sector gobierno	14	7.3
Total	192	99.9

Fuente: Elaboración propia con datos de catastro e información de cuestionarios y textos de "Mapping the World".

origen nacional o local, que por la forma tan atomizada en que se encuentran sólo tienen impacto a nivel local-regional, aunque en contraparte alcanzan profundidad temática por lo específico que pueden ser sus materiales o porque son por lo general bases de datos circunscritas a un sólo tema.

Así entonces, nos encontramos con una paradoja en el terreno de la oferta informativa y la condición de los centros de información, documentación y bibliotecas de América Latina; por un lado, la importancia de contar con una basta red de centros de información y documentación y la enorme oferta informativa representada por las distintas bases de datos de cada centro o biblioteca (con sus diversas temáticas) y por otro, el relativo bajo impacto debido a la atomización (dispersión) de la oferta informativa, su localismo y la poca eficacia que hasta ahora demuestran las diferentes redes documentales sobre género y mujer.

Por esta razón, la riqueza informativa que representan las ya numerosas bases de datos de la región latinoamericana y los centros que las administran, nos obliga a establecer compromisos para que esta riqueza pueda ser utilizada y compartida en la región por todas aquellas personas e instituciones interesadas en la información de género en Latinoamérica y el Caribe.

Cuadro 5. Bases de datos y acervos por país

País	Registros Totales	Número de Bases	Instituciones
Argentina	15,445	7	5
Bolivia	3,873	3	1
Brasil	14,300	8	4
Chile	23,345	7	4
Colombia	6,400	6	2
Costa Rica	9,595	5	3
Ecuador	22,931	3	2
Guyana	7,432	3	1
México	60,785	20	14
Nicaragua	4,500	4	1
Panamá	636	1	1
Paraguay	25,840	3	2
Perú	34,158	12	5
República Dominicana	3,156	5	2
Uruguay	6,700	2	1
Total	239,096	89	48

Fuente: Elaboración propia con datos de catastro e información de cuestionarios y textos de "Mapping the World".

Revisando el Cuadro 6, nos podemos percatar de las enormes bondades de microisis en procesos de automatización de bibliotecas y centros en instituciones sin recursos, para el caso tal vez no existe mejor ejemplo que el papel que este software cumple en cada centro vinculado al feminismo y/o a los estudios de género y mujer.

Según el mismo cuadro, otro conjunto de bibliotecas o centros, cuentan con software integrado de gran costo con el que pueden administrar todas y cada una de las actividades del trabajo bibliotecario. De estos solo se registran casos aislados y generalmente están vinculados a instituciones educativas que destinan un presupuesto fuerte para la compra de libros y equipamiento para la biblioteca, en tanto, otro conjunto de centros usan o diseñan sus bases de datos usando o programando en Cliper o Dbase, destacándose también el alto porcentaje de centros que no aportan información alguna.

Sobre las redes (véase Cuadro 7), si hay algún sector que gusta de trabajar en red, de estar "enredadas", ese es el movimiento feminista; no obstante en lo que toca a las redes latinoamericanas en el rubro del área de documentación, en realidad no existen, pese a que frecuentemente se mencione su necesidad.

La Fundación Carlos Chagas de Brasil menciona la existencia de la Red Latinoamericana de Información y Documentación pero en realidad no se

Cuadro 6. Uso de software para la
elaboración de las bases de datos

Software	Número de Centros o Bibliotecas
Microisis	43
Otros programas[a]	16
Centros sin información	54
Totales	113

a. Se consideran los siguientes programas: Dbase III y IV, Cliper, SDI/RB, SIAMDO, Ventura, FW3, Carbox, Works y ALEPH.

Fuente: Elaboración propia con datos de catastro e información de cuestionarios y textos de "Mapping the World".

siente su presencia; a su vez, en el cuadro mencionado se informa de la existencia de 12 redes de documentación de las cuales solo en tres países la misma red es mencionada en por lo menos dos centros: de esta manera, se confirma su participación. Los tres países son Brasil, Costa Rica y República Dominicana.

En Latinoamérica debemos de crecer en este sentido debido a que existen importantes recursos y experiencias que compartir, "Así, estar enredadas o en *networking* es una forma efectiva y abierta de crecer. Si es un proceso autorreferido o monopólico de algunos saberes, difícilmente se puede crear un sentido colectivo de accionar en la diferencia, reproduciendo así las limitaciones—en cuanto a impacto de retroalimentación, radio de acción, etc.—de las organizaciones".[4]

Por último existen otras peculiaridades que tipifican la situación de los centros de documentación de la región, por ejemplo, se caracterizan por ser centros pequeños, con pocos recursos económicos y materiales y sin personal calificado y/o profesional, situación que tiende a superarse en los centros con mayor claridad de tareas en el terreno informativo y que además cuentan con mayores recursos.

Conclusión

Se puede afirmar que el trabajo documental en el ámbito del movimiento y de los estudios de la mujer no es en modo alguno un asunto trivial, y debe considerarse como un trabajo importante dentro de una organización.

En la actualidad las diversas organizaciones y centros de estudios deben revalorar la actividad documental como una parte nodal de su trabajo de gestión académica y política, pues ninguna organización que se jacte de tener

Cuadro 7. Redes de documentación en América Latina

Redes	País	Centros Pertenecientes
Red Nacional de Documentación	Argentina	Consejo Nacional de la Mujer
Red Boliviana de Documentación sobre la Mujer (Nacional)	Bolivia	Centro de Información y Desarrollo de la Mujer
Red de Centros de Documentación Cochabamba (Local)	Bolivia	Oficina Jurídica para la Mujer
Rede Feminista de Documentação (REDOF)	Brasil	• Centro Informação Mulher (CIM) • Sos Corpo Género e Cidadania • Red Mulher
Red Latinoamericana de Información y Documentación	Brasil	Fundación Carlos Chagas
Women's Health Documentation Center Network	Chile	Isis Internacional, Santiago
Red Nacional de Información sobre la Mujer	Costa Rica	• Alianza de Mujeres Costarricenses • Centro Popular de Asesoría Legal
Red de Información Amazónica	Ecuador	Fundación Natura
Red Internacional de Centros de Documentación	México	CIDHAL
Red de Unidades de Información sobre la Mujer en el Perú	Perú	Centro de Documentación sobre la Mujer
Red de Centros de Documentación del Area de la Mujer	República Dominicana	• Centro de Servicios Legales para la Mujer • Centro Dominicano de Estudios de la Educación (CEDEE) • Coordinadora de Organizaciones No Gubernamentales del Area de la Mujer • Movimiento por la Identidad de la Mujer Negra • Instituto Internacional de Investigaciones y Capacitación para la Promoción de la Mujer (INSTRAW)

Fuente: Elaboración propia con datos de catastro e información de cuestionarios y textos de "Mapping the World".

liderazgo en este campo, podrá ejercerlo sin tener centros de información y documentación poderosos y un diestro manejo de los flujos de información que nutran su acción. La gestión de información de las organizaciones e instituciones en el ámbito de los estudios de género y del movimiento de la mujer, deberá ser lo suficientemente hábil para difundir su información, así como proveerse la necesaria para su trabajo político, académico y/o de investigación. El trabajo documental ya no debe ser la última prioridad sino la primera.

Con todo y las limitaciones, los centros de documentación de América Latina y el Caribe poseen una inigualable riqueza informativa, la cual se caracteriza por tener un marco de acción básicamente local. No obstante, han jugado, sin duda, un papel importante en la reproducción y ampliación del movimiento feminista y en el fortalecimiento de los estudios de género y mujer.

Las limitaciones y dificultades de los centros, expresadas en la escasez de recursos económicos, los espacios reducidos, la falta de equipo de cómputo y la falta de personal especializado, son factores que junto con la dispersión y localismo menguan el impacto de la información y la actividad de los centros, por eso es importante que se suscriban los más diversos convenios de colaboración y se inicie la red latinoamericana de documentación con fin de subsanar rezagos y avanzar hacia una gestión regional de nuestros recursos informativos con el fin de potenciar así nuestro trabajo local.

Termino aquí esta exposición con un texto de Victoria Jiménez:

La información en estudios de la mujer y género es indispensable para crear nuevo conocimiento y para suprimir la opresión y la ignorancia. No es sólo manteniendo documentos en las unidades de información documental como se logra el cambio, es dinamizando los servicios que en ella se ofrecen, es convirtiéndose la o el especialista de la información en un agente de cambio, es integrando redes de sistemas de información sobre la mujer. Es contribuyendo a hacer realidad la sociedad informada, como se puede operar un cambio positivo en la región latinoamericana (Jiménez s/f).

NOTAS

1. "Declaración: primer taller sobre organización y funcionamiento de centros de información y documentación en el tema de mujer en América Latina", *Mujeres en Acción* 14 (diciembre 1988), 20.

2. Vargas y Vargas, "Feminismo y autonomía".

3. Por ejemplo, el Fondo de Documentación del Programa de Estudios de Género, Mujer y Desarrollo de la Universidad Nacional de Colombia plantea como de sus objetivos: "Contribuir al proceso de desarrollo social y al cambio de las relaciones entre hombres y mujeres al hacer acequible la información sobre temas de mujer y género". En el folleto "Fondo de Documentación: Mujer y Género, 1994–1997", Programa de Estudios de Género, Mujer y Desarrollo, Facultad de Ciencias Humanas, Universidad Nacional de Colombia.

4. Vargas y Vargas, "Feminismo y autonomía", p. 4.

BIBLIOGRAFÍA

Barbieri, Teresita de. 1986. *Movimientos feministas*. Colección Grandes Tendencias Políticas Contemporáneas. México: UNAM-Coordinación de Humanidades.

Bonder, Gloria, ed. 1998. *Estudios de la mujer en América Latina*. Colección Interamer. Washington, DC: Organización de Estados Americanos.

Caracterización del feminismo en su trayectoria. S/a, s/f. Documento con folio 586 en el Centro de Documentación del Programa Universitario de Estudios de Género. México: UNAM.

Celiberti, Lilián. "Nubosidad variable". *Cotidiano* 23. http://www.chasque.apc.org/cotidian/nubosidad.htm.

Feijoó, María del Carmen. 1988. "Mujer y política en América Latina: el estado del Arte". En *Mujeres latinoamericanas: diez ensayos y una historia colectiva*, pp. 29–55. Lima: Flora Tristán, Centro de la Mujer Peruana.

Fernández, Ana María, comp. 1993. *Las mujeres en la imaginación colectiva*. Buenos Aires: Paidos.

"Fondo de Documentación: Mujer y Género, 1994–1997" (folleto de divulgación). S/f. Programa de Estudios de Género, Mujer y Desarrollo, Facultad de Ciencias Humanas, Universidad Nacional de Colombia.

Isis Internacional. 1995. *Centros de información, documentación y bibliotecas en el tema de la mujer en América Latina y el Caribe: análisis y catastro*. Documento para el Foro de ONG sobre la Mujer, Beijing '95. Isis Internacional, Santiago de Chile.

Jiménez, Victoria. S/f. *Nuevos paradigmas en información y comunicación para las mujeres centroamericanas*. Resumen de conferencia. S/d. Programa de Información para la Mujer del Instituto de Estudios de la Mujer, Universidad Nacional de Costa Rica.

Kanoussi, Dora. S/d, s/f. *El feminismo, hoy*. Documento con folio 630 en el Centro de Documentación del Programa Universitario de Estudios de Género (PUEG). México: UNAM.

La mujer en las Américas: cómo cerrar la brecha entre los géneros. 1996. Washington, DC: Banco Interamericano de Desarrollo.

Lavrín, Asunción. 1985. "Algunas consideraciones finales sobre las tendencias y los temas en la historia de las mujeres de Latinoamérica". En Asunción Lavrín, comp., *Las mujeres latinoamericanas: perspectivas históricas*, pp. 347–379. México: Fondo de Cultura Económica.

"Mapping the World of Women's Information Services". http://www.iiav.nl.

Molina G., Natacha. 1996. *El protagonismo de las mujeres en la construcción de la igualdad y ciudadanía en América Latina*. Santiago: Instituto de la Mujer.

Mujeres en Acción (Isis Internacional) 14 (diciembre 1988).

Navarro, Marysa. 1982. "El primer encuentro feminista de Latinoamérica y el Caribe". En Magdalena León, ed., *III Sociedad, Subordinación y Feminismo*, pp. 261–267. Colombia: ACEP.

Navas, Ma. Candelaria. S/f. *Los movimientos femeninos en Centro América: 1950–1985.* Documento con folio 633 en el Centro de Documentación del Programa Universitario de Estudios de Género (PUEG). México: UNAM.

Pisano, Margarita. 1987. "Feminismo: pasos críticos y deseos de cambio". *Edición de las Mujeres* (Isis Internacional) 9, 143–148.

Red de Información sobre Estudios de Género y Educación (Rige) en Internet. 1996. *Boletín No. 1* (octubre–noviembre). Guatemala: PUEG.

Suárez-López, Rocío y Leopoldina Rendón Pineda. 1988. "CIDHAL's Documentation Center: Helping to Build Feminism in Mexico". En Grace Jackson-Brown, *Libraries and Information Centers within Women's Studies Research Centers,* pp. 165–167. Washington, DC: Special Libraries Association.

Vargas, Virginia y Cecilia Olea. "Feminismo y autonomía". http://ekeko.rcp.net.pe/FLORA/rev-22/debate.htm.

Vargas, Virginia. 1988. "Las mujeres en movimiento: de cómo somos políticas, las mujeres". En *Mujeres latinoamericanas: diez ensayos y una historia colectiva,* pp. 249–272. Lima: Flora Tristán, Centro de la Mujer Peruana.

———. 1987. "Movimiento de mujeres en América Latina: un reto para el análisis y para la acción". *Mujeres, crisis y movimiento: América Latina y el Caribe.* Isis Internacional. Ediciones de las Mujeres 9 (junio), 83–90.

Werlhof, Claudia von. 1982. "Unidas como una bandada de águilas furiosas . . . Luchas femeninas y machismo en América Latina". En Magdalena León, ed., *III Sociedad, Subordinación y Feminismo,* pp. 238–260. Colombia: ACEP.

II. Culture

6. The Tango and the Buenos Aires Urban Identity

Simon Collier

The tango comes from Buenos Aires, the southern hemisphere's most stylish metropolis, a city of 1.5 million in 1914 and double that in 1947. It arose spontaneously in the city's poorer outer districts, the *arrabales,* sometime around 1880. Following the tango's spectacular triumphs on the dance floors of Europe and North America in 1913–1914, it became the dominant form of music and dance in Buenos Aires from the early 1920s to early 1950s, its golden age. The tango is once again immensely popular today in Buenos Aires, following its international revival in the 1980s, and the city remains the mecca for true tango-lovers.

Whether, or how, the tango reflects the urban identity of Buenos Aires is not altogether clear. The question of what constitutes an urban identity is indeed a difficult one, answerable (if at all) only in general terms. The world's great cities (Buenos Aires among them) possess distinctive characteristics: New York with its hustle and din and sky-embracing architecture, London with its shabby-genteel charm and leafy squares, Paris with its mix of village-like intimacies and gracious perspectives.

But let us assume that there is a Buenos Aires identity, and ask how the tango relates to it. The music and the dance came into existence through a spontaneous process of improvisation and fusion, in which the people of the *arrabales* used what materials they had on hand—the Cuban *habanera,* the mazurka, the local Argentine *milonga,* dance movements from the Afro-Argentine *candombe*—to create the tango. The elements that were rearranged into the tango and the shabby social setting where the improvisations actually occurred (probably around 1880) cannot be disassociated from a time and a place and a particular section of urban society. Whether the tango rhythm or the forms of the dance actually reflect the time, place, and society is another matter entirely, and one not easily investigated.

We should remember that the tango's "takeoff" into its local golden age was not simply a matter of dance bands and dancers. The tango also very quickly became a form of popular song, performed by many well-known vocalists, among them the legendary baritone Carlos Gardel. The tango song soon settled into a fairly standard shape: four sixteen-bar sections in an ABAB sequence, the second verse often repeated as the fourth. The first true tango song in this sense seems to have been the Samuel Linning–Enrique Delfino classic "Milonguita" (1920). Nearly all the songs that Gardel sang took that shape and form. As the tango song took hold of public taste, songwriters multiplied in Buenos Aires. Within a few years, an astonishingly rich tradition emerged—great tunes, wonderful lyrics. That the tango acquired *words* (rose from the feet to the lips, as dramatist Agustín Remón put it) sheds some light on its links to the Buenos Aires identity. For, as Jorge Luis Borges noted in 1930, "the words of tangos . . . form a vast and incoherent *comédie humaine* of the life of Buenos Aires."[1]

In fact, however, the *comédie humaine* was not quite as incoherent as Borges believed. The tango song came to constitute a kind of universe of its own, powerfully convincing though also rather stylized, but definitely self-contained, true to itself. This universe is peopled with its own stereotypes, stock characters, topics, and situations. Its geographical setting is largely that of the city. That marvelous Homero Manzi–Aníbal Troilo song of 1948, "Sur" ("South"), is not about the vast landscapes of Patagonia or the icy wastes of Antarctica. It is an evocation of the southern districts of Buenos Aires, safely within the city limits. And indeed, there are many tangos which uncomplicatedly but emotionally praise Buenos Aires as a great city (Carlos Gardel's "Mi Buenos Aires Querido" is the best-known example) or evoke particular neighborhoods or popular rituals of urban life, such as carnival, the circus, the racetrack. Clearly, the tango universe is rooted consciously and specifically in Buenos Aires.

One who has listened to tango songs for any length of time does not fail to notice the recurrence of certain themes. These can be broken down into broad categories, the largest being what I call the vicissitudes of love. Tangos are almost never straightforward love songs. In the tango universe, love is nearly always problematic or, better still, positively agonizing. Unrequited love, abandonment, betrayal, jealousy, rivalry are the preferred themes. Abandonment, perhaps the root concept, was the first great tango subject, introduced in Pascual Contursi's "Mi Noche Triste," the song that Carlos Gardel took to the theater in 1917 and that effectively started the tango song tradition.

The abandonment theme lends itself to an almost infinite number of variations. The abandoned lover hopes for reconciliation or vows eternal loyalty despite being thrown over. Alternatively, the injured lover takes refuge in a frenzied social life or drowns his sorrows in drink (the alcoholic strategy is recommended as early as "Mi Noche Triste," 1917). The jilted lover desires vengeance. This is where the fun begins, for vengeance against the faithless woman (nearly always that way around) should preferably be exacted with a knife thrust. It is doubtful whether early-twentieth-century Buenos Aires was the site of the number of knifings described in tango songs. Police statistics suggest the city was a rather nonviolent place compared with other great cities of the period. Murders averaged eighty per year between 1900 and 1910. Nonetheless, vengeance killings loom very large in the tango universe—sometimes described in tiny, self-contained stories, or often in the context of nostalgic settings (rooms, bars, or streets).

The nostalgic evocation of the past is the second broad category of tango themes. Knife fights, amorous vendettas, violent sexual rivalries, and a whole array of human stereotypes such as the *compadrito* (the street tough), the *payador* (old-style folk singer), the *malevo* (small-time crook), the *taura* (tough guy) had been associated with the ephemeral culture of the *arrabales,* the fringe districts from which the tango came and which by the 1920s were being overwhelmed by prosperity and respectability. I don't know whether the *arrabales* resembled their depictions in tango lyrics. But the image of that ephemeral culture came to exercise a powerful influence on the popular imagination of Buenos Aires, not only in tangos but also on the stage and (in the 1930s) on the screen.

Like abandonment, the theme of nostalgia is capable of almost infinite variation. Nostalgia can be triggered by old items of clothing, or by a return to the scene of past loves—perhaps the *bulín,* the rented room usually reserved for clandestine love affairs, or the old barrio, being demolished by the advancing tide of progress. Often nostalgia is related to somber reflections on the sheer transitoriness of life, the inevitable attrition of time. Perhaps the most celebrated example of this recurring theme is the 1935 Carlos Gardel classic, "Volver" ("Return"), one of the best-loved Latin American songs of the century and the one that introduced catchphrases into the Spanish language.

Remarkably, the same situations, the same stereotypes, turn up time and again, woven into the fabric of innumerable tangos: street lamps (inseparable from the tango universe), cabaret girls, knife-wielding *compadritos,* virtuous mothers. One could say a great deal about the standard human types who populate the tango universe—the virtuous mother, for instance, the *vieja* directly or obliquely eulogized in so many songs. Somebody once asked the great bandleader Aníbal Troilo why there were so many mothers in the tango. "Where else would you want them to be?" he replied.[2] In the tango universe the virtuous mother's children always go remorselessly to the bad. Her sons ruin themselves in expensive nightspots or in the world of crime and violence. Her daughters expose themselves to the delights of the cabaret and are fatally corrupted by rich young men or rich old men. There is an interesting time shift to be noted here. The world of the cabarets—a second common setting for many tango lyrics—was essentially a development of the 1920s. The rise of the cabaret was contemporary with the songs themselves, while the old *arrabal* was clearly receding into the past. The songs thus sometimes conflate two distinct periods of urban history, although many are firmly rooted in one or the other. But there is no reason for the tango universe to be absolutely consistent in every respect. Its vision of Buenos Aires may be partial and highly selective, but the universe itself has definite internal rules and conventions.

By the 1930s and 1940s, nostalgic evocations of the good old barrio—the *arrabal* culture—became more consciously stylized, almost self-caricaturing at times, with the same elements (street lamps, virtuous mothers, *compadritos*) repeated over and over again with a greater or lesser degree of skill. Some lyricists, Homero Manzi for instance, could pull it off superbly; in others, repetition becomes rather tedious.

It may seem from the foregoing that tango songs tend to emphasize the down side of life. Betrayal in love, vengeance, the transitoriness of everything, the decay of the good old barrio are omnipresent themes. Songs tell of disillusionment, cynicism, the feeling that despite whatever you manage to do, time will get you in the end. What emerges from these themes is a sort of tango philosophy. It is a rather stoical philosophy. The cards may be stacked against you (literally in one or two songs) but you do your best to carry on. "Don't you know," sings the protagonist of Francisco Canaro's tango "Sentimiento Gaucho" (1924), "don't you know that the condition of man is to suffer." There are a few comic tangos, a few nonsense tangos, and quite a few sarcastic or ironic ones, but the downbeat tone is nevertheless inescapable. The writer who expressed the down side of emotions most beautifully was undoubtedly Enrique Santos Discépolo, who wrote one of the finest single group of classics in the genre. Discépolo's lyrics often express deep contempt for modern society, which has led many to consider them protest songs. They are not really. Contempt for society is underpinned in Discépolo by deep feelings of ambiguity about life itself. Modern society may be a mess, but he does not suggest political remedies. Indeed, in his most celebrated song, "Cambalache" (1935), his vision is rather hierarchical, even elitist. One of the things he complains about is the leveling process of the twentieth century: "Everyone is equal, nothing is better or worse"—crooks and heroes, sportsmen and saints—all are mixed up in his tremendous image of the twentieth century as a junkshop.

"Cambalache"
("Junkshop")
Enrique Santos Discépolo
(1935)

Que el mundo fue y será una porquería, ya lo sé,
en el quinientos seis y en el dos mil también,
que siempre ha habido chorros, maquiavelos, y estafados,
contentos y amargados, valores y dublés,
pero que el siglo veinte es un despliegue de maldad insolente
ya no hay quien no niegue:
vivimos revolcados en un merengue
y en un mismo lodo, todos manoseados.

Hoy resulta que es lo mismo ser derecho que traidor
ignorante, sabio, chorro, generoso o estafador.
Todo es igual, nada es mejor,
lo mismo un burro que un gran profesor.
No hay aplazaos ni escalafón,
los inmorales nos han igualado.
Si uno vive en la impostura, y otro roba en su ambición
da lo mismo que si es cura, colchonero,
rey de bastos, caradura o polizón.

¡Qué falta de respeto! ¡qué atropello a la razón!
Cualquiera es un señor, cualquiera es un ladrón.
Mezclado con Stavisky va don Bosco y la Mignon,
Don Chicho y Napoleón, Carnera y San Martín.
Igual que en la vidriera irrespetuosa de los cambalaches
se ha mezclado la vida,
y herida por un sable sin remache
ves llorar la Biblia junto a un calefón.

¡Siglo veinte, cambalache, problemático y febril!
Él que no llora no mama
y él que no afana es un gil.
Dále nomás, dále que va . . .
que allá en el horno nos vamos a encontrar.
No pienses más, sentáte a un lado,
que a nadie importa si naciste honrado.
Es lo mismo él que labura noche y día como un buey,
que él que vive de los otros, que él que mata,
que él que cura, o está fuera de la ley.

The world has been and always will be a real mess, okay.
It was in 506, and will be in 2000 too,
there have always been thieves, schemers, suckers,
happy and bitter folks, genuine things and fakes,
but the twentieth century is a *real* display of mischief,
and that nobody can deny.
We all live flattened out in a meringue-like mess,
all rumpled up in the same mud-patch.

Today it's the same to be straight or treacherous,
ignorant, wise, thieving, generous, a swindler.
Everything's equal, nothing better or worse,
a dummy's the same as a great professor.
No failures any more, no proper scale of rewards,
people without morals have got to the same level as us.
Some live as impostors, others rob in their ambition;
it's all the same to be a priest, a mattress-maker,
King of Clubs, cheeky fellow, layabout.

What a lack of respect! What an assault on reason!
Anyone's a gentleman, anyone's a thief.
Mixed up with Stavisky go Don Bosco and Mignon,
Don Chicho and Napoleon, Carnera and San Martín.
Just like in the disrespectful windows of junkshops
life has got all muddled up,
and, half-wounded by a sword,
you see the Bible weeping next to an old stove.

Twentieth century, junkshop! Problem-filled, feverish!
If you don't whine, you don't drink,
if you don't steal you're a fool.
Go on, go on . . .
We shall all meet up together in the furnace.
Just stop thinking, sit down quietly to one side,
nobody cares if you were born honest.
It's the same for the guy who works like an ox all day,
the guy who lives off others, the guy who kills,
the guy who cures, the guy outside the law.

Notes:
Stavisky: Alexandre Stavisky, the villain in a famous French financial
      scandal, 1933–1934
Don Bosco: St. John Bosco, founder of the Salesian Order
la Mignon: archetypal prostitute figure '
Don Chicho: Juan Galiffi, celebrated Buenos Aires underworld figure of
      the time
Napoleon: Emperor of the French
Carnera: Primo Carnera, heavyweight boxer of the 1930s
San Martín: General José de San Martín, Argentina's national hero.

[This recording: Hector Blotta (1938–1998) with his own guitar
accompaniment, Medellín, Colombia, 1985.]

I am not sure I can explain why the particular configuration of topics
noted here came to occupy the predominant place in tango songs. One reason
may have been the sheer suddenness with which the tango song established
itself as an overwhelmingly popular form, at a time when radio and the phono-
graph were transforming popular life in Argentina. The tango was not folklore:
it was modern, urban, commercial popular music written for an apparently
insatiable public. Once the first handful of songwriters had marked out the terrain, their successors found it easy to fit into the established framework. It
never occurred to anyone to break seriously with the prevailing conventions. So
the tango song was stuck in a groove, albeit a rather magnificent groove. This
was what the public responded to, and this was what the public got.

Why the public responded to it is a hopelessly difficult question to answer.
The key, perhaps, lies in the cosmopolitan nature of Buenos Aires, an

immigrant metropolis. Its heterogeneous population turned away from the folk music of the countryside (music that was becoming popular between 1900 and 1920) toward something associated with the city itself, their city, even if a partly fantasized city, but a city, and an imagined past with links to the real world—"a dubious, unreal world which in some way *is* true," as Borges puts it in his great poem on the tango. The *arrabales* had existed; the cabarets were there; some of the stock characters of the tango universe had their counterparts in real life; the protagonists of at least a few songs were even based on real, identifiable individuals.

In the end, the tango managed to acquire its completely hegemonic role in popular taste (at least until the 1950s) pretty much on its own terms, that is, the terms of those who made it, the musicians and the writers. Whether it really reflected Buenos Aires, who can say? But Buenos Aires loved it, and so it became, forever, an inescapable part of the Buenos Aires identity.

How does a researcher set about studying a popular tradition like the tango? I came to the subject about twenty-five years ago and discovered immediately that there were no obvious guidelines. The tango did not (and does not) have an impressive research infrastructure like that available, for instance, to students of country music. The Country Music Foundation in Nashville, for example, holds extensive collections and resources and presents the best possible model of what such an organization should be. In Buenos Aires, the Academia Porteña del Lunfardo, founded in 1962, has assembled a library, and hundreds of short "academic communications" from its members and supporters have explored many aspects of the tango tradition and *lunfardo,* the distinctive Buenos Aires vocabulary so inseparably associated with it. More recently, the Academia Nacional del Tango, one of the seventeen official academies of the Argentine Republic, has aspired to promote research, but it is of very recent origin (1990), and its promise has yet to be fulfilled.

For serious research on tango, one must first become thoroughly immersed in (and conversant with) the tango tradition. As for the music, one can listen to recordings. Tangos have been recorded since 1902. The old 78 rpm discs and the vinyl LPs that succeeded them are now largely the preserve of collectors, of whom there are many. In the early 1980s multinational record companies and several independent labels like El Bandoneón in Spain and Harlequin in England began to reissue historic tango recordings on compact disc.[3] Similarly, reasonably good collections of the lyrics are available,[4] although they represent no more than the tip of the iceberg, given the tens of thousands of lyrics known to have been written. Unfortunately, anthologies tend to overrepresent the classics despite the fact that the more run-of-the-mill songs accounted for the majority of the pieces.

There is a much larger body of basic literature on the tango available now than there was twenty-five years ago, and it includes some serious general accounts of tango history.[5] Much of the work, especially the older literature, tends to be anecdotal and uncritical.[6] The same can be said of the autobiographies published by some of the leading bandleaders, singers, and songwriters,[7] although some useful biographies of such figures (of varying levels of seriousness) have begun to appear in recent years, and more are certainly to be expected.[8] There is also a considerable undergrowth of tango magazines; some of these serve the thousands of tango clubs around the world and are little more than bulletin boards, while others, though in no sense learned journals, publish contributions useful to the researcher.[9] Again the tone is often anecdotal and uncritical, picturesque rather than analytical, but the researcher, after determining what is useful and what is not, cannot afford to disregard these sources. Nor, of course, should we neglect work in related fields, studies that have a bearing on the tango tradition, such as literature on the social history of Buenos Aires, or local history studies of particular Buenos Aires *barrios,* many of which are inspired by genuine antiquarian enthusiasm.

As for primary materials, they are extremely miscellaneous. Interviews with surviving musicians and dancers (such as those collected by anthropologist María Susana Azzi)[10] are a potentially important source and often reveal a good deal about the distinctive culture that surrounded the tango in its golden age. Those who remember that period well are thinning out rather rapidly, and their commentaries need to be recorded before it is too late. Archival collections are scarce and are mostly in the hands of collectors. Whether the Academia Nacional del Tango will be able to acquire such collections in a central repository remains to be seen. Beyond these efforts, one of the richest sources of all can be found in the Buenos Aires press, which covered the tango extensively during its golden age. This was especially true of popular newspapers like Natalio Botana's *Crítica,* which ran from 1913 to 1963. In addition, popular music magazines like *Radiolandia* were effectively tango magazines during the golden age, and much information can be mined from their pages. The difficulties of working with press reports are mostly practical: Miguel Angel Morena, who has labored nobly (and for virtually no reward) for the past twenty-five years to establish a detailed chronology of the career of Carlos Gardel,[11] has told me real horror stories of decimated back runs of newspapers and magazines in provincial Argentine libraries in particular. Anyone who works with these sources must be prepared for considerable frustration.

But it is worth it. Popular traditions like the tango are part of the human record, a rather pleasant part of the human record, and their retrieval and study belong to history. Compared with many Latin American popular traditions, the tango has fared quite well at the hands of those who study it, but there is still much to be done. Thanks to the international revival of the tango as a dance since the 1980s, and the extraordinary international popularity of the music of the avant-garde tango composer Astor Piazzolla over the same period, there is every sign that this work will continue, just as the tango itself will continue. For, as Jorge Luis Borges puts it in his great poem:

Esa ráfaga, el tango, esa diablura
los atareados años desafía;
hecho de polvo y tiempo el hombre dura
menos que la liviana melodía.

That flash of light, that devilry, the tango
defies the overburdened years;
man, made of dust and time, does not endure
as long as the light melody.

NOTES

1. Jorge Luis Borges, *Obras completas* (Buenos Aires, 1974), p. 164.

2. María Esther Gilio, *Aníbal Pichuco Troilo: conversaciones* (Buenos Aires, 1998).

3. The discography of the tango is well advanced, thanks largely to the devoted labors of S. Nicolás Lefcovich in Buenos Aires, who has published discographies of scores of bandleaders and singers.

4. For example, José Gobello, ed., *Tangos, letras y letristas,* 6 vols. (Buenos Aires, 1993–1996), Vol. 1 with Jorge A. Bossio; Héctor Angel Benedetti, ed., *Letras de tangos* (Buenos Aires, 1997); Eduardo Romano, ed., *Las letras del tango,* 3d ed. (Buenos Aires, 1991); Jorge Sareli, *El libro mayor del tango* (Mexico City, 1974).

5. For example, José Gobello's beautifully written *Crónica general del tango* (Buenos Aires, 1980); Horacio Salas, *El tango* (Buenos Aires, 1980); Eduardo Stilman, *Historia del tango* (Buenos Aires, 1965); Simon Collier, Artemis Cooper, María Susana Azzi, and Richard Martin, *¡Tango!* (London and New York, 1995); Horacio Ferrer, *El siglo de oro del tango* (Buenos Aires, 1996). For the important story of the tango in Paris, see Nardo Zalko, *Un siècle de tango, Paris–Buenos Aires* (Paris, 1998). A moderately reliable basic reference work is Horacio Ferrer, *El libro del tango,* 2d ed. (Buenos Aires, 1977).

6. For example, the multivolume *Historia del tango,* 19 vols. (Buenos Aires, 1976–1987).

7. Julio De Caro (bandleader), *El tango en mis recuerdos* (Buenos Aires 1964); Francisco Canaro (bandleader), *Mis bodas de oro con el tango* (Buenos Aires, 1957); Edmundo Rivero (singer), *Una luz de almacén* (Buenos Aires, 1982); Libertad Lamarque (singer), *Autobiografía* (Buenos Aires, 1986); Carlos Marambio Catán (singer-songwriter), *60 años de tango* (Buenos Aires, 1973); Enrique Cadícamo (songwriter), *Bajo el signo de tango,* 2d ed. (Buenos Aires, 1987).

8. Sergio Pujol, *Discépolo, una biografía argentina* (Buenos Aires, 1997); Simon Collier, *The Life, Music and Times of Carlos Gardel* (Pittsburgh, 1986); Hamlet Lima Quintana, *Osvaldo Pugliese* (Buenos Aires, 1990); Osvaldo J. Sanguiao, *Troilo* (Buenos Aires, 1995); María Susana Azzi and Simon Collier, *Le Grand Tango: The Life and Music of Astor Piazzolla* (New York, 2000).

9. For example, *Club de Tango, Tango XXI, Tango y lunfardo, A puro tango* (all published in Buenos Aires); *Tango Reporter* (Los Angeles, Spanish-language).

10. *Antropología del tango: los protagonistas* (Buenos Aires, 1991). Some of the important interviews done by the brothers Luis and Héctor Bates in the mid-1930s, previously unpublished, are now appearing in the magazine *Club de Tango.*

11. Miguel Angel Morena, *Historia artística de Carlos Gardel,* 4th ed. (Buenos Aires, 1998).

7. The Body as Vehicle of Political Identity in the Art of José Clemente Orozco

Leonard Folgarait

José Clemente Orozco, one of Mexico's most important artists of the early to mid twentieth century, is probably the best known of the so-called Big Three mural painters active in the 1920s, '30s, and '40s, the other two being Diego Rivera and David Alfaro Siqueiros. This essay examines a selection of images—some drawings, some details of mural paintings—in the context of body theory. This interpretation of the human body as an active agent of meaningful articulation in and of itself and in partnership with other approaches, whether purely formalist or determinedly contextualist, is not limited to art history, certainly, but has widespread use in the humanities.

After review of the basic premises of body theory, I attempt its application to the art of Orozco for the purpose of determining how the human body is constructed to act as a politicized agent within the highly dramatic nature of Mexican history during and after its convulsive Revolution of 1910.

Body theory reads the human body as it would a discursive text, that is, it deconstructs aspects of the body such as anatomy, gender, pose, attitude, gesture, action, scale, relation to a spatial setting, relations to other bodies, relation to the viewer, how it affects the given narrative of the image, its state of dress or undress, and the manner in which it is drawn, painted, or sculpted, among other such qualities. The point of this body analysis is to determine how much of the overall meaning of the image is carried by the physical body proper and all of its attributes and behavior. In terms of formal considerations, we try to see the body as constructed by intelligible relations, the hipbone connected to the thighbone, and how those relations fit into the visual language of not only the larger painting but also of the larger culture and society in which it was produced. It is not enough, however, to simply decode the pose and action of a body according to its formal makeup. What is most necessary is to argue for that bodily expression to then be fully invested with ideological purpose, with political intent to articulate the agenda of some party driven by political interests. We look at the body along with other features of a picture because we are convinced that the body carries these serious messages mostly at an unconscious level, planted there not programmatically by the artist or the patron, but carried in covertly, as it were, by the political dynamics of the operative society at large, a society of which both artist and patron are members and the politics of which act out as unconscious consequences of their daily lives. The body carries these subliminal messages not only because it can but also because it has to; it has no choice but to speak with eloquence to the issues of its time, and it does so mostly because it is not aware that it is doing so. As the art historian Marcia Pointon has stated, "visual representations of the body work metaphorically and systematically to define and reinforce beliefs and social practices."[1] Therefore, body theory also involves some psychoanalytic methods on the part of the art historian, analyzing not the artist, but rather the image and its social world. Let us see if and how the images by Orozco bear this out.

Probably the most curious and challenging image to consider is not of the entire body, but simply of the head, such as the drawing for the cover page of the newspaper *La Vanguardia*, for the issue of May 10, 1915.[2] The date, 1915, puts this drawing at the very center of the most violent phase of the fighting of the Mexican Revolution, the period from 1913 to 1917. In 1915 there were many pitched battles between revolutionary and government forces and also between various factions of the revolutionary forces. In this drawing, the revolutionary camp represented is that of General Venustiano Carranza, who two years later would overpower his opponents and comrades and declare himself president of Mexico. In that case, the subtitle to this newspaper, "The Daily of the Revolution," has to be seen in the context of several claims to exactly what the revolution was at this time and who had the right to define it.

The drawing by Orozco attempts to do just that, to define political identity by the device of a face and its particular presentation. Several observations need to be pointed out: the caption, "Yo soy la Revolución, la destructora . . . ," "I am the Revolution, the destroyer . . . "; the happy expression; the exaggerated eyes; and the ax and knife crossed and superimposed over the side of the face. Apparently this head without a supporting body is speaking to us, identifying herself as an allegorical representation of the Revolution and warning of her destructiveness by word and by the display of the sharp-edged weapons.

But this is not an entirely sensible image, is it? How can such a bright and perhaps even joyful expression be squared with the violence of the rest of the message? Are the ax and knife attached to her head as ornaments or are they floating in space? Why are the eyes so large? Why are the weapons not held by her hands, or any other hands? Such questions, piling up so quickly, suggest that this is an image full of surrealistic rather than realistic suggestions, that the logic of illogic is in play here. All of these issues are based on the language of the human body, such as the overly large eyes, but also on the paradox of the meaning of the body as an *absent* body, such as her own missing body and the missing hands implied by the floating weapons. But even then, by calling these implements weapons we imply a body in violent conflict, when perhaps they can just as easily be read as tools of construction, farming, changing raw materials into useful objects for everyday life, such as chopping wood or trimming a leather hide. So the missing bodies may be engaged in nonviolent, domestic actions.

The body, then, in its bizarre presentation here, in both its presence *and* absence, begins to dissolve as a coherent entity of presentation. It begins to deconstruct any meaningful definition of its stated purpose, to be the visual representation of the Revolution, to be the Revolution itself.

But perhaps we are seeing this only from one side of the lens. Perhaps all these qualities of incoherence capture the second part of the caption, "I am the destroyer." What this image suggests with its surreal presentation is that the Revolution cannot be explained adequately in any terms at all; what the Revolution destroys is not only buildings and bridges and human lives but meaning itself; it destroys the mechanics by which we understand what we do and why we do it.

With this image the viewer does not know what is to be done with the ax, whether to cut down a tree or split the skull of a government soldier. Are these tools or weapons? The woman herself is given the heavy, dark, eye makeup that Orozco typically put on the faces of prostitutes to suggest that if the Revolution is a prostitute, then she offers no intellectual engagement with the purposes of the Revolution, no ideological justification for the fighting. She offers pure physicality, empty of content. She offers the Revolution as a commodity, bought for a bodily experience. But even then, the absence of her body is quite telling, as most of the functional anatomy of the prostitute is missing, making this an empty lure.

So the tools or weapons cannot be used, she cannot be used, so what happens now? The other side of the lens may suggest that this mismatch of connections, this lure toward emptiness of behavior and meaning, will take the viewer to a place where, if the rules no longer apply, either chaos or new rules will have to be invented, devised, in a moment and space that has been opened up by this chaos and that can be called revolutionary, where a new form of consciousness and life can be forged.

Maybe, in this moment of revolutionary possibility where the status quo has been destroyed, we can decide on our own to grab these implements as either weapons or tools, or both, that their sharp edges can cut two ways, that their multiplication of meaning is a moment of political emancipation. Maybe the eyes are supernaturally large due to this new enlightenment, this new vision; maybe the prostitute is happy because she has lost her body—as commodity—and can now invent a new one, one not for exploitation.

This image is about disconnectedness because that is the necessary condition before new connections can be made. All this has been articulated not by a landscape painting or an architectural setting, not by a political manifesto, but by the human body in a peculiar state of flux and redefinition, where even the inanimate objects represent bodies in different ways. This is an image of revolution at a time when the term itself was in a constant state of redefinition, as suggested above in the comments about the historical context.

A novel published that same year, 1915, titled *The Underdogs: A Novel of the Mexican Revolution*, by Mariano Azuela,[3] expresses this condition in a much-quoted piece of dialogue. The main protagonist, a peasant turned revolutionary soldier by force of circumstance, that very change in status speaking of the unstable political identities of the time, is asked by a comrade why he continues to fight, this as a way of asking what the Revolution is, to which he answers mutely but eloquently by pitching a stone into a ravine and remarking, "Look at that stone, how it keeps on going. . . . "[4] The stone, of course, will follow its own erratic course, pulled by gravity, bouncing off rocks, landing who knows where. It is propelled by a human body but then assumes its own chaotic logic and destiny, where anything can happen, where any meaning can assert itself. The falling stone is like this image.

Why was Orozco so conscious of the body? Maybe because he himself was deformed, having lost his left hand in a childhood accident involving explosives. In several other drawings of this time he exploits the potential of the body, sometimes in the style of caricature. One is especially telling, I believe, because of the mistake indicated, that the cubist painting on display is first misread as being a "nude descending a staircase," when actually it is a "microbe drinking beer with the ideal comic."[5] The fact that those cubes could possibly be mistaken as a body, and that his cruel joke on these effete and ridiculous characters is managed by the anatomical distortions, shows that, even in humor, Orozco treats the body with great seriousness.

Turning now to Orozco's mural paintings, I will discuss two examples, both in the city of Guadalajara.

One painting, titled *Man in Flames*, located inside the dome of the Hospicio Cabañas (Cabañas orphanage), is so quintessentially Orozcian that an early biography of the artist is titled *Man of Fire: J. C. Orozco*.[6] Orozco painted *Man in Flames* in 1939 as part of a complex program occupying much of the upper interior wall and ceiling surfaces of this large building.[7] It is enough for our purposes here to indicate that much of this project is devoted to allegorical human figures who represent the four elements, of which one is fire. It seems that Orozco was in a deeply philosophical and meditative state at this time and depended upon strongly symbolic concepts to carry the meanings of these images. Neither the artist nor critics and scholars, however, have given us a concrete explanation of the painting's meaning. We do not even know what, precisely, "the main in flames" is doing or what he represents.

Because of this odd lack of explanatory context, the figure comes across most strongly as a purely visual image, and what a strange one it is. The figure is most apparently on fire, but the longer we look, it seems that it is perhaps better described as being made *of* fire; rather than expiring and in doing so changing from the material of flesh and bone to ash, it remains in its constant material of flames. To look at a body not made of human tissue is to begin to consider an alien being, familiar in overall shape, but a foreigner in material, in content, and perhaps in consciousness. What is he doing? Is he dead or alive? What is he thinking? Do any of these questions apply to a being who has so few human qualities? All of these questions arise because Orozco denies this body (even that word resonates with doubt; perhaps "shape" is more appropriate) any grounding, whether literal or figurative. There is no ground or horizon line to orient the direction of the figure, and although the flames suggest constant movement across the surface of the shape, the question of whether the figure is in movement or not, floating or flying up, is completely unanswerable.

Let me shift now to another body, that of the viewer. In order to see this image most clearly, one needs to stand directly below the dome, with the head cast far back. The effect on the viewer's body is to lose sight of one's immediate surroundings of ground support and horizontal orientation. By looking straight up, we are detached from our normal sense of belonging to our body itself. The eye becomes detached from the body and reattached by an invisible cord to the zenith of the dome. So the two bodies are caught up in a choreography of weightlessness and dematerialization. This dynamic cannot be captured by looking at a reproduction on a flat page. The in-person viewing experience is brought down to, or elevated to, one of pure, abstract essence, of a visual connection to a fantastic vision unmediated by a sense of real bodies, ours or his, or real space or gravity or any sense of the laws of the natural world.

The main point here is that the effects I am describing, of the dissolving and disembodiment of the bodies of both flaming man and viewer, are made possible only by the particular position of the painted image, best seen by a viewer directly underneath. Those very exact requirements stage a process of transformation by which the viewer, eventually made very aware of her or his body because of the state of discomfort in peering straight up, is then encouraged to figuratively leave that strained pose and propel his or her vision and consciousness up toward the dome to hover below that flaming man.

So what does all this have to do with political identity? I would propose, in the briefest terms possible, that we are witnessing politics becoming spiritualized. Whatever causes that drive the flesh-and-blood human walking on the ground are here evaporating into the sheer ecstasy of a magical vision of the soul purified by flames in an extra-worldly place. All of this sounds rather cosmic, but it closely parallels Orozco's own disaffection, by the 1930s, with the founding principles of the Mexican Revolution. He had seen too much corruption and selfishness at the highest levels of government and had reached a point past disillusionment and embitterment in regard to the earthly struggles of his fellow Mexicans. What the flaming man looks like and how the viewer's body engages with him are symptoms of a wish to flee the world of the concrete into the abstract.

The other major figure Orozco paints in Guadalajara, also in 1939, this time for the staircase of the state government palace, is a dramatically over-sized portrait of Father Hidalgo, the great leader of the movement of Independence from Spain a century earlier.[8] Here again the quasi-mythical image floats above the viewer, the flames present this time on the edge of a machete he holds ready to strike. Yes, this is a historical figure, but *not* of the Revolutionary period. Hidalgo is from a period safe in the distant past, a period marked by leaders of unquestioned heroism and sacrifice, so different from the opportunists of the 1930s. With these images, Orozco disengages from the here and now and uses his depicted bodies to portray a political identity of profoundly negative criticism of the conditions at that time.

The last section on Orozco's mural paintings is related to the approach I have taken in my research on Mexican murals in Mexico and in the United States. Research in Mexico is an experience in paradox. On the one hand, newspapers and journals of the 1920s through 1940s are fairly well collected in the major libraries and archives. On the other hand, these runs are never quite complete, nor are they indexed, so it is still a matter of leafing carefully through countless pages to find useful items. The library staff is generally well trained and friendly, but overworked. This leads to long lines (seething mobs, really) at counters and long waits for the materials. The copy machines also tend to be cranky and poorly maintained.

Mexican scholars often remark on how much more efficiently they are able to conduct their research (on Mexican topics) in the United States than in Mexico. This is because certain major libraries in the United States collect Mexican newspapers and journals on microfilm and are quite aggressive in developing complete runs. The same is true for books. Where American collections fall short of those in Mexico is in ephemera, such as pamphlets and photographs. Since photographs of works of visual art are vital to my work, I have found the photo archives in Mexico City, especially those administered by the National Institute of Fine Arts (Instituto Nacional de Bellas Artes), comprehensive and of excellent visual quality.

In general, I have not encountered insurmountable problems in regard to access to materials. Owing to a supportive policy toward collection development in Mexican studies in all disciplines at Vanderbilt University, the resourcefulness of our bibliographers, and the efficiency of our Interlibrary Loan Office, I can do the bulk of my research here, with short trips to the Hispanic Division of the Library of Congress, the collections at the University of Texas at Austin and at UCLA, and with longer visits to Mexico City. I do not recall a single instance of a major item not becoming accessible to me with some detective work and some patience.

I do wish, however, that a major American collection, perhaps the Library of Congress, would contract with the Mexican collections to share photographic resources, by making the Mexican collections available online, on microfilm, or through some other medium that would offer easy access from this side of the border. This arrangement would be especially helpful to the scholar of mural paintings, as these works are much more difficult to photograph than easel paintings, for instance. I had to take many of my own photographs of these dimly lit paintings and, being an amateur rather than a professional photographer, captured only adequate representations at best. These limitations hamper study and presentations of arguments because so much depends on bringing the listener or reader as close as possible to the in-person experience of seeing these paintings.

How I became interested in body theory and began applying it to visual images may have some bearing here. Since the academic enterprise, especially in the humanities, is becoming more and more interdisciplinary, it would behoove art history librarians to regularly browse what their colleagues in related disciplines are ordering, especially in disciplines such as literature, history, philosophy, psychology, sociology, linguistics, and political science. Area studies, such as women's studies, are wonderful grounds for disciplines to cross over and encounter each other. Especially in terms of studies of the body, I began to search out gender studies and especially feminist methodologies in the disciplines listed above because most of the progressive work is now being conducted by feminists of both genders. Academic feminism has now become the intellectual site where the most radical and constructive rethinking is going on. The body, taken seriously by feminists, is making us look at it anew and at its powers of revelation; it is where the struggle for powers of different sorts takes place, where politics might show its full hand, so to speak, where it cannot or does not elsewhere.

Purely by training and by circumstance, I am an art historian who consults other art historians almost not at all. This is not done to further an agenda. On the contrary, I am caught by surprise when I peruse the endnotes to my own writing and notice the almost exclusive extradisciplinary references I make. I have made this personal digression to suggest that perhaps it is neither so personal or unusual to engage in this sort of widening intellectual horizon today.

The best way for libraries to serve me well today is to continue devising cross-reference and keyword systems that are sensitive to my sort of research style. I was intrigued to hear that Microsoft has recently bought software that allows online retailers of reading and musical materials to develop profiles of their customers in terms of either narrowly or broadly defined tastes; a customer inputs characteristics of her own profile and the program presents a tailored menu of choices that such an individual would otherwise miss. I do worry about the political implications of such software; it might limit us to *its* choices and would discourage those wonderful, random finds that unstructured browsing can produce, but I am willing to take that risk because I would still continue to conduct those nonelectronic searches.

What librarianship can best do to help a scholar of my inclinations is to improve the keyword search software by better understanding who is doing the searching. Vanderbilt has a service called UnCover Reveal, an automated alert service that sends tables of contents of selected periodicals to e-mail addresses. With customized search strategies, this service notifies users of the latest articles on selected topics. A system that allows a researcher and a librarian to customize searches in this manner, and that also incorporates constant, automatic searches to save and send titles regularly to such a user, would not only save researchers time but would also bring important titles to the attention of a wider audience and into the hands of specialists. Either way, more material would get read and all new work would build more on available knowledge, not only building the knowledge base, but advancing the sophistication of methodologies and new explanations of familiar issues. The most exciting development, perhaps, would be the development of new issues. That, we certainly need more of.

NOTES

1. In Marcia Pointon and Kathleen Adler, eds., *The Body Imaged: The Human Form and Visual Culture Since the Renaissance* (Cambridge, UK: Cambridge University Press, 1993), frontispiece.

2. For an illustration, see Clemente Orozco Vallardes, *Orozco, verdad cronológica* (Guadalajara: Universidad de Guadalajara, 1983), p. 70.

3. Translated by E. Mungía, Jr. (New York: New American Library, 1962).

4. Azuela, p. 147.

5. Illustrated in '*Sainete, drama y barbarie,' Centenario J. C. Orozco, 1883–1983* (Mexico City: Museo Nacional de Arte, Instituto Nacional de Bellas Artes, 1983), p. 56.

6. By MacKinley Helm (Westport, CT: Greenwood Press, 1953).

7. For an illustration, see Desmond Rochfort, *The Mexican Muralists: Orozco, Rivera, Siqueiros* (London: Laurance King, 1993), p. 118.

8. For an illustration, see Rochfort, p. 142.

8. Pan, Parang, and Chutney: Identity, Music, and Popular Cultural Forms in Trinidad and Tobago

Kathleen Helenese-Paul

Pan, parang, and chutney are three highly dynamic musical cultural forms that have found expression in the island of Trinidad and Tobago. All vie for musical and cultural space, but even as they have in recent times crossed over and transcended class and ethnic barriers, each was spawned in a particular folk/cultural milieu, with roots lying elsewhere: steelpan in Africa, parang in Spain/Venezuela, and chutney in India. Although this paper does not set out to present a comparative analysis, comparisons can be made and similarities noted between the birth of these folk cultures and their development.

This paper first looks briefly at the historical evolution of each form, then discusses the innovations, interchange, and syncretization between the art forms, and concludes by examining how this rich musical heritage is being documented.

Methodology

A small purposive sample was drawn from musicologists, lecturers, ethnomusicologists, steelband arrangers, and cultural researchers in an effort to solicit information on how the music examined here was being documented in a form that would lend itself to acquisition by The Main Library, the University of the West Indies, St. Augustine.

A shelf check of monographs was conducted at the St. Augustine library in order to determine the library's holdings in each area. In an attempt to determine to what extent the music was being electronically recorded, data were also secured by use of the catalogs or verbal reports of music producers and distributors in order to get some idea of the level of production of recorded music in each of the three areas. Using the Yellow Pages of the local telephone directory, nine of the recording studios were contacted, but catalogs were received from only three, with a verbal report via the telephone from one of the three. Six of the largest retail houses were contacted, but data in the form of an inventory were received from only one, since the others did not have catalogs or printed inventories of stock received. For a larger study, these shortages would have been a disadvantage, but apart from highlighting the setbacks to research, and for the purpose of this project, enough information was gathered to give some idea of the current recording status in each of the areas examined.

Limitations

Time did not allow for visits to individual recording studios of distributing houses nor for visits to other major libraries such as the Heritage Library to determine their holdings. This meant that only the collection at the St. Augustine library was examined both with respect to textual documentation and recordings. Radio stations, a very valuable source for ascertaining the volume of recorded music on master tapes, were also not visited. Regrettably, the "home" of pan, Pan Trinbago, burned to the ground in a fire on the morning of Monday, May 17, 1999. It is understood that they held the score sheets for many of the steelband competitions that took place under their auspices over the years; the music scores for the Music Festival; and photographs, trophies, and other primary material such as invitations and flyers for events extending back over several years. Had these materials had been deposited at the St. Augustine library, the story would have been different today.

Pan Music

Music's power to evoke time and place, its emotive force as both an individual experience and a representation of community fellowship, make it a preeminent symbol for collectivities such as nations, ethnic groups and subcultures. The supposed timelessness of musical traditions, coupled with a mythical belief in the uniqueness of a given musical expression can lead to musical forms being deemed representations of the genuine essence—the identity—of particular groups. But claims for the purity of music or any symbol or tradition are unfounded. Neither identities nor traditions are static. Both change with changing circumstances and with the continuous interaction of peoples.[1]

Born out of urban poverty and identified mainly with Afro-Trinidadians, pan music, or steelband or steelpan music, is inextricably linked with carnival and calypso. Carnival evolved during the nineteenth century along with the music that fueled it, and although pan music is now played all over the world, it is indigenous to Trinidad and Tobago and lays claim to the fact that these instruments are the only new percussion musical instruments invented in the twentieth century.

Its sociohistorical evolution can be roughly divided into three periods: 1783–1881, 1881–1900, and 1900 to the early 1930s. For many years after emancipation in 1838, Africans celebrated the anniversary of their freedom by organizing bands and marching in the streets. This pageant was called Cannes Brulées in memory of the burning of the canes in slavery days and comprised roving bands of stickfighters accompanied by African drumming and the singing of Kalinda songs (songs or chants to accompany stickfighting). This commemoration was eventually brought into the Mardi Gras, which the French celebrated on the island from Christmas to Ash Wednesday. White rulers resented this intrusion and sought to suppress it. Matters came to a head when in 1881 the police took to the streets to stop the bands, a riot ensued, and by 1884 a new ordinance was enforced which restricted the size of the bands and outlawed the use of the African drum.

Forced to become innovative in order to find a new way of making music, the Africans turned to tamboo bamboo, that is, varying lengths of bamboo which were either knocked together or struck on the ground to make sounds of varying pitch. These were used as the musical accompaniment of the bands at carnival time and were in existence in the 1920s and well into the early 1930s.

Many and varied are the oral accounts from pioneers and enthusiasts alike of the person or persons responsible for the evolution from the tamboo bamboo instruments to the steel drum. Suffice it to say that the instrument as we know it today emerged from the beating of metal (any piece of metal), biscuit tins, dustbin covers, in an attempt to produce a rhythmic percussive sound to accompany the band. By the late 1930s and early 1940s discarded oil drums from the oil industry began to be used and eventually developed into the steel drum instruments we know today.

In summary, then, the steelband, with a centuries-old tradition preserved through oral accounts and collective memory, was used by the unemployed and the outcasts of society to forge a sense of identity in a socially hostile environment fraught with social deprivation. J. D. Elder, commenting on Simmons's analysis of the history of steelband, states that he (Simmons) had

> without uncertainty, strung out steelband as the latest link in a cultural chain stretching backwards for centuries into the dim past of primitive music, rich with the voices of the African drums in the night, snatched up along with unsuspecting natives from the Gold Coast, the Ivory Coast, from Angola and the Congo littoral swamps. Captivated, these ancestors were brought to a new land to undergo pressures towards cultural change, but the musical instruments retained their basic percussional character though changing in form—skin drum, dustbin and finally steeldrum—in unbroken continuity through centuries of human struggle for freedom to sing, dance, and "play masque."[2]

With the passage of time, the steelband began to be gradually accepted as a grassroots cultural form of the masses, and by the 1960s it began to receive government support as it was seen as the means of forging national identity. As Elder put it, "the demonstration at State level of the admission that Trinidad popular music and music festivals are elements in a high order in the national culture . . . has also elevated the total folk cultural complex to a status never known in the past. Folklore in all its forms has suddenly attained an attractive status."[3]

Innovation, Integration, and Syncretization

As pan became institutionalized, it began to cut across class and ethnic lines, although it has remained embedded in grassroot communities. According to Stuempfle:

> For many Trinidadians the steelband is an indigenous creation that transcends ethnic heritage. . . . Though it was originally developed by Afro-Trinidadians and was most firmly rooted in Afro-Trinidadian folk music, the scope of the music was expanded to encompass other cultural traditions, and some members of other ethnic groups eventually participated in the movement. Many people, regardless of ethnic background, conceive of the pan as a unique local art form and central symbol of national identity.[4]

In 1992, however, the declaration of pan as the national musical instrument was met by a huge outcry from the Indo-Trinidadian community which opposed this move. Among the arguments they put forward was that pan was a symbol of Afro-Trinidadian culture and that aspects of Indian culture should be equally promoted, and that the harmonium as an Indian musical instrument should be equally treated. Nevertheless, the Indo-Trinidadian participates to quite a large degree in carnival and to a somewhat lesser extent plays pan music.

There is no doubt that Trinidad and Tobago is the home of pan, carnival, and calypso and that they are indeed sources of fusion in multifaceted, multicultural Trinidad and Tobago, a point that Weslynne Ashton summarizes well: "In Trinidad and Tobago, while it is true for a large number of people, we have forged a unique culture and identity. Where else can you find someone of Syrian descent singing chutney soca, or someone of Indian descent conducting classical music on a steelpan orchestra? We have blended our differences and created an identity that is entirely our own."[5]

Documentation

The documentation of pan music is examined here from two main perspectives—the written, or textual, and the electronic recording of the music. Textual documentation takes the following forms: monographs including theses, discographies, oral history transcripts (transcripts of tape recordings of the Oral History Programme at the library), and Caribbean Studies Projects (projects submitted by final-year students in the Faculty of Arts and Humanities). With regard to the recorded medium, the most common forms are audio cassettes, video cassettes, compact discs, record albums, and tracks or tapes done either in a recording studio or by the radio station.

The textual holdings at the St. Augustine library included: 59 monographs on the steelpan, 24 Caribbean Studies Projects, 2 oral history transcripts, and 1 discography. Among the recordings were 20 audio cassettes, 13 video cassettes, 21 long-playing albums, and 5 compact discs. Since journal articles were not included, these figures represent a fair amount of documentation.

There is consensus in some quarters about the need for more research in this area. Erin Ryan, an American graduate student in ethnomusicology, echoes the sentiments of the Sparrow's calypso, "Document de Pan," when she states that "Trinidadian calls for pan research derive from not only the desire to document and explore the whos, whats, wheres and hows of the steelband movement, but also from a collective desire to acknowledge the national and cultural importance of pan by committing Trinbagonian resources to the undertaking of such a project, preferably by other Trinbagonians."[6] Ryan also laments the fact that "individuals lack the financial means or educational access to carry out large-scale ethnomusicological documentation of the steelband movement. However, foreigners from economically privileged nations . . . are able to afford the luxury of graduate and professional research into pan in Trinidad."[7]

The introduction to *Play Mr Pannist Play*, which includes a transcription, by American researcher Dr. Jeannine Remy, of a tune composed for pan, states that "Since 1989, Remy had been the recipient of several grants to continue her research on Trinidadian music [and that the] score was made possible by a grant award from Idaho State University Faculty Research committee and the Idaho Commission on the Arts."[8]

Both *Play Mr Pannist Play* and Ryan's thesis are housed in the West Indiana Collection at the St. Augustine library. While we are able to derive the benefit of having the research done through the largesse of the metropole, it supports Remy's observation of the need for us to do more of it ourselves.

The situation is not altogether bleak. The 59 monographs held in the West Indiana section of the library include many by our own pan innovators, published personal accounts, descriptive overviews, studies on the characteristics of pan, scientific analyses, and texts on how to play the instrument.

RECORDED DOCUMENTATION

Catalogs from recording studios and distributors were examined to assess the current scene in the recording industry for pan music. One of these belonged to the Sanch label produced by Sanch Electronix Limited, owned and operated by Simeon Sandiford, who stated that he has in stock more than 500 hours of digitally recorded pan music.[9] The catalog showed that 36 cassette recordings have been produced so far. Many of these have been released on the Panyard Series because they were recorded at the panyards while the steelbands were rehearsing for the Panorama competition. Fourteen compact discs of his music were produced in conjunction with Delos International of California, U.S.A., which also distributes them in the North American market. Five more compact discs were produced on other foreign labels. According to Sandiford, 1999 is the first year he has produced all of the tunes played at the Panorama competition. Even so, he is the first to produce a compact disc of pan music in conjunction with Delos International. This corroborates a statement by Pat Bishop, musicologist, arranger, and conductor of The Lydian Singers, one of the foremost chorales in Trinidad, that only the electronic media can save pan music.[10] The other catalogs acquired did not list any pan music.

A discography that proved very useful in verifying the state of documentation of pan music was *Forty Years of Steel: An Annotated Discography of Steelband and Pan Recordings, 1951–1991*, by Jeffrey Thomas. This discography represented "commercially available recordings of steelbands of any size and configuration . . . and also any commercial recording on which one or more steel pans were featured and /or used in an accompanying role."[11]

The discography highlights the fact that two of Trinidad and Tobago's major local radio stations—the National Broadcasting Service of Trinidad and Tobago (NBS 610 Radio, now part of the International Communications Network I.C.N. group of companies) and Radio Trinidad—are great repositories of pan music, but that 18 of the audio cassettes listed are also in the Sanch catalog, as are 4 of the compact discs, 2 on the Delos label, and 1 long-playing album. Of the 776 recordings listed, approximately 336 were housed at the National Broadcasting Service (NBS) and 154 at Radio Trinidad. Most of the recordings included in the count noted Trinidad as the geographic location of origin. Others not thus designated were selected because they were housed at the local radio stations. Thomas found 15 record albums in the audio-visual collection at St. Augustine library, but a recent check revealed that the library held 21 albums of pan music.

SCORING AS DOCUMENTATION

One area of major significance in the documentation of pan music is scoring, since it provides a format for acquisition, storing, and eventual retrieval. This was an important topic to be covered in interviews. The findings were corroborated in the debate between the oral transmission of the music to the pannist, versus, according to Ryan, one of the common-sense notions of a modern musical instrument, that it is affiliated with "transcribed, published or reproduced scores for the transmission of written ideas."[12] The fact that few pannists read music creates a difficult situation for composers. They do not produce scores because of the widespread absence of music literacy. The lack of scores limits the amount of documentation for research, acquisition, and posterity. According to Remy, "The aural transmission of parts is the panmen's learning process. Requiring them to read written music would slow down the whole learning process and would inhibit them and keep them away from the pan yards."[13] However, in reference to the Panorama tune "Life's Too Short" by composer and arranger Ray Holman, which Remy transcribed, she states, "This type of documentation has never been done before. This score is valuable to scholars who want to further their knowledge of authentic steel drum arranging. This score is also valuable to Trinidadians like Ray Holman who said he would like to see his music preserved in print."[14] However, in the recent past many individuals and pan schools in the general community have tried to address this situation.

One such effort occurred on May 22, 1999, at "Panorama Champions of the Twentieth Century: A Tribute to Excellence," a concert that brought together eleven of the Panorama champions of the event's thirty-seven-year history to play their winning tunes. The brochure that accompanied the program contained the following statement:

> As we approach the end of the 20th century, it is fitting that an event such as this be staged, not only as a tribute to excellence, but also to create an opportunity to capture for the cultural archives unscored music that would be lost to our future generations. This would be achieved via the production of a CD that would undoubtedly be a collector's item second to none.[15]

This is further evidence of the unscored music of our principal cultural resource and of the crucial part played by the electronic media in its documentation.

Following are some of the comments from individuals interviewed on the debate over the value of scoring versus oral transmission. According to Pat Bishop, conductor of The Lydian Singers, "The concept of the idea for the music changes between times. Therefore it is difficult to score . . . it goes from head to hands. They are still preliterate and the mechanisms to put music into systems for retrieval are not in place. Only the electronic media can save us."[16]

Clive Bradley, a leading arranger who led Desperadoes to victory in the 1999 Panorama competition said, "It is time consuming. I keep the scores in my head."[17]

A leading cultural researcher, Gideon Maxime, spoke of the need for a combination of the two concepts of literacy and the "grassroots experience" and said that "the gut feeling of having lived the occasion would assist him [the pannist] at a higher level."[18]

At least two of the interviewees spoke of the enormous cost of transcribing the music with little or no return. The music is seasonal, most of it being produced in relation to carnival and climaxing at the Panorama competition. It was felt that low demand and poor sales would not be sufficient to support the industry.

As Satanand Sharma, lecturer at the Creative Arts Centre of the University of the West Indies, St. Augustine, explained, "Who would want to play the music of a rival band anyway? The demand would probably come from universities abroad but not locally."[19]

Speaking about another pan festival, "Pan Is Beautiful," where the emphasis is on classical music, Pat Bishop again noted that "classical pan poses some very special challenges. The players do not read music . . . the arranger must therefore transpose, transcribe, and condense a symphonic score and teach it by rote. . . . The only solution is musical literacy which will not occur in my lifetime."[20]

Thus the debate continues. It must be borne in mind that there are some arrangers capable of scoring the music. Eddie Wade, proprietor of Eddie Wade Music Scores Ltd. and part-time lecturer at the Creative Arts Centre, explains that while there are no consistent arrangements in place for the scoring of Panorama tunes, test pieces for the "Pan Is Beautiful" festival are scored and usually held at the office of Pan Trinbago and/or kept by some of the judges. He himself scored music, but only on demand because of the time and cost involved.[21]

On November 27, 1990, The Trinidad and Tobago Methanol Company Limited (TTMC) "embarked on a joint venture project with Pan Trinbago to publish the scores of outstanding steelband arrangements from the 1991 Panorama competition. TTMC launched this project in an effort to preserve steelband music, to improve the literacy of today's pan players and make steelband music available internationally. The written preservation of this music is an important step in the overall growth and development of the art form."[22]

In subsequent years this project was repeated through the collaboration of Major & Minor Productions, MultiMedia Limited, and Panyard Inc., an American-based company. This cooperation took place between 1991 and 1994 and, despite the difficulties surrounding the scoring of pan music, showed that individual effort and corporate sponsorship can help assure that scoring takes place, thus contributing to the body of documentation. Eight of the scores are housed at the library of the Creative Arts Centre, attesting to the effort to acquire locally produced material.

Foremost in the arena of forging pan literacy is the Creative Arts Centre at the University of the West Indies. The Centre offers a Certificate in Music (Pan) and the B.A. degree in Musical Arts. According to Satanand Sharma, lecturer, pan arranger, and conductor at the Centre, all students are taught to read and write music. Thus, a body of scores is being built which allows for the teaching of pan music in schools. Another lecturer at the Centre, Mervyn Williams, explained that "Students at the Centre are taught to read, write, compose and arrange music, with the 'ethno' part of it being an important component, since the steelband movement is looked upon as a music culture, and that it is more than a humanly organized sound and instrumentation."[23]

Apart from the curriculum noted above, each student is required to complete a research project which is kept at the Centre's library. Eleven such projects have been done on the steelband, two of which deal specifically with the scoring of pan music. It is also interesting to note that in the process of teaching pan theory and practice, the Centre is producing scored pan music which is used widely by teachers in the schools. The Centre is also now the examining body for pan music, providing graded pan examinations which are used in other islands of the Caribbean such as St. Lucia and St.Vincent.[24]

Commercial Base

Considering documentation in a global perspective, it is important to mention Panyard Inc., a prolific and consistent producer of music sheets of scored pan music. In contrast to the one-time Methanol Project, part of their operations is to produce these sheets thereby providing a constant source of pan music. Since 1994 and its involvement in Trinidad with the Methanol Project, Panyard's catalog shows that the company has transcribed at least half a dozen sheets of Panorama music. It would perhaps be worthwhile for the University library or the Creative Arts Centre to begin purchasing this resource. This proposal brings up once again the issue of inadequate financial and human resources to do this ourselves and the need to turn to the foreign market to purchase at whatever price it sets.

Apart from sheet music for Panorama arrangements, Panyard Inc.'s 1998 catalog advertises at least 10 printed arrangements for the Pan Ramajay competition, another premier steelband competition, while the 1997 catalog advertises 17 compact discs of pan music, 8 cassette recordings (also listed in the Sanch catalog), and steelband recordings from all over the United States of music produced by school, university, and other steelband fraternities.

Remy again remarks that her transcription of the Panorama tune "Life's Too Short" was performed in the United States in the fall of 1989 by the University of Arizona Steel Band, the first college group to perform a complete authentic Trinidadian Panorama composition from beginning to end.[25] This reinforces Sharma's prediction that the demand for our scored music would most likely come from universities abroad. The evidence therefore points to a need for us in Trinidad and Tobago, and by extension the Caribbean, to do more of the work ourselves.

International Scene

"Japanese to Stage World Panorama" screamed the headlines of the *Express* newspaper of Friday, April 16, 1999, when Patrick Arnold, president of Pan Trinbago, said, "Pan Trinbago fears that the announcement by a Japanese producer about his plans to host a Steelband Panorama Competition next year may signal the end of an era in which Trinidad and Tobago was considered the world leader in steelband affairs." He showed that this trend was already a reality when he noted, "Already in North America, with Ellie (Mannette) turning out tunes like crazy at West Virginia University, and customers saying that you cannot tell the difference between their pans and ours."[26]

Arnold rationalized that fears about the internationalization of pan were not unfounded especially since Panyard Inc. had recently boasted that there was now no discernible difference between the pans that their former Trinidadian tuner Ronald Harrigin produced and those of the American tuners.[27]

Selwyn Tarradath also alluded to the vast commercial potential of which others were taking full advantage:

> Northern Illinois University not only appointed Cliff Alexis as an associate music professor, but is the first university to offer a music degree to steelband majors. Our own Harold Headley recently completed his Master's thesis there on a scholarship from the University . . . other American universities have Trinidadian panmen on their faculties. Leonard Moses, a former Desperadoes man, is a professor of percussion studies at the University of Pennsylvania, while Orville Wright is the head of a department at the famous Berkeley College of Music, Boston.[28]

While beyond the scope of this paper, an analysis of the implications of the internationalization of pan music and its teaching and documentation abroad is an area for further research.

A final point relates to the composition and documentation of music specifically designed for the pan. One sterling effort in this regard is *Soca Hits Volume 9*, by Alvin Daniell, former chairman of the Copyright Association of Trinidad and Tobago (COTT). Released in April 1999, the book contains scores for 13 songs, the majority of which were played by steelbands in the 1999 Panorama competition.[29] In a recent awards ceremony the composers, pannists, and steelband music arrangers received trophies for their contribution to the art form.

Despite the debate over issues like those discussed here, Trinidad and Tobago continues to celebrate the pan. The major steelband festivals are described briefly below.

Steelband Music Festival.—In 1952 the first competition for steelbands took place, under the direction of the Music Festival Association with the steelband as a separate class. In 1964 for the first time a separate competition was held for the steelband under the auspices of the Steelband Association. After a hiatus of some years (1968–1972 and 1974–1980), the event was revived by Pan Trinbago in 1980 with a new name, "Pan Is Beautiful." This competition is biennial and the secondary schools have participated since 1981.

Panorama.—At this premier pan event, held at carnival every year, steelbands compete for the top prize. It is said to be the most popular musical event in the pan calendar of Trinidad and Tobago.

Pan Ramajay.—This event, held in May each year, is an opportunity for soloists to display their virtuosity in an atmosphere of freedom and spontaneity. The festival began in 1989 under the auspices of the Exodus Steel Orchestra and is limited to an ensemble of ten players.

Pan on the Move.—This festival is held annually in May in the Borough of Point Fortin in south Trinidad. As the name suggests, the steelband performs while on the move rather than concert style, although there is a time during the day's events when the band stands and plays at a fixed position for the competition.

Pan Jazz.—Held in November, this festival features local and international steelband and jazz musicians.

Parang Music

> Just as calypso and pan are the music of Carnival, parang is the music of Christmas. Regarded as Christmas music, it comprises Spanish lyrics, Venezuelan music, and Trinidadian rhythms.[30]

The term parang refers to a custom belonging to Trinidad's Hispanic heritage. Neither Spanish nor English, the word is the colloquial term for parran, the abbreviation of Spanish *parranda,* a spree, or carousal, or a group of more than four people who go out at night singing to the accompaniment of musical instruments. There are two theories that identify parang with the Hispanic world, as an offspring from Spain or from neighboring Venezuela. According to Daphne Pawan-Taylor, the first maintains that "the custom was introduced from Spain during the Spanish occupation of Trinidad (1498–1797), adapted to the social environment of the island, influenced by contact with neighboring Venezuela and kept flourishing after the Spanish capitulation to Britain in 1797 through continued communications with Venezuela."[31]

The second theory suggests that "the custom came from Spain to Trinidad via Venezuela during the Spanish administration of the island and was continued after the capitulation because of constant interchange between the people of Trinidad and Venezuela."[32]

Each theory has its adherents among academics and practitioners. Noteworthy here is the fact that parang is closely related to the music played by the "peons" who were brought to Trinidad as contract labor for the cocoa and coffee plantations. On the identity of these "peons" Sylvia Moodie-Kublalsingh explains that among the clusters of subcultures that emerged in Trinidad during the nineteenth century were

> Individuals referred to as peons and conqueros, i.e. Spanish labourers and peasants. More recently they have been identified because his language and customs were Spanish and he was an agricultural worker who lived in the valleys and foothills of the cacao-producing areas of the island. Language, customs, occupation and even place of residence distinguished him from the rest of the society. . . . Life was celebrated in the environs of the cacao estate and *conuco* . . . the musicians, the troubadours, the craftsmen, the galleros (who reared and trained fighting cocks) were all prestigious members of the rural Spanish community.[33]

In cultivating the customs of his native country, the peon celebrated the "velorio de Cruz" and the Christmas parang, and "whereas formerly it was known mainly in the rural areas where the 'panyols' lived, it grew to become a widely known part of local folklore."[34]

> Traditionally, in Trinidad, the Christmas parang has been crystallized into the season that is Christmastime—from the last week in November to the "Day of Kings" (Magi), or "Dia de los Reyes" which is January 6 . . . merrymakers [visit] the homes of families, friends or patrons to sing songs in Spanish to the accompaniment of certain musical instruments; usually, the guitar, the cuatro, the maracas or chac-chacs, the mandolin, the bandolin, the violin, and the bandola and sometimes the cello.[35]

Nowadays, the official parang season begins in October and ends in January, and whereas it was originally confined to the villages where the peons had settled, for example Arima, St. Joseph, Santa Cruz, Paramin, Lopinot, and others, today the music can be heard throughout Trinidad and Tobago.

Innovation, Interculturation, and Syncretization

Like any musical heritage that exists in an intercultural environment, parang has undergone changes and has absorbed aspects of other art forms of the host country. This evolution is evidenced by the emergence of young parang groups, the addition of nontraditional instruments such as the steelpan and percussion, change of dress, greater ethnic diversity within the groups, and the emerging presence of women in the group. Also pronounced are the tendency to flavor the songs with non-Spanish words and the poor pronunciation of Spanish by those who often do not even understand Spanish. Moodie-Kublalsingh, in one of her numerous interviews with traditional parranderos, solicited the following comment from a respondent from one of the strongholds of the panyol communities: "and them *hombre negro* singing, is not their fault, but they do not have the pronunciation! What they know about parang? And they singing it wrong. Every dam thing mix up like hell! They ent know what they singing self!"[36]

Documentation

The analysis of the documentation of parang music follows the same format as the discussion of pan music. The data come from an examination of the holdings of the West Indiana Collection and the audio-visual collection of the University of the West Indies St. Augustine library. In the West Indiana and Special Collections Division, there were 6 monographs, 1 oral history transcript, 7 Caribbean Studies Projects, 4 audio cassettes, and 1 video cassette. The Library at the Creative Arts Centre holds 1 project.

Many of the monographs and Caribbean Studies Projects were found to contain English translations of parang songs and samples of songs in Spanish with notation. Worthy of special mention is Francisca Allard's thesis, "The Evolution of Parang (Music and Text) in Trinidad and Tobago, 1900–1997."[37] Apart from a sociohistorical analysis of the presence of the panyols and the birth of parang in Trinidad, the work also presents linguistic, musical, textual, rhyming, and thematic analyses of some of the songs made famous by leading parang groups in Trinidad and Tobago.

In an interview, Simeon Sandiford mentioned that he has been trying for the past four years to persuade the Lara Brothers, one of the oldest traditional parang groups in Trinidad, to write the lyrics of their songs, many of which are original compositions. When asked about transcribing the songs, Sandiford indicated that it would pose some difficulty because of the language. His catalog lists one parang tune that he has produced on audio cassette, but the Lara Brothers celebrated their fiftieth anniversary in the business with the release of a compact disc in 1997.

RECORDED DOCUMENTATION

Other forms of documentation also exist. An examination of the most recent catalogs received from two commercial enterprises—Crosby's Music Centre and the KMP Recording Studio—showed: 10 compact discs available on the local market, of which 3 were also available on cassette tapes; 3 long-playing records; 2 songs stored on 24-track two-inch tape, and 9 on 12-track half-inch tape awaiting release.

Radio broadcasts have been very instrumental in promoting the art form. Consequently, like pan, a lot of the parang music is held on tape by the radio stations. According to Allard, "It was not until 1950 that parang music was broadcast over the radio through the efforts of Holly Betaudier. . . . The Old Oak Serenaders from St. Joseph were the first parranderos invited to participate in this special parang broadcast . . . it was not until 1960, when Radio 610 (spearheaded by Leo de Leon) began to broadcast parang music that the popularity of the art form began to spread."[38]

The rise of two registered associations (the National Parang Association of Trinidad and Tobago [NPATT] and the Trinidad and Tobago Parang Association) also led to parang's increasing popularity through the broadcasting of competitions and festivals. Local television was also used extensively to broadcast the competitions and contributed to the high visibility of the art form. Radio and television stations are thus important repositories for the documentation of parang music.

Commercial Base

An element that has intruded very significantly into the art form is soca parang, or parang soca, a blend of soca, calypso, and parang. With the birth of the NPATT in 1971, parang moved from traditional rural areas to center stage through the competitions the association introduced. This expansion naturally brought with it the innovations mentioned above, including the introduction of Latin rhythms and a changed image. As parang became more and more commercial, traditional calypsonians entered the fray and began to produce soca parang songs in the period leading up to Christmas. Many of these songs have moved away from the tradition of the *aguinaldos* and place more emphasis on the merriment of Christmas, and the food, drink, and numerous holiday preparations. Spanish words (mostly pidgin Spanish) are often loosely interspersed in order to retain the Spanish flavor, but most of the soca parang songs are sung in English. Other modifications include variations in the music and melodies, the use of electronic instruments, the introduction of pan, and the music's non-religious character. Naturally these innovations have their adherents and their detractors. Non–Spanish-speaking Trinidadians welcome them because in the main, they cannot understand what is being sung, while the traditional parranderos decry them as a bastardization of their parang tradition and its religious significance. Many calypsonians have benefited economically from the tremendous pre-Christmas sales and the new avenues for revenue in addition to their calypso music.

Parang soca has had an impact not only on the local scene but also internationally. It represents local Christmas music, has spawned an annual soca parang competition, and now represents a new musical art form. According to Sylvia Moodie-Kublalsingh, "The language of the parranda in future years may well be Trinidad English rather than Trinidad Spanish. This is all part of the never ending dynamic process of acculturation in a heterogeneous society."[39]

Chutney Music

> [Chutney is] a product of Indian classical music in the Bhojpuri style. This was the music brought by the Indian indentures from the Gangetic plains of Bihar and Uttar Pradesh. Those who came were simple country folk who had a tradition of song and dance in their culture dating back thousands of years. . . . In their isolated environment, their religious, cultural and social traditions survived almost intact to this day. Indian classical music was mainly of a religious nature and was adapted from religious texts; its earliest form was probably the bhajans sung at prayer meetings. Life on the plantations was not easy, and the indentures, like the slaves, gathered in the evenings after work, at weddings, childbirth, deaths and other ceremonies to socialize and ease their frustration in song and dance.[40]

While this passage provides a definition of chutney music, chutney itself is actually a hot spicy sauce made from a fruit or vegetable such as tamarind or mango and served as a side dish. The songs, like the dish, are usually hot and spicy with a fast musical beat, simple catch tunes, and sexual overtones.

The modern chutney phenomenon had its beginnings in the earliest cultural folkways. Originally, rituals such as Kartik, Holi, the prenuptial celebrations, and the birth of children were primarily celebrated within the family, and some even as closed-door affairs, such as the Batwaan. In identifying these

songs as the progenitors of the chutney dance, Indian classical dancer Satnarine Balkaransingh explains that "Some were burlesque in their interpretation of
the love and sex act. Sung on the night preceding the wedding, they were used
as instructions to young brides inexperienced in the art of love and sex . . . in
this popular village type theatrical event, the vulgar becomes natural, and the
obscene joyous."[41] He went on to ask if a parallel could not be drawn between
this expression and calypso and soca in carnival.

Whatever the occasion for the celebration, it is clear that all these rituals,
like the pan for the Africans, were the foundation for forging a new identity in
their new and hostile surroundings. By the mid 1960s, chutney began to emerge
from being a closed-door affair and entered the public domain. "But the chutney boom really started in the 1980's when commercial dances began to attract
massive crowds of working class Indians who decided that chutney was just
too much fun to be limited to occasional weddings and single-sex dancing in
stuffy rooms and damp field. The public fetes soon became a fixture of Indo-
Trinidadian life."[42] It is now a well-organized affair attracting thousands of
patrons at large cultural complexes mainly in south and central Trinidad where
there is a concentration of the Indian population.

Innovation, Interculturation, and Syncretization

In a multicultural, multiethnic island like Trinidad, blending of the art
forms is inevitable. The resulting hybrid is called chutney soca or soca chutney,
a blend of chutney and soca. Author Susan Gosine describes chutney soca: "In
a relatively new crossover beat which is emerging, not only the Indian community but a substantial portion of Afro-Trinis, and only recently two Chinese
. . . you'll find them all on one stage wining and swaying to the rhythms of
chutney, soca, blending the pulsating throb of the dholak and the irresistible
tassa drums with the scintillating, titillating soca rhythms."[43]

Not unlike parang's incorporation of soca beat, chutney moved away from
the traditional folk songs and bhajans to the singing of light-hearted, frivolous
songs, sung either in Hindi or in English or a mixture of both. Allard explains
it this way:

> Music, especially popular at Hindu weddings and celebrations, that has
> blended Afro-Trinidadian rhythms with East Indian melodic lines. Sung in
> either Hindi, English or English and Hindi, frivolity of theme has been
> retained. The infectious nature of this music has been enhanced by its assim-
> ilation of soca rhythms. On the other hand, the adoption of the calypso's
> "double entendre" had led to the employment by some artists of lewd-
> sounding lyrics that border on the obscene.[44]

With respect to change, other authors have observed what they call "tan
singing" at the "tent night" or "cooking night" (the night before the wedding).
They observe:

tan singing is a mixture of old folk songs from the Bhojpuri-speaking area of North India, somewhat garbled elements of North Indian classical music, and some features unique to Indo-Caribbean culture, all reinterpreted by local musicians who stress original composition and creation. . . . Although singers don't really know Hindi, they know the words to the Hindi songs and are generally steeped in Hindu folk lore. For their part, audiences don't understand Hindi either, but they like the sound of it and prize its use as an emblem of Indianness.[45]

The case of chutney music is not unlike that of secular parang. Attempts to popularize and internationalize the art form by blending it with soca and modifying the traditions and symbols associated with it have caused some controversy. As with parang, dissidents have raised their voices in protest over the ribald and often raunchy lyrics of the chutney songs. Undoubtedly, the music will eventually settle into a form that is acceptable and at the same time commercially viable.

Documentation

Because chutney music is of rather recent origin, most of the information about it is to be found in the newspaper clippings file in the West Indiana Division of the University of the West Indies St. Augustine library. The collection contains: 2 monographs, 2 Caribbean Studies Projects, 4 audio cassettes, and 1 compact disc. The library at the Creative Art Centre has 1 project.

RECORDED DOCUMENTATION

The KMP catalog listed 2 songs on 24-track two-inch tape and 21 on 12-track half-inch tape. Inventory at Planet Rock, a chutney musical outlet in Couva Central Trinidad, included production of 52 compact discs between 1994 and 1998; 32 of these contained chutney music produced in Trinidad and the rest consisted of music produced mainly in Guyana. I was informed, however, that these figures are only approximate because the inventory records for the period were not kept on a consistent basis.

Studios devoted to such recordings have been established, although two of the pioneering ones, Saarana and Windsor, no longer exist. Mohan Jaikaran, based in Queens, New York, has his own label, Jamaica Me Crazy Records, Inc. Data from Ribiero's 1992 study show that chutney is quite a lucrative business, with audio cassette sales topping the 5,000 mark annually on the local market with a similar retail figure for the international market.[46] My own sampling, though small, revealed that chutney has spanned a whole new cultural industry, with a uniquely indigenous sound, with its blend of African drums, the dholak, chantal, harmonium, and guitars.

Commercial Base

Having enjoyed commercial success since the late 1980s, chutney music came into its own in 1996 with the synthesis of chutney and soca music and hits like "Chutney Bacchanal" by Chris Garcia and "Lota Lah" by Sonny Mann. Artists from the Afro-Trinidadian calypso arena began entering the big Chutney Monarch competition, the first of which was held in 1995. Commenting on this show, Felix Paul said, "and what has been described as the 'soca chutney mix' in the music, there is every likelihood that not only East Indians will be following this show, but their African brothers and sisters as well."[47]

More lies beneath the surface of this seemingly innocent comment, however. As Gordon Rohlehr explains, "Thus, while Indo-Trinidadians have been identified as a target community for the marketing of chutney-soca crossover music, the details of this aspect of inter-ethnic interface suggests that it involves a fierce contestation of space in which little quarter is being given on either side."[48] This statement is corroborated by Ribiero, who says that the chutney art form is "an attempt at counter acculturation of the community and represents cultural persistence and continuity. . . . Chutney is now a useful medium for social and political commentary by Indo-Trinidadians along similar lines to that of the calypso. . . . "[49] While this jostling for space in an arena colored by politics may be the reality, the interculturation continues among music lovers.

The first Pan Chutney festival took its place on the national agenda in 1995 and when the first Spectacular Chutney Soca Review opened its "tent" in 1997, its proprietor stated that "Chutney is now as much part of Carnival as is soca, and what can be more beautiful than the blending of the two."[50]

As noted above, the commercialization of chutney music led to a vigorous marketing industry headed by the media, mainly radio, and recording studios. According to Rohlehr, "The Indo-Creole quest for specific cultural visibility had led since independence to complaints that a disproportionately small amount of radio and television time was being devoted full-time to various types of Indian music. This situation has changed, and since the mid 90s there are at least four radio stations devoted full time to various types of Indian music."[51] These radio stations, therefore, apart from being purveyors of the chutney music, would also be sources of documentation. Moean Mohammed, one of the pioneers of radio programs and recently inducted into the Hall of Fame at the first Indo-Caribbean Music Awards, presented the first program, "Indian Talent on Parade," on Radio Trinidad. In 1970 Moean, together with his brother Sham, produced the first edition of "Mastana Bahar," "one of the few forums which provides an avenue for show-casing live local East Indian talent, on Trinidad and Tobago Television."[52] Peter Manuel describes the proliferation of Indian radio and television programs: "While some non-Indians in Trinidad, Guyana and Suriname continue to regard such shows as ethnically divisive, most are coming to accept the fundamentally multicultural nature of their societies, and the increased role that Indians will play therein. For its part, Trinidad—the proverbial land of steelband and calypso—may eventually become known more universally as the land of steelband, calypso and chutney."[53]

Conclusions

Although this paper did not set out to be a comparative study of the popular cultural art forms in Trinidad and Tobago, similarities and differences can be easily discerned.

In a society as cosmopolitan as that of Trinidad and Tobago, where the African and Indian populations are of almost equal size, it can be expected that in the confined space of a small island intercultural exchanges would occur, along with the inevitable modification of traditions and symbols.

In the area of pan music, Lennox Bobby Mohammed, the one-time leader of the now defunct Guinness Cavaliers who led them to becoming the first band from the southern region of Trinidad to win the National Panorama competition in 1965, was honored at the championship event on May 22, 1999. Composer/arranger Jit Samaroo has been associated with the Amoco Renagades Steel Orchestra since 1971 and has led them to nine National Panorama victories. He too was honored at the championship event. He also received the national Humming Bird Medal of Merit for his outstanding contribution to the culture of Trinidad and Tobago. Satanand Sharma, of the University of the West Indies Creative Arts Centre, is one of the steelband arrangers/composers at the Centre and conducts the Centre's pan ensemble.

When aficionados, pannists, and well-wishers are added to the above group, pan music truly can be said to have been instrumental in forging a national identity, integrating the island's ethnic groups through the power of the music. With regard to parang and chutney, evidence of cultural encounters diversely affecting their musical styles is apparent. But whereas pan has cut across class, ethnic, economic, and political boundaries, chutney especially is still evolving. It is all to the good, however, and it is the opinion of Kampta Karran that "through the power of musical fusion, the sharing of the stage floor and chart, growing cross-cultural appreciation, increasing integration, and the quest for equality, are on the upswing."[54]

NOTES

1. Nancy Morris, "Cultural Interaction in Latin American and Caribbean Music," online posting ehost@epnet.com. April 8, 1999.

2. J. D. Elder, *From Congo Drum to Steelband: A Socio-Historical Account of the Emergence and Evolution of the Trinidad Steel Orchestra* (St. Augustine, Trinidad: University of the West Indies, 1969), p. 20

3. Ibid., p. 12.

4. Stephen Stuempfle, *The Steelband Movement: The Forging of a National Movement in Trinidad and Tobago* (Mona, Jamaica: The Press, University of the West Indies, 1995), p. 221.

5. Weslynne Ashton, "Down South," *Sunday Express,* May 3, 1999, Section 3, p. 6.

6. Erin Ryan, "Pan on the Verge of the 21st Century: Issues on the Evolution of the Trinidad Steelband," Ph.D. dissertation, Wesleyan University, 1994, p. 11.

7. Ibid., p. 12.

8. De Fosto, *Play Mr Pannist Play* (music composed by De Fosto, arranged by Nervin Saunders "Teach" for The Petrotrin Invaders Steel Orchestra; score transcribed by Dr. Jeannine Remy, 1993), p. ii.

9. Simeon Sandiford, personal interview, April 22, 1999.

10. Pat Bishop, personal interview, April 13, 1999.

11. Jeffrey Thomas, *Forty Years of Steel: An Annotated Discography of Steelband and Pan Recordings, 1951–1991* (Westport CT: Greenwood Press., 1992), p. xviii.

12. Ryan, p. 153.

13. Jeannine Remy, "A Historical Background of Trinidad and the Panorama Competitions with an Analysis of Ray Holman's Panorama Arrangement of 'Life's Too Short,' " Ph.D. dissertation, University of Arizona, 1991, p. 39.

14. Ibid., p. 41.

15. Pan Trinbago, *Panorama Champions of the Twentieth Century: A Tribute to Excellence* [Brochure] (Port-of-Spain: Pan Trinbago, 1999).

16. Pat Bishop, personal interview, April 13, 1999.

17. Clive Bradley, personal interview, April 15, 1999.

18. Gideon Maxime, personal interview, April 11, 1999.

19. Satanand Sharma, personal interview, April 27, 1999.

20. Pan Trinbago, *Pan Is Beautiful VII: World Steelband Music Festival* (Port-of-Spain, Trinidad: Pan Trinbago, 1994), pp. 15–16.

21. Eddie Wade, personal interview, April 13, 1999.

22. Taken from front page of one of the score sheets.

23. Mervyn Williams, personal interview, April 14, 1999.

24. Satanand Sharma, personal interview, April 27, 1999.

25. Remy, Preface to score, p. 87.

26. Patrick Arnold, "Japanese to Stage World Panorama," *Express,* April 16, 1999, Section 2, p. 1

27. Ibid., p. 1.

28. Selywn Tarradath, "Maybe Pat Bishop Was Right: TT Does Not Deserve the Steelband," *Trinidad Guardian,* June 5, 1992, p. 11.

29. Terry Joseph, "Daniell Releases 'Soca Hits,' " *Express,* April 23, 1999, Section 2, p. 4.

30. Trinidad and Tobago, Ministry of Public Administration and Information (Information Division), "The History of Parang" [Leaflet] (Trinidad and Tobago: The Author, 1996), p. 1.

31. Daphne Pawan-Taylor, *Parang of Trinidad* (Trinidad and Tobago: National Cultural Council, 1997), p. 8.

32. Ibid., p. 8.

33. Sylvia Moodie-Kublalsingh, *The Cocoa Panyols of Trinidad: An Oral Record* (London: British Academic Press, 1994), pp. xi, 10.

34. "Survival of Hispanic Religious Songs in Trinidad Folklore," *Caribbean Quarterly* 29:1 (March 1983), 4.

35. Pawan-Taylor, p. 15.

36. Moodie-Kublalsingh, p. 78.

37. Francisca Carol Allard, "The Evolution of Parang (Music and Text) in Trinidad and Tobago, 1900–1997," Ph.D. dissertation, University of the West Indies, St. Augustine, 1998.

38. Ibid., p. 109.

39. Moodie-Kublalsingh, p. 24.

40. Unanan Persad, "Calypso and Chutney: Parallel Development and Integration," *Caribbean Dialogue* 3:4 (October–December 1997), p. 78.

41. Satnarine Balkaransingh, "Chutney, an Indian Search for Roots," *Express,* October 25, 1998, p. 24, from a paper "Chutney Crosses Over into Chutney Soca in Trinidad and Tobago Carnival" presented at the International Development Seminar on Carnival at the State University New York, September 12, 1998.

42. Peter Manuel, "Chutney Wine: Dance Music from India via Trinidad Hits Queens," online posting ehost@epnet.com. April 21, 1999.

43. Susan Gosine, "Fever in the Chutney Soca," *Sunday Express,* January 17, 1999, Section 2, p. 2.

44. Allard, notes, p. 83.

45. Peter Manuel, Kenneth Bilby, and Michael Largey, *Caribbean Currents: Caribbean Music from Rumba to Reggae* (Philadelphia: Temple University Press, 1995), p. 215.

46. Indra Ribiero, "The Phenomena of Chutney Singing," Caribbean Studies Project (St. Augustine, Trinidad: University of the West Indies, 1992).

47. Felix Paul, "First Local Chutney Monarch a Hit," *Trinidad Guardian,* May 12, 1995, p. 12.

48. Gordon Rohlehr, "We Getting the Kaiso We Deserve," online posting ehost@epnet.com. April 21, 1999.

49. Ribiero, p. 27.

50. Terry Joseph, "Chutney Soca Rising," *Express,* January 10, 1997. p. 15.

51. Rohlehr, p. 7.

52. Ribiero, p. 54.

53. Manuel, *Caribbean Currents*, p. 220.

54. Kampta Karran, *Trinidad and Tobago's Parang, Calypso and Chutney* (n.p.: n.p., 1996).

9. Preserving Our Heritage: The Work of Al Ramsawack, Folklorist of Trinidad and Tobago

Jennifer Joseph

Since information about the social history of a country is derived largely from the stories handed down through the generations, it becomes extremely important to gather and record this information. Al Ramsawack, folklorist of Trinidad and Tobago, recognized the value of the stories he had been told during his childhood in a small, rural village in northeastern Trinidad. During his career as a school-teacher, he made a decision to actively seek out these stories which are a major part of the nation's oral tradition. As part of the Oral History program of the library at the University of the West Indies St. Augustine,[1] Al Ramsawack shared with us his methods and experiences in documenting the stories.

This paper examines the work of Al Ramsawack who for more than thirty-years has committed himself to documenting, writing, and communicating sto-ries that form an essential part of our heritage and popular culture. It describes the author's experiences in collecting and recording these stories and legends which have their origin in West Africa and India and have been influenced by aspects of the culture of Britain, France, and Spain. The paper highlights some of the central characters in the folklore of Trinidad and Tobago and how Ram-sawack uses them to tell his story of life in Trinidad and Tobago. Ramsawack skillfully uses the folklore to develop "lessons of life" for our people, and in the process he records some of the country's social history through numerous illus-trations of the folk characters. The paper also considers the role of libraries in recording and preserving the oral tradition in small, developing countries.

The Oral Tradition, Folklore, and Caribbean Society

Folklore has been defined in several ways and is generally accepted as being the body of traditional customs and belief that has been handed down largely by word of mouth (Adams 1973). Folklore is the entire body of stories, legends, and myths of a people and is indeed a part of society's oral tradition which must be explored in order to arrive at an understanding of human behav-ior. In essence, folklore is an essential part of the popular culture of a country and provides an invaluable insight into the social history of its people. For countries such as Trinidad and Tobago and the several Caribbean islands that have been colonized and influenced by the British, the Dutch, the French, and the Spanish and that are populated by more than one ethnic group, a knowledge of the folklore is important for tracing and recording our heritage. In Trinidad and Tobago, our customs, beliefs, and legends have come from a variety of cultures. These form the core of a rather unique cultural heritage since the styles and lives of various peoples have been woven and interwoven into a special form. The phenomenon of folklore therefore becomes extremely important for Trinidad and Tobago which does not have a major tradition of reading and which is a relatively young country in the context of world civilization.

The Folklorist Gathers

Al Ramsawack, the sixth child in a family of nine, was born in Sangre Grande, a rural village in northeastern Trinidad which was heavily forested and had several cocoa plantations. He recalls that his father, who was of East Indian descent, entertained them as children by relating a series of folktales[2] from India and Africa. Ramsawack indicates that as a result of his contacts with the hunters and agricultural workers who lived in the environs of his village, he was also told numerous stories of the adventures in the forest. His interest in researching the folklore came when he had to tell stories to his own children.[3]

In a 1994 interview at the Main Library of the University of the West Indies, St. Augustine, Ramsawack explained his data collection methods.[4] The first stage of his research involved a return to his hometown to speak with the older persons to whom many of the stories had been handed down and who also claimed to have actually had various experiences. He indicated that he spoke with some descendants of the native peoples of the island who said they actually had some of the encounters. Ramsawack utilized the personal, informal encounter to gather the oral data. He paid several visits to the local "Rum Shop," a place where people gather to "have a beverage" and to chat about the politics and activities of the day.[5] Ramsawack states that after a few hours of imbibing these "beverages," the tongues became looser and he was able to draw pertinent information and a wide variety of stories from the "limers"[6] in the Rum Shop. The encounters in the Rum Shop also provided him additional names of older inhabitants of the village who could be used to verify some of the stories. He was therefore able to gather additional data by visiting and talking with the older villagers.

Informal, unplanned encounters also provided additional data. Ramsawack relates one occasion when he sat on the roadside with an old man who had seen him pass by but who had mistaken him for someone else. In this rather informal setting, Ramsawack was told numerous stories. He took mental notes and wrote the stories down when he returned home.

Finally, the local "wake" generated the greatest number of stories. A "wake" is an old African tradition still very much alive in Trinidad and Tobago and the Caribbean. On someone's death, friends and family gather every night at the home of the deceased person to "keep company" or "stay awake" with the dead person's spirit before the spirit moves on to the next stage of its existence (Herskovits and Herskovits 1947:457–461). In this setting, where people talk freely and exchange stories, Ramsawack was able to collect several stories. He describes sitting in a small thatched hut lit only by a small flambeau, trying to write down the stories. In the semi-darkness of the hut, he would write over his own writing and would therefore have some trouble deciphering his own notes at a later date. Ramsawack has utilized the memories of those settings in the preparation of his own stories.

The Influences

The majority of the stories used by Al Ramsawack have their origin in the folktales that came from West Africa and India. After the arrival of Christopher Columbus in 1492 and the subsequent need to supply labor for the sugarcane, coffee, and cocoa plantations, the islands were populated in the ensuing centuries by slaves from West Africa. The islands changed hands on more than one occasion and have been governed by the French, Spanish, and British (Abrahams 1967:457–461). The years after emancipation brought the Portuguese, Chinese, and East Indians to the islands of the Caribbean as indentured laborers. However, the main inhabitants of Trinidad and Tobago are the descendants of the African slaves and the Indian indentured laborers. The African slaves brought with them their culture and folk style which have largely survived despite attempts by the colonial masters to destroy their various customs. Much of the Indian culture has also remained intact even though there has been a level of fusion. It is said that the slaves and later the Indian indentured laborers shared their stories at night as a form of entertainment and as a way to preserve a link with their homeland. Of significance is the fact that the stories told by the slaves were related to their daily lives and their experiences with the white slave masters on the plantations. Since the slaves could not communicate openly about their treatment by the white slave masters, they created animal characters to disguise various incidents and to express their discontent and desire to be rid of the burden of the slave master. These, then, are the stories that form the core of Ramsawack's writing and that reveal something about the lives of the slaves and their struggle against the domination of the slave master. In the folklore, animals assume human roles. For example, Anansi is the small, insignificant spider or the poor slave, who is forever hunted and taken advantage of by the Lion, the white slave master. An understanding of the Anansi stories researched and developed by Ramsawack provides some insight into the historical relationship between Caribbean peoples of African descent and the white plantation owners (Abrahams 1967:457–461).

Lessons of Life

Al Ramsawack's stories assume a didactic role as he skillfully uses folklore to establish moral values and to offer guidance to all. In addition to the numerous stories he collected, Ramsawack has also created several original stories through which he offers his special "lessons of life."

Ramsawack's effort to preserve local culture is reflected in his use of local animals and local dialects. In many stories, the introductioin of local animals such as the manicou and the agouti serves to document indigenous information about the country for children and nationals in general, who have never been to the forest. As an illustrator, Ramsawack is also able to document images of the animals that inhabit the forests of Trinidad and Tobago and that are in danger of becoming extinct.[7]

The creation of stories set against the local landscape has been used to teach a variety of values. The importance of preserving the environment is highlighted in the folklore of Trinidad and Tobago and is even more relevant today in a society grappling with environmental issues. The folklore of Trinidad and Tobago is replete with stories about confrontations between the hunters and Papa Bois, the country's first Champion of the Environment. In a special collection of stories, Ramsawack uses folklore to build consciousness about the need to preserve the country's flora and fauna (Trinidad and Tobago 1980). Papa Bois, King of the Forest, or Father of the Woods (as he is known), fiercely performs his task of protecting the animals and the forest from being destroyed by hunters. Ramsawack therefore highlights several stories that tell of eerie encounters between the hunters and Papa Bois who is depicted as a stocky man with a long beard whose entire body is covered with long hair like that of a donkey. His cloven hoof on one foot makes him the eerie, supernatural character.

Several lessons of life are documented through Anansi, the Spiderman, the colorful character whose main aim in life was to survive. His survival was sometimes to the detriment of another character whom Anansi manages to out-fox. The stories usually carry a strong moral which forces the listener or the reader to stop and think before pursuing a particular course of action. His stories give rules and guidelines for living and are particularly useful for teaching young children.

In one instance, Ramsawack describes Anansi's encounter with Lion who is tricked by Anansi into going into the river to retrieve a nonexistent piece of cheese. The story highlights the moral that greed will always lead to the loss of something that may already be in one's possession. In another instance, Anansi does good and gets his just reward. In another story, Anansi finds an old violin, restores it to life, and provides parang[8] music at Christmas time for all the villagers. Late on Christmas he realizes that he has spent all his time in this way and has not provided the basic necessities for his family for Christmas day. It is on his way home, a sad and forlorn character, that the violin speaks to Anansi and tells him that he should not be sad for while he may think that his family had been neglected, he has in fact been doing good and bringing music and joy to so many, including the Violin "himself" who had previously been discarded by so many. When Anansi awakes on Christmas morning, he finds that his family has been well provided for with food and gifts.[9]

Authenticity

A large portion of Ramsawack's work is indeed built around the legendary characters that have become part of the folklore of Trinidad and Tobago. Many of these, whose names have been influenced by the French, also appear in the work of other folklorists and researchers of the culture. M. P. Alladin, for example, cites many of the major characters who play a part in Ramsawack's work. For example, La Diablesse, the she-devil of the folklore, is common to the work of Alladin and Ramsawack. She is usually depicted as a beautifully dressed woman in a white gown with frills cascading from the waist down. She also wears a wide-brimmed straw hat which hides her face. Her right foot is a human foot while the left is a cloven hoof like that of a cow. She wears a strong perfume to which men are attracted and she lures her unsuspecting victims into the forest and to their death. The dead man's soul becomes the devil's property and is used to create other "jumbies" for his kingdom. The illustrations of Ramsawack are similar to Alladin's and other folklore artists. The soucouyant is also depicted in the same way in Alladin's work and in Ramsawack's. The soucouyant, known as the old woman who has connections with the devil, is a nocturnal creature who at midnight removes her skin and puts it into a wooden mortar. She then turns into a ball of fire and flies through the night to suck the blood of her enemies. She trades this blood with the devil in return for further evil powers. Another example is the Douens, the souls of infants who were not baptized and died before the age of seven. They are either depicted as nude or dressed in long, loose flannel shirts and wear broad-rimmed straw hats.[10]

In their stories, both Ramsawack and Alladin use the Boot ghost featured in the stories derived from Indian tales. The ghost can appear in different forms. Sometimes they are not seen, but their presence is felt. The Churile, which also originated in the Indian tales, is a specialized boot or ghost that came from the soul of a woman who died in childbirth.[11] These characters are similar to some of the others already described.

Al Ramsawack continues to write and present work in the folklore tradition. He has introduced some new elements to the folk material and appears to have given extra powers to the fiction. He is in the process of creating a new series of myths based on his own characters such as Monkey Polo and Pahyorl,[12] thereby making his own contribution to the body of myths that already exist in the folklore. Al Ramsawack has indeed recognized that folklore is dynamic and should be contemporary and should relate to the issues surrounding life in Trinidad and Tobago and the Caribbean. He has written over five hundred stories—folklore stories, folktales, and general stories about people in society, as well as his own original fairy tales. Very much aware of the negative effect that the electronic media can have on reading, particularly in a society already without a long tradition of reading, Ramsawack has written new stories for younger children with themes that will attract and hold their attention. He has therefore deliberately created a new set of fiction to address contemporary problems. He has expressed concern about the decline in the use and teaching of the folk traditions in schools. He has continued to produce stories and to use the medium of the newspaper to disseminate them. These stories are published weekly in the children's magazine of one of the country's leading newspapers.

The Role of Libraries

What, then, is the role of libraries in preserving a nation's heritage? Society has a responsibility to ensure that a record of its culture is maintained and communicated in a variety of ways. Society can fulfill its role by funding and supporting the work of libraries and archives, the main custodians of the written cultural heritage. Preservation of the oral tradition is of great importance and it therefore falls within the domain of libraries to find ways to document and preserve the heritage. This becomes even more important in small, developing societies, such as Trinidad and Tobago, which are affected and influenced by powerful external forces under which the indigenous culture tends to be subsumed. The advent of the electronic information age and the consequent reliance on "packaged" information has led to a further decline in the reading habit in a society which already lacks a long-standing reading tradition.

While the UNESCO Public Library Manifesto places the responsibility for promoting cultural heritage and for supporting oral traditions on public libraries in general, university libraries must share that responsibility in view of the research needs of its particular clientele. In the case of Trinidad and Tobago, which is now in the process of building a national library, the university libraries at the St. Augustine campus have assumed the responsibility of collecting and recording oral data. Through the library's Oral and Pictorial Record Programme, numerous interviews have been conducted with persons who, in some instances, are the sole repositories of some of society's experiences. It becomes even more important for libraries to not only provide access to indigenous information but also to assume the responsibility for documenting the culture. Libraries in the Caribbean need to make full use of information technology in order to institute and promote the development of multimedia access to the country's folklore.

Conclusion

The work of Al Ramsawack is an important part of the efforts of nationals of Trinidad and Tobago to preserve our heritage which, because of the country's multicultural and multiethnic community, is a special blend of the cultures of the several countries that have had an impact on the islands of the Caribbean. The work of folklorists like Al Ramsawack needs to be gathered and published.

The preservation of a nation's heritage is the ultimate responsibility of the custodians of the world's knowledge.

NOTES

1. Under the auspices of the Oral and Pictorial Records Programme, Main Library, University of the West Indies, St. Augustine, Trinidad, interviews are conducted with persons who contribute in some way to the life of the country.

2. Indian folktales, known as "Kheesahs," were shared by the Indian indentured laborers when they came to the West Indies. These have been handed down through generations and Al Ramsawack has used several of them in his books.

3. Ramsawack provided some biographical information in 1972. His interest in writing and art began at high school. His interest in researching the folklore came later when he wanted to tell stories to his own children.

4. Ramsawack shared this information as part of the University Library's Oral and Pictorial Record Programme.

5. A "Rum Shop" in Trinidad and Tobago is the traditional "bar," a place where people meet to have an alcoholic drink.

6. "Liming," a term used in Trinidad and Tobago, means meeting and talking in an unstructured, relaxed mode. People engaging in this activity are called "limers." North Americans might say "hanging out."

7. Al Ramswack has written and illustrated more than five hundred stories, some of which have been published. Some of these titles are included in the bibliography.

8. The influence of the Spanish has given parang music to Trinidad and Tobago. This particular style of music is played at Christmas time since the main themes of the lyrics are about the birth of Jesus Christ.

9. These examples of Anansi stories are cited in Trinidad and Tobago (1980).

10. The descriptions of the various folklore characters are found in several texts including the work of Al Ramsawack, M. P. Alladin, and Gerry Besson.

11. Stories based on characters created by Al Ramsawack are recorded in Ramsawack (1983).

12. The Boot and Churile are characteristic of the folktales which were derived from India.

BIBLIOGRAPHY

Abrahams, Roger D. 1967. *The Shaping of Folklore Traditions in the British West Indies.* (Reprint from *Journal of Inter-American Studies* 11:3 [July 1967].) Coral Gables, FL: University of Miami Press.

Adams, Robert J., ed. 1973. *Introduction to Folklore.* Columbus, OH: Collegiate Publishing.

Alladin, M. P. 1968. *Folk Stories and Legends of Trinidad.* Port of Spain, Trinidad: M. P. Alladin.

————. 1980. *12 Short Stories.* Maraval, Trinidad: Dial.

American Folklore Society. 1984. *Folklore, Folklife.* Washington DC: The American Folklore Society.

Besson, Gerard, ed. 1989. *Folklore and Legends of Trinidad and Tobago.* Port of Spain, Trinidad: Paria Publishing Company Limited.

Dundes, Alan. 1965. *The Study of Folklore*. Englewood Cliffs, NJ: Prentice-Hall.

Ethnographic Society of Trinidad and Tobago. N.d. *Panel Discussion on Folklore*. St. Augustine, Trinidad: U.W.I. Faculty of Social Sciences.

Henige, David P. 1982. *Oral Historiography*. London: Longman.

Herskovits, Melville J., and Frances S. Herskovits. 1947. *Trinidad Village*. New York: Alfred A. Knopf.

Maharaj, Ashram B. 1990. *Indo-Trinidadian Folk Tales in the Oral Tradition*. Beucarro, Trinidad: Indian Review Committee.

Mills, Therese. 1972. *Caribbean Christmas: A Book for Children*. Port of Spain, Trinidad: Therese Mills.

Ramsawack, Al. 1972. *Flamme Belle: A Caribbean Folk Tale Told and Illustrated by Al Ramsawack*. Marabella, Trinidad: Lyrehc Productions.

_____. 1983. *Sermon of the Drunkard and Other Selections*. Marabella, Trinidad: Lyrech Productions.

Trinidad and Tobago. Ministry of Agriculture, Lands and Fisheries. Forestry Division. 1980. *Forest Folklore of Trinidad and Tobago: Selections from Al Ramsawack, a Local Author*. Port of Spain, Trinidad: Ministry of Agriculture, Lands and Fisheries.

10. The Way We Live: Fetes and Festivals of the English-Speaking Caribbean

Elmelinda Lara

Lesser-known festivals of the English-speaking Caribbean mesmerize the visitor, interest the scholar, and challenge the information professional. This paper examines national, religious, and cultural fetes and festivals throughout the region, with particular emphasis on Trinidad and Tobago, and the institutions and organizations that play a crucial role in ensuring their survival. I begin with a brief history of the English-speaking Caribbean from colonialism to the present showing the impact of conquest, colonialism, slavery, and plantation capitalism, as well as free trade and American influence on the cultures of the societies. The work of researchers and information professionals in documenting and preserving the cultural heritage of the English-speaking Caribbean and the challenges of information collection, processing, and handling are also examined.

Historical Overview

Movement has always been a feature of the Caribbean landscape. The original inhabitants, Arawaks and Caribs, moved from island to island and a number of place names owe their origin to the presence of these groups. According to historical accounts, the Caribs seemed the more mobile of the two, and today there are still descendants of Caribs in places such as Dominica, Guyana, and Trinidad and Tobago. Carib communities still exist in these islands and attempts are being made to record and preserve what remains of the culture of this group.

Columbus's arrival in 1492 established contact between Europeans and the West Indies and opened the way for settlements and immigrants. The Spanish were the first to dominate the region, subjugating the Indians and establishing the Roman Catholic Church, a government, and ways of life. Some of the islands still exhibit elements of Spanish heritage, and Spanish influence is evident in some of the present-day fetes and festivals.

Following the Spanish, the British, French, Portuguese, and Dutch established settlements and colonies in the islands and introduced sugarcane cultivation and European capitalism. Portuguese slavers introduced the slave trade in the sixteenth century, and during the seventeenth century France, England, and Holland established colonies in the islands and brought African slaves to the plantations from West and Central Africa.

The introduction of African slaves altered the ethnic composition of the Caribbean. It is estimated that by the nineteenth century some six million slaves were brought to the Caribbean and the British Caribbean imported 1,401,000 between 1791 and 1801 (Parry, Sherlock, Maingot 1987:88). People of African descent predominate in the older plantation islands such as Barbados, Tobago, the Leewards and Windwards, and Jamaica and account for a large proportion of the population of Guyana and Trinidad.

With the abolition of the slave trade in the nineteenth century and labor shortages on the sugar plantations in the Caribbean, indentured laborers were imported from India and China. Laborers were also imported from Portugal, the Canary Islands, and other parts of Europe. Even free Africans came to the Caribbean under contract. Large numbers of East Indians and Chinese were also imported to Trinidad, Guyana, and Jamaica while smaller numbers went to other parts of the Caribbean. With each new movement of people to the Caribbean the ethnic mix was further altered and the cultures diversified result- ing in truly heterogeneous societies.

The breakup of the British Empire and the formation of newly indepen- dent Caribbean territories marked the period from 1962 to 1972. Jamaica, Trinidad and Tobago, Barbados, Guyana, and Belize all achieved independence during this period.

As a result of historical forces, ethnic, religious, linguistic, and cultural diversity are characteristic of the English-speaking Caribbean. West Indians are of Amerindian, African, East Indian, European, Chinese, and Middle Eastern origin. Caribbean people practice Catholicism, Islam, Hinduism, varieties of Protestantism, and variants of African religions. Caribbean festivals combine aspects of different influences and reflect the multiracial, multireligious, mul- ticultural nature of the societies.

Cultural Diversity

Defining Caribbean culture presents difficulty for the researcher since the Caribbean is a region of great diversity and it is more appropriate to think in terms of a heterogeneous cultural area which is well exemplified in the Trinidad and Tobago scenario. There are, however, similarities in cultural forms and practices owing to a similar socioeconomic and sociocultural her- itage among the islands. The influence of Africa, Europe, India, and recently America has had an impact on the cultures of Caribbean peoples. "The cultures of Caribbean peoples resulted from a profound cross-fertilization of cultures to which, over a period of four centuries, the various races present in the area had been subjected" (Arguelles 1981:35).

In spite of the commonality of historical experiences that shaped the cul- tures, the uniqueness of the festivals from island to island highlights the resilience of Caribbean peoples and their ability to establish their own iden- tity, thereby creating a national consciousness and festivals with national characteristics. It shows their ability to respond creatively to a changing environment while at the same time acting as change agents.

The history and influences of the region suggest that in the Caribbean context it is not completely accurate to refer to a Caribbean culture but rather Caribbean cultures. There is ongoing dialog and debate about the notion of a Caribbean culture. M.G. Smith (1965) referred to the disparate cultural and social elements and observed that these communities do not combine socially and culturally. He attributed this phenomenon to the plurality of the societies. In 1965 this view might well have been valid, but the mixing, the innovation, the hybrids evident in the festivals of the Caribbean today cannot support Smith's position. In fact, Brathwaite (1974, quoted in Allahar 1993) and Hall (1977, quoted in Allahar 1993) viewed the Caribbean as a "melting pot" and referred to the process of "cultural homogenization" or "creolization" which suggest a common Caribbean culture. Latin American cultural theorists refer to the blending of culture or cultural elements as "cultural hybridization" or "cross-fertilization."

At the level of popular culture the islands have to be viewed individually, each with its unique identity and culture owing in part to its racial, ethnic, religious, and social makeup. Each island has a distinct blend of African, East Indian, European, and indigenous culture in varying proportions. Allahar supports the hybridization theory, stating that "Upon emancipation clandestine cultural practices asserted themselves publicly among the liberated groups, while new hybrid cultures that reflected various degrees of socio-ethnic combinations of European, indigenous, Chinese, East Indian, and African elements were also in evidence" (1993:74). In Trinidad and Tobago, cultural practices that were once dormant or even nonexistent are now competing for attention among the various festivals already present.

Lesser-Known Popular Festivals

Although there are a number of fetes and festivals throughout the English-speaking Caribbean, these have received very little scholarly attention and any attempt at examining festivals inevitably focuses on carnival and carnival-type celebrations. The other festivals receiving some attention are the Jonkonnu festivals of Jamaica and the Bahamas and Hosay of Trinidad.[1]

Trinidad and Tobago commemorates a number of festivals by granting a public holiday. The issue of holidays engenders fierce debate since each group in the society views a holiday as recognition of its social, political, religious, and cultural contribution to the national community. Holidays also contribute to greater understanding among the community.

There are about thirteen official public holidays in Trinidad and Tobago, and while carnival Monday and Tuesday are not official public holidays, the public regards them as holidays. The official public holidays are New Year's Day, Good Friday, Easter Monday, Eid-ul-Fitr, Spiritual Baptist/Liberation Shouter Day, Indian Arrival Day, Corpus Christi, Labour Day, Emancipation

Day, Independence, Divali, and Christmas. Apart from these, several festivals are significant to the population and are eagerly anticipated. It is said that Trinidad and Tobago is a nation of fetes and festivals and lives from fete to fete. At the Caribbean level, one can identify public holidays that are common to some of the islands.

National Festivals

Independence Day

Independence Day is celebrated by Jamaica (August 7), Trinidad and Tobago (August 31), St. Kitts (September 19), Antigua and Barbuda (November 1), Dominica (November 3), Barbados (November 30), St. Vincent and the Grenadines (January 22), Grenada (February 7), St. Lucia (February 22), Guyana (May 26), and Bahamas (July 10).

Independence Day is a significant event in these islands and marks their progress from colonial status with ties to the British Empire to self-rule. The event is celebrated by a public holiday with church services of various denominations, military and street parades, lectures, and much fanfare and jubilation. In Trinidad and Tobago partying and pyrotechnic displays also form part of the celebrations. In Barbados the National Independence Festival of Creative Arts held during October and November culminates in Independence Day on November 30. The festival gives prominence to the creative arts and artists of the island. Professional and amateur performers, photographers, artists, and writers are recognized. In Grenada the day is celebrated by church services followed by a parade. In the Bahamas parades, pyrotechnics, and amusement regattas commemorate independence. In St. Lucia a craft exhibition is held every year as part of the celebrations. The exhibition showcases the artistry of the island, which has been passed down from the Arawaks. In Jamaica a heritage festival featuring traditional Jamaican food, Jonkonnu competitions, and general merry-making takes place during the week before Independence Day.

Emancipation Day

Emancipation Day is celebrated in Barbados and Trinidad and Tobago (August 1), Guyana, Jamaica, Bahamas, Grenada, and St. Lucia (August 2). Emancipation Day marks the end of slavery in the British West Indies and has historic, social, political, and psychological significance for the region. All of these islands now commemorate the day by a public holiday but until 1996 Trinidad and Tobago was the only island that had such a public holiday. Owing to the efforts and support of the Emancipation Support Committee of Trinidad and Tobago and the Caribbean Historical Society based in Trinidad, Guyana, Jamaica, and Barbados started with a public holiday in 1997. Jamaica previously celebrated emancipation with a holiday but removed the holiday from the national calendar on attaining independence. The holiday has now been reinstated after thirty years.

Emancipation Day celebrations in Trinidad, Jamaica, and Barbados take on great significance. In Trinidad commemorations take the form of public lectures, exhibitions, radio and television programs, street processions, and the re-creation of an African village. The Lidg Yasu Omowale Village at the Queen's Park Savannah is a permanent feature of the celebrations. The celebrations highlight the contributions of Africans to Trinidad and Tobago's cultural heritage and citizens can be seen proudly attired in colorful African garb to mark the occasion.

Emancipation Day celebrations in Trinidad and Tobago attract prominent participants from abroad including dignitaries, scholars, and artists. Some of the distinguished guests of past celebrations include Oba Okunade Sijuwade Olubuse; Ooni of Ife (1988), whose visit marked the 150th anniversary of Emancipation; President Jean-Bertrand Aristide of Haiti (1992); astronaut Mae Jemison (1993); and Chief Emeka Anyaouku, Secretary General of the Commonwealth (1995), who delivered a lecture titled "From Political Intellectual Emancipation—The African Diaspora." The president of Ghana, Jerry Rawlings, visited in 1997 and delivered the feature address to mark the celebrations. In 1999 Femi Biko, a Nigerian professor now lecturing at the University of London, is scheduled to deliver the keynote address. Artists from other parts of the Caribbean, Suriname, and Latin America will also participate in the celebrations and the book titled *The Evolution of the Steelband Phenomenon in Tacarigua* will be launched.

In Jamaica emancipation farms and parks are created where traditional dances are performed and foods displayed. There are exhibitions at libraries and town halls and activities lead straight into independence celebrations. Unlike Trinidad, there is no need to re-create an African village since celebrations take place in the town of Accompong, an old Maroon town where the inhabitants still feel "closely connected to Africa spiritually and culturally" (de Bourg 1997:3). Celebrations include reenacting Maroon-style ambush of British troops and blowing of the abeng, a Maroon horn.

In Barbados, public lectures, articles in the press, and a series of cultural activities mark the celebrations. The Barbados Museum and Historical Society keeps alive the legacy of all that contributed to the demise of slavery and oppression. Government and high-level officials also participate in the celebrations. Bahamian celebrations take the form of public commemorations of the abolition of slavery.

The Caribbean Historical Society has undertaken an initiative to make Emancipation Day officially recognized in various countries. As a consequence, it will be observed in Ghana for the first time on August 1, 1999.

Information on Emancipation Day can be obtained from articles in the press, exhibitions, radio and television programs, and public lectures and from Ministries of Culture and Information as well as organizations responsible for the celebrations.

Religious Festivals

The number of religious festivals and holidays in the English-speaking Caribbean and in particular Trinidad and Tobago reflects the diversity of our religious beliefs. Many forms of Christianity exist side by side with Hinduism, Islam, and African religions. Religious practices have been reinterpreted, refashioned, and refined to ensure survival. Creative ways have been found to accommodate diverse groups in celebratory activities.

In Trinidad as elsewhere in the Caribbean Afro-Caribbean religions have merged with Christianity (Protestant) to produce new faiths. One example is the Shouter or Spiritual Baptist religion, which persists to this day and is celebrated by a public holiday commemorating the removal of the prohibition of worship by this group. A recent addition, the holiday was declared in 1996. The existence of this faith today highlights the struggles of a group to defend and preserve their unique religion. Spiritual Baptist/Liberation Shouter Day is celebrated on March 30 by church services, lectures, and cultural activities. Because of the public holiday, increased attention is being focused on this group as the subject of serious research.[2]

Similarly, the survival of a number of East Indian religious and cultural practices is the result of cultural resistance and triumph over hostility and persecution in an alien land.

Different groups adapted their religious practices in order to survive and continue to hold on to these customs to sustain them. As a result of East Indian immigration, the festivals of Divali, Phagwa, Hosay, Eid-ul-Fitr, and a host of others enrich some Caribbean societies. Divali and Phagwa are the legacy of the Hindus while Hosay and Eid-ul-Fitr represent Moslem contributions. Divali and Eid-ul-Fitr are commemorated by national holidays in Trinidad and Tobago to enable and encourage participation by the society. Hosay is observed in Guyana, Jamaica, and Trinidad and Tobago while Phagwa and Divali are national holidays in Guyana.

Historical records confirm that the indentured laborers who came to Trinidad were a heterogeneous group comprising people from different provinces with different languages, customs, and religious practices. According to Jha, "These settlers who carried only pots, pans and blankets on recruitment bequeathed to their children and grandchildren the cultural heritage of India" (1974:1–2).

Divali

Divali, the festival of lights, is rooted in Indian mythology and signifies Lord Rama's return to his throne in Ayodhya, in the state of Uttar Pradesh, after seventeen years of exile. Thousands of indentured immigrants came from that state, which explains the festival's presence in the Caribbean. Other legends surrounding the festival are the victory of Lord Krishna over the demon

Narakusara and the emergence of goddess Lakshmi from the oceans when the earth was being formed.

For over a hundred years Divali was confined to Hindu homes and temples, but in 1966 it was first celebrated as a national holiday owing to the efforts of the Hindu community. Today the national community supports the festival by actively participating in the celebrations. It is celebrated in most districts of Trinidad by people of different races and religious persuasions. Non-Hindu women adorn themselves with saris and *shalwars* signaling their support and appreciation of the festival.

Important features of the celebration are the lighting of *deyas* (small earthen clay pots) on Divali night and Lakshmi *puja* (prayers). Prior to the actual day of the festival, much activity takes place, in the form of house cleaning, shopping, and public celebrations. On the day itself friends are entertained at Hindu homes, there are family reunions, gifts are exchanged, and a ceremonial meal is prepared.

Divali is a very popular festival in Trinidad, where it has undergone some modification. There is the crowning of a Divali queen, in some instances electric bulbs replace deyas, and the popularity of the festival has encouraged increased commercial activity. In fact, the festival has a permanent home at Divali Nagar or Divali Village, a centalized location for the pre-Divali activities. At the Divali Nagar one gets the opportunity to understand Hindu thought, practices, and philosophy. Traditional aspects of the festival and the religion are highlighted and cultural practices and artists are given prominence. The Divali Nagar attracts both local and overseas visitors.

In Guyana there are processions, illumination, fairs, and cultural concerts for Divali. As in Trinidad, ceremonial dress is common on these occasions. Months of preparation, sacrifice, and fasting precede Divali celebrations. The festival symbolizes the victory of good over evil and the triumph of light over darkness.

Organizations such as the Hindu Prachar Kendra, the Hindi Foundation, and the National Council of Indian Culture ensure the continuation of this festival as well as many others. The National Council of Indian Culture publishes a Divali Nagar souvenir brochure annually and various newspapers publish articles as well as a Divali Supplement to the newspapers. The brochures feature papers by Hindu scholars and thinkers from Trinidad and abroad, poetry, photography, and personality profiles.

Phagwa

Like Divali, the Hindu festival of Phagwa has grown in popularity and there have been calls for it to be recognized as a national festival. In fact, in Guyana it is celebrated as a public holiday. Phagwa, the spring festival of India, is based on legends, the most popular being the destruction of the demon king Hiranya-Kashipu and the burning of Holika, the sister of Hiranya. Phagwa is celebrated late February to early March and involves a huge bonfire symbolizing the attempt by Holika to burn the little hero saint Prahalaad. Phagwa, an old world harvest festival, is also connected to the harvest of sugarcane in Trinidad and Tobago. The festival has been described by Ravi-Ji as a "raucous affair" (1999). Lively singing (*chowtal* or folk songs), the clash of *dholaks* (small drums), dancing, the lighting of the bonfire, and the throwing of *abeer* (red powder and perfumed water) on the bodies of celebrants characterize the celebrations

This festival has accommodated innovation and creativity. One element of the festival native to Trinidad and Tobago is the "pichakaaree" competition. Pichakaaree, originally an instrument used in the celebrations for squirting abeer onto participants, also refers to "a song in English with Hindi/Bhojpuri words which articulate the Hindu viewpoint on events local and international" (Maharaj 1999:13). Pichakaaree, like calypso and soca, is a vehicle for social and political commentary and shows heavy influences of the two art forms. Pichakaaree has also been described as a medium for "stimulating Hindu pride and consciousness and articulating Hindu hope and vision for the future" (Blood 1999:15). Phagwa celebrations held outdoors in open areas are colorful events. The existence of a National Phagwa Association ensures the growth and survival of this festival.

Hosay

The region's Muslims are concentrated in Trinidad, Guyana, and Suriname. Trinidad and Tobago is considered the focus of Muslim life in the Caribbean. Indian Muslims have contributed the festivals of Hosay and Eid-ul-Fitr to national life.

Hosay has been celebrated in Trinidad since 1846. The celebrations commemorate the martyrdom of Hassan and Hussain, the grandsons of the Holy Prophet Muhammad. Hussain was killed at Kerbala in Iraq in 640 A.D. and Hussain's brother Hassan was killed by poisoning in Medina.

Hosay is observed by Shi'ite Muslims worldwide but unlike other religious observances it began to be celebrated by Muslims and Hindus alike in Trinidad and Tobago. The history also points to the involvement of Afro-Trinidadians in the tassa drumming aspects of the celebrations. This festival served as an integrative mechanism during the period of indentureship and survives today as a unifying force in the society. Hindus participated in the building of *tadjahs* (temples), the processions, the drumming and the ritual mock battles. Today Hosay transcends creed and race barriers and is celebrated by all segments of Trinidad and Tobago society.

The Hosay festival takes place in the month of Muharram, the first in the Muslim calendar and lasts for four days. It is characterized by street processions each beginning with flag night, when red and white flags are paraded at the Hosay yard signifying the battle at Kerbala. On the second night miniature

Hosay is paraded through the streets accompanied by singing and tassa drumming. On the third night there is a spectacular procession of "rajahs" or "model mausoleum of the martyrs" (Singh 1988). The procession is accompanied by Taos drumming, singing, dancing, and gay abandon. The procession is the reenactment of the tragedy at Kerbala. On the fourth day or night the processions come together and the Hosay is dumped in a nearby river or sea.

Hosay is also celebrated in Jamaica and Guyana but seems to be of little religious significance; contemporary Hosay is dominated by drumming, dancing, and drinking. It is an occasion for revelry.

In Trinidad there have been recent attempts to emphasize the religious character of the festival and participants have been urged to observe the solemnity of the occasion and to desist from consuming alcohol during the street processions. Hosay's turbulent and violent history has been well documented.[3] As a subject of scholarly research Hosay continues to receive attention. As a festival it represents community involvement, creativity, and much partying.

Eid-ul-Fitr

Unlike Hosay, the festival of Eid-ul-Fitr is a more sedate affair. Eid-ul-Fitr marks the end of the holy month of Ramadan for Muslims. Eid is preceded by one month of fasting, prayer, and meditation. At the end of Ramadan there is fasting and praying at mosques throughout the country followed by greeting of friends and relatives and alms giving to the poor.

This festival has been celebrated as a public holiday in Trinidad and Tobago since 1967, which has increased the awareness of it among non-Muslims. During the month of Ramadan the media call attention to the festival by devoting time for the breaking of the fast and the call to prayer on each day.

Trinidad and Tobago is home to a number of Islamic organizations which keep the faith alive and promote the festival. The largest of these, the Anjuman Sunnat Ul Jamaat Association, publishes an annual Eid-ul-Fitr brochure.

La Divina Pastora or "Siparia Fete"

The festival of La Divina Pastora links Trinidad to its Spanish heritage. Devotion to Mary, La Divina Pastora, began in southern Spain and is believed to have spread to Trinidad and Tobago through the Spanish Capuchins around 1715. Controversy surrounds the origin of the festival and many legends recount the existence of the statue. The festival is a particularly interesting one because Christians and non-Christians worship through the same medium.

The main festival is celebrated in the town of Siparia, South Trinidad, on the third Sunday after Easter. Features of the festival include devotions on the second Sunday of each month from November to April culminating in a colorful procession through the streets of Siparia on the Feast Day. On this day pilgrims— Catholics and non-Catholics—converge on Siparia for the annual Siparia Fete.

East Indians also worship the statue and organize a separate festival that takes place on Holy Thursday until Good Friday. Referred to as Siparee Mai, the statue represents an East Indian deity. East Indian observances are characterized by singing, dancing, and alms giving.

Legend has it that La Divina Pastora possesses special powers and worshipers go to the shrine to request special favors. La Divina Pastora is a fascinating festival, and many stories that have been passed on orally about it are now part of the documentation (see, for example, Jaggassar 1992).

Cultural Festivals

Tobago Heritage Festival

The first Festival of Tobago was held in 1975, the forerunner of today's Tobago Heritage Festival. The brainchild of anthropologist J. D. Elder, the Tobago Heritage Festival showcases the rich folk heritage and unique culture of the island. African influences predominate in Tobago and much of the cultural fare include legends, myths, tales, proverbs, music, art, drama, rituals, practices and beliefs, and culinary arts showing the African influence.

The festival incorporates old-time wedding and courtship codes, the Salaka feast of African ancestral worship, an Amerindian village reminiscent of the Amerindian culture of the island, the Bele festival reminder of European struggles over the island, and re-creations of black revolts. Music is an integral part of these celebrations. The tambourine, the only indigenous musical instrument, is featured in the celebrations.

The Tobago Heritage Festival enjoys a high degree of participation by Trinidad and Tobagonians and attracts visitors from abroad. The growth of the festival is evident in the increase in the number of villages participating each year. The festival is also being promoted abroad by shrewd marketing. A contingent of performers and officials recently toured New York and Washington. This year the festival will host the director of the Senegal Tourist Office and the head of the South African Tourist Board, and it is expected that the Senegalese will send a performing contingent for the 2000 festival.

Each year a special supplement of the daily newspapers in Trinidad and Tobago covers the festival and the Oral and Pictorial Records Programme of the Main Library, University of the West Indies, St. Augustine, ensures that some record of the rich cultural elements of the festival is preserved.

Information Sources

Information sources on fetes and festivals of the English-speaking Caribbean are as diverse as the cultures that produce them. This presents challenges for libraries, librarians, and researchers throughout the region. While we do not possess all the information in our libraries, we can advise researchers where to look for sources. The *Encyclopedia of World Cultures: Middle*

America and the Caribbean provides very basic information on the cultural heritage of the islands, and while it does not address the specifics it is an important starting point. Another source is *Fetes and Festivals of Trinidad and Tobago* (Rajnarinesingh 1991), which contains basic descriptions of a number of festivals, photographs, and annotations. It needs updating since more festivals have been added to our calendar of events.

Other important sources are handbooks of the region, guidebooks, newspapers, popular magazines, diaries, calendars, handbills, flyers, leaflets, audio and video cassettes, and Internet resources. As mentioned above, organizations and associations with responsibility for specific festivals are important sources since a lot of information is generated within these bodies. Ministries of culture and ministries of information also generate records of national festivals and holidays. The libraries of the University of the West Indies have important West Indiana collections containing information on festivals. The Oral and Pictorial Records Programme at St. Augustine campus, the Library of the Spoken Word, and the Social History Project at Mona campus point to valuable information sources for the researcher.

Researchers and academic staff of the University of the West Indies writing in newspapers and journals also contribute to the dialog and discourse on festivals, and researchers from foreign universities who utilize the resources of libraries in the region also contribute to the literature on festivals of the region.

Conclusion

Through an examination and study of Caribbean festivals, one can understand the historical, economic, cultural, and religious life—past and present—of Caribbean societies. Libraries in the English-speaking Caribbean play an important role in recognizing national, religious, and cultural observances and festivals, and facilitate exhibitions and lectures. They also highlight materials in their collections and promote and assist research activities for these occasions.

NOTES

1. See Nunley, Bettelheim, et al. (1988); Cowley (1991); and Lent (1990). A search of the online database *EBSCOhost,* under Caribbean festivals, produced a carnival calendar for the islands.

2. Recent studies of this group include DePeza (1996, 1999); Jacobs (1992, 1996).

3. See Singh (1988); Parmasad (1983); de Verteuil (1984); Wood (1968); and Brereton (1981).

BIBLIOGRAPHY

Allahar, Anton L. 1993. "Unity and Diversity in Caribbean Ethnicity and Culture." *Canadian Ethnic Studies* 25(1), 70–85.

Alleyne, Mervyn. 1990. "African Roots of Caribbean Culture." In Alan Gregor Cobley and Alvin Thompson, ed., *The African-Caribbean Connection: Historical and Cultural Perspectives*. Bridgetown, Barbados: University of the West Indies. Pp.107–122.

Alleyne-Pilgrim, Vernella. 1995. "Ethnological Dimensions of the Tobago Heritage Festival." *OPRep Newsletter* 30.

Arguelles, Luis Angel. 1981. "Socio-Cultural Unity in the Caribbean." In *Caribbean Cultures: Proceedings of the Meeting of Experts Held in Santo Domingo* (Dominican Republic), September 18–22, 1978. Paris: Unesco.

Blood, Peter Ray. 1999. "Songs of Hope and Belonging." *Sunday Guardian* (March 14).

Brathwaite, Edward. 1974. *Contradictory Omens: Cultural Diversity and Integration in the Caribbean*. Mona: Savacou Publications.

Brereton, Bridget. 1981. *A History of Modern Trinidad, 1783–1962*. Kingston, Jamaica: Heinemann.

Cowley, J. 1991. *Carnival and Other Seasonal Festivals in the West Indies, U.S.A, and Britain: A Selected Bibliographical Index*. Coventry: Centre for Research in Ethnic Relations, University of Warwick.

DeBourg, Carlene. 1997. "Marooned in Accompong." *Sunday Express* (August), 3.

De Peza, Hazel Ann Gibbs. 1996. "Glossolalia in the Spiritual Baptist Faith: A Linguistic Study." Master's thesis, University of the West Indies, St. Augustine.

_____. 1999. *My Faith: Spiritual Baptist Christian*. St. Augustine: University of the West Indies.

De Verteuil, Anthony. 1984. *The Years of Revolt: Trinidad 1881–1888*. Port-of-Spain, Trinidad: Paria Publishing.

Duff, Ernest A. 1993. "Attack and Counterattack: Dynamics of Transculturation in the Caribbean." *Studies in Latin American Popular Culture* 12:195–202.

Friday, Edmie. 1975. "La Divina Pastora: Legends and Traditions." Caribbean Studies project, University of the West Indies, St. Augustine.

Giles, D. 1991. "Carnival Calendar." *Black Enterprise* 21:10 (May), 80–82.

Hall, Stuart. 1977. "Pluralism, Race, and Class in Caribbean Soceity." In *Race and Class in Post-Colonial Society*. Paris: Unesco.

Jacobs, C. M. 1992. *Joy Comes in the Morning: Elton Griffith and the Shouter Baptists*. N.p.

_____. 1996. "The Spiritual Baptist Faith as an African Religion." Paper presented at a seminar as part of the 2nd Annual Spiritual Baptist Week, March 26.

Jaggassar, Laurence. 1992. "La Divina Pastora Analysed as a Manifestation of Popular Religion." B.A. thesis, University of the West Indies, St.Augustine.

Jha, J. C. 1974. "The Indian Heritage in Trinidad." In John La Guerre, ed., *Calcutta to Caroni: The East Indians of Trinidad*. Port-of-Spain: Longman Caribbean.

Lent, John A., ed. 1990. *Caribbean Popular Culture*. Bowling Green, OH: Bowling Green State University Popular Press.

Mahabir, Noor Kumar. 198– . *Hindu Festivals, Ceremonies and Rituals in Trinidad.* Tunapuna, Trinidad: Chakra Publishing.

Maharaj, Indira. 1999. "Pichakaree, a Voice for Hindus." *Express* (March 5).

Mansingh, Ajai, and Laxmi Mansingh. 1989. "Hosay and Its Creolization." Paper presented at Festival of Arts, Smithsonian Institute, Washington, DC.

Marks, P. 1991. "Caribbean Festival Arts." *Art Journal* 50:1(Spring), 89–92.

Mintz, Sidney W., and Sally Price, eds. 1985. *Caribbean Contours.* Baltimore, MD: Johns Hopkins University Press.

Nunley, John W., John Bettelheim, et al. 1988. *Caribbean Festival Arts: Each and Every Bit of Difference.* Seattle: University of Washington Press in association with the St. Louis Art Museum.

Parmasad, Kenneth Vidia. 1983. "The Hosea Riots of 1884 (Trinidad)." Master's thesis, University of the West Indies, St. Augustine.

Parry, John H., Philip M. Sherlock, and Anthony P. Maingot. 1987. *A Short History of the West Indies.* New York: St. Martin's Press.

Rajnarinesingh, Mala. 1991. *Fetes and Festivals in Trinidad and Tobago.* Port-of-Spain, Trinidad: Imprint Caribbean.

Ravi-Ji. 1999. "Memories of Long Time Phagwa." *Trinidad Guardian* (March 5).

Singh, Kelvin. 1988. *Bloodstained Tombs: The Muharram Massacre 1884.* London: Macmillan.

Smith, M. G. 1965. *The Plural Society in the British West Indies.* Berkeley: University of California Press.

Walton, Chelle Koster. 1993. *Caribbean Ways: A Cultural Guide.* Westwood, MA: The Riverside Co.

Wood, Donald. 1968. *Trinidad in Transition.* London: Oxford University Press.

11. In Their Own Words: The Folk Literature of South American Indians Series

Colleen H. Trujillo

Folk Literature of South American Indians is a twenty-four-volume series dedicated to the narrative art of aboriginal South America. The first volume appeared in 1970 and the last, the General Index to the entire series, in 1992. The project was conceived by Johannes Wilbert, professor of anthropology at UCLA, who served as the senior editor of the twenty-four volumes (Table 1). The Latin American Center at UCLA published the series. This paper discusses the reasons for undertaking the series, its objectives, the methodology, and its contribution to folklore scholarship.

The project had two goals: (1) to provide a readily accessible and uniquely comprehensive source of the oral literature pertaining to the marginal Indian societies of lowland South America, and (2) to present a classification of the narratives according to their constituent elements, or motifs (Wilbert and Simoneau 1992). The volumes do not attempt to analyze the tales nor to explain their sociocultural significance. The editors simply felt that presentation of the narratives and identification of their motifs were necessary prerequisites to future analytical research.

Background

In the 1960s South Americanists became increasingly concerned about the alarming rate at which aboriginal societies were being destroyed and their traditions relegated to oblivion before they could have been recorded. Even the existing body of oral literature—collected by travelers, missionaries, soldiers, naturalists, and ethnographers over some five hundred years—remained largely unavailable. The disappearance of indigenous groups and the inaccessibility of existing source materials were not good signs for future studies in South American myth and narrative.

There was some good news, however. At about this time, convenient battery-operated tape recorders were introduced—which revolutionized ethnographic fieldwork in general, and accelerated the compilation of large bodies of narrative in native vernacular. Ethnographers and language specialists who were traveling to the region in large numbers in the early 1960s soon began to record oral traditions of entire regions.

Table 1. Folk Literature of South American Indians
Johannes Wilbert and Karin Simoneau, Editors

Folk Literature of the Warao Indians (1970)
Folk Literature of the Selknam Indians (1975)
Folk Literature of the Yamana Indians (1977)
Folk Literature of the Gê Indians, Volume One (1978)
Folk Literature of the Mataco Indians (1982)
Folk Literature of the Toba Indians, Volume One (1982)
Folk Literature of the Bororo Indians (1983)
Folk Literature of the Gê Indians, Volume Two (1984)
Folk Literature of the Tehuelche Indians (1984)
Folk Literature of the Chorote Indians (1985)
Folk Literature of the Guajiro Indians, Volume One and Two (1986)
Folk Literature of the Chamacoco Indians (1987)
Folk Literature of the Nivaklé Indians (1987)
Folk Literature of the Mocoví Indians (1988)
Folk Literature of the Toba Indians, Volume Two (1989)
Folk Literature of the Ayoreo Indians (1989)
Folk Literature of the Caduveo Indians (1989)
Folk Literature of the Yanomami Indians (1990)
Folk Literature of the Yaruro Indians (1990)
Folk Literature of the Makka Indians (1991)
Folk Literature of the Cuiva Indians (1991)
Folk Literature of the Sikuani Indians (1992)
Folk Literature of South American Indians: General Index (1992)

But the other problem remained—the lack of access to already published narrative material. The physical inaccessibility of widely scattered documents—even in libraries with large South American holdings—in addition to the fact that the texts were rendered in many different European languages were formidable obstacles to the study of South American oral literature.

Aware of these circumstances, Johannes Wilbert began to design a plan to assemble the published and unpublished texts in a continent-wide, multivolume reference work of aboriginal South American folk literature. Given the vast amount of published narrative and the proliferation of tale collection, the undertaking was clearly an ambitious one. A number of decisions were made to make the project more feasible and to assure its eventual completion.

First, the series would include only marginal (that is, nonagricultural or incipient agricultural) groups of open lowland South America (grassland, scrubland, savanna, steppes, bushland, an area that constitutes about two-fifths of the subcontinent). It was decided to further limit the series to the narratives of thirty-one native groups of the surviving marginal societies in Argentina, Brazil, Colombia, Paraguay, and Venezuela (see map). The estimated population of the

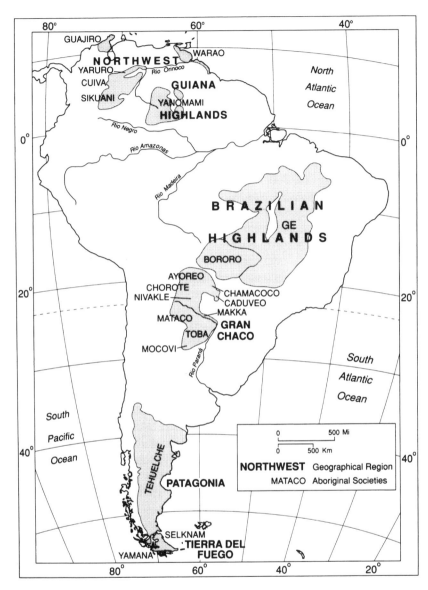

Distribution of aboriginal societies treated in the Folk Literature of South American Indians series.

Source: Johannes Wilbert and Karin Simoneau, *Folk Literature of South American Indians: General Index* (Los Angeles: UCLA Latin American Center Publications, 1992), p. 5.

area concerned was some 240,000 in the 1960s, which amounted to about one-third of the aboriginal inhabitants of the five countries. The geographic distribution includes the southern lowlands, Brazilian highlands and Mato Grosso, the Guiana highlands and the Orinoco Delta, and the continental northwest (Table 2).

The second major decision with respect to the delivery of the series was to present the material in English in order to make it as widely available as possible. Approximately half of the narratives are published for the first time in this series; the remainder were previously published. Many of them, published and unpublished, had to be translated into English—from any one of eight European languages, depending on the native language of the collector— Czech, Danish, French, German, Italian, Portuguese, Spanish, and Swedish. Co-editor Karin Simoneau, who possesses extraordinary linguistic skills, did the bulk of the translations.

Once the English-language manuscript of a particular volume was assembled, it was carefully copyedited. Much attention was given to assuring the accuracy of native terms and scientific and botanical names, consistency in the orthographic rendering of proper names, and, most of all, readability, while at the same time preserving the tone and rhythm of the story as told by the informant.

Scope and Logistics

Upon its completion, the series published 4,259 narratives and tale fragments. All the volumes are arranged in the same fashion. The preliminary material includes biographical information about the contributing authors (or

Table 2. Societies and Their Distribution

Southern Lowlands
Yamana* and Selknam* of Tierra del Fuego
Tehuelche* of Patagonia
Mocoví, Toba, Mataco, Nivaklé, Chorote, Caduveo, Chamacoco,
    Ayoreo, and Makka of the Gran Chaco

Brazilian Highlands and Mato Grosso
Bororo of the Mato Grosso
Gê of central Brazil

Guiana Highlands and the Orinoco Delta
Yanomami of northern Brazil and southern Venezuela
Warao of the Orinoco Delta

Continental Northwest
Yaruro, Cuiva, and Sikuani of the Venezuelan and Colombian llanos
Guajiro of the Venezuelan and Colombian La Guajira Peninsula

*Now extinct.

"collectors"), a description of the field conditions under which the narratives were gathered or recorded, and a summary of the geographic, linguistic, demographic, and cultural characteristics of the group. In the body of the book, the narratives are organized according to general topics. The narratives tend to cluster around themes pertaining to the establishment of the universe, the heavens, and the earth; cataclysms; the creation and ordering of human, animal, and plant life; extraordinary creatures and events; animals; and a number of recurring story lines.

Each story is followed by the name of the informant or storyteller (if known), the source (contributing author), a summary of the tale, and a listing of its motifs. Each volume concludes with a Motif Index, in four parts: motif distribution by narrative, a topical (or subject) motif index, an alphabetical index, and a listing of motif distribution by motif group. Each volume also contains a glossary of scientific, botanical, and native terms and a bibliography

The narratives were recorded by 111 individuals, through, in most instances, the process of fieldwork. They in turn were assisted by some 500 native storytellers, or informants, 10 percent of whom were women. The number of field assistants, interpreters, and translators is probably even higher, given that many of the early collectors did not record the names of their assistants. After recounting their oral traditions, storytellers were usually asked to assist in transcribing, translating, and verifying recorded tales. Thus the contribution of field assistants, both named and unnamed, is significant.

About a third of the tales were collected before 1960. Without the help of the tape recorder, texts were documented by hand, a tedious, time-consuming process. About two-thirds of the material was collected after 1960.

Manuscript acquisition and preparation required correspondence with some sixty-six authors from fifteen different countries and numerous copyright holders. Often published in small editions or in obscure or discontinued journals, much of the material was located and then obtained only after considerable effort. On occasion Wilbert traveled to the region in search of collections or to arrange for additional fieldwork to be done or for transcription assistance. Given the abundance of South American Indian folktales, a wealth of oral literature no doubt remains in storage as manuscript or untranscribed tapes in archival drawers.

Motif Indexing

The scholarly study of South American Indian folk literature dates to the early 1900s, contemporaneous with work among North American Indians. The description and classification of growing numbers of narratives led to the realization that certain basic story plots and component elements of American folk narratives turned up time and again among peoples living in different regions and on different continents. As scholars began to undertake comparative folk literature studies, the need arose for definitions of the narrative features to be compared. In short, a motif index was needed. To address this problem, the American Folklore Society recommended preparation of a concordance of American myths and in 1905 named a committee to carry out the task. To make a long story short, no comprehensive concordance of North American Indian myths materialized from this initiative.

In the 1930s, Stith Thompson, a philologist and bibliographer, published his six-volume *Motif-Index of Folk-Literature* (1932–1936; revised and enlarged edition, 1955–1958). While Thompson was working on an earlier compilation, *Tales of the North American Indians* (1929), he noticed a number of recurring episodes and elements and began to assign alphanumeric codes to them. This phase of his work ultimately formed the basis for his *Motif-Index of Folk-Literature*. Its purpose was to serve as a reference aid to the classification and analysis of large bodies of folk narrative.

The editors of the UCLA Folk Literature series recognized that in order to facilitate comparative studies of prose narrative like the South American Indian literature, it would be necessary to classify it in an orderly and systematic fashion. This meant identifying the constituent elements by means of brief designations or phrasings in order to provide uniform terminology for comparative analysis. Despite earlier criticisms from the scholarly community of the Thompson index, including complaints about the complexity of its alphanumeric system, inadequate bibliography, arbitrariness, and geographic bias, the editors determined that Thompson's *Motif Index* offered the best concordance of motifs available at the time. Thus, through the analytical methodology of motif indexing, the Folk Literature series facilitates reliable, consistent access to a large collection of traditional South American Indian narrative.

The General Index, which concludes the series, compiles the data from the individual tale listings of motifs in the previous twenty-three volumes into four separate indexes: a motif distribution by narrative, according to major groups and subgroups; a topical, subject-based motif index; an alphabetical index of keywords from each individual motif; and a concordance of specifically South American motifs. The General Index to the series is the most comprehensive regional folktale index published to date. The creation of this specifically South American motif database was one of the major contributions of the Folk Literature series.

A total of 10,150 motifs occur either singly or repeatedly, a total of 54,637 times. Fifty-eight percent of the motifs had been registered in the Thompson index, which enabled the indexer to simply adopt a particular code and its phrasing. In 42 percent of the cases (4,256 motifs), however, the indexer created a "plus motif" to accommodate elements found in South American narrative, using the alphanumeric code of a closely related or broadly collective Thompson motif followed by a plus sign but modifying the phrasing. In the General Index and the individual volume indexes, the original Thompson motif appears in parentheses after the plus motif, for comparative purposes.

Plus motifs were created either by (1) making a general Thompson motif more specific or by (2) altering the wording of an already specific motif. In most instances, the indexer used the first method.

An example of the first method:

D110.+. Transformation: man to coati. (D110. Transformation: man to wild beast [mammal].)

An example of the second method:

A714.4.+. Sun mirror in sky. (A714.4. Sun and moon metal mirrors in sky.)

The 4,256 plus motifs constitute the specific New World contribution of Folk Literature of South American Indians series to the Thompson index. The large number (42 percent) of new motifs shows that Thompson's *Motif-Index* is potentially worldwide in scope and infinitely expandable in number of motifs. As illustrated by the contributors to the Folk Literature series, ethnologists are in an excellent position to expand world coverage of oral literature further by indexing collections in their own fields of interest.

A look at the motif distribution by motif group and subgroup shows some interesting patterns and reveals the value of motif indexing. Of the 54,637 motifs, the two largest groups are Mythological motifs (22 percent) and Magic (17 percent), followed by Marvels (11 percent), Animals (8 percent), Deceptions (8 percent), and The Wise and the Foolish (7 percent).

Subgroups show a similar pattern. The five largest subgroups belong to the three largest motif groups: Transformation (7 percent), Magic powers and manifestations (6 percent), Creation and ordering of human life (6 percent), Marvelous creatures (5 percent), and Magic objects (4 percent).

Looking at the data another way, that is, counting each motif only once (instead of the total of motif occurrences), reveals something different. The four largest categories are the same, but the percentages differ. Mythological (25 percent) and Magic (21 percent) motifs together constitute 46 percent of the total number of motifs, followed by Marvels (11 percent) and Animals (9 percent). As for subgroups, Transformation is again the largest (8 percent), while Animal characteristics and Magic objects follow with 8 percent and 7 percent, respectively.

As noted above, new (plus) motifs constitute 42 percent of the total motifs (counting single motifs rather than total motif occurrences). Closer analysis shows that certain groups and subgroups show a high incidence of these new, specifically South American motifs. In two groups, Mythological and Animal motifs, plus motifs constitute more than half of the total—52 percent each, and in the group Magic, plus motifs account for 47 percent of the total, followed by Marvels (37 percent) and Deceptions (20 percent).

As for subgroups, the statistics present an intriguing picture as well. Plus motifs account for 71 percent of all the motifs found in the subgroup Animal characteristics and 63 percent of those in Transformation. In Creation and ordering of human life they account for 52 percent of the total, and in Magic objects 40 percent, Marvelous creatures 38 percent, and Magic powers and manifestations 30 percent.

Without pursuing a detailed analysis of the figures, it is clear that the higher percentages of plus motifs turn up in categories that are either culturally or environmentally specific for the South American societies studied in the Folk Literature series, categories dealing with animals, culture, and transformation. More universal categories, such as Deceptions, exhibit a lower incidence of plus motifs.

It is important to keep in mind that the motif indexing in the series took place over nearly a twenty-year period. Because all volumes except the first were indexed by the same person, co-editor Karin Simoneau, there is remarkable uniformity in the manner in which motifs were identified and assigned to specific groups and subgroups. Nevertheless, when the comprehensive General Index was generated, inconsistencies, duplications, misclassifications, and other errors were apparent. At that point the editors decided to make the necessary corrections in order to produce a reliable database for future indexers of South American narrative material.

Final Comments

In addition to the series editors, contributing authors, and informants, another important player was the computer programmer. The indexes to the first seven volumes were done by hand, a process that entailed handwriting thousands of slips of paper, typing, proofreading, and retyping. In the early 1980s, a graduate student in anthropology at UCLA, Yehuda Afek, volunteered to write a program to generate the index for each volume as well as the comprehensive General Index. This development not only made an enormous difference in both speed and accuracy, but also enabled the editors to manipulate the data in a variety of ways, opening the way to comparative cross-cultural research on a scale previously not possible.

Since its inception in 1970, the series has been recognized for its quality and scholarship. For example, Johannes Wilbert received a University of Chicago Folklore Prize for 1980 for the fourth volume in the series, *Folk Literature of the Gê Indians*. The Chicago Folklore Prize is awarded annually for important contributions to the study of folklore. In 1998 Wilbert was chosen for a PEN Literary Career Achievement Award, the Gregory Kolovakos Award, which is given to a scholar whose life's work has brought the literature of the Hispanic world to English-language readers. The Folk Literature series played a major part in his being selected for this award.

The Folk Literature of South American Indians series is the product of a collaboration among Indian storytellers, an international assembly of contributing authors, and co-editors Johannes Wilbert and Karin Simoneau, whose dedication to the project and, at times, sheer perseverance assured its completion. The series has given the Indians an opportunity to reveal their world in their own words.

REFERENCES

Thompson, Stith. 1929. *Tales of the North American Indians*. Cambridge: Harvard University Press.

———. 1955–1958. *Motif-Index of Folk-Literature: A Classification of Narrative Elements in Folktales, Ballads, Myths, Fables, Mediaeval Romances, Exempla, Fabliaux, Jest-Books and Local Legends*. 6 vols. Revised and enlarged edition. Bloomington: Indiana University Press.

Wilbert, Johannes, and Karin Simoneau, eds. 1992. Introduction to *Folk Literature of South American Indians: General Index*. Los Angeles: UCLA Latin American Center Publications.

12. "Yo vivo de lo que escribo": Antonio Paredes Candia, Bolivian Folklorist

John B. Wright

Eighteen years ago I lived in a small village called Tahri, located on the Altiplano of Bolivia. I was a nineteen-year-old young man serving as a Mormon missionary assigned to work with the Aymara people. I was known as Elder Wright. A man in the village, Germán Mendoza, wanted to make an addition to his home, and my missionary companion and I went to help him make the needed adobes. It was my job to mix the straw into the mud. I didn't realize how difficult and uncomfortable that job could be. Before growing numb because of the cold water in the mixture, my tender feet felt the scratch and discomfort of every small pebble. It hurt! It soon began raining, and Germán insisted that we wait out the downpour in his home. We went in and had a little lunch while the rain passed by. When lunch ended the rain continued, and I found it enjoyable to speak to and play with Germán's newborn son. After the rain passed we went back outside ready to jump back into the mud and continue making adobes. The weather had turned very cold, and Germán told us that we would stop for the day. Elder Walker and I returned home.

The next morning we were awakened at 6:30 by someone pounding on our door. Elder Walker opened the door, and a young man entered. He told us that Germán's baby son had died during the night, and that he had been sent to get us. We hurriedly dressed and ran to Germán's home. Sure enough, the baby I had played with the day before had died during the night. It was Germán's third child and the third one to die.

Elder Walker and I were asked to wash and dress the body, preparing it for burial. The baby had been wrapped in swaddling clothes and a blanket. As we loosened these, it appeared to me that the baby must have suffered greatly as it died. The hands and feet of this little child were clenched tightly into balled fists as though he had fought a great fight. We washed the body and dressed it in the special clothing provided. The burial clothing was different from what I was accustomed to seeing at funerals in the United States. We put the baby in a white shirt that was long like a nightgown. We covered his head and face with a white hood that had holes cut for the eyes and mouth. We then placed white cardboard *wisc'unaca* (sandals) on his feet. Last, we attached white cardboard wings to his back by tying a black sash around his body. The body was placed on an *awayu* (multicolored blanket) along with an egg and all of the baby's other belongings. The *awayu* was tied up as a *k'epi* (bundle).

After eating a light lunch provided by Germán and his wife, our little funeral party began its procession to the cemetery. I carried the *k'epi*. Upon arriving at the cemetery Elder Walker and I took turns digging the grave and, apparently, were not doing it precisely as required, for a member of our party, another of Germán's friends, took the shovel from us, and with a few quick slices, perfectly squared the walls of the hole. We placed a layer of rocks on the bottom of the grave. The walls were lined with four pieces of sod. A handful of straw was placed inside this newly created sod box on top of the layer of rocks. We lowered the *k'epi* on top of the straw. Another piece of sod was used to enclose the *k'epi* in a sod coffin. We all took turns shoveling dirt on top of the sod to complete the burial.

I hope you can appreciate the impact this experience had on me. I had never before been involved with death in such a way; I had never before dressed and buried a dead person. As I dressed the body in the clothing provided by Germán and his wife, I most assuredly recognized the fact that I was dressing the body to appear like an angel. I did not, however, understand the cultural significance of this event in the lives of Germán and his wife. During the intervening years, I have occasionally reflected on this experience, trying to understand its meaning according to my own culture's experience with death. It wasn't until I was exploring possibilities for a presentation at the 1999 SALALM meeting that I came to understand the significance of that event in the culture of Bolivia.

As a cataloger I see many books cross my desk. Over the years I have seen a lot of books by a Bolivian writer named Antonio Paredes Candia. I remembered that all his books seemed to deal with the popular culture and folklore of Bolivia. I thought his writings might include something that would lead to an exciting paper and I retrieved all of his books in our library hoping to find such a lead. During my search, I opened one of his books, *Tukusiwa, o, La muerte*. Several Bolivian customs dealing with different aspects of death and burial are recorded in this book.

Chapter five has the title "Entierro del angelito." Reading this chapter caused the experience recounted above to come flooding back to my mind. I learned from reading this chapter that the parents of the dead child are not to grieve because the child has not committed any carnal sin and, referring to original sin, has been made clean through baptism. When the child dies, the soul rises directly to heaven. The godparents are the first to be notified of the child's death because they have the responsibility to make all the burial arrangements. It is also the obligation of the godfather to bathe the body of the dead child and to dress it in its burial clothing. For a male child who dies, the clothing is fashioned after the image of Saint Raphael and Saint Michael. It consists of a long white shirt, with adornments and applications of paper which are sewn to the fabric. Also, a set of small wings are fashioned from the same material as the adornments and included on the back of the body.[1]

Knowing the seriousness of the responsibilities of a child's godparents, I have come to realize the great honor paid to my companion and me. We were asked to participate in an event—a significant spiritual event—reserved primarily for family members and close friends. I'll return to this topic later.

The information documented in this book helped me understand what happened to me. It was then that I knew I wanted to share this with you. I knew that I must introduce you to Antonio Paredes Candia and his work. Who is Antonio Paredes Candia? How does he gather and organize information for his books? Of what value are his writings? This paper answers these questions. I will introduce you to Antonio Paredes Candia by (1) sharing with you glimpses into his life, (2) describing the way he gathers and organizes Bolivian folklore, and (3) discussing how he documents the popular culture of Bolivia in his published monographs.[2]

The Life and Research of Antonio Paredes Candia

Antonio Paredes Candia was born July 10, 1923, in the city of La Paz, Bolivia, in his family home. His father was Manuel Rigoberto Paredes Iturri and his mother was Haydeé Candia Torrico. He was born the eleventh of fourteen children of whom ten survived to adulthood. He grew up in an affluent family, his father being involved in politics and serving in various ministerial and judicial posts under various presidencies, eventually becoming the Dean of Bolivia's Corte Suprema de la Justicia. Although raised in an upper-middle-class family in an area of La Paz that appeared to have all the trappings of Spanish high society, Paredes considers himself a mestizo. His ancestry includes Spanish immigrants from the Canary Islands and indigenous *caciques* from Carabuco, a small village on the shores of Lake Titicaca. This combination of the races, Spanish and Indian, makes Paredes very proud. He believes that the mixture of both cultures is what gives Bolivia her cultural strength.

He spent his childhood—as do most youth—playing, doing chores, and attending school. Paredes did play some of the games common to Bolivian children such as marbles and tops. He did not enjoy participating much in team sports such as soccer. He preferred to sit in the window of his home and read books and talk with his mother. He also took care of the chickens and sheep, which were penned in one of the three patios that were part of the family home. As a youth he enjoyed attending parties where the teenagers associated with one another, listened to 78 rpm records, drank punch, and ate cakes, cookies, and candies. Paredes began his education in La Paz. He finished the *ciclo primario* and the *quinto curso del secundario*. He then became disinterested in school. He felt that he could learn more from his books. He never completed nor graduated from secondary school, preferring instead to teach himself.

Like all Bolivian young men, Paredes was required to serve in the military. He was part of the 1st Cavalry unit, stationed in the hinterlands of Bolivia along the Chilean border. He found that he thoroughly enjoyed riding a horse. He was the tallest in his group and, therefore, had the biggest horse whose name was El Moro. While in the military he had the good fortune of being associated with a commander who lived his life in accordance with strict moral values. His commander, Captain Armando Escobaduría, once asked him if he was going to take a leave one weekend to visit his family, and he said no. Of course, he did not have enough money to buy passage and was too embarrassed to reveal the real reason. The captain got wind of this and ordered him to return to his office. "Paredes, you don't have any money to travel? I will lend you the money on one condition, that you carry this box of eggs to my wife and family." Paredes delivered the box to the captain's wife. He was able to visit his family. He learned from this experience that men who are true to their values can gain the respect of their subordinates.

His father obtained for him a post in the Ministerio del Exterior. It was supposed by his father and perhaps even himself that he would eventually enter the career of diplomacy and would be part of the Bolivian embassy in Paris. Over a three-year period, Paredes sensed a growing conflict of values between his supervisor and himself. His supervisor was a very competent and capable man, but a man who seemed to lack any sense of morals. This conflict led to Paredes's decision to leave the Ministerio. He had no degree, no job experience. His father had paved the way for him to enjoy a successful career as a diplomat, but now any future in a government post was destroyed. Paredes's career options looked bleak, but even more damaged was his relationship with his father. The senior Paredes was very displeased and confused with his son's decisions. How could a son be so ungrateful, so short-sighted, so pig-headed?

Paredes found a solution to his career problem by getting a job teaching seven-, eight-, and nine-year-old children in a rural school in Quechisla, a mining village in southern Bolivia. Running after this teaching post, however, did nothing to solve his problem with his father. In fact, it probably aggravated the problem. Concern for the well-being of his son led the senior Paredes to ask questions similar to these: What kind of job is that, teaching a bunch of small children in a mining camp? What kind of career will that lead to? What security will that offer you for your future? We will see, however, in the long run, that seeds would be sown during this teaching experience that would satisfy even the anxieties of his father. Paredes arrived in the small mining camp and began teaching. He found it thoroughly to his liking to immerse himself in textbooks and prepare lessons for his young students. He was appalled, however, at their inability to pronounce the Spanish language correctly.

In an attempt to help them with their pronunciation skills, Paredes began to tell them of Little Red Riding Hood, the Big Bad Wolf, and other similar children's stories. As he concluded a story, a girl named Agustina Balajar raised her hand and said, "Teacher, I also know some stories." He invited her to tell them to the class. She began to tell stories of the fox, the rabbit, and the condor, narrating them in a mixture of Spanish and Quechua, her native language. Paredes was enthralled by her stories. When she finished, a boy, Asencio Titizano, indicated that he, too, knew more stories, and that his grandmother knew them all. That day, the seeds were sown for the long-term solution to Paredes's career troubles and his troubled relationship with his father. He knew that he had to collect and document these natural and national treasures of Bolivia. When the children left that day, Paredes had an agreement with the boy that he would visit him and his grandmother the following Sunday and collect their stories.

As part of his responsibilities as a teacher, Paredes planned for his students' tactile, as well as their intellectual, development. He decided that he would help them make puppets. He believed that this was the best way for the children to develop their tactile skills. Creating puppets and the scripts that puppet shows require would be a great way to develop their artistic abilities and their imaginations. He also saw a pragmatic benefit to the puppet shows. The puppet productions would provide a much-needed pastime for the children and their mining families, something other than drinking. The puppet shows became a success. They performed several shows for their families and neighboring communities.

Another way of helping the children develop physically was playing games and sports. Paredes tells of being out on the playground with the children during a recess period. He heard a plane and instinctively looked up, shielding his eyes to see the plane fly overhead. He looked and looked, scanning the sky to see the plane, but could never locate it. He soon heard laughter from the children. They said, "No, teacher, the plane is not up there, it's down there." Paredes shifted his gaze to the sky in the lower valleys and soon discovered the plane. Paredes casually says that this event helped him realize how high he was living in the mining camp located on Mt. Chorolque. I believe, however, that this story, told by Paredes in a casual, matter-of-fact way, illustrates the significant, life-changing impact his years as a rural teacher had on him. While living in Quechisla, Paredes saw the sad reality of people living in poverty and ignorance. His experience taught him to reexamine—to truly see—the value of the view of life held by the Indians. He learned that his upper-middle-class upbringing did not prepare him for the realities of life experienced by the lower social classes living in the mines.

In 1950, while Paredes was away teaching, he received word that he should return home immediately: his father was dying. He secured train passage back to La Paz. Upon entering his father's room, his father, who was lying in bed, grasped his hand, clutched it to his ear, and died. Soon after his father's death, Paredes's four-year contract expired. He left the mining school. Although he had a wonderful experience teaching school, Paredes was ready to turn his efforts full-time to his interests kindled in the mining camps—gathering folklore and combating poverty and ignorance.

This was the beginning of Paredes's planning and conducting book fairs. His book fairs had two purposes: (1) he carried books and culture to the people and (2) he gathered folklore from the people. Traveling into the various towns, both urban and rural, Paredes was able to live like the people he visited. He ate the same food, slept in the same type of bed, and witnessed what made the people laugh and cry. He was able to participate with them in the daily activities of living. While sitting at his table with books, he would ask people questions to clarify and understand the events he experienced, the food he ate, the stories he heard, the language he heard, and so on; and he recorded their answers in little notebooks. This was in the days before the portable tape recorder. He wrote down the data in pencil. Upon arriving home he would transfer the information onto worksheets which were later typed and classified according to topic and filed into a drawer. These drawers have since become his folklore archive. He draws from these cards the data necessary to create monographic works.

Paredes's style of living—traveling the countryside, living with various groups of people, sharing in their experiences, and documenting them—has produced many interesting experiences in his own life. One such experience happened while he was gathering folklore in the valleys surrounding the city of Cochabamba during the 1950s. He says:

> Yo recorrí el valle de Cochabamba a pié, con mi mochila a la espalda en la que guardaba la elemental muda de ropa y mis cuadernos de apuntes, muchos lápices y tajadores. Vivíamos el tiempo que según la gente de la ciudad era peligroso caminar por el valle de Cochabamba, ya que el partido imperante, por conveniencia propia y mala fe, había politizado al campesino, y el señor de vida y haciendas de la región era el Secretario General del Sindicato Agrario, de Apellido Rojas. Al hablar de aquél líder, los citadinos temblaban de miedo porque muchas veces había amenazado invadir y saquear la ciudad. Muchos me aconsejaban que no cometiera la imprudencia de viajar allí, podía sufrir atropellos me decían, y los más timoratos aseveraban hasta que podían fusilarme. Yo me reía, no por audaz, ni por jactarme de valiente, sino porque conocía al indio aymara y quechua, y sabía de las altas cualidades humanas que tienen, cualidades que están ausentes en la conducta de los mestizos y blancoides. Llegué a Cliza y bajé del vehículo. Inmediatamente dos campesinos armados se me acercaron y me dijeron que debía explicar a su jefe el motivo que me llevaba a esa región. El líder Rojas, tenía el despacho en la escuela y su secretaria era la profesora. Primero me observó desconfiado y estuvo hasta reticente en su actitud, no podía ser de otra manera; ellos recién conocían la libertad después de cuatro siglos de esclavitud. Yo tomé la palabra y le expliqué el motivo de mi presencia en esos lugares. Rojas cambió de gesto del rostro por cordial, era un valluno moreno, alto, fornido. Me hizo recuerdo a Pancho Villa y como al líder mejicano sus paisanos, a este los vallunos le obedecían ciegamente y tenían fe en

su palabra. Inmediatamente ordenó a su secretaria me extendiera un memorándum que era el pasaporte para que todos los sindicatos y rancheríos del
valle me recibieran, me alojaran y me dieran los informes que yo les pediría.
Ese memorándum escrito a máquina con cinta roja, en papel cuadriculado de
cuaderno escolar, me abrió las puertas del Paraíso, y fuí tratado a cuerpo de
rey por el campesino valluno. Entonces saboreé la auténtica comida campe-
sina, agradable, nutritiva y sana, y conocí el cordial trato humano de esos
hombres.[3]

He has been all over the country, conducting book fairs and gathering folklore.
He claims that forty to fifty years ago, when he gathered the majority of his
data, the folklore of the people was authentic. Many people today have learned
that by making up ceremonies or dances, they can earn dollars from the field
researchers. He therefore believes that the folklore gathered today is not as
valid.

Paredes established the practice of taking the books to the people. In Bolivian society the indigenous peoples, the *cholas* and the *cholos*, were not wel-
comed in bookstores. They really had no access to the written word. After his
experience in the mining school and traipsing around the countryside gathering
folklore, Paredes realized the power the written word had in changing the lives
of people, for he witnessed it. He would take his backpack full of books into
towns, and the local people could look at the books with no pressure to buy.
Those who wanted a book frequently had no money to buy it, so they offered
to barter with him. They would bring potatoes, chickens, corn, and other food-
stuffs to exchange for books. The book fairs became very popular. He now
operates book fairs throughout the country. When asked how the people
received his book fairs, he told the following story:

> En Potosí viene un indio y me dice, "Y por qué no llevas [libros] a mi
> comunidad?"
>
> "Dónde es[tá] tu comunidad?"
>
> "Es un pueblo que se llama Visijsi."
>
> "Bueno, voy a ir, pero cómo se va?"
>
> Y el indio me dice, "Cuándo vas a ir?"
>
> Yo le digo, "Voy a ir el domingo."
>
> "Ah," me dice, "vas a tomar el camión en tal parte." Me da todo lo
> señal. "Te voy estar esperando."
>
> Cuando tomo el camión, llevo dos cajoncitos de libros y llego ya lo
> distingo en el camino un hombre. Y mientras nos acercábamos era él
> que me había invitado ir. Hago parar el camino me bajo. Todavía el
> chofer me mira un poco extrañado, que en un lugar tan desolado
> hago parar el camión y me bajé. Bueno y al indio se alegró mucho.

Y con su burrito, los dos cajones y caminamos. Caminaríamos una hora máxima, y en una ondonadita estaba la comunidad, las casas de la comunidad. Llegué fue una fiesta para ellos. Entonces, puse los libros en exhibición y ocurre que no había plata, no había dinero y me dice, "No te podemos pagar con dinero, pero te pagamos con los productos que tenemos."

"Ay," yo le digo, "Pero he encontrado, pues, bueno, yá."

Y entonces cambiaba un libro, digamos, por cinco huevos. O otros cuantos libros por una cantidad de papas, o así. Y hasta gallina, hasta un patito tierno, o sea que regresé a Potosí con una cantidad de productos. . . . Pero, lo interesante de esa, mi visita a Visijsi, es que había muerto uno de los comunarios y esa noche se lo enterraba, o al día siguiente, y esa noche era el velatorio. Y allí recojí juegos ceremoniales que están en mi libro de juegos.[4]

The people of Bolivia, especially the indigenous communities, have been very supportive of and interested in his book fairs. He has run into some problems, however. For years, Paredes has conducted his book fair in the city of La Paz along its main boulevard, El Prado, which runs through the center of town in the business district. In 1990 the mayor of La Paz decided that having a book fair with all of its tables and books lying around did not contribute to the image of an advanced city that he was trying to create. There was also some pressure by local bookstores to do something with the book fair where many pirated books were being displayed and sold. Using members of the municipal police force, Mayor Ronald Mac Lean Abaroa shut down the book fair. The police came in one night and demolished the book displays. Paredes took the case to the Supreme Court of the Department of La Paz because he believed that he was within the law—he had received authorization from the municipal government to operate his book fair prior to its opening. The Court decided in his favor. Many people congratulated Paredes for winning the case, but he defiantly insists that he did not win, the Bolivian people won. Anytime the laws are followed and enforced, the people win.

In the aftermath of his experience with Mayor Mac Lean, Paredes and the other book exhibitors have moved the book fair a block north on the pedestrian street Paseo Marina Núñez del Prado. Here there have been constructed 65 kiosks which are operated by independent book exhibitors, all members of the Asociación Nacional de Expositores de Libros "Antonio Paredes Candia" which was founded in 1970. The members of this association have invested a great deal of time and money to create an area of the city which is very beautiful. The Paseo, formerly a place of prostitution, drug trafficking, and filth, has now been converted into a place of culture. The kiosks line both sides of the Paseo which runs two city blocks. The Paseo is paved with beautiful tiles and is adorned with lawns, planters, and benches. It is Paredes's hope that financial support can be found to create a permanent puppet theater at the west end of the Paseo. Finally, he says, this has become a lasting positive tribute to the great Bolivian sculptress whose name it bears. Although this arrangement seems to be satisfactory, Paredes warns that nothing is certain.

Paredes never married. He did, however, wish to share his life and feelings with other people so he adopted an Aymara boy named Huáscar, who has since grown to adulthood, married, and has four children. The oldest child, Kantutita, has three children. This has been a great joy in the life of Paredes. His roles as father and grandfather are important to him for they have taught him more about life. He has learned that as a father, he can only suggest, not counsel. As a grandfather he has learned the special relationship a grandparent shares with a grandchild. His grandchildren, and now his great-grandchildren, visit him often and share their lives with him. Paredes indicates that he thought he understood the Aymara people from his trips into their communities over the years, but he really came to appreciate the values of these people after adopting Huáscar and being his father. He has also appreciated greatly the fact that Huáscar married a young Aymara from the Altiplano. Interacting with his family has truly given him insights into the Aymara people.

Presently, Paredes lives in his home of more than forty years located on Avenida Manco Kapac across the street from the old train station on the west end of the city of La Paz. His home is filled with colonial era furniture, walls of books, and many art treasures, paintings, and sculptures. His daily schedule is as follows: He gets up at 7:30 A.M., tends to his bed (airing out the sheets and blankets, then making it), washes, dresses, eats breakfast, and works on his research until 10:30 A.M. when he goes downtown to work at his kiosk. He returns at 1:00 P.M. and eats lunch and then naps until 3:00 P.M. In the afternoons he works on his research. He returns to his kiosk until 6:00 P.M. He returns home and eats dinner, after which he sometimes watches the news. He works on his research until 1:00 A.M. Sometimes he will be so excited about what he is reading, or the notes he is making from his cards, that he totally forgets about the time and ends up going to bed at 2:00 or 3:00 in the morning. He does not experience insomnia and he doesn't dream; he sleeps like a child. He lives a very modest life. He does not experience loneliness as he advances in age. He says he will continue in this pattern until the end.

Documenting His Research

The publications of Antonio Paredes Candia span almost a half a century. As mentioned, his first book, *Literatura folklórica*, was published in 1953. He originally took it to the Ministerio de Educación, which had advertised its desire to publish national authors whose works deal with Bolivia. His work was rejected; he was told that it was complete nonsense. He continued his efforts to see his work published and was successful when A. Gamarra agreed to publish the manuscript. When the book was published and printed, available for sale, Paredes did not have any money to pay for the printing. He gave the publisher a stove with three burners in payment. It was accepted. From the introduction we read:

> El estudio del folklore de una región o de un grupo étnico, es labor patriótica y plena de sacrificios cuando se trata de naciones como la nuestra, en la que no se ha inquietado el ánimo de los intelectuales por el conocimiento de esta ciencia, cuyo estudio y divulgación en la mayoría de las repúblicas sudamericanas avanza notablemente. El folklore en sí, representa la explicación de la idiosincracia de un pueblo mediante sus costumbres, danza, música, creencias, mitos, leyendas y alimentación. Bolivia, en el continente, es uno de los países más ricos en este sentido. . . . Su enorme población indígena . . . es fecundo campo para que el estudioso recopile datos sobre tan interesante tema. . . . Se ha llegado al convencimiento de que un pueblo que no guarda celosa y sobre todo honestamente su folklore, dá a entender que reniega de la herencia de antecedentes que estructuran su existencia. Es lamentable que en nuestra Patria no se haya tomado en serio la recopilación y divulgación del nuestro, que es amplísimo.[5]

The following year, 1954, Paredes received a book from Efraín Morote Best, a Peruvian folklorist. This book, *Elementos de Folklore* (1950), encouraged Paredes to continue in his new career of investigator and researcher of Bolivian folklore. The book contains a detailed history of the principles and practices of the discipline of folklore. It also contains a lengthy classification scheme for organizing and classifying the different forms of folklore. This book became the basis for Paredes's future work. Since publishing that first book, Paredes has taken advantage of the richness of Bolivia's folklore and has published several more. He decided, however, not to have to wonder how each book would be published. Paredes established his own imprint to publish the results of his research. He chose the name Ediciones Isla because he believes that the culture of Bolivia is an island. Paredes worked cooperatively with Librería-Editorial "Popular," a publishing house headquartered in La Paz, to print all of the books produced under the Ediciones Isla imprint. His relationship with this printing house began early when he contracted with doña Elena Lucía de Villamor, a woman with great business acumen, to publish his books. She and Librería-Editorial "Popular" helped to make Ediciones Isla successful. When it came time to pay for the publication, doña Elena would say, "Bring another book. With the sale of the new book, you can pay me for the publication of the earlier book." The company is now presided over by her son, Germán Villamor Lucía. The Librería operates bookstores in several Bolivian cities and in Argentina. It also controls about 60 percent of the greeting card industry in Bolivia which is what they primarily produce now—greeting cards, calendars, date books. Paredes is the only author who has books produced by the Librería.

Since 1953 Paredes has published 95 titles, the majority as monographs.[6] Primarily they focus on topics of folklore: documenting popular practices, speech, dances, food, anecdotes, stories, and so on. Some works were written specifically for Bolivian children because he wants them from an early age to begin to love Bolivia. This they will do, he believes, as they learn about her people, legends, stories, geography. These include the following two books: *Cuentos bolivianos para niños* (1984) and *Cuentos de maravilla para niños* (1988). He has published books dealing with the folklore of different regions of Bolivia: *Folklore de Potosí* (1980), *Tradiciones orureñas* (1980), *De la tradición paceña* (1982), *Literatura oral del Beni* (1992), *Folklore de Cochabamba* (1997). Another group deals specifically with popular usage in folk language: *Refranes, frases y expresiones populares de Bolivia* (1976), *Voces de trabajo pregones, juramentos e invocaciones* (1976), *El apodo en Bolivia* (1977), *Estribillos populares de carácter político* (1993), *Lenguaje mímico* (1997). Anecdotes are another favorite collection for Paredes. He watches the news every night and reads several regional newspapers, combing them for new anecdotes worth saving. He believes that anecdotes are important because the anecdote "en muchos casos da lugar a la creación de cuentos populares. Con el correr del tiempo se olvidan los personajes protagonistas de la anécdota. Queda el hecho iniciándose así el proceso de folklorización hasta que llega el tiempo en que se cuenta la anécdota anteponiendo 'dice que ha pasado', 'le contaron a mi abuela', o 'occurió en tiempos antiguos.' "[7] Paredes has written several short novels dealing with social injustices commonly practiced in his native land. Each of these short novels is important in its own right because it demonstrates for the reader positive ways to break out of the pattern of victimization accompanying these forms of social injustice: *El zambo salvito* (1982), *Aventuras de dos niños* (1986), *Ellos no tenían zapatos* (1989), *Los hijos de la correista* (1990), and *La historia de Gumercindo* (1994). He wrote two biographies of two men who have deeply influenced him: *La vida ejemplar de Antonio González Bravo* (1967) and *La trágica vida de Ismael Sotomayor y Mogrovejo* (1967). One a musicologist the other a traditionalist/historian, both were authentic, no illusions; both were quiet, unassuming researchers who, for the most part, have been forgotten by their countrymen. Paredes believes that all of his books should be considered as a single grain of sand that will someday be used to reclaim the true Bolivian culture which has been neglected and destroyed by decades of corrupt politics and politicians.

Paredes is principally a collector, an arranger, and a describer of Bolivian folklore. The discipline of folklore is, of course, concerned with gathering and preserving knowledge of the people. The collection of this data is crucial for the student of folklore. Current trends in the discipline, however, also require the serious scholar to evaluate and analyze the importance of the performance of the folklore and the environment of its performance in addition to the collection of the data. Paredes's work seems to be lacking in this important facet of folklore scholarship, but this is a topic for another paper. The collection of folklore—the preservation of culture—is the greatest contribution Paredes has made to the study of Bolivian folklore. In fact, he states in the *notículas* of many of his books that his sole motivation in doing his work was to preserve the culture, to prevent it from disappearing. Because of Paredes's work, many facets of Bolivian culture have been kept alive for generations to come. His books are a seedbed for future scholars in Bolivian folklore. His writings will help all Bolivians come to a better understanding of their own culture. After conducting an interview with Paredes, one person described the significance of his work as follows: "Antonio Paredes-Candia, admirado por muchos, criticado por otros, respetado por todos, constituye el más importante investigador de nuestro folklore. A lo largo de sus cien obras ha recopilado tradiciones, leyendas, cuentos, personajes, en fin, nuestra identidad cultural. Conocer la obra de Paredes-Candia es requísito para entender y reconocer lo que somos."[8]

Conclusion

I have offered you a brief glimpse into the life of Paredes. I described his manner of doing research and I have explained how he documents his research by publishing books. I have mentioned the impact his writings had on me at the beginning of this paper. I would like to return now to that book, *Tukusiwa, o, La muerte.* By reading this book, I gained insights into the historical practice of burying children. This information helped me clarify the meaning of my experience assisting in the burial of a Bolivian child. I now understand what a privilege it was for me to act as the child's godfather, at the request of his parents, and wash, dress, and bury the child. Now, however, I have more questions. Why was I, a Mormon missionary, chosen to act as godfather? Was it because my missionary companion and I were the only available religious leaders? Were the child's godparents unavailable? Did the child not have godparents? If he didn't have godparents, does that mean that he was never baptized? If not, what impact would that have on the status of his soul? Could he be an *angelito?* I still do not know exactly what the significance of that event was for Germán Mendoza and his wife. I do not know if I understand what the dressing of their child in an angel's clothing meant for them. I do know, however, that this was their third child and the third one to die. I would hope that they were comforted in knowing that their son was every bit as beautiful as was his angel costume. I would hope that they had the consolation that their son could return to the presence of God. In anyone's language, customs, or folklore I would hope that this would be the case.

Aymara is a language that is very capable of expressing the depths of a human soul. The first word in the title of Paredes's book is *tukusiwa.* The word *tukusiwa* is Aymara. It is constructed from the verb *tukuña*—meaning to finish, complete, come to an end, come full circle; the suffix *-si* is added to make the verb reflexive; the suffix *-wa* changes the reflexive verb into a noun. An

English translation of *tukusiwa* might be then the state of completing oneself by bringing oneself to an end or coming full circle or simply finishing one's cycle. This is not the usual word used for death in Aymara. That word is *jiwaña*. Why does Paredes use it here? I think he chose it to express the feeling that death has for the Aymara people. Death is not a crisis for the Aymara. It is something natural and logical for someone who has completed his life cycle.

Paredes himself knows that one day he will complete his life cycle. Does he feel complete? What does he feel about his work, his attempt to document Bolivian folklore? I will let him speak for himself as he explains the significance of the dedication written by Morote Best in the book Paredes received in 1954. He explains the following:

> El libro que me mandó tiene una dedicatoria muy significativa para mi. Se lo voy a leer:
>
> Mi querido amigo Sr. don Antonio Paredes Candia,
>
> Deposito en sus manos este libro que ojalá sirva para que usted continúe la admirable obra de su ilustre padre. Tengo fe en lo que usted logrará y por eso, le envío también mi espíritu.
>
> Su amigo,
> Efraín Morote Best
> Cuzco, Perú 1954
>
> Yo creo que ni a mi padre, ni a Morote he defraudado. Creo he cumplido con lo que dice en esta dedicatoria Morote Best.[9]

The life Paredes has lived and the books he has written have been a direct result of his decision to accept the position of rural teacher in the mining town of Quechisla. He says in a letter I received in February 1999, "Yo soy uno de los raros escritores de mi Patria, que vive de lo que escribe." He repeats later in the letter, "Yo vivo de lo que escribo," and adds this important qualifier: "Mi oficio no me da para lujos ni derroches, pero sí, para una vida honesta y honrada."[10] The gathering of folklore and the writing of books based on this folklore has allowed Paredes to sustain himself. More important, by conducting his research he is "sumergido en la verdadera Bolivia . . . porque me enseña a conocer a mi patria, a conocer a mi pueblo, a poder saber sus inquietudes, sus confesiones, todo."[11] This understanding has allowed Paredes to continue honestly and honorably the work of his father which most definitely, I believe, has satisfied the senior Paredes's more important concerns for his son.

NOTES

1. Antonio Paredes Candia, *Tukusiwa, o, La muerte* (La Paz, Bolivia: Librería-Editorial Popular, 1995), pp. 126–127. In this passage Paredes is actually recording the events surrounding the death of children in Tarata, Department of Cochabamba, Bolivia. Although my experience took place on the Altiplano in the Department of La Paz, I found the events discussed here strikingly

similar to those surrounding my experience in Tahri. I am assuming the meanings of the events are similar as well.

2. In April 1999 I traveled to La Paz, Bolivia, and conducted an oral history interview with Antonio Paredes Candia. We met April 9–10 and 12–14 at his home from 3:00–5:00 P.M. Each session of the interview was videotaped and tape recorded. The biographical sketch was created from information I learned during the interviews. I am in the process of transcribing the interviews. I will record subsequent references to this interview in the following manner: Interview, date of interview.

3. Antonio Paredes Candia, *Folklore de Cochabamba* (La Paz, Bolivia: Ediciones Isla, 1997), pp. 9–10.

4. Interview, April 10, 1999. The ceremonial games that he refers to are recorded in his book *Tukusiwa, o, La muerte*, pp. 356–358.

5. Antonio Paredes Candia, introduction to *Literatura folklórico: (Rocogida de la tradición oral boliviana)* (La Paz, Bolivia: Tall. Gráf. A. Gamarra, 1953).

6. When I first spoke with Paredes during the interviews, I understood that the 95 titles represented monographic titles. I believe, however, after trying to create a bibliography of his complete works, that the number represents the total number of titles published by him regardless of format. I believe that my bibliography is complete as far as listing all of the titles of his monographic publications. I have also listed different editions if I could discover them. (See "Selected Works of Antonio Paredes Candia" at the end of this paper.) More work will have to be done to complete the bibliography of all of Paredes's work.

7. Antonio Paredes Candia, *Cuentos populares bolivianos: De la tradición oral,* 3. ed. (La Paz, Bolivia: Librería-Editorial "Popular," 1984), p. 20.

8. Ramiro Calasich, "Conversación con Antonio Paredes-Candia," *Presencia-Dominical* (La Paz, Bolivia), July 14, 1991, p. 5.

9. Interview, April 9, 1999.

10. Antonio Paredes Candia, letter to author, February 9, 1999, p. 4.

11. Interview, April 12, 1999.

SELECTED WORKS OF ANTONIO PAREDES CANDIA

Monographs (Chronological Order)

Literatura folklórica: (Recogida de la tradición oral boliviana). La Paz, Bolivia: Tall. Gráf. A. Gamarra, 1953.

Folklore en el valle de Cochabamba: Dos fiestas populares. La Paz, Bolivia: n.p., 1957.

El folklore en la ciudad de La Paz. Separata de la revista de arte y letras "Khana," año V, vol. 2, nos. 25 y 26, julio de 1957.

Bibliografía del folklore boliviano. La Paz, Bolivia: Separata de la revista de arte y letras "Khana," correspondiente al no. 35, diciembre 1961.

Todos Santos en Cochabamba: Folklore. La Paz, Bolivia: Separata de la Revista "Khana," no. 36, septiembre 1962.

Vocablos aymaras en el habla popular paceña: Folklore. La Paz, Bolivia: Ediciones Isla, 1963.

La danza folklórica en Bolivia. La Paz: Ediciones Isla, 1966.

Juegos, juguetes y divertimientos del folklore de Bolivia. La Paz, Bolivia: Ediciones Isla, 1966.

Artesanías e industrias populares de Bolivia. La Paz, Bolivia: Ediciones Isla, 1967.

La trágica vida de Ismael Sotomayor y Mogrovejo: (Bio-bibliografía). La Paz, Bolivia: Ediciones Isla, 1967.

La vida ejemplar de Antonio González Bravo. La Paz, Bolivia: Ediciones Isla, 1967.

Antología de tradiciones y leyendas bolivianas. 3 tomos. La Paz, Bolivia: J. Camarlinghi, 1968.

La Navidad paceña: Fiesta popular. La Paz, Bolivia: H. Municipalidad de La Paz, 1968.

Selección del teatro boliviano para niños. La Paz, Bolivia: Camarlinghi Editor, 1969.

Comercio popular de la ciudad de La Paz: Folklore. La Paz: Prefectura del Departamento de La Paz. Separata de la Revista de Cultura "Pukara," correspondiente al no. 1 y 2, 1970.

Brujerías, tradiciones y leyendas. 2. ed. La Paz, Bolivia: Ediciones El Amauta, 1972.

Cuentos de curas: Folklore secreto. La Paz, Bolivia: Ediciones Isla, 1972.

Diccionario mitológico de Bolivia: Dioses, símbolos, héroes. La Paz, Bolivia: Ediciones Puerta del Sol, 1972.

Cuentos populares bolivianos: De la tradición oral. 1. ed. La Paz, Bolivia: Ediciones Isla, 1973.

Las mejores tradiciones y leyendas de Bolivia. La Paz, Bolivia: Ediciones Puerta del Sol, 1973.

Antología de tradiciones y leyendas bolivianas. Tomo I. La Paz: Editorial "Los Amigos del Libro," 1974.

Leyenda de Patacamaya. La Paz, Bolivia: Ediciones Isla, 1974.

Anécdotas bolivianas. La Paz, Bolivia: Ediciones Isla, 1975.

Cuentos de curas: folklore secreto. 2. ed. La Paz: Ediciones Isla, 1975.

Leyendas de Bolivia. La Paz: Editorial "Los Amigos del Libro," 1975.

Las mejores tradiciones y leyendas de Bolivia. 2. ed. La Paz, Bolivia: Ediciones Puerta del Sol, 1975.

Adivinanzas de doble sentido: Folklore secreto. La Paz, Bolivia: Ediciones Isla, 1976.

Brujerías de Bolivia. La Paz: Editorial "Los Amigos del Libro," 1976.

Fiestas populares de Bolivia. 2 tomos. La Paz, Bolivia: Ediciones Isla/Librería-Editorial "Popular," 1976.

Refranes, frases y expresiones populares de Bolivia: 1.495 paremias. La Paz, Bolivia: Ediciones Isla, 1976.

Tradiciones de Bolivia. 2. ed. La Paz: Editorial "Los Amigos del Libro," 1976.

Voces de trabajo, pregones, juramentos e invocaciones: Folklore de Bolivia. La Paz, Bolivia: Ediciones Isla, 1976.

Adivinanzas bolivianas: (De la tradición oral). La Paz, Bolivia: Ediciones Isla, 1977.

El apodo en Bolivia. La Paz, Bolivia: Ediciones Isla, 1977.

El sexo en el folklore boliviano. La Paz, Bolivia: Ediciones Isla, 1977.

Cuentos kjuchis: Folklore secreto. La Paz: Ediciones Isla, 1978.

Otros cuentos de curas: Folklore secreto. La Paz, Bolivia: Ediciones Isla, 1978.

Penúltimas anécdotas bolivianas. La Paz, Bolivia: Ediciones Isla, 1978.

Brujerías, tradiciones y leyendas. La Paz, Bolivia: Ediciones El Amauta, 1979.

Las mejores tradiciones y leyendas de Bolivia. 3. ed. La Paz, Bolivia: Ediciones Librería-Editorial "Popular," 1979.

Costumbres matrimoniales indígenas. La Paz, Bolivia: Ediciones Isla, 1980.

Folklore de Potosí: Algunos aspectos. La Paz, Bolivia: Ediciones Isla, 1980.

Tradiciones orureñas. La Paz, Bolivia: Ediciones Isla, 1980.

Adivinanzas de doble sentido: Folklore secreto. 3. ed. La Paz, Bolivia: Ediciones Isla, 1981.

Diccionario mitológico de Bolivia: Dioses, símbolos, héroes. 2. ed. La Paz, Bolivia: Ediciones Isla/Librería-Editorial "Popular," 1981.

Poesía popular boliviana. La Paz, Bolivia: Ediciones Isla/Librería-Editorial "Popular," 1981.

Las alacitas: Fiesta y feria popular de la ciudad de La Paz: Monografía. La Paz, Bolivia: Librería Editorial "Libertad," 1982.

De la tradición paceña: Folklore y tradiciones de la ciudad de La Paz. La Paz, Bolivia: Librería-Editorial "Popular"/Ediciones Isla, 1982.

Kjuchi cuentos: (Folklore secreto). 2. ed. La Paz, Bolivia: Ediciones Isla, 1982.

Las mejores tradiciones y leyendas de Bolivia. 4. ed. La Paz, Bolivia: Ediciones Librería-Editorial "Popular," 1982.

El zambo salvito: Vida y muerte. La Paz, Bolivia: Librería-Editorial "Popular," 1982.

Once anécdotas del Libertador. La Paz, Bolivia: Ediciones Isla, 1983.

Cuentos bolivianos para niños. La Paz, Bolivia: Librería-Editorial "Popular," 1984.

Cuentos populares bolivianos: De la tradición oral. 3. ed. corr. y considerablemente aumentada. La Paz, Bolivia: Librería-Editorial "Popular," 1984.

La danza folklórica en Bolivia. 2. ed. La Paz, Bolivia: Editorial Gisbert y Cía., 1984.

La comida popular boliviana: Apuntes y recetario. La Paz, Bolivia: A. Paredes-Candia, 1986.

Leyendas de Bolivia. La Paz, Bolivia: Librería-Editorial "Popular," 1986.

Otras anécdotas bolivianas. La Paz, Bolivia: Librería-Editorial "Popular," 1987.

Tradiciones de Bolivia. La Paz, Bolivia: Librería-Editorial "Popular," 1987.

Cuentos de maravilla para niños: De almas, duendes, aparecidos. La Paz, Bolivia: Librería-Editorial "Popular," 1988.

Ellos no tenían zapatos. . . . La Paz, Bolivia: Librería-Editorial "Popular," 1989.

Otros cuentos de curas: Folklore secreto. La Paz, Bolivia: Ediciones Isla, 1989.

Antología de tradiciones y leyendas bolivianas. 3 tomos. La Paz, Bolivia: Librería-Editorial "Popular," 1990.

Artesanías e industrias populares de Sucre. La Paz, Bolivia: Librería Editorial "Popular," 1990.

Ellos no tenían zapatos. . . . 2. ed. La Paz, Bolivia: Librería-Editorial "Popular," 1990.

Los hijos de la correista: Novelín. La Paz, Bolivia: Librería-Editorial "Popular," 1990.

La danza folklórica en Bolivia. 3. ed., aumentada. La Paz, Bolivia: Librería-Editorial "Popular," 1991.

La chola boliviana. La Paz, Bolivia: Ediciones Isla, 1992.

Literatura oral del Beni. La Paz, Bolivia: Ediciones Isla, 1992.

Estribillos populares de carácter político. La Paz, Bolivia: Ediciones Isla, 1993.

El molino quemado: Novelín. La Paz, Bolivia: Ediciones Isla, 1993.

El rutuchi: Una costumbre antigua. La Paz, Bolivia: Ediciones Isla, 1993.

El zambo salvito. Aymara trans. La Paz, Bolivia: Ediciones Casa de la Cultura, 1993.

La historia de Gumercindo: Novelín. La Paz, Bolivia: Librería-Editorial "Popular," 1994.

Quehaceres femeninos. La Paz, Bolivia: Librería-Editorial "Popular," 1995.

Tukusiwa, o, La muerte: Algunas costumbres bolivianas. La Paz, Bolivia: Librería-Editorial "Popular," 1995.

Ultimas anécdotas bolivianas. 4. entrega. La Paz, Bolivia: Librería-Editorial "Popular," 1995.

Isolda: La historia de una perrita. La Paz, Bolivia: Ediciones Isla, 1996.

Costumbres matrimoniales indígenas: Y de otras capas sociales. La Paz, Bolivia: Ediciones Isla, 1997.

Folklore de Cochabamba, 1949–1955. La Paz, Bolivia: Ediciones Isla, 1997.

Lenguaje mímico: Folklore. La Paz, Bolivia: Ediciones Isla, 1997.

La muerte del dictador Germán Busch. La Paz, Bolivia: Librería–Editorial "Popular," 1997.

Relaciones históricas de Bolivia. Tomo 1. La Paz, Bolivia: Ediciones Isla, 1997.

Bandoleros, salteadores y raterillos. La Paz, Bolivia: Ediciones Isla, 1998.

De rameras, burdeles y proxenetas. La Paz, Bolivia: Ediciones Isla, 1998.

Periodical Articles

"Los pájaros en los cuentos de nuestro folklore: (Recogidos de la tradición oral)." *Khana*, vol. I, nos. 3–4 (julio de 1954), 80–84

"El folklore escrito en la ciudad de La Paz. *Khana* (julio de 1955), 53–98.

"Folklore en el valle de Cochabamba: El sombrero." *Khana* (octubre de 1956), 136–152.

"Folklore en el valle de Cochabamba: Dos fiestas populares." *Khana* (marzo de 1957), 145–151.

"El folklore de la ciudad de La Paz: Dos fiestas populares." *Khana* (julio de 1957), 160–177.

"Antología de cuentos del folklore boliviano: (Recogidos de la tradición oral)." *Khana* (octubre–diciembre de 1957), 64–70.

"Folklore de la Hacienda Mollepampa." *Khana*, vol. II, nos. 31 y 32 (julio de 1958), 135–141.

"Antología de cuentos del folklore boliviano: (Recogidos de la tradición oral)." *Khana* (julio de 1959), 300–313.

"Bibliografía del folklore boliviano." *Khana*, vol. I, no. 35 (diciembre de 1961), 119–172.

"Todos Santos en Cochabamba: (folklore)." *Khana* (septiembre de 1962), 66–82.

Newspaper articles

"Cuando Dios quiere dar: Tradición paceña." *La verdad: Una voz con fe en Tarija*. Año VII, Tarija, jueves, 18 de marzo de 1982, no. 800, p. 8, columns 3–6.

"La leyenda de la coca." *Chulumani: Publicación del Centro Cultural y Deportivo*. No. 1, 24 de agosto de 1984, p. 5.

"De Santa Marta a los barrancos de Llojata: tradición." *Tiahuanacu*. Septiembre de 1987, p. 9, columns 1–3.

"El banquete en el cielo." *Opinión: El esolar*. Año III, no. 141, Cochabamba, 20 de febrero de 1990, pp. 6–7.

"La bodega." *Pausa Semanal*. Sucre, jueves, 7 de junio de 1990, no. 18, año I, p. 2.

"Los aldabones o llamadores en puertas de casas coloniales de Sucre." *Correo del Sur*. Guía Semanal. Sucre, domingo 10 a sábado 16 de junio de 1990, año 2, no. 86, pp. 12–13.

"Francisco Perro." *Prensa Libre*. Sucre, 15 de agosto de 1992, p. 14.

"Una oreja es una oreja (tradición)." *Prensa Libre*. Sucre, 22 de agosto de 1992, p. 14.

"Caín los habría enviado." *Prensa Libre*. Sucre, 29 de agosto de 1992, p. 18.

"El carnaval de antaño era una diversión sana." *Ultima Hora*, La Paz, domingo, 21 de febrero de 1993, p. 7.

"La poesía popular boliviana." *Sociedad Hoy*. La Paz, domingo, 8 de mayo de 1994, p. 8.

"El Alto: Ciudad Túpac Katari." *Presencia*. La Paz, Bolivia, viernes, 8 de octubre de 1998.

"Calendario Folklórico del Departamento de Potosí." *La Voz de Potosí*. Sucre, sábado, 10 de noviembre, año I, no. 1, pp. 6–7.

"Nuevas anécdotas bolivianas: Sin guardar las apariencias." *Opinión: Pueblo y Cultura*. Año III, no. 117.

13. Los esfuerzos por recuperar y preservar el cine puertorriqueño

Víctor Torres

Cualquier aproximación al cine puertorriqueño tiene que comenzar con la pregunta obligada, ¿existe realmente un cine puertorriqueño? La respuesta es afirmativa, aunque en términos cuantitativos el mismo esté muy lejos del cine mexicano o argentino, por mencionar dos de los países latinoamericanos que cuentan con una amplia y sostenida producción cinematográfica.

Etapas del cine puertorriqueño

La trayectoria del cine puertorriqueño se puede dividir en cuatro etapas.

1. Etapa inicial

A comienzos del siglo XX dos pioneros del cine puertorriqueño, Rafael Colorado y Juan Viguié, producen las primeras películas. El primero realizó en 1912 la película *Un drama en Puerto Rico* y en 1916 funda la primera compañía de cine del país, la Sociedad Industrial Cine Puerto Rico, para la que dirige tres películas: *Por la hembra y el gallo*, *El milagro de la virgen* y *Mafia en Puerto Rico*. En 1917 se funda otra compañía nativa, la Tropical Film Company, que contaba en su Junta Directiva con los conocidos hombres de letras Nemesio Canales, Luis Lloréns Torres y Antonio Pérez Perret. Ese mismo año producen *Paloma del monte* dirigida por Lloréns Torres. Otra compañía con capital nativo y norteamericano, la Porto Rico Photoplays, se funda en 1919 y produce *Amor tropical* con dos estrellas del cine silente norteamericano. Este primer periodo culmina con *Romance tropical*, primer largometraje sonoro del cine puertorriqueño que produjo y dirigió Juan Viguié en 1934 con libreto de Luis Palés Matos (Torres 1994:14–21).

2. Cine de la División de Educación a la Comunidad

Luego de un periodo de inactividad, la producción fílmica resurge con la creación de la División de Educación de la Comunidad. Aunque se crea oficialmente mediante la ley número 372 del 14 de mayo de 1949 como una agencia adscrita al Departamento de Instrucción Pública (actualmente, el Departamento de Educación), la División comenzó a producir cine a mediados de los años 40 cuando Jack e Irene Délano, junto a Edwin Rosskam, comienzan la producción y distribución de películas, carteles, folletos y otros materiales visuales en un taller ubicado en el sótano de la Comisión de Parques y Recreo Público

(Délano 1994:44). Así se inicia un proyecto abarcador para educar al pueblo, especialmente a los habitantes de la zona rural, que combinaba el uso de carteles y folletos con películas.

La División produce más de un centenar de películas a lo largo de su existencia, en su mayoría corto y mediometrajes. Su producción consistió principalmente de documentales o películas dramatizadas filmadas en ambientes naturales con actores no-profesionales. Según Ramón Almodóvar Ronda, las películas de ficción se utilizaron para trabajar los temas sociales y el documental se utilizó para los temas culturales (1994:88). Este cine respondía a los objetivos ideológicos y programáticos del Partido Popular Democrático. Como tal, tenía unos claros objetivos didácticos encaminados a elevar el nivel y la calidad de vida de la población y señalar problemas sociales o algunas de las necesidades básicas de las comunidades. El enfoque didáctico estaba dirigido a que la población, en particular las comunidades, resolvieran motu proprio, sus problemas o necesidades: "la necesidad de obras públicas en las comunidades, la educación del consumidor y el mercadeo, el autoritarismo o caciquismo, los derechos de la mujer, el cooperativismo, el trabajo y el bienestar social, la cultura popular y la historia" (Mongil Echandía y Rosario Albert 1994:32–33).

Estudiosos del cine puertorriqueño coinciden en señalar las aportaciones indiscutibles del cine de la División. En primer término, sienta las bases del cine puertorriqueño al producir un corpus sostenido de alta calidad artística y técnica. En segundo término, desarrolla al personal técnico necesario para la producción de cine. En este renglón hay que destacar que a los pioneros del proyecto, los esposos Délano y Rosskam, se unieron escritores de la talla de René Marqués, Emilio Díaz Valcárcel y Pedro Juan Soto en calidad de guionistas; Rafael Tufiño y Lorenzo Homar, entre otros, en las artes gráficas y los compositores Hector Campos Parsi y Amaury Veray. A este cuadro de talento puertorriqueño hay que añadir al grupo de realizadores que se forjan bajo la División: Amílcar Tirado, Luis A. Maysonet, Angel F. Rivera y Marcos Betancourt, entre otros.

3. Cine comercial

El auge económico de Puerto Rico durante los años 50 y la popularidad que adquieren los artistas de la televisión, motivó a que varios productores independientes y compañías reiniciaran durante esta década la producción de largometrajes. Uno de estos esfuerzos fue el del realizador dominicano Rolando Barreras que produjo tres películas a fines de los años 50 y principio de la década del 60. Sin embargo, ninguna de estas películas alcanza el éxito de *Maruja*, película de la compañía PROBO Films que se estrenó en 1959. Todavía es común referirse incorrectamente a *Maruja* como el primer largometraje del cine puertorriqueño. Lo cierto es que esta película abre una brecha en lo que se refiere al cine comercial que había de durar 20 años al promover la producción ininterrumpida de largometrajes con capital nativo o en coproducción con México. Durante este periodo se producen 46 filmes que, en su mayoría, siguen de cerca las fórmulas convencionales del cine mexicano: melodramas o comedias ligeras con un fuerte ingrediente de música. Entre las mejores producciones de este periodo se encuentran: *Ayer amargo*, *El alcalde de Machuchal* y *Mientras Puerto Rico duerme* producidas, respectivamente, por Gerónimo Mitchell, Paquito Cordero y Damián Rosa, los tres productores más consecuentes de esta etapa.

4. Período actual

Aunque todavía no podemos referirnos a una industria de cine, se considera que en el periodo actual el cine puertorriqueño alcanza su madurez. El ciclo se inicia en 1980 a raíz de *Dios los cría*, película de Jacobo Morales que alcanza, junto al éxito comercial, un nivel artístico y técnico que la lleva a competir internacionalmente en festivales de cine. A este periodo pertenecen *La gran fiesta*, *La guagua aérea* y otros filmes de Jacobo Morales.

A pesar de que la nueva generación de cineastas tiende a identificarse y resaltar el cine de este periodo, a tal grado que suele menospreciar o subestimar el cine del periodo anterior, la producción de estos 20 años resulta exigua en lo que a largometrajes se refiere. En cambio, cobra fuerza la producción de documentales independientes, de cine experimental y de animación, gracias, entre otros factores, a los nuevos formatos que surgen: el video y el Super 8.

Preservación y conservación del cine puertorriqueño

Los dos esfuerzos que existen por preservar y conservar el cine puertorriqueño, ambos de creación reciente, son el Archivo de Imágenes en Movimiento y el Proyecto Cine Nuestro.

Archivo de Imágenes en Movimiento

El Archivo de Imágenes forma parte del Archivo General de Puerto Rico y, como tal, está adscrito al Instituto de Cultura Puertorriqueña. El mismo se crea mediante la Resolución Conjunta 129 de la Legislatura de Puerto Rico que encomendó al Instituto de Cultura Puertorriqueña la organización del primer archivo de cine y televisión del país. El archivo se organiza propiamente en 1988 como un centro especializado en la conservación, preservación y divulgación del material fílmico producido principalmente por las distintas agencias del gobierno de Puerto Rico.

La colección incluye imágenes en movimiento en distintos formatos: películas de 8 mm, 16 mm y 35 mm y cintas videomagnetofónicas (videotapes) de ½", ¾", 1" y 2". El material refleja la vida política, cultural y social de Puerto Rico desde finales del siglo XIX. Como dato curioso, cabe destacar que una de las imágenes fílmicas es la de la invasión de las tropas norteamericanas a Guánica en el 1898. La colección primaria incluye los siguientes fondos.

• La colección completa de las películas realizadas por la División de Educación a la Comunidad desde 1946 hasta 1974 incluye las películas que realizara la División en sus orígenes bajo el nombre de la División de la Educación Visual de la Comisión de Parques y Recreo Público.

- La colección de Felisa Rincón de Gautier presenta algunos aspectos de la vida y la gestión pública de la alcaldesa de San Juan durante su incumbencia de 22 años, entre 1946 al 1968.

- Películas y cintas videomagnetofónicas de la Administración de Fomento Económico muestra la promoción industrial de esta agencia a través de actividades como la inauguración de fábricas, reuniones profesionales y noticieros.

- La colección de noticieros fílmicos comprende los noticieros *Al día con Kresto y Denia*, *Deportes Kresto y Denia*, *El Mirador Kresto y Denia* y *El noticiero Viguié* que se presentaban en las salas de cine como parte de la función durante las décadas del 50 y 60.

- Películas comerciales entre los títulos que posee la colección se encuentran *Maruja*, *El otro camino*, *Diez años de nostalgia*, *Más allá del capitolio* y *Obsesión*.

- La Colección de Kinescopio de personalidades puertorriqueñas incluye imágenes de varias figuras de la vida pública y del ambiente artístico, entre ellas Luis Muñoz Marín, Inés Mendoza, Ramón Ortiz del Rivero (Diplo) y Johnnie Rodríguez.

Otros fondos añadidos a la colección son la Colección WIPR que consta de varios de los programas de la estación del gobierno WIPR en cinta videomagnetofónica, entre estos *Mirador puertorriqueño* (80 ediciones) y las telenovelas *Pueblo chico*, *El regreso* y *Los dedos de la mano* producidas por el Instituto de Cultura Puertorriqueña durante los años 70. Además, varios cineastas puertorriqueños han donado su producción fílmica, entre ellos José Artemio Torres y Enrique Trigo (Luna Films).

Como medida de preservación, la producción fílmica se transfiere al formato de video (VHS ½") que facilita y permite su uso y manejo. En lo que se refiere a conservación, el Archivo trabaja en la restauración de películas y, hasta la fecha, ha restaurado 25 filmes entre los que figuran *Maruja*, *Modesta* y *Los peloteros*. Toda la colección está localizada en una bóveda climatizada que reúne los requisitos de temperatura y permite el control apropiado de la humedad.

Como se desprende de esta breve descripción, la colección del Archivo de Imágenes en Movimiento recoge principalmente documentales, noticieros y programas de televisión, relacionados de una forma u otra al gobierno, dejando al descubierto el cine comercial que se produce en el país desde principio de siglo.

Proyecto Cine Nuestro

Es precisamente para cubrir esta necesidad que un grupo de ciudadanos acoge la iniciativa de Roberto Ramos Perea, conocido dramaturgo y Director

Ejecutivo del Ateneo Puertorriqueño. Este proyecto, conocido como Cine Nuestro, e impulsado por la Sección de Cine y Video del Ateneo Puertorriqueño, intenta localizar y rescatar una copia en video de cada película producida en el país, ya sea con capital nacional o extranjero. El proyecto resulta ambicioso pues contempla, además, incluir las películas realizadas por artistas y técnicos puertorriqueños en el extranjero, principalmente en México y los Estados Unidos.

La tarea inicial consistió en realizar un inventario de las películas producidas en Puerto Rico. Para este trabajo se utilizó como fuente de consulta principal la filmografía del cineasta puertorriqueño Joaquín (Kino) García Morales (García Morales 1997). El inventario realizado arrojó un total de 508 títulos que incluyen cortometrajes, mediometrajes y largometrajes producidos por agencias del gobierno, productores independientes o compañías privadas. Incluye, asimismo, las co-producciones realizadas, principalmente con México. Luego de identificar los títulos se procedió a localizar las películas en colecciones públicas y privadas de Puerto Rico y el extranjero, en filmotecas, distribuidores de video, bases de datos en Internet y otras fuentes. Se logró ubicar un 70% de los títulos. Los restantes, que ascienden a 44 títulos, se han declarado "desaparecidas" por el momento, esto es, se desconoce si existe alguna copia disponible o su paradero. Se declararon también como "desaparecidas" varias películas que si bien se conoce localización, los dueños o custodios no han permitido su acceso. En la actualidad, el proyecto está enfrascado en la tarea de recuperar estos títulos y, a tales fines, comenzó a circular una lista y a recabar la colaboración de personas e instituciones.

El siguiente paso, aún inconcluso, está encaminado a conseguir una copia en video de cada una de las películas identificadas y localizadas. Salvo en los casos en que el video se encuentre accesible en el mercado, la labor requiere transferir al formato de video todas las películas que se puedan recuperar. En algunos casos, el propio curador del proyecto ha transportado los rollos de películas a un laboratorio para realizar esta labor (Ramos Perea, entrevista personal, 7 de abril de 1999). La lista de "desaparecidas" incluye a todas las películas de lo que hemos llamado la etapa inicial del cine puertorriqueño, películas que con toda probabilidad se han perdido para siempre dada la naturaleza inflamable del material fílmico de la época. Sin embargo, las películas desaparecidas no se limitan a las primeras décadas del siglo XX ya que incluye películas de los años 50, 60 y aún de los años 70. Entre estos títulos sobresale *Ayer amargo*, una adaptación libre de *Yerma,* de García Lorca, trasplantada al ambiente boricua y filmada en San Germán, que dirigió Amílcar Tirado y protagonizó Marta Romero.

Según el curador del proyecto, una de las explicaciones para que películas de época reciente no puedan localizarse obedece a que durante esta época fue práctica común que los productores recibieran dinero de la casa distribuidora, en la mayoría de los casos la Columbia Pictures, y entregaran el producto final a la compañía perdiendo así el control de la película (Ramos Perea, entrevista personal).

Control y acceso

No existe un acceso adecuado para estas colecciones. La colección primaria del Archivo de Imágenes en Movimiento se encuentra catalogada, pero dicha catalogación no está accesible al público. El único acceso al acervo es a través de las listas que son propiamente un inventario de la colección (Marisel Flores Carrión, entrevista personal, 1999). El proyecto Cine Nuestro ha realizado una lista por título, que se puede consultar en el Ateneo, y que indica dónde está ubicada la película, el año de producción, y una clasificación por género. Muchos de los títulos que aparecen, especialmente la producción de la División de Educación de la Comunidad, se encuentran en el Archivo de Imágenes en Movimiento. Algunas permanecen en custodia de su productor y las más recientes (*Angelito mío, Cuentos para despertar*) están a la venta en video. Las proyecciones de los encargados de ambas colecciones, Marisel Flores Carrión del Archivo y Roberto Ramos Perea de Cine Nuestro, contemplan instalar la información en un banco de datos de manera que la misma esté accesible a través de Internet.

Ambas colecciones cuentan con un acervo documental relacionado con el cine en Puerto Rico. El Archivo de Imágenes posee revistas especializadas, artículos de periódicos, carteles, fotografías y libretos. El Archivo también permite y cuenta con facilidades para la duplicación del material fílmico, aunque este servicio se limita estrictamente al material de entidades gubernamentales considerado de dominio público. La colección de videos del Proyecto Cine Nuestro está abierta al público en general que puede examinar cualquiera de las películas del acervo en la biblioteca del Ateneo Puertorriqueño.

A pesar de las limitaciones señaladas, estos esfuerzos resultan encomiables si tomamos en cuenta que ninguna otra institución se ha preocupado por nuestro patrimonio fílmico. El acceso y la utilidad de estos recursos, particularmente para el investigador, dependerán de un control bibliográfico adecuado que permita identificar el material y provea una descripción. En gran medida, esta tarea se encuentra supeditada al reclutamiento o asesoramiento de personal bibliotecario especializado.

BIBLIOGRAFÍA

Almodóvar Ronda, Ramón. 1994. "Archivo de la memoria: el documental, la animación y el cine experimental en Puerto Rico". *Idilio Tropical: la aventura del cine puertorriqueño*. San Juan: Banco Popular de Puerto Rico.

Délano, Jack. 1994. "Mi participación en los comienzos de la División de Educación de la Comunidad". *Idilio Tropical: la aventura del cine puertorriqueño*. San Juan: Banco Popular de Puerto Rico.

García Morales, Joaquín (Kino). 1997. *Cine puertorriqueño, filmografía, fuentes y referencias.* San Juan: Ateneo Puertorriqueño.

Mongil Echandía, Inés y Luis Rosario Albert. 1994. "Cine con un propósito". *Idilio Tropical: la aventura del cine puertorriqueño.* San Juan: Banco Popular de Puerto Rico.

Torres, José Artemio. 1994. "Apaga misiú: los primeros pasos del cine puertorriqueño". *Idilio Tropical: la aventura del cine puertorriqueño.* San Juan: Banco Popular de Puerto Rico.

III. Women and Identity

14. A Bolivian Literary Minority: Women Writers

Nelly S. González

Between 1945 and 1999, Latin American literature witnessed a dramatic explosion in both the volume and quality of literary production. Creative styles developed and flourished during this period which were nourished by the environment before, during, and after the "boom." This surge in literary activity is evidenced by the fact that five Nobel Prizes for Literature were awarded to Latin American writers for work created during this period. Even while this boom was flourishing, women writers were largely ignored by publishers and scholars. When Isabel Allende entered the limelight with her novel *The House of Spirits*, women's literary works began to gain importance among publishers and literary critics.

Literary historians, in analyzing the evolution of Latin American women writers in Spanish America, concur that female authors record their knowledge with a unique vision, both of their immediate surroundings and of the world as a whole. This often relates to how they express their feelings and the constant conflict with their sociocultural position in society.

Lucía Guerra Cunningham in the introduction to her work on Latin American women writers[1] acknowledges progress in the status of women in society today, but states that in spite of these advances, in the specific case of Latin American literature it has not yet reached the importance it deserves. Women's writing and their culture in general are undergoing an important reevaluation and change.

If that is true of the literary corpus by women writers in Latin America, the case of Bolivian literature is even worse, since literary critics, scholars, bibliographers, and compilers of works by women writers seldom include Bolivia in their works. Josep M. Barnadas and Juan José Coy wrote that in Bolivian literature up to 1959 there is a profound symbiosis between the text and the context making it impossible to separate one from the other.[2] Thus, the themes and scope present in its literature range from the mountains through the valleys and tropics, the rural space as well as the urban, life in the mines, social conditions, politics and government, and so on. Anything is a source of inspiration for these literary writers. It is their way to express their feelings.

Bolivian literature was not in the avant-garde of the modernizing process that challenged Latin American writers. Only a couple of writers were known beyond its borders. This explains why in the *Historia de la literatura boliviana*[3] Bolivian women writers could be counted on the fingers of one hand.

The *Encyclopedia of Latin American Literature*[4] is among the most recent works devoted to the region's literature. The editor's note states that one goal was to stimulate "interest in some of the smaller countries of the region such as Ecuador and Bolivia." However, a careful reading in search of Bolivian women writers revealed scant references, mostly in passing. More specific titles such as *Women Writers of Latin America: Intimate Histories*[5] do not include Bolivia at all. Reviewing works that provide information on Bolivian literary history, its writers and their works, and some literary criticism, I found no Bolivian women writers included, with the exception of Adela Zamudio, and maybe a couple more.

The bibliographic tools available for Latin American literature are not scarce; on the contrary, there is a myriad of works, indexes, dictionaries, and other reference sources. The problem arises when scholars want to research the literary production of lesser-known countries. Furthermore, works with titles such as *Latin American Writers* or *Spanish American Women Writers*, which seem to be comprehensive, and where researchers could hope to unequivocally find the information they are looking for, often fail to provide even basic data on these countries. Unfortunately, all these research tools keep repeating the same information about the more prevalent countries, and continue to omit treatment of the less important ones.

For example, in Diane E. Marting's *Spanish American Women Writers: A Bio-Bibliographical Source Book* (1990), an update of the 1987 edition, Bolivia is not represented at all. One might think: Are there no Bolivian literary women? Although the editor states that this work was compiled with the help of numerous scholars and provides the "names of seventy-eight readers who commented on the entries in a cooperative spirit of help and reinforcement rather than one of mere acceptance or rejection,"[6] Bolivian women writers are not included. The only references to Bolivian women writers are made in the chapter "Indian Women Writers of Spanish America," written by Nancy Gray Díaz.[7]

Yet there are several reasons why Bolivian women's literature should be of interest to publishers and scholars. The fact that Bolivia is a multiethnic society in which Aymara and Quechua peoples coexist with populations of Hispanic descent makes multiculturalism an important issue in the country. The testimonies of two indigenous women, Domitila Barrios de Chungara[8] (*Si me permiten hablar*, 1977) and Basilia[9] (*Dos mujeres indígenas*, 1976) have illuminated the role and vision of women within this context. These stories of Domitila and Basilia, as told to Moema Viezzer and June Nash respectively, in which they relate their social and political struggles in Bolivian society, are exemplary of how women negotiate their roles in this complex social environment. Indeed, Domitila sheds light on the organized labor movement and revolutionary politics of the period. In spite of the fact that Gray Díaz devotes a complete chapter to the coming of age of indigenous women's literature, the surface has only been scratched, and only the future will bring to light their contribution to society.

Most of the works by Bolivian women writers share some common political inclinations and denounce in their works the violence that sprang from the social and economic conditions to which they have been submitted. Ironically, this chauvinistic society was one of the few to appoint a female president (Lydia Gueiler). Either directly or indirectly, political and social movements shape and influence the literary expression of a country, and within it, its women writers.

Enrique Finot, describing the history of Bolivian literature, cites Adela Zamudio as one of the "independent" writers of what was known as modernism. Although her life was dedicated to education, it is important to note that her feminism remained "invisible" during the period in which she lived. It manifested itself in the expression of her honest feelings and plight against the unjustifiable treatment of women in society, where she was condemned to fill a secondary role which for her was unworthy of a civilized society.[10] Carmen Castillo[11] states that there is always a moment in the intellectual history of nations when the valiant and loud feminine voice is heard. For Chile it was Gabriela Mistral, and for Bolivia, Adela Zamudio. Born in Cochabamba, Bolivia, in 1854 she led a prolific life dedicated to teaching. Among her writings there are various essays, short stories, and poetry. Perhaps her poem *Nacer hombre*[12] best portrays her philosophy and conviction of her equality, and maybe superiority, toward men. Indeed, Adela Zamudio expresses clearly in this poem her struggle with the "machismo" that was not only inscribed in the culture, but given legitimacy in the country's legislation at that time. It reads:

> Cuánto trabajo ella pasa
> Por corregir la torpeza
> De su esposo, y en la casa,
> (Permitidme que me asombre).
> Tan inepto como fatuo,
> Sigue él siendo la cabeza,
> Porque es hombre!
> Una mujer superior
> En elecciones no vota,
> Y vota el pillo peor.
> (Permitidme que me asombre).
> Que a ella se llame el "ser débil"
> Y a él se le llama el "ser fuerte,"
> Porque es hombre!

Zamudio also wrote short stories. In her own words her best stories are *La reunión de ayer* and *Noche de fiesta*,[13] the latter being also a rebellious critique of her contemporary society. Perhaps the best recognition of her struggle for equal rights for women in society is the fact that in 1980, more than a century later, her grandniece wrote Adela Zamudio's biography.

On occasion, women have been forced to become writers by circumstances outside their control. An interesting example is Julia Urquidi Illanes. When Mario Vargas Llosa published his work *La tía Julia y el escribidor*,[14] in which he recounts his erotic adventures with Urquidi, ten years his senior, she felt compelled to write her own version of the affair. In 1983 she published *Lo que Varguitas no dijo*,[15] literally "what [little] Vargas did not say," later translated into English as *My Life with Mario Vargas Llosa*.[16] This work sheds light not only on Vargas Llosa the man, but also on the creative process and the relationship between an author's personal life and his fiction.

The Unión Nacional de Poetas y Escritores de Cochabamba published its *Primera antología* in 1994.[17] It lists twenty-five writers, nine of them women. This representative sample, in which women make up 36 percent of the total, is encouraging and signals the changing times.

Fire from the Andes[18] reflects a work of love by the compilers, who gathered the information and translated into English the short stories of nine contemporary authors included in this anthology. Furthermore, they provide a short biography and list of works by each writer, with a more extensive bibliography at the end, including works by women writers. Because of the accessibility that the language provides, this work opens a great path for the dissemination of Bolivian women writers and their literary works, and it will serve as a catalyst for awakening interest among the literary community. Also, it will help to introduce high school students to the literature of the country. In addition, Kathy S. Leonard compiled an *Index to Translated Short Fiction by Latin American Women in English Language Anthologies*[19] and in it there is a selected list of Bolivian women writers and their works.

Marjorie Agosín[20] clearly demonstrates the lack of attention that Bolivian women writers had to endure, when she states that when invited to write the foreword for *Fire from the Andes* she "felt great enthusiasm, but at the same time, great fear. Enthusiastic at the possibility of collaborating in the effort to make the silenced voices of Latin American authors known, voices often destined for oblivion. Bolivia, Ecuador, and Peru have remained somewhat anonymous, and their literature largely unknown."

The *Bio-bibliografía boliviana*[21] is the best source for books published in Bolivia and by Bolivian writers. Published yearly, it is an excellent up-to-date bibliography arranged by author. It includes the imprints of the year and journals. Since Bolivia does not have a national bibliography, through the years, this work has served that purpose very well. Although not very well organized (i.e., author, subject, title), it provides brief information about the authors and their works. This is where I found the authors that I present in this paper. This is not a comprehensive and complete list of women writers, but it is a start and a step toward achieving bibliographic control of Bolivian literary women. The purpose of this paper is to stimulate interest among scholars and students in Bolivian women's literature. It is hoped that that this will encourage Bolivian women writers to continue producing their works, knowing that they are not being ignored by the literary community. To this end, I have reviewed the reference works dedicated to Latin American and Bolivian literature for the past fifty years, and I have compiled a bibliography of works by Bolivian women writers. I hope it will serve to open the road for the cultivation of a literary environment that will offer variety, vitality, and promise for future women writers and scholars.

NOTES

1. Lucía Guerra Cunningham, *Splintering Darkness: Latin American Women Writers in Search of Themselves* (Pittsburgh, PA: Latin American Literary Review Press, 1990), p. 8.

2. Josep P. Barnadas and Juan José Coy, *Realidad sociohistórica y expresión literaria en Bolivia* (Cochabamba, Bolivia: Los Amigos del Libro, 1977), pp.11–12.

3. Enrique Finot, *Historia de la literatura boliviana* (La Paz, Bolivia: Gisbert, 1964).

4. Verity Smith, ed., *Encyclopedia of Latin American Literature* (London, Chicago: Fitzroy Dearborn, 1997), p. ix.

5. Magdalena García Pinto, *Women Writers of Latin America: Intimate Histories,* Trudy Balch and Magdalena García Pinto, tr. (Austin: University of Texas Press, 1991).

6. Diane E. Marting, ed., *Spanish American Women Writers: A Bio-Bibliographical Source Book* (Westport, CT: Greenwood Press, 1990), pp. xi–xii.

7. Marting, pp. 546–547.

8. Domitila Barrios de Chungara, *Si me permiten hablar: Testimonio de Domitila, una mujer de las minas de Bolivia* (Mexico: Siglo Veintiuno, 1977).

9. Basilia, in *Dos mujeres indígenas* (Mexico: Instituto Indigenista Interamericano, 1976).

10. Finot, pp. 158–159.

11. Carmen Castillo, *Una visión personal de la poesía boliviana* (La Paz, Bolivia: Universidad Mayor de San Andrés, 1967), p. 53.

12. Finot, pp. 159–160.

13. Gabriela Taborga de Villarroel, *La verdadera Adela Zamudio* (Cochabamba, Bolivia: Editorial Canelas, 1980), p. 343.

14. Mario Vargas Llosa, *La tía Julia y el escribidor* (Barcelona: Seix Barral, 1977).

15. Julia Urquidi Illanes, *Lo que Varguitas no dijo* (La Paz: Khana Cruz, 1983).

16. Julia Urquidi Illanes, *My Life with Mario Vargas Llosa* (New York: P. Lang, 1988).

17. Unión Nacional de Poetas y Escritores de Cochabamba, *Primera antología* (Cochabamba, Bolivia: The Union, 1994).

18. Susan E. Benner and Kathy S. Leonard, *Fire from the Andes* (Albuquerque: University of New Mexico Press, 1998), pp. 3–50.

19. Kathy S. Leonard, comp., *Index to Translated Short Fiction by Latin American Women in English Language Anthologies* (Westport, CT: Greenwood, 1997), p. 58.

20. Benner, p. vii.

21. *Bio-bibliografía boliviana* (Cochabamba, Bolivia: Los Amigos del Libro, 1975–).

SELECTED BIBLIOGRAPHY OF BOLIVIAN WOMEN WRITERS

Abrego, Guadalupe. *Los Cruceños y la cultura: Un diagnóstico de la Cultura en Santa Cruz*. Santa Cruz: Edición Municipal, 1990. 399p.

Aguirre de Ballivián, Virginia. *Poemas: Club del Libro Número Dos "Virginia Aguirre de Ballivián.*" Cochabamba, Bolivia: Editorial Serrano, 1993. 282p.

_____. *Poemas a una sombra de su sombra (Breviario)*. Cochabamba, Bolivia: Editorial Universitaria, 1971. 63p.

_____. *Waldo Ballivián, legendaria figura de lealtad*. Cochabamba, Bolivia: Editorial Canelas, 1976. 140p.

Aguirre Gainsborg de Méndez, Aída. *Instantes de una vida*. La Paz, Bolivia: Editorial Offset Boliviana, 1995. 170p.

_____. *Teatro*. La Paz, Bolivia: Editorial Offset Boliviana, 1995. 304p.

Alemán de Uribe, Sonia. *El baúl de los recuerdos: Cuentos*. La Paz, Bolivia: Editorial Don Bosco, 1990. 81p.

_____. *Potosí—Por siempre inmortal: Poemas*. La Paz, Bolivia: Garza Azul, 1991. 62p.

Aliaga Raygada, Daisy. *Un recuerdo en la distancia: Poemas*. La Paz, Bolivia: E. Burillo, 1968. 168p. [Also in Microfilm.]

Amelunge de Lavayén, Paquita. *Hilvanando recuerdos*. Santa Cruz, Bolivia: Sociedad Cruceña de Escritores, 1994. 121p.

Anaya de Urquidi, Mercedes. *Evocaciones de mi vida y mi tierra*. Cochabamba, Bolivia: Editorial Canelas, 1965. 113p.

Andrade S., Lupe. *La tía Eduviges y otras historias*. La Paz, Bolivia: Ediciones Vaca Sagrada, 1993. 178p.

Antelo Aguilar, Peggy. *Como veo La Paz, mi ciudad*. La Paz, Bolivia: Casa Municipal de la Cultura "Franz Tamayo," 1982. 73p.

_____. *Simón Bolívar niño (y otras páginas)*. Biblioteca Popular Boliviana de Ultima Hora, 1979. 153p.

Anzoátegui de Campero, Lindaura. *Don Manuel Ascencio Padilla: Episodio histórico*. La Paz, Bolivia: Librería Editorial Juventud, 1976. 172p.

Aranzaes V. de Butrón, Emma. *Arminda: Historia de una vida polifacética*. La Paz, Bolivia: Gramma Impresión, 1990. 77p.

_____. *Narraciones verídicas*. La Paz, Bolivia: Impr. y Librería Renovación, 1986. 89p.

_____. *Novela infantil: Vivir con alegría*. La Paz, Bolivia: Industrias Gráficas "Sagitario," 1990. 106p.

_____. *Para tí, mujer boliviana*. La Paz, Bolivia: Empresa Editora Proinsa, 1980. 117p.

Arnal Franck, Ximena. *Visiones de un espacio*. Bolivia: Ediciones Piedra Libre, 1994. 99p.

Arze, Silvia. *Mujeres en rebelión: La presencia femenina en las rebeliones de Charcas del siglo XVIII*. La Paz, Bolivia: Ministerio de Desarrollo Humano, 1997. 158p.

Avendaño Siles, Dilma. *Pedrito*. Potosí, Bolivia: División de Extensión Universitaria, U.B.T.F., 1976 or 1977. 27p.

Avila, Silvia Mercedes. *Tu nominas los sueños*. La Paz, Bolivia: Empresa Editorial "Universo," 1980. 11p.

Ayllón Soria, Virginia. *Búsquedas: Cuatro relatos y algunos versos*. Potosí, Bolivia: Artes Gráficas Potosí, 1996. 53p.

_____. *Las campeonas: Mujer y deporte en la prensa nacional 1991*. La Paz, Bolivia: Centro de Información y Desarrollo de la Mujer, 1992. 42p.

_____. *De tanto haber andado yo ya soy otra: Bibliografía de la mujer Boliviana, 1986–1991*. La Paz, Bolivia: Centro Documental de la Mujer "Adela Zamudio," 1991. 110p.

_____. *Gritos sin eco: Violencia contra la mujer en la prensa boliviana*. La Paz, Bolivia: Centro de Información y Desarrollo de la Mujer, 1989. 38p.

_____. *La memoria de las ciudades: Bibliografía urbana en Bolivia, 1952–1991*. La Paz, Bolivia: CED-ILDIS, con el auspicio de la Honorable Alcaldía Municipal de La Paz, 1992. 474p.

_____. "Prayer to the Goddesses." In *Fire from the Andes*. Susan E. Benner and Kathy S. Leonard, eds. Albuquerque: University of New Mexico Press, 1997. Pp. 4–6.

_____. *Volar entre sonidos, colores y palabras: (Mujer y actividad cultural en la prensa boliviana 1991)*. La Paz, Bolivia: CIDEM, 1992. 112p.

Balcazar Rossell, Gaby. *En el recodo del tiempo*. Santa Cruz de la Sierra, Bolivia: Industrias Gráficas, 1993. 66p.

Bedregal de Conitzer, Yolanda. *Almadía*. La Paz, Bolivia: Editorial "Juventud," 1977. 114p.

_____. *Antología de la poesía boliviana*. La Paz, Bolivia: Editorial Los Amigos del Libro, 1991. 94p.

_____. *Antología mínima*. La Paz, Bolivia: Editorial El Sigma, 1968. 280p.

_____. *Ayllu: El altiplano boliviano*. La Paz, Bolivia: Museo Nacional de Etnografía y Folklore, Los Amigos del Libro, 1984. 94p.

_____. *Bajo el oscuro sol*. La Paz, Bolivia: Editorial Los Amigos del Libro, 1991. 241p. Premio Nacional de la Novela "Erich Guttentag."

_____. *Ecos*. La Paz, Bolivia: Editorial "Juventud," 1977. 76p.

_____. *Escrito*. Quito, Ecuador: Printer Graphic, 1994. 315p.

_____. *Nadir*. La Paz, Bolivia: Editorial "Juventud," 1977. 107p.

_____. *Naufragio*. La Paz, Bolivia: Editorial "Juventud," 1977. 77p.

_____. *I [Primera] antología poética*. Caracas, Venezuela: [s.n], 1961. 64p.

_____. *Poemar*. La Paz, Bolivia: Editorial "Juventud," 1977. 92p.

_____. *Poesía de Bolivia, de la época precolombina*. Buenos Aires, Argentina: Editorial Universitaria, 1969. 119p.

_____. "The Traveler." In *Fire from the Andes.* Susan E. Benner and Kathy S. Leonard, eds. Albuquerque: University of New Mexico Press, 1997. Pp. 8–13.

Bruzonic, Erika. *Historias inofensivas.* La Paz, Bolivia: Impresiones Arellano, 1995. 83p.

_____. *Cegados por la luz.* La Paz, Bolivia: Editorial Don Bosco, 1992. 85p.

Bruzonic, Erika. *El color de la memoria.* La Paz, Bolivia: Editorial Don Bosco, 1989. 106p.

_____. *Ecos de guerra.* La Paz, Bolivia: Editorial Don Bosco, 1987. 79p.

_____. "Inheritance." In *Fire from the Andes.* Susan E. Benner and Kathy S. Leonard, eds. Albuquerque: University of New Mexico Press, 1997. Pp. 15–16.

Bruzzone de Bloch, Olga. *Hondo, muy hondo: Poemas.* La Paz, Bolivia: Don Bosco, 1960. 99p.

_____. *Torbellina de horas: Novela.* La Paz, Bolivia: Editorial Los Amigos del Libro, 1984. 277p. Colección Premio novela "Erich Guttentag."

Bullón, Emma Alina. *Espiral de Alivio: Sonetos y romances.* La Paz, Bolivia: "Unidas," 1978. 121p.

Cajías, Lupe. *Don Flavio Machicado Viscarra: 1898–1986.* La Paz, Bolivia: Ediciones Gráficas, 1994. 106p.

_____. *Valentina: Historia de una rebeldía.* Cochabamba, Bolivia: Editorial Los Amigos del Libro, 1998. 252p. Besides the above works, she has also published extensively on politics and related subjects.

Calvimontes de Rodríguez, Velia. *Abre la tapa—y destapa un cuento.* Cochabamba, Bolivia: Oficialía Mayor de Cultura, 1991. 65p.

Canedo de Camacho, Georgette. *Creeis en fantasmas?* La Paz, Bolivia: Imprenta Editora Andegrafía, 1989. 169p.

_____. *Creeis en fantasmas? No, pero les temo: Ensayos literarios.* La Paz, Bolivia: Summa Artis, 1991. 190p.

_____. *Letra desleída.* La Paz, Bolivia: Ediciones Casa de la Cultura: Alcaldía Municipal, 1993. 77p.

Cárdenas Pacheco, Ruth. *Poesías.* La Paz, Bolivia: Casa Municipal de la Cultura "Franz Tamayo," 1977. 322p.

_____. *Telegramas a Fermín.* La Paz, Bolivia: Casa Municipal de la Cultura "Franz Tamayo," 1979. 57p.

Cardona Torrico, Alcira. *Carcajada de estaño y otros poemas.* La Paz, Bolivia: Ediciones Arcoiris, 1949. 16p.

_____. *De paso por la tierra: Cuento.* La Paz, Bolivia: Ediciones IPRA. 24p.

_____. *Letanía de las moscas: Tragedia en tres actos.* La Paz, Bolivia: Ediciones IPRA, 1980. 149p.

_____. *Mesa redonda sobre el problema del litoral boliviano.* La Paz, Bolivia: Municipalidad de La Paz, 1966. 325p.

_____. *"Positivismo generacional de Gesta Bárbara."* La Paz, Bolivia: Separata de la revista *Khana* no. 36, septiembre 1962. 13p.

_____. *Rayo y simiente.* La Paz, Bolivia: Editorial Benavides, 1995. 172p.

_____. *Tormenta en el Ande: Cuatro cantos.* La Paz, Bolivia: s.n., 1967. 103p.

Casazola Mendoza, Matilde. *El espejo del ángel: Una canción y cuatro poemas.* La Paz, Bolivia: Universidad Mayor de San Andrés, 1991.

_____. *La noche abrupta.* La Paz, Bolivia: Universidad Mayor de San Andrés, 1996.

_____. *Obra poética.* Sucre, Bolivia: s.n., 1996. 969p.

_____. *Poesía y naturaleza = Poesie und natur.* Crista Fabry de Orías, tr. Sucre, Bolivia: Instituto Cultural Boliviano-Alemán, 1993.

Castellanos de Ríos, Ada. *Buenos días, señorita!* Potosí, Bolivia: Departamento de Extensión Universitaria de la Universidad Boliviana, 1976. 129p.

_____. *Teatro boliviano.* La Paz, Bolivia: Instituto Boliviano de Cultura, 1977. 80p.

_____. *Un viernes de Miguelito.* Potosí, Bolivia: Universidad Boliviana "Tomás Frías," 1976. 28p.

Charbonneau de Villagómez, Nicole. *Antología de autores cruceños: Desde el siglo XVII hasta nuestros días.* Santa Cruz, Bolivia: Editorial Casa de la Cultura Raúl Otero Reiche, 1988. 265p.

Contreras, Pilar. *Existencias insurrectas: La mujer en la cultura.* La Paz, Bolivia: Ministerio de Desarrollo Humano; Secretaría de Asuntos de Género, 1997. 448p.

Dávalos Arze, Gladys. *Corazones de arroz: Sátiras.* Cochabamba, Bolivia: Colorgraf Rodríguez, 1989. 104p.

_____. *Piel de bruma: Poemas.* La Paz, Bolivia: Hisbol, 1995. 112p.

Dorado de Revilla Valenzuela, Elsa. *Las bacterias no hacen huelga: Cuentos.* La Paz, Bolivia: s.n., 1994. 95p.

_____. *Filón de ensueño: Cuentos.* La Paz, Bolivia: 1977. 140p.

_____. *La Libertadora Juana Azurdui de Padilla: Guerrillera de la independencia de América.* La Paz, Bolivia: Gráfica Alianza, 1980. 53p.

_____. *"The Parrot."* In *Fire from the Andes.* Susan E. Benner and Kathy S. Leonard, eds. Albuquerque: University of New Mexico Press, 1997. Pp. 26–31.

Estenssoro, María Virginia. *Cuentos y otras páginas.* La Paz, Bolivia: Editorial Los Amigos del Libro, 1988. 149p.

_____. *Ego inútil.* Cochabamba, Bolivia: Editorial Los Amigos del Libro, 1971. 83p.

_____. *Memorias de Villa Rosa.* La Paz, Bolivia: Editorial Los Amigos del Libro, 1976. 167p.

_____. *Obras completas.* La Paz, Bolivia: Editorial Los Amigos del Libro, 1988.

Estenssoro, Quica. *Violeta de oro: Cuentos.* La Paz, Bolivia: Escuela Tipográfica Salesiana, 1925. 170p.

Estrada Sainz, Milena. *Corola de Agua.* Oruro, Bolivia: Imp. de la Universidad Técnica de Oruro, 1946. Unpaged.

Fajardo de Perelman, Leticia. *Pampa, metal y sangre: Poemas.* La Paz, Bolivia: Editorial La Paz, 1959. 118p.

Fernandois de Ballón, Marina. *Cartas a la vida.* La Paz, Bolivia: Editorial Los Amigos del Libro, 1992. 274p.

Ferrufino Llach, Clara. *Pensamiento filosófico de Franz Tamayo*. La Paz, Bolivia: Producciones CIMA, 1995. 188p.

_____. *Tamayo y el hombre boliviano*. La Paz, Bolivia: Editorial Gisbert, 1987. 203p.

Flores Saavedra, Mery. *Bruma* [microform]. Potosí, Bolivia: Editorial Potosí, 1958. 70p.

_____. *Poesías*. Potosí, Bolivia: Departamento de la Cultura de la Universidad Mayor y Autónoma, 1965. 14p.

_____. *Poemas de la sombra*. La Paz, Bolivia: Ediciones de la Casa de la Cultura "Franz Tamayo," 1975. 35p.

_____. *Los silencios de Dios*. La Paz, Bolivia: Ediciones de la Casa de la Cultura "Franz Tamayo," 1988. 65p.

_____. *Sonetos*. La Paz, Bolivia: Editorial "16 de Julio," 1965. 39p.

Fortún, Julia Elena. *Antologia de Navidad*. La Paz, Bolivia: Alcaldía Municipal, 1956. 77p.

_____. *La danza de los diablos*. La Paz, Bolivia: Ministerio de Educación y Bellas Artes, Oficialía Mayor de la Cultura Nacional, 1961. 108p.

Garnica, Blanca. *De la tierra y de las preguntas*. Cochabamba, Bolivia: [s.n.], 1992. 36p.

_____. *La razón del musgo: Poemas de amor*. Cochabamba, Bolivia: Ediciones Altiplano, 1986. 73p.

_____. *Retama y lombriz*. Cochabamba, Bolivia: Senda, 1986. 65p.

_____. *Siempre el amor*. Cochabamba, Bolivia: Ediciones Puente, 1993. 109p.

_____. *Vastago del sol*. Cochabamba, Bolivia: Ediciones Altiplano, 1993. 35p.

_____. *La vocal de la higuera*. Cochabamba, Bolivia: Ediciones Altiplano, 1986. 83p.

Gutiérrez, Marcela. *Diario de campaña: Cuentos eróticos*. La Paz, Bolivia: Ediciones del Ventarrón, 1994. 85p.

_____. "The Feathered Serpent." In *Fire from the Andes*. Susan E. Benner and Kathy S. Leonard, eds. Albuquerque: University of New Mexico Press, 1997. Pp. 33–38. She also works as a journalist.

Gutiérrez Aguilar, Raquel. *Las armas de la utopía: Marxismo, provocaciones heréticas*. La Paz, Bolivia: Punto Cero, 1996. 350p.

Jiménez Bullain, Maritza. *Podemos ser—desde nosotras mismas*. La Paz, Bolivia: Fundación La Paz, 1996. 54p.

Kavlin, Alicia, and Susana Kavlin. *Susurros*. Mexico: Federación Editorial Mexicana, 1977. 62p.

_____. *Holocausto: Poemas*. La Paz, Bolivia: Editorial Los Amigos del Libro, 1975. 87p.

Kuramoto Medina, Beatriz, and Estela Bringas Cruz. *Fuego de tiempos*. Santa Cruz, Bolivia: Editorial Pynda, 1992. 135p.

_____. "The Agreement." In *Fire from the Andes*. Susan E. Benner and Kathy S. Leonard, eds. Albuquerque: University of New Mexico Press, 1997. Pp. 40–43.

Loayza Millán, Beatriz. "The Mirror." In *Fire from the Andes*. Susan E. Benner and Kathy S. Leonard, eds. Albuquerque: University of New Mexico Press, 1997. Pp. 44–47.

Maldonado, Clara Isabel. *Arcoiris de sueños = Rainbow of Dreams*. Sydney, Australia: Cervantes Publ., 1993. 93p. Poems and prose in Spanish with selections in English translated by the author.

Melgar de Ipiña, Rosa. *El amor y la gloria del Libertador*. Sucre, Bolivia: s.n., 1993. 432p.

_____. *La ciudad crece*. La Paz, Bolivia: Los Amigos del Libro, 1968. 280p.

_____. *Lo sabía: 26 cuentos*. La Paz, Bolivia: Editorial Educacional, 1988. 244p.

_____. *Maura: Novela*. La Paz, Bolivia: s.n., 1964. 359p.

Monje Landívar, Mary Luz. *Abalorios*. La Paz, Bolivia: [s.n.], 1967. 87p.

_____. *Dulce y amargo*. Oruro, Bolivia: Editorial Universitaria, 1968. 33p. Also available in microform.

Monroy, María Eugenia. *Ensueño entre sombras, poemas*. La Paz, Bolivia: 1967. 49p.

Montenegro, Raquel. *Cuentos bolivianos*. La Paz, Bolivia: Alfaguara, 1966. 190p.

Nava, Paz Nery. *Distancias interiores: Poemas*. Santiago?, Chile: Ediciones Renovación, 1965?. 44p.

_____. *Lina: Novela*. La Paz, Bolivia: Librería "Renovación," 1971. 174p.

Palacios Parada, María del Rosario. *Volemos al infinito*. Santa Cruz, Bolivia: Offset Landívar, 1995. 70p.

Patiño de Murillo, Blanca. *Himnos y canciones en Aymara*. La Paz, Bolivia: Imprenta Visión, 1978. 30p.

Paz, Blanca Elena. *Breve poésia cruceña*. Santa Cruz, Bolivia: s.n., 1991.

_____. "The Light." In *Fire from the Andes*. Susan E. Benner and Kathy S. Leonard, eds. Albuquerque: University of New Mexico Press, 1997. Pp. 49–50.

_____. *Teorema*. Santa Cruz, Bolivia: Litera Viva, 1995. 146p.

Peña de Rodríguez, Martha. *Hoy, mañana y siempre*. Santa Cruz, Bolivia: Sociedad Cruceña de Escritores, 1994. 102p.

Peralta Soruco, Pepita. *Espigas al viento*. Santa Cruz, Bolivia: Editorial Serrano, 1979. 112p.

Quiroga, Giancarla de. *Aurora: A Novel*. Seattle, WA: Women in Translation, 1999. 178p.

_____. *"Une Chambre à Soi" à Saint Nazaire*. Saint-Nazaire, France: M.E.E.T., 1995. 77p.

_____. *De angustias e ilusiones: Cuentos*. Cochabamba, Bolivia: Editorial Serrano, 1990. 59p. Also published in English: "Of Anguish and Illusions." In *Fire from the Andes*. Susan E. Benner and Kathy S. Leonard, eds. Albuquerque: University of New Mexico Press, 1997. Pp. 18–24.

_____. *La discriminación de la mujer en los textos escolares de lectura*. La Paz, Bolivia: Ministerio de Desarrollo Humano; Cochabamba, Bolivia: Universidad Mayor de San Simón, 1995. 93p.

_____. *La flor de La Candelaria*. Cochabamba, Bolivia: Editorial Los Amigos del Libro, 1990. 188p.

_____. *Los mundos de "Los deshabitados"*: (Estudio de la novela de Marcelo Quiroga Santa Cruz). Cochamba, Bolivia: Offset Casema, 1980. 125p.

Quiroga, María Soledad. *Ciudad blanca*. La Paz, Bolivia: P.A.P., 1993. 133p.

_____. *Recuento del agua*. La Paz, Bolivia: Plural Editores, 1995.

_____. *Strengthening Voluntary Environmental Organizations in Bolivia*. La Paz, Bolivia: The Office, 1992. 39p.

Richardson, Hermila Armida Clemente. *Encadenada en infernal drama de violencia*. La Paz, Bolivia: H. Richardson, 1995. 426p.

Rivera Cusicanqui, Silvia, and Denise Arnold. *Ser mujer indígena, chola o birlocha en la Bolivia postcolonial de los años 90*. La Paz, Bolivia: Ministerio de Desarrollo Humano, 1996. 451p. Most of her works are in the social sciences with occasional publications in literature.

Rizo A. de Alfonso, Fanny Luz. *"Niño grande, niño niño" : Poemario*. Santa Cruz de la Sierra, Bolivia: Casa de la Cultura, 1989. 85p.

Sánchez de Hoss, Bertha, et al. *Estos cuatro*. Cochabamba, Bolivia: Vientos Nuevos, 1976.

Schulze Arana, Beatriz. *En el diente de la noche*. Madrid, Spain: s.n., 1951.

_____. *Luces mágicas*. La Paz, Bolivia: Editorial Juventud, 1986. 104p. She writes extensively children's literature.

Suárez de Antelo, Berta. *Ilusión mágica: Poemas infantiles*. Santa Cruz de la Sierra, Bolivia: Sociedad Cruceña de Escritores, 1994. 97p.

Taborga de Requena, Lola. *Cuadros incásicos*. La Paz, Bolivia: Editorial Don Bosco, 1952. 159p.

Vallejo de Bolívar, Gaby. *Encuentra tu ángel y tu demonio*. Cochabamba, Bolivia: Editorial Los Amigos del Libro, 1998. 174p.

_____. *Leer: Un placer escondido*. Bolivia: Ediciones Puente, 1994. 149p.

Vásquez de Arizcurinaga, Olga. *Poemario para todos*. La Paz, Bolivia: Tall Gráf. de Mundy Color, 1993. 90p.

_____. *Tres figuras del modernismo latinoamericano*. La Paz, Bolivia: Librería y Editorial Puerta del Sol, 1990. 99p.

Von Borries, Edith. *En un atardecer violeta: Poemas y cuentos*. La Paz, Bolivia: Editorial e Imprenta Gramma Impresión, 1988.

Wilde Lavayén de Disch, Güiomar. *Legado de libertad*. Cochabamba, Bolivia: Editorial Serrano, 1992. 111p.

_____. *Relatos bolivianos*. Cochabamba, Bolivia: Editorial Serrano, 1986. 192p.

Zamudio, Adela. *Cuentos breves*. La Paz, Bolivia: Difusión, 1975. 155p.

_____. *Noche de Fiesta*. La Paz, Bolivia: Ediciones Isla, 1983.

_____. *Peregrinando: Poesías*. Cochabamba, Bolivia: Editorial Canelas, 1965. 191p.

_____. *Redon y Rondin: Cuento*. La Paz, Bolivia: Ediciones ISLA, 1976. 15p.

Zapata Parrilla, Norah. *De las estrellas y el silencio*. La Paz, Bolivia: H. Municipalidad de La Paz, 1975. 100p.

_____. *Diálogo en el acuario*. Cochabamba, Bolivia: Ediciones Casa de los Pueblos, 1985. 29p.

_____. *Gémenis en invierno*. La Paz, Bolivia: Editorial Casa Municipal de la Cultura Franz Tamayo, 1978. 79p.

15. Memory and Identity in Selected French Caribbean Women Writers: Maryse Condé and Simone Schwarz-Bart

Marian Goslinga

At a recent conference sponsored by Florida International University's Women's Studies Center, the keynote address was delivered by Marjorie Agosín, noted writer and human rights activist originally from Chile and author of more than twenty books of fiction, poetry, memoirs, and essays. Her work ranges from a book on Chilean women during the Pinochet era, to fiction about "women who only desire to live a good life," to collections on Latin American women writers and artists, as well as two highly regarded family memoirs.

The presentation was billed as the Minerva Bernardino Keynote Address in honor of the feminist from the Dominican Republic who died at the age of ninety-one. Bernardino was one of only four women to sign the Charter of the United Nations (the others being Eleanor Roosevelt from the United States, Jean McKenzie from New Zealand, Evdokia Uralova from the Soviet Union, and Ellen Wilkinson from Great Britain) and was a founding member of the U.N. Commission on the Status of Women. At the Charter Conference in San Francisco in 1945, it was she who insisted that the document include the phrase "to ensure respect for human rights and freedoms without discrimination against race, sex, condition or creed." She chaired the Inter-American Commission on Women and is remembered as an honored leader of Acción Feminista Dominicana.

Agosín's presentation, "A Passion for Memory: Women Writers in Latin America," dealt with some of the issues facing contemporary authors throughout the region. Colonialism, dependency, gender, and class friction are but some of the realities of everyday life across the border. She pointed out that, despite these obstacles, the women's movement is alive and well in most Latin American countries and that it is the writers who can most often be found on the front lines of any cause dedicated to improving women's lives.

Agosín traced this vigorous and committed role of Latin America's women writers to the concept of "memory"—the ability to remember the past, to use reality for their own purposes, and to create a new sense of engagement and continuity in their fiction. Past experiences—no matter how traumatic—should not be forgotten and should be preserved with the same veneration awarded the present. Claribel Alegría (El Salvador) and Elena Poniatowska (Mexico) are but two examples of this contemporary trend, according to Agosín.

In the case of Caribbean women writers, the concept of "memory" is strong and invigorated, to a certain extent, by the issue of race. In all four major language areas in the region, women use "memory"—collective or individual—to trace and return to the past in search of their true identity. They go back to the era of slavery, the legacy of an African homeland, and the invisible scars of displacement, captivity, and exile to tell their story. Race is a powerful ingredient and is frequently reflected in the use of "Creole" as the language of choice. Indeed, race and language have become close allies in the quest for cultural identity.

The next section of this paper addresses the related issues of "memory" and "identity" through the eyes and in the works of selected Caribbean women writers, specifically writers from the French Caribbean—in particular the island of Guadeloupe. Nowhere, I believe, has the women's search for some kind of separate "identity" made greater inroads or has had greater influence than in the small Caribbean island known as Karukéra (the island of the beautiful waters) in pre-Columbian days.

It was a French Caribbean author Aimé Césaire, from neighboring Martinique, who in the first half of the twentieth century—together with Guyanese Léon-Gontran Damas and Sengalese Léopold Sedar Senghor—developed the theory of Négritude while studying in Paris. At the core of Négritude was the exaltation of an African cultural identity long repressed and despised in the West Indies, where the assumption of white superiority over black was a basic tenet of the institution of slavery. Césaire's key text of 1939, *Cahier d'un retour au pays natal (Return to My Native Land)*, gave poetic form to the yearning for reconciliation with ancestral Africa. Its searing text became the cornerstone of modern Francophone West Indian literature, and Césaire's theme of black cultural exile was picked up by many writers concerned with the search for identity. Writers from all parts of the Caribbean—Spanish, English, French, and Dutch—raised the doctrine to an absolute truth and lingered on it incessantly.

However, within the relatively short span of nineteen years, this privileged position which Césaire had accorded to Africa—a step intended as a corrective to Europe's long dismissal of African civilization—was challenged and opposed on the grounds that it encouraged West Indians to bypass their own country in their quest for spiritual roots.

Hence, it was in 1958 that another French Caribbean academic, Edouard Glissant, brought forth the concept of Antillanité, which offered another interpretation of cultural identity—one more tuned in to geographical reality and historical truth. Viewing the recovery of an African identity as a practical impossibility owing to the intervening, alienating centuries of slavery, Glissant preferred to focus his attention not on a distant, imagined continent but on the real country of his birth—Martinique. Rather than a total emotional affiliation with Africa, Antillanité instead sought to incorporate the history and traditions pertaining to the despised institution of slavery and all its accompanying evils. Négritude was not repudiated; rather, it was adapted and adjusted to conform to the Caribbean reality. For Glissant, therefore, the real issue became one of authentication rather than denial—Négritude was fused into Antillanité not only to provide a historically correct basis for identity theories but to give it a stamp of legitimacy as well. In founding the journal *Acoma* in the early 1970s, he initiated a forum for a lively psychological and socioeconomic debate dealing with the new doctrine and its implications for Martinique and Guadeloupe.

This Glissantian insistence on the value of history despite the imperfections of "memory" has had a marked effect upon succeeding generations of novelists, dramatists, and essayists in the French Caribbean. The two women writers I have chosen to discuss here—Maryse Condé and Simone Schwarz-Bart—are both from the French Caribbean island of Guadeloupe and, in their literary works, best exemplify this cultural transition from Césairian Négritude to Glissantian Antillanité.

Maryse Condé

Maryse Condé was born in 1937 in Pointe-à-Pitre, Guadeloupe, the eldest in a family of eight children (four boys and four girls). At the young age of sixteen, she left her native island to continue her studies in France where, in 1959, she married Mamadou Condé, an actor from Africa. Soon afterward, the newlyweds moved to Africa—the Ivory Coast—and Condé taught school for a year in Bingerville. After the disintegration of her marriage, she set out on her own for Ghana. Yet she was not happy, and in the 1970s she left Africa and returned to France where, in 1975, she earned a doctorate in comparative literature from the Sorbonne. In 1982 she married Richard Philcox, who was to become the English translator of the majority of her novels. Since then, she has been back to Guadeloupe but is currently residing in the United States teaching at Columbia University in New York. Condé has received many honors and awards and is generally regarded as one of the most criticized and complicated as well as one of the most prolific writers the Caribbean has produced—eleven novels over twenty years.

The work of Maryse Condé not only highlights the tensions in Caribbean culture between traditional and modern values but those among ethnic groups and between the sexes as well. She combines a representative view of a Caribbean writer's specific concerns with a postmodern view of literature as a multicultural, polymorphous intersection. It has been argued that Condé bypasses the conventional notions of Antillanité in favor of affirming her own particular style, selectively choosing one or the other idea at her discretion. A careful analysis of the chronology of her literary production proves otherwise and places her firmly within the parameters set by Glissant. For Condé, the

concept of "memory"—an integral part of Antillanité—is of the utmost importance as she carefully weaves together personal experiences and meticulous
historical documentation to develop plot and style in her fiction. Within the
context of the complex and traumatic West Indian heritage of slavery, colonization, and assimilation, her fictional characters are searching for an identity
which reflects that of a larger community. And as a black woman novelist from
a geographically, culturally, and politically marginal world, Condé self-consciously attempts to represent the interrelated issues of race, gender, and class.
With this is mind, it is possible to divide Condé's works into three distinct
stages chronicling this trajectory from Négritude to Antillanité.

In the first stage of Maryse Condé's writing, the influence of Césairian
Négritude is clearly dominant as references to Africa are everywhere and the
return to the past is her main source of inspiration. With *Hérémakhonon* (which
ironically means "welcome home" in Malinké) and *Une saison à Rihata (A
Season in Rihata)*, Veronica and Marie-Hélène, the two female protagonists
(both from Guadeloupe), are in search of their African roots. Veronica seeks in
Africa an elusive sense of belonging, but finds instead a continent torn by violence, ambition, opportunism, and lost hope. Marie-Hélène, married to Zek
and living in the sleepy African town of Rihata with their six daughters,
becomes involved in a variety of intrigues, corruption, and power struggles.
Mirroring the antinomies of their colonial backgrounds, neither is able to define
a role for herself on the African soil and to break free from a Westernized
frame of reference.

The quest for the African past is also the main focus of *Ségou (Segu)*, the
two-volume saga of the mythical Bambara empire of eighteenth-century Segu.
In this award-winning best-seller, Condé re-creates a high civilization of a pre-
colonial Africa that practiced slavery well before the Europeans and entertained extensive contacts with the Christian and Islamic worlds.

After *Ségou*, Condé entered the second stage of her writing by resolutely
turning to the Americas and the African diaspora with *Moi, Tituba, sorcière
noire de Salem (I, Tituba, Black Witch of Salem)*, a historical subject which
begins her series of fictional works set in the New World. The novel's female
protagonist, Tituba, asserts her presence and her role within the puritanical and
racist U.S. society of the seventeenth century, as well as within the institution
of sugarcane plantations on the Caribbean island of Barbados. Tituba's first-
person narrative—the story of her escape from domination by colonial and
patriarchal forces—allows Condé to rewrite a new Caribbean history from a
woman-centered point of view.

In *La vie scélérate (The Tree of Life)*, Condé proceeds one step further and
finally returns to Guadeloupe where, as she herself has said in a recent interview,
she comes to terms with her quest and is at peace with herself. In this stage of
her development, she has become convinced that being black is no longer a historical appendage but an ideological construction. Criticizing Négritude, she

writes "Or le nègre n'existe pas. L'Europe soucieuse de légitimer son exploitation le créa de toutes pièces" ("Négritude césairienne," p. 413).

La vie scélérate, based on the "memories" of Condé's own family, is a multicultural narrative that explores the historical and cultural significance of race, gender, and class relationships in the diverse contexts of the New World— Panama, the United States, Jamaica, Haiti—and of France. Using "memory" against the backdrop of the slave-like conditions of the building of the Panama Canal, she raises unrelentingly the questions of exile, estrangement from the motherland, relations to the "others" of the diaspora and to the whites, and a return to roots.

In what is perhaps her most celebrated novel, *Traversée de la mangrove (Crossing the Mangrove)*, Condé presents the reader with another vision of her native Guadeloupe in what can only be construed as the final stage of her quest for a separate identity and the culmination of her affiliation with Antillanité.

Set at a wake, the novel not only explores the diversity of the voices of the community but also suggests the impossibility of retrieving a collective "memory." The mysterious figure of the dead man, Francis Sancher, and the solemn backdrop of the wake provide Condé with the crucial tools to formalize the quest for identity within a typical Caribbean framework.

As Ruthmarie H. Mitsch so aptly points out in her "Maryse Condé's Mangroves," the search for identity within the framework of a Caribbean landscape is the central theme in the novel with the mangroves as the appropriate vehicle and symbol of Caribbean authenticity.

In *La colonie du nouveau monde*, published in 1993, Condé returns to the same themes—the African heritage, the destructive consequences of colonialism, the concept of alienation—as well as other aspects that keep the Caribbean locked in a certain space. The novel is ably criticized by Bettina Anna Soestwohner in her "Uprooting Antillean Identity: Maryse Condé's *La colonie du nouveau monde*." Creativity, says Soestwohner, quoting Condé, means to wander, which might mean geographically, as well as exploring one's cultural and historical heritage.

Simone Schwarz-Bart

Simone Schwarz-Bart was born Simone Brumant in 1938 in Guadeloupe. After graduating, she went to Paris where she met André Schwarz-Bart, a French Jew, whom she married in 1960 and with whom she has had two children. These two people, separated by color, religion, and culture, were, for a time, to become inseparable and form one of the most successful literary alliances in the French Caribbean. In collaboration they wrote *Un Plat de porc aux bananes vertes* and *La mulâtresse Solitude*, the latter patterned after a historical Guadeloupean figure from the eighteenth century. Unfortunately, they have recently separated, signaling the collapse of one of the French Caribbean's most celebrated "power teams."

In *Un Plat de porc aux bananes vertes*, the female protagonist, Marie, a seventy-two-year-old Martinican woman, living in an institution for the aged in Paris, narrates her failed efforts to reclaim her lost Caribbean identity through a voyage to the past and the rediscovery of the Creole language. Using the connotations of Antillanité to the fullest, the novel becomes a celebration of life manifest through a story told—the "memories."

In 1972 Simone published her masterpiece, *Pluie et vent sur Télumée Miracle (The Bridge of Beyond)*, which follows the lives of three generations of women from a small remote village in Guadeloupe. The focus of the text is on Télumée's struggle for survival against poverty, dispossession, betrayal, discrimination, and work in the cane fields. Poetically written, the novel is based on the true story of a Guadeloupean peasant reliving the past. It matters little to Schwarz-Bart that slavery as an institution was abolished long before Télumée's time. The dishonor and spiritual displacement suffered by her ancestors linger on in her "memory," leaving psychological and social scars and interiorized but no less damaging shackles.

Ti Jean l'Horizon (Between Two Worlds), written upon Schwarz-Bart's return to Guadeloupe, where she settles with her husband in Goyave, is based on the adventures of Ti-Jean, a Guadeloupean folk hero who journeys to other countries and the netherworld in search of the knowledge needed to defeat the Beast that has swallowed the sun. In his quest, Ti-Jean travels through history and space, recalling Caribbean folktales, legends, and myths.

Her play *Ton beau capitaine (Your Handsome Captain)*, published in 1987, relates the ending of a proletarian love story through a counterpoint of poignantly restrained French-speaking voices and insistent, wailing Creole song.

Conclusion

Although they have pursued questions of racial ancestry and cultural identity in their own way, both Schwarz-Bart and Condé have adhered to Glissant's basic notion of a special West Indian reality and have used different aspects intermittently. Both writers have consistently, for instance, used the French Creole language as a vehicle for defining the parameters of their identity quest—although not always in the conventional way. In *Pluie et vent sur Télumée Miracle*, for example, Schwarz-Bart conveys the essence of a peasant community without ever actually employing Creole dialogue. Rather, her richly metaphoric French text contains frequent echoes of Creole proverbs and habitual expressions that re-create the social ambience of rural Guadeloupe.

The select bibliography at the end of this paper focuses on the theories of Négritude and Antillanité and the impact of these ideologies on the literary development of Guadeloupeans Maryse Condé and Simone Schwarz-Bart. The bibliography is in no way exhaustive and should only be considered an introduction to the subject. At the same time, it seems appropriate to call attention to some of the difficulties involved in isolating pertinent works.

The documentation of a controversial and illusionary multidisciplinary concept such as *identity* is rife with contradictions and has, as yet, not been successfully completed for the Caribbean. References abound—especially in literature—but always in relation to specific literary works and/or authors. No general theoretical framework nor record exists covering all disciplines, all writers, and all aspects.

Frederick Ivor Case's groundbreaking *The Crisis of Identity: Studies in the Guadeloupean and Martiniquan Novel*, published in 1985, effectively deals with just two women writers from Guadeloupe—Michèle Lacrosil and Simone Schwarz-Bart—while ignoring similar contributions made by others.

Compounding the issue further is the general state of neglect of French Caribbean area studies in U.S. academic circles. While the quest for a separate identity has been most pronounced in the French Caribbean and among the area's women writers, in particular, it is precisely these areas that have traditionally been relegated to a back burner. Were it not for the heroic efforts of Richard Philcox and other qualified translators, the possibility exists that both Maryse Condé and Simone Schwarz-Bart would still be laboring in relative obscurity.

BIBLIOGRAPHY

Arnold, James. "Poétique forcée et identité dans la littérature des Antilles francophones." In *L' héritage de Caliban*. Maryse Condé, ed. Pointe-à-Pitre, Guadeloupe: Jasor, 1992. Pp. 15–27.

Arowolo, Olubukoye. "Maryse Condé: un retour aux sources africaines." M A. thesis, University of Ife, 1984.

Balutansky, Kathleen M., and Marie-Agnes Sourieau, eds. *Caribbean Creolization: Reflections on the Cultural Dynamics of Language, Literature, and Identity.* Gainesville: University of Florida Press, 1998.

Bernstein, Lisa. "Ecrivaine, sorcière, nomade: la conscience critique dans *Moi, Tituba, sorcière . . . noire de Salem* de Maryse Condé." *Etudes Francophones* 13:1 (Spring 1998), 119–134.

Bouchard, Monique. *Une lecture de Pluie et vent sur Télumée Miracle de Simone Schwarz-Bart*. Paris: L'Harmattan, 1990.

Busia, Abena P. A. "This Gift of Metaphor: Symbolic Strategies and the Triumph of Survival in Simone Schwarz-Bart's *The Bridge of Beyond*." In *Out of the Kumbla: Caribbean Women and Literature*. Carole Boyce Davies and Elaine Fido Savory, eds. Trenton, NJ: Africa World Press, 1990. Pp. 289–301.

Case, Frederick Ivor. "In the Grips of Misery and the Absurd: The Nihilism of Simone Schwarz-Bart." In *The Crisis of Identity: Studies in the Guadeloupean and Martiniquan Novel*. Frederick Ivor Case, ed. Sherbrooke, Canada: Naaman, 1985. Pp. 133–177.

Césaire, Aimée. *Cahier d'un retour au pays natal*. Paris: Bordas, 1939.

Clark, Vèvè. "Developing Diaspora Legacy: Allusions in Maryse Condé's *Hérémakhonon*." In *Out of the Kumbla: Caribbean Women and Literature*. Carole

Boyce Davies and Elaine Fido Savory, eds. Trenton, NJ: Africa World Press, 1990. Pp. 303–319.

Colloque sur l'oeuvre de Maryse Condé (1995, Pointe-à-Pitre, Guadeloupe). L'oeuvre de Maryse Condé: à propos d'une écrivaine politiquement incorrecte—actes du "Colloque sur l'oeuvre de Maryse Condé," 14-18 mars 1995, organisé par le Salon du Livre de la ville de Pointe-à-Pitre (Guadeloupe). Paris: L'Harmattan, 1996.

Condé, Maryse. *La colonie du nouveau monde*. Paris: R. Laffont, 1993.

_____. *Les derniers rois mages*. Paris: Mercure de France, 1992.

_____. *Hérémakhonon/En attendant le bonheur*. Paris: Seghers, 1976.

_____. *Moi, Tituba, sorcière . . . noire de Salem*. Paris: Mercure de France, 1986.

_____. *Pays mêlé (nouvelles)*. Paris: Hatier, 1985.

_____. *Pension Les Alizés*. Paris: Mercure de France, 1988.

_____. *Une saison à Rihata*. Paris: Laffont, 1981.

_____. *Ségou*. Paris: Laffont, 1984–1985.

_____. *Traversée de la mangrove*. Paris: Mercure de France, 1989.

_____. *La vie scélérate*. Paris: Seghers, 1987.

_____. "Négritude césairienne, négritude senghorienne." *Revue de Littérature Comparée* 48:34 (1974), 409–419.

Condé, Maryse, and Vèvè Clark. "Je me suis réconciliée avec mon île: une interview". *Callaloo* 12:1 (Winter 1989), 86–133.

Condé, Maryse, and Françoise Pfaff. *Conversations with Maryse Condé*. Lincoln: University of Nebraska Press, 1996.

Crosta, Suzanne. "Corps, écriture, et idéologie dans *Les derniers rois mages* de Maryse Condé." In *Elles écrivent des Antilles: Haïti, Guadeloupe, Martinique*. Susanne Rinne and Joëlle Vitiello, eds. Paris: L'Harmattan, 1997. Pp. 193–205.

_____. "La réception critique de Glissant." *Présence Francophone* 30 (1987), 59–70.

DeVille, Jennifer Suzanne. "La parole créole dans *Traversée de la mangrove* de Maryse Condé." M. A. thesis, University of Georgia, 1997.

Glissant, Edouard. *Le discours antillais*. Paris: Seuil, 1958.

_____. "Le romancier noir et son peuple." *Présence Africaine* 16 (October–November 1957), 26–31.

Gyssels, Kathleen. "Dans la toile d'araignée: conversations entre maître et esclave dans *Pluie et vent sur Télumée Miracle*." In *Elles écrivent des Antilles: Haïti, Guadeloupe, Martinique*. Susanne Rinne and Joëlle Vitiello, eds. Paris: L'Harmattan, 1997. Pp. 145–157.

_____. *Filles de Solitude: essai sur l' identité antillaise dans les (auto)biographies fictives de Simone Schwarz-Bart*. Paris: L'Harmattan, 1996.

_____. *Le folklore et la littérature orale créole dans l'oeuvre de Simone Schwarz-Bart (Guadeloupe.)* Brussels: Académie Royale des Sciences d'Outre-Mer, 1997.

Heady, Margaret Loren. "From Marvelous to Magic Realism: Modernist and Postmodernist Discourses of Identity in the Caribbean Novel." Ph.D. dissertation, University of Massachusetts, Amherst, 1997.

Knutson, April. "Maryse Condé: créer les textes de la diaspora antillaise". In *Elles écrivent des Antilles: Haïti, Guadeloupe, Martinique*. Susanne Rinne and Joëlle Vitiello, eds. Paris: Seuil, 1997. Pp. 163–173.

Lionnet, Françoise. *Autobiographical Voices: Race, Gender, Self-Portraiture*. Ithaca, NY: Cornell University Press, 1989.

_____. *"Traversée de la mangrove* de Maryse Condé: vers un nouveau humanisme antillais?" *French Review* 66:3 (February 1993), 475–486.

McKinney, Kitzie. "Second Vision: Antillean Versions of the Quest in Two Novels by Simone Schwarz-Bart." *French Review* 62:4 (March 1989), 650–660.

Mekkawi, Mod. *Maryse Condé: Playwright, Critic, Teacher—An Introductory Biobibliography*. Washington, DC: Howard University Libraries, 1991.

Mitsch, Ruthmarie H. "Maryse Condé's Mangroves." *Research in African Literatures* 28:4 (Winter 1997), 54–70.

Morrison, Anthea. "The Question of Identity in the Work of Maryse Condé and Simone Schwarz-Bart." Paper presented at the 16th Annual Conference of the Caribbean Studies Association, May 1991, Havana, Cuba.

Moudileno, Lydie. "Les écrivains de Maryse Condé: face à la filiation et l'affiliation." In *L'écrivain antillais au miroir de sa littérature*. Lydie Moudileno, ed. Paris: Karthala, 1997. Pp.141–171.

Nichols, Yanik Kerr. "L' identité réconstruite: une quête de soi dans *La vie scélérate* de Maryse Condé." Ph.D. dissertation, University of Rochester, 1997.

Oeudraogo, Jean. "Récits de l'indicible: articulation, translation de l'histoire chez Maryse Condé et Ahmadou Kourouma." Ph.D. dissertation, University of Georgia, 1997.

Pierre, Alix. "L'image de la femme résistante chez quatre romancières noires: Maryse Condé, Simone Schwarz-Bart, Toni Morrison et Alice Walker." Ph.D. dissertation, Florida State University, 1995.

Prouix, Patrice J. "Situer le 'moi' dans *Pluie et vent sur Télumée Miracle*." Whitney Sanford, tr. In *Elles écrivent des Antilles: Haïti, Guadeloupe, Martinique*. Susanne Rinne and Joëlle Vitiello, eds. Paris: L'Harmattan, 1997. Pp. 135–143.

Rogers, Nathalie. "Oralité et écriture dans *Pluie et vent sur Télumée Miracle*." *French Review* 65:3 (1992), 435–448.

Rosello, Mireille. *"Les derniers rois mages* et *Traversée de la mangrove*: insularité ou insularisation?" In *Elles écrivent des Antilles: Haïti, Guadeloupe, Martinique*. Susanne Rinne and Joëlle Vitiello, eds. Paris: L'Harmattan, 1997. Pp. 175–192.

Scharfman. Ronnie. "Mirroring and Mothering in Simone Schwarz-Bart's *Pluie et vent sur Télumée Miracle* and Jean Rhys' *Wide Sargasso Sea*." *Yale French Studies* 62 (1991), 88–106.

Schwarz-Bart, Simone. *Pluie et vent sur Télumée Miracle*. Paris: Seuil, 1972.

_____. *Ti Jean l'Horizon*. Paris: Seuil, 1979.

_____. *Ton beau capitaine*. Paris: Seuil, 1987.

Schwarz-Bart, Simone, and André Schwarz-Bart. *Un Plat de porc aux bananes vertes*. Paris: Seuil, 1967.

Smith, Arlette. "Maryse Condé's *Hérémakhonon:* A Triangular Structure of Alienation." *CLA Journal* 32:1 (September 1988), 45–54.

Soestwohner, Bettina Anna. "Uprooting Antillean Identity: Maryse Condé's *La colonie du nouveau monde.*" *Callaloo* 18:3 (Summer 1995), 690–706.

Sourieau, Marie-Agnès. *"La vie scélérate:* une écriture de l'histoire." In *Elles écrivent des Antilles: Haïti, Guadeloupe, Martinique.* Susanne Rinne and Joëlle Vitiello, eds. Paris: L'Harmattan, 1997. Pp. 207–219.

Toureh, Fanta. *L'imaginaire dans l'oeuvre de Simone Schwarz-Bart.* Paris: L'Harmattan, 1987.

Veldwachter-Sapotille, Germina N. "Tracées de la 'négritude' au féminin; ou, L'art de conter les Antilles dans *Pluie et vent sur Télumée Miracle* et *Juletane.*" M. A. thesis, University of New Mexico, 1998.

Williams, Helen Teresa. "Female Identity Through Language in Simone Schwarz-Bart's *Pluie et vent sur Télumée Miracle.*" M. A. thesis, University of British Columbia, 1986.

Wood, Jacqueline E. "Cracked Roots: Identity in Maryse Condé's *Hérémakhonon.*" M.A. thesis, Florida Atlantic University, 1991.

Zimra, Clarisse. "Righting the Calabash: Writing History in the Female Francophone Narrative." In *Out of the Kumbla: Caribbean Women and Literature.* Carole Boyce Davies and Elaine Savory Fido, eds. Trenton, NJ: Africa World Press, 1990. Pp. 143–159.

_____. "What's in a Name?: Elective Genealogy in Simone Schwarz-Bart's Early Novels." *Studies in Twentieth Century Literature* 17:1 (Winter 1993), 97–118.

16. Menchú, Stoll, and Ideology: Oral History and Documentation

Mark L. Grover

The April 1999 photograph of fifty-four Nobel Peace Prize recipients and Pope John Paul II was historic because so many previous Prize winners had come together in one place. Standing next to the Pope was a small, native-American woman in distinctly Guatemalan Indian dress, quite a contrast in the group of mostly white men in business suits.[1]

The Indian woman, Rigoberta Menchú, has been the focus of much interest over the past fifteen years. Even before the 1983 publication of her passionate autobiography, *I, Rigoberta Menchú,*[2] she had attracted attention because of the cause she espoused and the manner in which she presented her message. The autobiography thrust her into the international spotlight and she became a frequent guest and speaker at conferences and meetings around the world. Her high visibility as the principal spokesperson for indigenous groups led to her being awarded the Nobel Peace Prize in 1992, five hundred years after Columbus set foot in the Americas. For twenty years the stimulus to her activities and the reason for her passion was the horrific civil war and senseless violence in Guatemala that resulted in thousands of deaths.

An unexpected by-product of her book was the unusual attention accorded her by the academic community. Menchú suggests that over 1,500 thesis and dissertations have been written about her.[3] Nevertheless, she found this type of intensive scrutiny of her writings and life unsettling. The most well known of these works is anthropologist David Stoll's *Rigoberta Menchú and the Story of All Poor Guatemalans.*[4] On the basis of oral documentation and archival research, Stoll challenges the veracity of some of the incidents Menchú describes in her autobiography and then uses these inconsistencies to suggest a different interpretation of the Guatemalan conflict and to criticize the involvement of the world academic community in it. His assertions about the accuracy of parts of Menchú's story were supported in a front-page *New York Times* article by Larry Rohter who also went to Guatemala and interviewed family members whose recollections of events differed from Menchú's.[5]

The aftermath of the appearance of these two critical publications typifies the polemics surrounding the conflict in Guatemala. The conservative right immediately took the offensive and used Stoll's arguments to question the legitimacy of all worldwide revolutionary or indigenous movements. The right also attacked the academic community for supporting the movements and questioned why anyone would continue to have students read Menchú's autobiography in light of what it considers a complete repudiation of her story. The left rallied around Menchú and pointed out the veracity of the general descriptions in the book, while acknowledging that some of the details are not completely accurate. The left's response was to question Stoll's political motives and to suggest that his writing of the book was influenced by racism. Some even hinted at a religious motive, making frequent reference to Stoll as a "Protestant scholar." One wonders if either side read the book, since most of the commentary, regardless of politics, fails to address the primary thesis of the book which questions the motives of the international academic community in the Guatemalan conflict.[6]

This paper examines the issues surrounding oral history in relation to the Stoll/Menchú controversy. The focus is neither truth (Menchú's) nor motive (Stoll's). Little that libraries collect is not tainted by issues of veracity or ideological motive. Although we librarians may have strong feelings about volatile issues, we cannot allow such feelings to affect how we do our job. Our work should not be compromised by political or ideological beliefs or personal concerns. Our responsibility is to collect and make available the documentation that scholars and students need in order to carry out their research, regardless of their motivation.

What does the controversy about Menchú's autobiography have to do with libraries and the role of librarians in collecting and disseminating information about Latin America? I suggest that librarians look at the entire episode in terms of what documentation was used and what the incident suggests about what we should be collecting. In order to do so we need to understand issues related to oral documentation.

Oral History

The role of oral documentation in research varies according to discipline. For scholars in anthropology, folklore, and sociology, the collection of oral data is essential. In these disciplines evidence is generally gathered not to obtain information about one person or one event but to assemble an accumulation of opinions. Often the concern is not to establish the veracity of something but to arrive at a description of a group or communal perception. When the use of oral documentation in these disciplines extends beyond these primary purposes, its value and authenticity have to be assessed.

The use of oral documentation in history is much more controversial. For historians, the goal is the re-creation of the past. Consequently, historians prefer documentation that was created contemporaneously with the events under study. The value of oral history is questionable because of the time between the interview and the actual event. There is also concern about distortions that occur during the interviews. Oral history is of greater value in social history when other documentation is not available and is similar to sociological research when multiple interviews are conducted in order to gather the desired information. The use of oral history to establish specific information such as dates and chronology is problematic. Oral history's greatest value is in supplementing and adding details and body to a description of an event. For most historians the use of oral history is limited to this function.[7]

I, Rigoberta Menchú is the result of an interview. Rather than oral history, life history, or autobiography in the traditional sense, it falls into the category of *testimonio*. John Beverley defines this genre as a "novel or novella-length narrative in book or pamphlet (that is, printed as opposed to acoustic) form, told in the first person by a narrator who is also the real protagonist or witness of the events he or she recounts and whose unit of narration is usually a 'life' or a significant life experience."[8]

One difference between the testimonio and oral history is its purpose. An oral history interview is normally conducted to gather historical and background information about the subject's life and work. In the case of the testimonio, however, the narrator is generally motivated by a desire to bring about change. The document is often political and intended to elicit a reaction. There is a reason, for example, for describing repression, imprisonment, or struggles. Unlike a novel, a testimonio focuses on issues, not on "literariness." In most cases the narrator speaks for, or acts on behalf of, a group or community. The genre is well developed in Latin America.[9]

Questions arise about the value of the testimonio with respect to its description of events and establishment of fact. One concern is whether the descriptions were modified to evoke emotion and encourage support. If the narrator wants the testimonio to establish the description of events as legitimate, then the document must pass the scrutiny of historical evidence. If the expectation is different—the narrator's presentation is more fictional than historical—then the process for evaluating the document is different.

Menchú's book was promoted as fact, the true story of the author's life. Whether that was the purpose when she told her story on tape is not known, but that was the way readers perceived it. As a result, the book has been unusually effective in generating sympathy for the author and support for revolutionary movements in Guatemala. Note how Allen Carey-Webb describes his reaction to the book and the way his students responded to it:

> [It] is one of the most moving books I have ever read. It is the kind of a book that I feel I must pass on, that I must urge fellow teachers to use in their classes. . . . My students were immediately sympathetic to the Menchú story and were anxious to know more, to involve themselves. They asked questions about culture and history, about their own position in the world, and about the purposes and methods of education.[10]

The Process

Understanding how a document such as Rigoberta Menchú's autobiography is constructed will assist librarians in understanding the value of collecting all components of the oral interview. Collecting only the finished product, such as a copy of an oral interview or a published volume, suggests a disregard for the complexities of the oral history process. In the case of *I, Rigoberta Menchú,* the process is important because the document was created from both oral and written components. The more complex the process, the greater the possibility of introducing unintended changes.

Rigoberta Menchú was unique in the revolutionary movement against the Guatemalan military government because of her very personal connection to the widespread violence and destruction. She was able to speak forcefully about what was happening to the indigenous population under military dictatorship because of her Indian background and her family's history of opposition to the Guatemalan government. Several members of her family, including her parents, died in the violence or were victims of it. She was also unusually astute and articulate.

The leaders of the revolutionary movements in Guatemala, particularly the January 31st Popular Front, recognized her potential and used her as an international spokesperson to further their cause. The idea to have Menchú tell her story appears to have come while she was in Paris in January 1982 as part of a European tour with the Popular Front. The group was to be in Paris for a week before traveling to Holland for a conference and could arrange for Menchú to be interviewed during that time.

The group contacted Elisabeth Burgos-Debray, a longtime friend of the Guatemalan guerrilla movement. From an upper-class family, Burgos was a political exile with a long history of activism in her native Venezuela and other parts of Latin America. In Bolivia, she married Régis Debray, the French revolutionary and member of Ernesto "Ché" Guevara's revolutionary troops in Bolivia. Debray had written the famous *Revolution in the Revolution* and was active in Latin American insurgencies in Cuba and Chile. He eventually became an advisor to French president François Mitterand.[11]

In 1982 Burgos was in Paris working on a Ph.D. in anthropology. She had begun to question some of the theories of revolutionary war, wondering whether it could actually be successful. She had become particularly interested in indigenous movements and had organized at least one demonstration in support of the Guatemalan revolutionary movements. Because of her political ideology and experience, combined with her academic training, she appeared to the Guatemalans to be the right person to do the history of Menchú the way they thought it should be done, despite the fact that she had never been to Guatemala and came from an upper-class Venezuelan family.[12]

It is important to understand how the interviews were conducted, transcribed, edited, reviewed, and finally published in book form as Menchú's story. First, Menchú did not write the autobiography. Beyond what the interviewer and interviewee bring as preparation, the interview session is a creative process which often results in unique outcomes as well as distortions and mistakes. The interviewer is very important because in most cases he or she controls the course of the interview. Certain information is elicited according to the way the interview is conducted and what questions are asked.[13]

Elisabeth Burgos-Debray's interview of Rigoberta Menchú was conducted over the course of a week and took place in Burgos's apartment. Burgos says her involvement in the interview was limited because of the way Rigoberta spoke. Although Burgos had prepared an outline for the interview, she says she soon put it aside because Menchú needed little encouragement. According to Burgos, "Rigoberta made more and more digressions, introduced descriptions of cultural practices into her story and generally upset my chronology. I therefore let her talk freely and tried to ask as few questions as possible."[14] This kind of situation often occurs when there is an overarching purpose for the interview and frequently indicates that the interviewee prepared extensively in advance.

David Stoll, who listened to two hours of the interview, agrees with Burgos's description of the course of the interview and suggests that Burgos interrupted Menchú only to ask for clarification. He says, "Never does Elisabeth raise new subjects, change the direction of the interview, or prod a reluctant subject into continuing."[15] Obviously Burgos's role can be assessed only by listening to all the tapes and comparing them to the final Spanish version of the book.

Another issue in the transformation of an oral interview to its published form is the role of the transcriber and editor (most often the interviewer). The editor becomes a creative partner in the process. Oral interviews are never completely smooth and error free: accounts are told out of chronological order, grammar is incorrect, terms are undefined, discussions are incomplete, and so on. The sequence of stories and events in the chronology affects meaning and understanding. Additional information almost always has to be added for clarity and continuity. Although the editor seldom intends to alter meaning, such changes are known to occur.

The final version of the document, incorporating all changes and additions, needs to be approved by the interviewee. This part of the process can also introduce changes and adjustments to the text. Exactly what happened during this phase of the preparation of the Menchú volume is unclear. Burgos suggests that little of the original interview was changed. She and her assistant transcribed the tapes, producing a document of more than 500 typed pages. Burgos then rearranged the story according to the original chronological outline she had made in preparation for the interview. Organizing the document was so difficult that she had to cut the interview into sections, identify each part, and then reorder the parts. She states that the only corrections she made to the text were grammatical. Burgos says, "Yes, I corrected verb tenses and noun genders, as otherwise it would not have made sense, but always trying to retain her own powerful form of expression."[16]

Burgos then gave the completed manuscript to Arturo Taracena, a friend of Menchú, who delivered it to the revolutionary organization. The document was read and changes suggested. According to Burgos, only minor changes were requested and most were done. Menchú is said to have delivered the manuscript herself to Burgos, who then made all the publication arrangements.

Menchú has given different versions of her role in the process. In her recent book *Crossing Borders,* she describes a very diminished role for Burgos. She says that Taracena, a Guatemalan historian, was the most influential person in the book's creation. "He had a significant hand in the book, though he is a modest man and was not interested in self-aggrandizement." She never states that Burgos actually conducted the interview and says that Burgos was involved in the publication of the book only because she had "a reputation and an entrée into the academic and publishing world." She says that the Guatemala Solidarity Committee in Paris "helped with the transcription." When the text was finished, Menchú kept it for more than two months "trying to understand it." She even got help from friends in Mexico in the editing of the manuscript. She had them read the text to her so that she could understand it. She requested that several passages be omitted.[17] This version of the publication process suggests a very limited role for Burgos and a more important one for Arturo Taracena.

In another version of the story, Menchú says she was not allowed any involvement in the editing of the document and that the final version was a surprise to her. "Elisabeth Burgos took those manuscripts, arranged them according to her own criteria, and added and suppressed what suited her. . . . Never did she permit that I or Dr. Taracena know the final version, much less make observations or corrections to the text."[18] Although Menchú has never clarified exactly what happened, the fact that she has distanced herself from the book over the past few years suggests she is dissatisfied with it. Problems with the payment of her royalties have also played a part in the conflict between Menchú and Burgos.

In recent interviews and writings Burgos has talked about why she believes Menchú was not accurate in telling her story.

> I have become aware that they (Menchú and another person she interviewed) relate, as their own experiences, what they could not have witnessed directly, what instead happened in proximity to their own histories. It is not that they act in bad faith, nor that they lie. Instead, they are moved by a feeling of belonging. . . . The act of telling a story orally required recreating what

happened through images, it requires setting a stage, like a theater director would, and requires what theater does—to demonstrate. Rigoberta's objective with her testimony was to demonstrate, to shake public opinion to the maximum to win support, and that she has accomplished.[19]

Conclusions

This account of the creation of *I, Rigoberta Menchú* points out several issues concerning the use of oral interviews and histories in academic research. An analysis of David Stoll's use of oral documents would likely yield another set of problems with his sources. I am not suggesting that the potential problems with oral documents preclude their use in academic research. On the contrary, they are vital and important resources. What I am suggesting, however, is that libraries need to carefully collect all the components of the oral documentation and make all of them available to scholars.

Many scholars use oral documentation in their work, but most do not recognize the long-term importance of these documents, nor do they acknowledge that they should become part of the library's collection. Librarians need to make scholars aware of the value of these sources for the library and to advise them on how to conduct the interviews and gather the proper documents so that the complete documentation can be made available to other researchers.[20]

Once the interview is complete, librarians need to be involved in the transcription process. Researchers need to know the proper format and structure for the interview. They need to understand the importance of retaining the original copy of the transcription. If the transcript is then given to the interviewee for additions and corrections, a copy of the suggested changes needs to be kept as well. Correspondence containing information about the interview should be retained as part of the record. Thus the file in the library should include a copy of the original tape recording, the original transcription, all correspondence, the document listing suggested changes and additions, and the corrected final manuscript.

Regardless of one's position on the Menchú/Stoll controversy, the story of Rigoberta Menchú's autobiography underscores the importance of libraries as collectors and preservers of oral documentation. These are valuable research resources. Collecting these documents enables us to better serve our patrons.

NOTES

1. "Trimble Meets Pope at Vatican," *The Times*, April 23, 1999, p. A2.

2. First published in Spanish in 1983 (Barcelona: Editorial Argos Vergara). The English translation was published one year later by Verso (New York).

3. An example of the interest in Menchú can be found in Allen Carey-Webb and Stephen Benz, eds., *Teaching and Testimony: Rigoberta Menchú and the North American Classroom* (Albany: State University of New York Press, 1996). The authors describe how the book is used in the classroom.

4. Boulder, CO: Westview Press, 1998.

5. Larry Rohter, "Nobel Winner Finds Her Story Challenged," *New York Times*, December 15, 1998, pp. A1, 8. See also "Guatemala Laureate Defends 'My Truth,'" *New York Times*, January 21, 1999, p. A8. It should be pointed out that there have been questions about the book for several years. See, for example, Doris Sommer, "Rigoberta's Secrets," *Latin American Perspectives* 18 (Summer 1991), 32–50.

6. See Frei Betto, "Rigoberta Menchú e um tal Stoll," *O Estado de São Paulo*, March 24, 1999, p. A2; Diane Nelson, "Rigoberta Menchú, Is Truth Stranger Than Testimonial?" Http://www.vanderbilt.edu/AnS/Anthro/GSN/nelson.htm Guatemala Scholars Network; David Horowitz, "I, Rigoberta Menchú, Liar" Http://www.frontpagemag.com/dh/dh01-11-99.htm Right On? See also several letters to the editor, *New York Times*, December 20, 1998, Section 4, p. 12.

7. For a good discussion of the problems of subjectivity in oral history, see Olga Rodrigues de Moraes Simson, organizer, *Os desafios contemporâneos da história oral* (Campinas, Brazil: Centro de Memória, UNICAMP, 1997). See also Paul Thompson, *The Voice of the Past: Oral History*, 2d ed. (Oxford: Oxford University Press, 1988), and Arthur Marwick, *The Nature of History* (New York: Macmillan, 1970), pp. 133–137.

8. John Beverley, "The Margin at the Center: On *Testimonio* (Testimonial Narrative)," in Sidonie Smith and Julia Watson, eds., *De/Colonizing the Subject: The Politics of Gender in Women's Autobiography* (Minneapolis: University of Minnesota Press, 1992), pp. 92–93.

9. John Beverley, " 'Through All Things Modern': Second Thoughts on *Testimonio*," in Steven M. Bell et al., *Critical Theory, Cultural Politics, and Latin American Narrative* (Notre Dame, IN: University of Notre Dame, 1993), pp. 125–151.

10. Allen Carey-Webb, "Teaching Third World Auto-Biography: Testimonial Narrative in the Canon and Classroom," *Oregon English* (Fall 1990), 8.

11. Burgos and Debray have since divorced.

12. For a discussion of the role of Burgos see Marc Zimmerman, *Literature and Resistance in Guatemala: Textual Modes and Cultural Politics from El Señor Presidente to Rigoberta Menchú;* Volume Two, *Testimonio and Cultural Politics in the Years of Cerezo and Serrano Elias* (Athens: Ohio University, 1995), p. 55.

13. Two episodes in my personal experience illustrate the important role of the interviewer. Several years ago when I was beginning a research project I was given a large collection of oral interviews conducted by a colleague. As I listened to the tapes, I quickly realized that the interviewer asked certain questions in order to elicit certain information. If the person did not respond in the desired way, a particular line of questioning was pursued until the desired response was given. Dissatisfied with these interviews, I decided to re-interview each person in order to gather the data needed for my research.

In another instance, earlier in my career, I was doing an interview on a sensitive topic. The interviewee stopped the interview and said that he could tell which side I was on and what my interpretation would be by the way I phrased the questions. He walked out in anger and was unwilling to be part of the project.

14. Elisabeth Burgos-Debray, "Introduction," in *I, Rigoberta Menchú: An Indian Woman in Guatemala* (New York: Verso, 1984), pp. xix–xx.

15. Stoll, *Rigoberta Menchú*, p. 188.

16. Ibid, p. 185.

17. Rigoberta Menchú, *Crossing Borders* (New York: Verso, 1998), pp. 113–114.

18. "Carta de Rigoberta Menchú," *El Periódico*, December 12, 1997, quoted in Stoll, *Rigoberta Menchú*, p. 301. Another version from Menchú's organization, since discounted, is that Burgos had interviewed several Guatemalans and combined the stories.

19. Quoted in Stoll, *Rigoberta Menchú*, pp. 198–199.

20. For more on the role of libraries in the preservation of oral documentation, see Stephen Humphries, *The Handbook of Oral History: Recording Life Stories* (London: Inter-Action Imprint, 1984), and Thad Sitton and O. L. Davis, Jr., *Oral History: A Guide for Teachers (and Others)* (Austin: University of Texas Press, 1983).

17. The Urban Woman in the Electronic Age: A Survey of Electronic Resources

Mina Jane Grothey

I have been selecting materials and conducting research on women in Latin America and the Caribbean for more than fifteen years. At SALALM XL (1995, Athens, Georgia) I presented preliminary findings about my work on the topic "Women in the Urban Economy of Latin America and the Caribbean." When asked to prepare a paper for SALALM XLIV, I decided to return to this topic and pursue the goal of compiling an annotated bibliography on the subject to update earlier research (Bourque 1989). I realized quickly that much had changed since 1995 in the way we search for and find information. I also wondered whether, given the advances in information systems and technology, bibliographies were still useful. Had the Internet made the bibliography obsolete?

I decided to do a literature search on the question "Is the bibliography dead?," a task that turned out to be more problematic than I had expected. It is difficult to search for bibliography as a form rather than actual bibliographies. I did find one article, "Bibliography as an Interdisciplinary Information Service," which argues that a bibliography is still a valid tool. The author, Joan Fiscella, argues that "although published subject bibliographies would seem to have lost their value due to the availability of electronic catalogs and indexes, they still play an important role in winnowing the vast amount of information derived from these resources" (Fiscella 1996:280). A bibliography is not just the result of a gathering activity or list making. Bibliographies, especially for interdisciplinary studies, add value by "cull[ing] the materials retrieved in an efficient and effective way" (ibid.:293). Fiscella states that "the growing numbers of electronically accessible bibliographic tools have not substituted for skillfully compiled bibliographies, since electronic indexes are not constructed to identify functionally relevant materials or to identify patterns, analogies, etc." (ibid.).

In following up on several of Fiscella's references, I found a chapter by Howard D. White titled "Literary Forms in Information Work: Annotated Bibliographies, Bibliographic Essays, and Reviews of Literatures." White says that the most useful form is the review of literatures prepared by someone knowledgeable in the field. In good reviews of literatures, the arrangement of materials by function provides insight (White 1992:142).

> Reviews of literatures are of central importance because they indicate how
> readers can read convergently with insiders' definitions of the field. . . . The

review of a literature, if good of its kind, will resemble a course given by an intelligent and critical teacher. It establishes contexts and priorities. It screens out. It synthesizes claims, perhaps even obviating the need to read some or all of the writings it covers. It is an essay. The guide to a literature, in contrast, will resemble one or more sections of a library. While not disorganized, its level of organization is not as high as the review's. It says in effect, "If you are interested in this subject, *this* may be useful, and *this* may be useful, and *this* may be useful . . . etc." There is no synthesis, merely agglomeration. The guide cannot substitute for any of the writings it covers; it simply points to them. (Ibid.:148.)

I would add that a bibliography can also be a time saver. Today there are so many places to search for information that a bibliography can save the researcher time by indicating the most reliable, relevant sources.

A major change in the way we look for information relates to the availability of electronic resources. This paper examines, in particular, general databases, specialized databases for Latin American subjects, and Web resources and evaluates their general usefulness for research on Latin America, women, and economics.[1] (See Appendix 1 for a list of the databases and resources and Appendix 2 for a detailed account of search results.)

General Databases

At the University of New Mexico General Library (UNMGL) we are reevaluating the general databases we provide to users to determine whether we are making the best use of resources and are meeting user needs. In summer 1998 we switched from Expanded Academic Index to EBSCOhost Academic Search FullTEXT Elite. The Library also joined the consortium subscribing to Lexis-Nexis Academic Universe. In winter 1999 the New Mexico State Library began providing access to ProQuest Direct–UMI for all public, high school, and college and university libraries.

1. EBSCOhost

The UNMGL subscribes to the Academic Search FullTEXT Elite version of EBSCOhost. The database provides abstracts and indexing for over 3,100 scholarly journals in the social sciences, humanities, education, and other fields. It also offers full text for over 1,000 journals including 380 journals dating to 1990. Total coverage includes over 3 million articles. The user may search by keyword, advanced, and natural language and may limit the search to peer-reviewed journals and to full text.

The natural language search is a special feature of EBSCO which allows the user to enter a phrase or question. The results are relevancy ranked so one can easily get the maximum number of hits—250. Another feature is the availability of links to Web results, although these Web sites may have little relevancy to the search. I did a search for the "role of urban women workers in latin american economy." Even when limited to full text and peer reviewed the search still produced the maximum of 250 hits. The citations show declining relevancy starting with 100 percent, and by record number 90 relevancy is down to 69 percent. Journals indexed include *Latin American Research Review* (full text 7/96–), *Latin American Perspectives* (full text 1/90–), *NACLA Report on the Americas* (full text 7/96–), *Economic Development and Cultural Change* (not full text), and *Urban Studies* (full text).

2. ProQuest Direct–UMI

The ProQuest Direct–UMI database provides access to magazines, journals, and newspapers. It covers over 2,200 magazines and journals, 1,400 of which are full text. The searching is divided into current (1997)– and backfile (which I find frustrating). The search can also be limited to peer reviewed and full text and can be done using basic or advanced search screens. I had some difficulty using ProQuest, perhaps because I am more familiar with EBSCO-host and how it searches.

One significant difference between EBSCOhost and ProQuest is that the latter turns up more news-type articles, such as those from *Inter Press Service* (full text, but only through 7/98). The searches I conducted found articles from *Journal of Third World Studies* (full text), *World Development* (not full text), and *Journal of Latin American Studies* (full text). ProQuest is updated more frequently and provides full text quicker than EBSCO. *Latin American Research Review* is full text in ProQuest from 1/94 while *Latin American Perspectives* is only full text from 1/97. *NACLA Report on the Americas* is also in ProQuest with full text from 9/97.

3. Lexis-Nexis Academic Universe

Considerable practice and experimentation by trial and error is required to do a good search using Academic Universe. I understand that some modifications are planned to make searching easier, such as the ability to search by publication and by multiple publications at once.

For my research, I concentrated on the Foreign Language News category, Source Material: Spanish language news. In addition to *El País* from Spain and EFE, the Spanish news agency, most of the newspapers included are from Mexico. I searched the General News category, Source Material: All Magazines with little success. I also searched the General News category, Source Material: Newsletters and found more on my subject than in the All Magazines category.

How did I decide to search in this particular Source Material? I thought that Lexis-Nexis included the title *Market Latin America*, which I found while searching Info-Latinoamerica. When I determined which part of Lexis-Nexis included this title, I was led to Newsletters. There I found *Inter-Press Service*, *Latin America Weekly Report*, and *NotiSur*. To my surprise, I found only articles from 1994 and 1995 from *Market Latin America* while in Info-Latinoamerica

I found items as recent as 1999. According to the Lexis-Nexis Source Locator, coverage is through 1997. I attempted to determine, by reviewing the pages about content, whether *Market Latin America* had been dropped but found no helpful information.[2]

4. Social SciSearch

This electronic database is based upon the Social Science Citation Index (SSCI), an international, multidisciplinary index to social science journal literature produced by the Institute for Scientific Information. The search interface is the same as that for SciSearch via Los Alamos National Laboratory (LANL). The UNMGL subscribes to both databases through the Library Services Alliance of New Mexico, a consortium of science and technology libraries in New Mexico. Currently, we provide coverage only back to 1991.

I found the search interface easy to use and retrieved better results than when I searched SSCI on Dialog five years ago, although searching "women and economic and latin america" still retrieves citations dealing with health issues. Results are listed by relevancy ranking. The citation indexes enable the user to search by cited reference in addition to general searches by keyword, author, or source. I found Social SciSearch helpful for finding current citations.

5. FirstSearch

FirstSearch contains more than sixty databases including WorldCat. In my research, I searched Contemporary Women's Issues, EconLit, and PAIS International. I had difficulty doing a clean search in Contemporary Women's Issues, a full text database. This database is updated weekly and indexes 1,500 titles with coverage from 1992 to the present. It includes standard journal and newsletter articles; research reports from nonprofit groups, governments, and international agencies; and "fact sheets." (The content of this database will be added to Lexis-Nexis Academic Universe.) I have yet to determine how to do a clean search for a geographic name, which is apparently not the same as geographic region found as a field label in a record. When I did a country as subject keyword search it can be pulled from anywhere in the record which includes notes and bibliography.

Using "development" as subject keyword instead of "economic" produced more relevant citations. The problem in using "economic" is that it occurs in articles on the economic status of women in relation to other factors such as reproduction. As with other full text databases, it is important to use a variety of words, such as "labor force" and "employment," rather than relying only on a term that would appear in a subject heading.

Produced by the *Journal of Economic Literature*, EconLit provides citations and abstracts for articles from more than 500 journals, books, dissertations, and the Cambridge University Press Abstracts of Working Papers in Economics (AWPE). Coverage goes back to 1969, and the database is updated monthly. Because it provides access to working papers, it is an excellent resource. Once scholars are aware of institutions doing work in their area of interest, a visit to that institution's Web site can also be helpful. For example, my search turned up two working papers from the Economic Growth Center, Yale University

The other database in FirstSearch that I tested was PAIS International, from Public Affairs Information Service. Updated monthly, the database includes articles, books, conference proceedings, government documents, book chapters, and statistical directories going back online to 1972. This database is a good source for foreign language materials.

All the FirstSearch databases proved to be good resources, each with a particular strength. For example, Contemporary Women's Issues brings up non-journal references that are difficult to find elsewhere; EconLit includes working papers; and PAIS has foreign language materials including government documents from other countries.

Latin American Databases

This section reviews the standard interdisciplinary databases that focus on Latin America and the Caribbean: Hispanic American Periodicals Index (HAPI), Handbook of Latin American Studies, Info-Latinoamerica, and Latin America Data Base (LADB).

HAPI includes citations to articles, documents, book reviews, and original literary works in approximately 400 social science and humanities journals that regularly contain information on Latin America, the United States–Mexico borderlands, and Hispanics in the United States from 1970 to date.

The Handbook of Latin American Studies has a long tradition of indexing and abstracting. A special feature is the introductory essays which discuss recent research trends in a particular field. Now that the Handbook is available on the Web, I no longer use the CD-ROM version. Both HAPI and the Handbook present preliminary information on works to be included in future volumes. For example, when I searched the Handbook I was able to select up through volume 60 (2003).

Info-Latinoamerica is easy to use. The current citations I retrieved were from business publications such as *Market Latin America*. The most recent journal article was from 1994, in contrast to the very current news articles retrieved.

When I searched the Latin America Data Base I discovered that the newsletter *EcoCentral* had been renamed *NotiCen* in line with *NotiSur*. LADB has links to *The Columbia Guide to Online Style* and other sites of interest (primarily economic), as well as to SALALM. My search in the economic journals section was very productive.

Each database has particular strengths. LADB is a good source for keeping up with what is happening in Latin America. Info-Latinoamerica is an excellent supplement to LADB for additional articles. I recommend HAPI to students doing basic undergraduate research and the Handbook for more in-depth searching.

World Wide Web Resources

Because Web resources are in a state of constant flux, this section of the discussion makes no claim to being exhaustive.

I began my search using the University of Texas at Austin's Latin American Network Information Center (LANIC) in the section "Women & Gender Studies," also called "Women, Gender & Sexuality in Latin America,"under "Society and Culture." As with other subject areas, it starts with the broad heading "Latin American Resources," then lists resources by country, followed by "International Resources." Other areas of interest are "Economy" under "Economy in Latin America" and "Development" under "Sustainable Development." The amount of information is overwhelming, although some sites ultimately did not deliver what I had hoped. For example, the section on Latin America and the Caribbean in Women in Development Network (WIDNET) provided links to other sites but no original information. The section on statistics gives very brief statistical information from other sources. I did not find a statement outlining the purpose of the site.

It is helpful to be able to go directly to sites such as the World Bank (where I searched the publication list) and JOLIS (Joint Libraries Information System), the combined library for the World Bank and the International Monetary Fund, rather than relying on other library catalogs. Another useful site is the Inter-American Development Bank and its library. When I tried to access the Web site for the Comisión Económica para América Latina y el Caribe (CEPAL), however, I could get to the homepage but no further.

In addition to LANIC, another important resource for finding Web sites is the Spanish language version of Yahoo, "Yahoo en español." Spanish language search engines provide access to sites not found by English language search engines. Sites can be searched in Spanish as well as by using the categories provided. For example, under "ciencias sociales" is the subcategory "economía" which is further subdivided into such categories as "Revistas" (1), "Bancas centrales@", "Bibliotecas" (1), and "Educación y formación" (18). Many of the sites are from Spain rather than Latin America. A search on the words "centro" and "mujer" brought up six sites, of which two where in Houston, Texas, two in the Gran Canarias, and two for Flora Tristan in Peru.

Additional Spanish language search engines can be found at Motores de Búsqueda en Español, which includes a link to Yahoo en español (Withers 1999:363). The site is a collection of more than a dozen Spanish language search engines. Also, Yahoo Brasil, a Portuguese language search engine, provides access to Brazilian sites.

Has the proliferation of access to electronic resources eliminated the need for bibliographies? My answer is no. As access has increased, so has the need for more help in, as Fiscella says, "culling" through what is available. The content of bibliographies will change to include more electronic resources. Bibliographies will remain useful tools if they provide added value and information not available elsewhere. The best bibliographies will offer guidance in determining the usefulness of a particular source and will suggest strategies for navigating through the overwhelming amount of material available.[3]

APPENDIX 1

Databases and Web Resources

General Databases

EBSCOhost Academic Search FullTEXT Elite
FirstSearch
        Contemporary Women's Issues
        EconLit
        PAIS International
        WorldCat
Lexis-Nexis Academic Universe
ProQuest Direct–UMI
Social SciSearch

Latin American Databases

Hispanic American Periodicals Index (HAPI) (http://hapi.gseis.ucla.edu)
Handbook of Latin American Studies (http://lcweb2.loc.gov/hlas)
Info-Latinoamerica (http://biblioline.nisc.com)
Latin America Data Base (LADB) (http://ladb.unm.edu)

World Wide Web Resources

Inter-American Development Bank Library (http://www.iadb.org/int/lib)
Joint Libraries Information System (http://jolis.worldbankimflib.org)
World Bank and International Monetary Fund Library
Latin American Network Information Center (LANIC) (http://lanic.utexas.edu)
Latin American and Iberian Collections and Resources, University of New Mexico General Library (http://www.unm.edu/~libibero)
Motores de Búsqueda en Español (http://www.aered.com/miscelanea/buscador.htm)
Women in Development Network (WIDNET) (http://www.focusintl.com/widnet.htm)
World Bank (http://www.worldbank.org)
Yahoo Brasil (http://br.yahoo.com)
Yahoo en español (http://espanol.yahoo.com)

APPENDIX 2

Search Histories

General Databases

1. EBSCOhost Academic Search FullTEXT Elite

Keyword: women and economic and latin america; retrieved 18 citations, 12 full text.

Advanced: (women or female) and labor and brazil; 10 citations, 3 full text.

Natural language: role of urban women workers in latin american economy. With natural language searching, the results are relevancy ranked so the user can easily get the maximum number of 250. Another feature is the availability of links to Web results, although these Web sites may have little relevancy to the search. Even when limited to full text and peer reviewed, the search still came up with the maximum of 250. The citations have declining relevancy starting with 100 percent and by record 90 the relevancy is down to 69 percent.

2. ProQuest Direct–UMI

(Searched March 18, 1999, and May 17, 1999)

Basic

women and economic and latin america, 1997– ; 20 citations, 6 full text

women and economic and latin america, – 1997; 22 citations, 6 full text

Basic limited to peer reviewed

1997– ; 1 citation, full text, a book review

–1997; 6 citations, 2 full text

Advanced peer reviewed

(women or female) and labor and brazil, 1997– ; none

(women or female) and labor and brazil, –1997; 8 citations, 2 full text

Basic peer reviewed

urban women and latin america, 1997– and –1997; none

urban and women and latin america, 1997– ; none

urban and women and latin america, –1997; 6 citations, none full text

Basic all databases

urban and women and latin america, 1997– ; none

urban and women and latin america, –1997; 9 citations, none full text

Advanced all databases

(women or female) and labor and brazil, 1997– ; 3 citations, one full text

(women or female) and labor and brazil, –1997; 18 citations, 7 full text, earliest from 1974

3. Lexis-Nexis Academic Universe

(Searched March 16, 1999)

Foreign News Category, Source Material: Spanish language news, 6 months

> mujer! and econom!; more than 1,000 documents

>> mujer! and econom! and urbana; 69 documents. Using only "and" did not produce relevant documents. Searched again using "w/p", but the definition of paragraph was very broad, sometimes the whole article. Searched again substituting "w/10" for "w/p" but found nothing. Actually, "w/s" works better than "w/p".

> mujer! w/10 empleo; 44 citations

Broadened date period to two years

> mujer! w/10 econom!; 656 citations

> mujer! w/10 econom! and additional terms: brasil or mexico; 455 citations

(Searched May 18, 1999)

General News Topics: All Magazines to retrieve English language magazine or journal articles

> women w/s economic in key term, additional term: latin america, 6 months; 2 citations. Note: to find relevancy use "KWIC view" to see where words are located.

> Redid search using "w/5" instead of "w/s" and retrieved the one relevant citation from previous search.

Foreign Language News: Spanish language news, 6 months

> (mujer or mujeres) w/s econom! in key term and ecuador in additional term; 17 citations Queen Sofia traveling to Ecuador in April '99!

(Searched May 21, 1999)

General News Topics: Newsletters

> women and economic and latin america as keywords for all available dates; 31 citations

> women and latin america for previous year; 38 citations

> women and latin america and urban for previous year; 2 citations (both to the same article)

4. FirstSearch: Contemporary Women's Issues

(Searched March 18, 1999)

women and economic and latin america (all as subject keyword); 85 citations many dealing with health and reproduction

same search adding NOT health; 24 citations

There is a difficulty with geographic name, which is apparently not the same as geographic region found in records. When one does a country as subject keyword it can be pulled from anywhere in the record which includes notes and bibliography (attempted again May 18 with no success). It is also difficult to retrieve relevant citations. A search using "development" in subject heading keyword worked better than "economic" as subject keyword (May 18).

5. FirstSearch: EconLit

(Searched May 13, 1999)

women and urban and latin america; 6 citations. (No need for "economic" since it is an economic database.)

women and latin america; 44 citations

6. FirstSearch: PAIS International

(Searched March 19, 1999)

women and economic and latin america, 1995– ; 7 citations

women and labor and latin america, 1995– ; 6 citations including 3 found in the previous search

women and employment and latin america, 1995– ; same 6 citations as above

women and urban and latin america, 1995– ; none

women and urban and brazil, 1995– ; 1 citation

women and economic and brazil, 1995– ; 7 citations

women and labor and brazil, 1995– ; 14 citations, including 4 in previous set

women and employment and brazil, 1995– ; 10 citations, all found in previous searches

7. Social SciSearch at LANL

(Searched March 19, 1999)

women and economic and latin america as keywords, 1997–98, 1994–96; 2 citations (not relevant)

women and labor and latin america; 4 citations, which also came up in search using women and employment and latin america. (The term labor force worked better in order to exclude labor as in giving birth.)

women and economic and limit language to Spanish 1991– ; 9 citations

Latin American Databases

1. Hispanic American Periodicals Index

(Searched March 19, 1999)

women and economic in keyword limited to 1995–1999; 22 citations

2. Handbook of Latin American Studies

(Searched March 19, 1999)

women and economic in full text, 1995 (v. 54); 41 citations. (The system searched the word "and".)

women economic in full text, 1995 (v. 54); reached the 100-item limit, 15 exact phrase, 85 citations contain the two words

economic development women as subject, 1995– ; reached the 100-item limit with 2 exact phrase, 14 all words, and 84 with one or more words

women urban in full text, 1995– ; reached 100-item limit with 6 exact phrase, 68 all
    words, and 26 containing 1 or more words. Using the starting date of 1995
    retrieved citations from 1989.

3. Info-Latinoamerica

(Searched May 13, 1999)

women and economic; 472 citations

and urban; 80 citations

limiting by date 1998; 28 citations

4. Latin America Data Base

(Searched May 13, 1999)

Searched in NotiSur for women and economic, 1998– ; 14 articles

Explored the economic journals section: (mujer or mujeres) and economica; 37
    articles

NOTES

1. Since it has been a while since I worked in economics, I want to thank Carolyn Mountain,
Latin American Specialist at the Parish Memorial Library, the business and economic library of the
University of New Mexico General Library (UNMGL) system, for assisting me with the economic
portion of this research.

2. I want to thank Harold Colson and an alert staff member of UNMGL, Rebs Bauer-
schmidt, for leading me to these pages.

3. For more on the usefulness of bibliography, see Chapter 19 (herein), Lesbia Verona,
"Escritoras cubanas en el exilio." Verona points out the problem of tracking writers of Cuban
descent who are born elsewhere since the Library of Congress classifies these authors with the literature of the country of birth rather than as Cuban. See also Chapter 14, Nelly González, "A Bolivian Literary Minority: Women Writers." González discusses the difficulty of finding Bolivian
women writers listed in sources that claim to cover women writers of Latin America. According to
her findings, which provide information not easily found elsewhere, women writers of less important countries are often ignored. At the SALALM 1999 meeting, Earl Fitz, Vanderbilt University,
presented a paper titled "Latin American Identity in an Inter-American Context: The View from
Literature" (not published in this volume), in which he discussed the new field of inter-American
studies, an area in need of bibliographic help. For example, it is difficult to find listings of novels
by theme so that a researcher can find works to compare.

BIBLIOGRAPHY

Bourque, Susan C. 1989. "Urban Development." In K. Lynn Stoner, ed., *Latinas of the
    Americas: A Source*. New York: Garland Publishing. Pp. 581–594.

Fiscella, Joan B. 1996. "Bibliography as an Interdisciplinary Information Service."
    Library Trends 45:2 (Fall), 280–295.

White, Howard D. 1992. "Literary Forms in Information Work: Annotated Bibliogra-
    phies, Bibliographic Essays, and Reviews of Literatures." In Howard D. White,
    Marcia J. Bates, and Patrick Wilson, eds., *For Information Specialists: Inter-
    pretations of Reference and Bibliographic Work*. Norwood, NJ: Ablex Pub. Pp.
    131–149.

Wilson, Patrick. 1992. "Pragmatic Bibliography." In Howard D. White, Marcia J. Bates, and Patrick Wilson, eds., *For Information Specialists: Interpretations of Reference and Bibliographic Work*. Norwood, NJ: Ablex Pub. Pp. 239–246.

Withers, Rob. 1999. "Foreign Language, Literature, and Culture: A Look at What's New for Students and Scholars." *C&RL News* 60:5 (May), 361–363, 410.

18. Frances Toor and the Mexican Cultural Renaissance

Peter Stern

Frances Toor, the *gringa folklorista,* was one of a host of political and cultural pilgrims who flocked to Mexico in the decade after the Revolution. In the same way that travelers, mostly European and American intellectuals, journeyed to Russia after the triumph of the Bolsheviks to see socialism in action and to find their long-sought Utopia, many North Americans headed for Mexico City to witness for themselves the new Mexico that Alvaro Obregón and José Vasconcelos were building after the Revolution. Toor, along with visitors like Tina Modotti, Edward Weston, Carlton Beals, D. H. Lawrence, and many others, sought to discover a Mexico that met their particular political or cultural needs. Others, like Julio Antonio Mella, came seeking refuge from persecution; still others, like Bertram Wolfe and Vittorio Videlli, came to Mexico for political reasons both altruistic and sinister. All these visitors had longings and needs which they believed Mexico could fulfill; few were disappointed in what they found there.

Toor, together with other *gringas* like Anita Brenner and Alma Reed, championed the cultural and artistic revival which flourished in Mexico in the decade of the 1920s. These women made it their mission to explain the new Mexico to a suspicious United States and beyond, and to spread the word about the work of Mexican artists, composers, anthropologists, and educators who were bringing about this *renacimiento*. Even more, each of them made a deep personal commitment to Mexico and to the Mexican people; each had a life-long "love affair" with the ideals of the Mexican Revolution, ideals which were all too briefly and incompletely fulfilled by a recalcitrant government. A recent biographer of Tina Modotti summed it up in this way:

> In 1923 Mexico City teemed with fanatics, bohemians, idealists, radicals, and visionaries. Intellectuals who had once looked to Europe for cultural revelation now turned their backs upon the old continent, embracing instead the genius of peasants and indigenous peoples whose inclusion in the Mexican community promised to bring forth the "regeneration and exaltation of the national spirit." Military chieftains had retreated to their ranches or ensconced themselves in plush ministries. Artists and writers were unfurling the blueprints of a more authentic culture, forging new values and constructing a modern utopia.

Lured by such vibrancy and ferment, anticipating inspiration, and titil-
lated by skirmishes between marauding guerrilla bands, foreign pilgrims
shook off their own tired affairs to board trains and boats bound for Mexico.
Some came as intellectual sightseers; others seized the opportunity to
embroil themselves in the artistic, social, and political experimentation, the
nation-building, and the fiestas.[1]

Frances Toor was born in Plattsburgh, New York, in 1890. She earned
bachelor's and master's degrees at the University of California, Berkeley
(studying with Herbert Eugene Bolton, the father of borderlands studies) before
coming to Mexico in 1922 to attend the summer school at the National University. She admitted later that she knew little about Mexico, but was overwhelmed by an exhibition sponsored by the Secretariat of Industry, Commerce
and Labor. She wrote almost twenty years later that "The beauty of it was one
of the motivating factors in my remaining. I wanted to know more of the country in which humble people could make such beautiful things." [2]

> Like most foreigners, when I came to Mexico I was ignorant of what
> Mexico really is. In those days there was not the literature that there is now
> on its history, culture, and art. But the Ministry of Industry and Labor had
> just financed the collection of an exhibit of folk art to be sent to the United
> States. Textiles, pottery, lacquer work, gold and silver jewelry had been col-
> lected by artists from the entire republic. I saw the exhibit many times, and
> I grew ever more enthusiastic over the beauty of an art produced by a hum-
> ble and practically enslaved people and also over the work of modern artists,
> so alive, virile, passionate. [3]

Another member of Mexico City's Bohemian circles was Anita Brenner,
who was in fact not a *gringa* at all, but a Mexican citizen, born in 1905 in Aguas-
calientes to immigrant Jews from Latvia. (She was delighted, much later in life,
to be able to decline the Mexican government's award of the Aguila Azteca on the
grounds that she could not accept an award meant only for foreigners.) Her family were small landowners and merchants; they fled the Revolution's fighting
several times, the last time in 1916. They settled in San Antonio, where Anita was
schooled at a Catholic girls' school before attending the University of Texas at
Austin for only a year. (As a Jew and a Mexican, she felt like a social misfit in
Austin.) She managed to persuade her father to let her go back to Mexico in 1923
to finish her education at the National University. The head of the B'nai Brith
office in Mexico City assured Isidore Brenner that the capital was now quite safe,
inasmuch as Carranza, Villa, and Zapata were dead and Obregón was president.
Brenner supported herself by teaching English in the capital.[4]

Toor later related in a 1932 issue of *Mexican Folkways* how she founded
her magazine. She came to attend summer school and stayed on, supporting
herself like Brenner by teaching English in government schools and attending
the University. "Every vacation," she wrote, "I visited some villages. As I knew

enough Spanish to carry on a conversation, I made friends easily with the Indians, and became fascinated by their courtesy and customs as well as by their modes of artistic expression. Because of my own joy in the discovery of an art and civilization different from any that I had previously known, I thought it would interest others as well. Thus I conceived the idea of the magazine."[5]

With no experience in publishing, she consulted friends who did; the Americans, like Ernest Gruening (who was then managing editor of *The Nation* and a reporter working in Mexico), tried to dissuade her; the Mexicans encouraged her efforts. Manuel Gamio, Sub-Secretary of Education, offered to contribute 100 pesos a month to support the effort and wrote a piece for the first number. Toor remarked later that, as she was making seven and a half pesos a day (three dollars *yanqui*) as an English teacher, working only ten hours a week, she had little to lose: "I had the time, and not much to lose if I were not successful, so I walked where angels feared to tread." Writing seven years after she started her enterprise, Toor described her intentions:

> I did not take existing folk-lore magazines for models. As I wanted Mexican Folkways to express the Mexico that interested me so keenly, it has not only described customs, but has touched upon art, music, archaeology, and the Indian himself as part of the new social trends, thus presenting him as a complete human being. And in order that the magazine might mean something to the Mexicans as well as to outsiders, everything has been published in both English and Spanish.[6]

Volume one, number one of *Mexican Folkways* appeared in June–July of 1925. The first issue carried an editor's foreword; an article titled "The Utilitarian Aspects of Folklore," by Manuel Gamio; pieces on Mexican pottery, Coatlicue, an Aztec goddess, "the magic of love among the Aztecs," the legend of Tzuatzinco; and articles about the petate, "a national symbol," by Anita Brenner and the passion play at Tzintzuntzan by Toor herself. The government's small subsidy did not suffice to pay for printing, and *Mexican Folkways* carried from its first issue through its last advertisements from various commercial enterprises operating inside Mexico, particularly those appealing to tourists. Thus the inside back cover had ads for the American Hotel Geneve, the Tlaquepaque Art Store (corner of López and Juárez Avenues)—and a small ad for a photography studio operating at 42 Avenida Veracruz; the ad simply said "Photographs—Edward Weston–Tina Modotti."

In her foreword, Toor spelled out her aims and objectives, and the philosophy underlying them:

> "Ya se va pasando," I am told wherever I go. Legends and stories are being buried with the "ancianos" and forgotten. Fiestas, dances, marriage customs and other celebrations are no longer as they used to be before the revolution. The Indians are coming more into contact with white civilization and they are growing self-conscious, ashamed.

In Mexico there are about ten million, at least two-thirds of the population living in the remnants of their ancient civilizations. It is these ten million that President Calles has promised to incorporate into modern life. The task will be a tremendously slow and difficult one. But it would be even slower and more difficult if it were not that through his folkloric expression the Indian has kept alive that something which has prevented him from degenerating into a mere beast of burden, compatible with his mode of living. The poorest Indian woman who lives with her whole numerous family, and perhaps with her animals also, in a one-room hut, who sleeps on the floor and has not a chair to sit upon, can embroider the most exquisite napkins or weave marvelously beautiful sashes or bags. Children of five begin to imitate their fathers in the artistic fashioning and painting of pottery; others weave fine, lacy baskets or serapes. The primitive Indian producer has not made the unfortunate separation between utility and beauty which so greatly distorts our modern life.[7]

Although to our postmodern sensibilities Toor may sound patronizing, her enthusiasm and delight in rural Mexican life swept up many collaborators who agreed to contribute to her magazine (almost certainly for little or no remuneration). Manuel Gamio (often called the father of modern Mexican anthropology) was especially encouraging, as was Franz Boaz, who urged that both Spanish and English be retained as the two languages of the enterprise. No doubt printing the magazine in both languages (with the attendant costs of translation and increased expense of more pages) placed a greater financial burden on Toor, but she hoped that *Mexican Folkways* would be of use to high school and university students of Spanish as "material for the study of social background, which gives insight into language and literature, as well as to those who are interested in folklore and the Indian for their own sakes." She did concede that much beauty might be lost in translating.[8]

It is not my intention to catalog the many and varied topics which *Mexican Folkways* explored during its ten years of intermittent existence, but rather to show how this magazine and its devoted band of contributing editors and authors typify attitudes and opinions in post-Revolutionary Mexico, and how *Mexican Folkways* served as a sounding board for many prominent artists and intellectuals who tried to bridge the immense historical chasm between *gringos* and *mexicanos*. Suffice it to say that in a decade of existence, *Mexican Folkways* explored indigenous dances, masks, village festivals, children's art, the muralist movement, Mexican theater, pre-Columbian deities, weaving, poems, corridos and other folk songs, maguey and *pulque* making, Tarahumara runners, Indian psychology, *piñatas*, Zapotec rites, passion plays, the cult of the Virgin, Mesoamerican architecture and archaeology, burial customs, the day of the dead, Mayan symbolism, and a few hundred other topics. Frances Toor visited *curanderas* and related her experiences. She and colleagues drove or rode pack animals into remote villages, always, she said, made welcome by the poorest of Indian peasants. *Mexican Folkways* also reviewed recent books on Mexico (the reviews included a good-natured panning of D. H. Lawrence's *The Plumed Serpent,* titled "Mexico through frightened eyes"; Toor wrote "Poor Lawrence! How scared he was in Mexico").[9]

Very quickly, *Mexican Folkways* became the focus of those Bohemians who had taken up residence in the capital. Issue two carried a piece on the esthetics of Indian dances by Jean Charlot, who was one of the first artists to execute a public mural at the behest of José Vasconcelos. Dr. Atl, *nom de pin̄cel* of Gerardo Murillo, former head of the Academy of San Carlos and mentor of most of the muralists, contributed an article on the purple fabrics of Oaxaca. By issue three Diego Rivera was weighing in on the issue of *retablos* as the true and only pictoric expression of the Mexican people; before *Mexican Folkways* was a year old Rivera was on the masthead as its art editor.

The magazine itself reflected what one critic has called a quasi-official stance of "romantic nationalism." *Mexican Folkways*, with articles by linguists and writers, musicians and anthropologists, as well as professional and amateur folklorists, mirrored the times, since post-Revolutionary Mexico "seemed to find its reflection in all things popular; poets, musicians, and painters all cultivated this approach."[10]

The journal, as befitted its name, concentrated on the rapidly changing culture of Mexico's Indian, determined to record native arts, crafts, and customs even as its writers applauded the integration of the Indian into national life. *Mexican Folkways* carried a series of articles through the years about the new government programs in education; Moisés Sáenz wrote, "Without neglecting the city schools, preference has been given in the present administration to rural schools." When Puig Casauranc replaced Vasconcelos as Secretary of Education in 1924, there were 700 functioning rural schools; by 1928 that number had been increased, according to the Secretary, to over 4,000. Calles's call to incorporate the Indian into modern civilization was reflected in both material resources and zeal: ". . . there has been a definite and intensive effort to make these schools really serve the community, according to the statement of aims by Moisés Sáenz, Sub-Secretary of Education. . . ." Sáenz stated that "It is necessary to establish a spiritual relationship in the community, give the teacher a social conscience, make the school the home of the people and the village the home of the school. This is not an easy task."[11]

The Ministry, Sáenz reported, had been holding "Cultural Missions" for the previous two years for rural school teachers, with courses on educational methods, hygiene, agricultural and home industries, cooking, sewing, and so on. Federal inspectors followed up these courses with inspection trips to see how well teachers were carrying out the new "socialized school of action." Sáenz reported on a trip to the Puebla Sierra, where he visited 37 schools. "This," he wrote, "is an entirely indigenous region, in which Aztec is spoken to the exclusion of Spanish, excepting in the schools. The people are ruled by an

Aztec cacique, who represents the government, and they still conserve the customs of their ancestors before the Conquest." Although everywhere he and his companions went they were received with courtesy, music, flowers, and fireworks, his conclusions on the state of the pueblos were largely negative:

> In some the children were dirty and the scholarship bad; the social work insignificant. On the whole, however, the report on the schools is infinitely more hopeful than on the people. The standard of living is low. Due to primitive methods, the agricultural production is insufficient, even though the land is good. Alcoholism in this region, as in many another, is a scourge. Their [sic] is a resistance to the Spanish language, and the people cling to their primitive customs. Mr. Saenz conclusion [sic] is that the school alone cannot uproot the old and implant the new, but that "The Ministries of Industry and Commerce, of Agriculture, of Communications and the Department of Health—all have their responsibility and their place in these regions. Unless all of them come with us to share in the work of the Rural School, our labor will be lost and within a few years we shall have another desilusion [sic] to hang on our necks." [12]

Sáenz went on to report that when inspecting schools in the San Luis Potosí region, he found some excellent and others in poor condition, but he was more hopeful about their chances for improvement, as the inhabitants of this region were not Indians, but *mestizos*. The last paragraph of the report highlights the dilemma of both the government and champions of indigenous culture: "There are other Mexican scholars who hold the opinion that the Indians must become mestizos in order to progress." Toor and her collaborators championed the old ways while urging greater integration of the Indian into national society, and while *Mexican Folkways* alludes from time to time to the contradictions inherent in such attitudes, it was never able to reconcile them.

A longer report on rural education placed the idealized school at the center of village life, alongside the church, a secular temple sometimes named the "House of the People." In each village inspectors asked questions designed to elicit the desired information on the great project of national unity:

How many children speak Spanish fluently?

How many can read and write with ease?

Is there a Mexican flag in the school?

Do the children know about Mexico?

Do they know the name of our President?

What names of great Mexicans do they know?

Do they raise chickens, pigs, bees, and silkworms?

Have they a garden?

Is there water in the school? Do they use it?

Is the school socialized? In which grade?

Has it a parents club?

Does the teacher do any social work in the community?

Sáenz freely admitted that the school routine did not particularly interest the authorities, and questions of method and technique were of secondary interest. "... but we are passionately interested," he wrote, "in having a vital school, contributing to social organization and national unity . . . in which the raising of chickens is as important as undertaking the learning of a poem."[13] The teacher in these villages acted as pedagogue, librarian, correspondent, even pharmacist and rural doctor! Sáenz was careful to distinguish between a "socialist school" and a "socialized school," which he said represented a community of effort between the government and the children and adults of rural Mexico. The Mexicans took their inspiration directly from the American educator and philosopher John Dewey, who visited the country at the invitation of the Mexican government and praised its program; he wrote that "there is no educational movement in the world which exhibits more of the spirit of intimate union of school activities with those of the community than is found in this Mexican development." He also praised the attention to music and design in the plastic arts, for which he said the Indians displayed a marked genius, which took place in many schools.[14]

The aim of all this effort, Sáenz wrote, was to create in peasant classes a rural spirit:

> To integrate Mexico. To incorporate into the Mexican family the millions of Indians; to make them think and feel in Spanish. To incorporate them into that type of civilization that constitutes Mexican nationalism. To bring them into that community of ideas and emotions that means Mexico.[15]

Between the path of segregation, which Sáenz believed would finally lead to annihilation, and of assimilation and mixing, the government chose the latter path. It was in this perhaps unrealistic belief that Toor and her collaborators on *Mexican Folkways* placed their faith.

That faith was a compound of fierce Mexican nationalism and an undoctrinaire, simplistic Marxism of the 1920s. The people with whom "Paco" Toor mixed in Mexico City were mostly unabashed admirers of the Russian Revolution, as well as Americans fiercely opposed to their own country's colonialism in Latin America. *Mexican Folkways* was first and last a magazine dedicated to showing Americans the "true" face of Mexico, through its arts and folkcrafts. It was never a political journal. While many who contributed to it were without any doubt "reds" (in the sense that they belonged to the Mexican Communist Party), neither Toor nor her journal could be said to be so. But both might be said to have been slightly "pink." The American ambassador to Mexico, James Rockwell Sheffield (a New York Republican with no diplomatic experience who was convinced that the Calles government was radical, fanatically anti-American, and altogether too cozy with the Soviet Union), described Toor as a Mexican agent, a Soviet sympathizer, and a close friend of

Alexandra Kollentai, the first ambassador of the U.S.S.R. to Mexico.[16] Toor even permitted Diego Rivera to draw a cover for her magazine which featured two stylized Mexican peasants flanking an eagle with an ear of corn in its mouth; on second glance, one notices that one of the Indians holds a hammer, the other a sickle!

From time to time the naïve sentiments of revolution showed up in the pages of *Mexican Folkways*. The same issue that published Moisés Sáenz's report on rural schools also carried a song titled "Corrido del ejido de 'Garrapata y Misión Unidas,'" which celebrated land reform and included the verse:

> Gritaban los agraristas
> Cuando estaba la reunión
> ¡Que viva el problema agrario
> Y que muera la reacción!

Somewhat more blatant was a ballad in the October–December 1929 issue, titled "Thus Will be Proletarian Revolution," accompanied by a photo of a Diego Rivera fresco titled "The Insurrection," which showed Frida Kahlo and Tina Modotti handing out rifles and ammunition to the workers. The song celebrated the time when:

> the people overthrew the kings
> And the mercenary bourgeois governments.
> And installed their councils and laws
> And established the proletarian authority.[17]

But mostly *Mexican Folkways* stuck to an optimistic hope (oftentimes misplaced) that the Mexican government would live up to its revolutionary ideals and promises to the people. More typical of its political philosophy was a corrido titled "El 30-30," which is a common caliber of rifle ammunition. The short song expressed all the disappointed hopes of frustrated farmers:

> How poor we are all,
> Without bread to eat,
> Because our bread is spent
> By the boss in his pleasure.
>
> While he has clothes
> And palaces and money,
> We go about in rags
> And live in pigsties.
>
> Everything we sow
> And everything we reap,
> But, all the harvest
> Is for the good of the masters.

> Everything we suffer,
> Exploitation and war;
> And yet they call us thieves
> Because we ask for land!
>
> And then the mean little priests
> Excommunicate us...
> I suppose they think that Christ
> Was like our bosses!
>
> Comrades of the hoe
> And of all the tools of labor,
> Only one way is left us:
> To grasp the thirty-thirty.[18]

Still, the editor's note to the song explained that the *agraristas* who sang it were ready to fight for President Calles during the Cristero rebellion. The rebels, explained Toor, hoped to find support in Morelos, Puebla, and Veracruz, but met with defeat, "because the peasants are for Calles and Obregón, the two presidents who have already given them land, irrigation, roads, and schools."[19] (When Bertram Wolfe, who was ostensibly in Mexico to teach English, but had been secretly ordered by the American Communist Party to Mexico to bring some order to the quarreling factions of the Mexican Communist Party, was expelled from the country without a hearing under Article 33 of the Mexican Constitution as a "pernicious foreigner," the police, upon detaining Wolfe, asked him whether he preferred "33" or "30-30"!)[20]

But Toor never quite bit the hand that subsidized her. A year into the magazine's existence, Toor celebrated *Mexican Folkways*'s financial survival and carried a tribute from the highest levels of the Mexican government. President Calles, upon examining several numbers, wrote ". . . besides being very original in its class, it is making known to our own people and to foreigners the real spirit of our aboriginal races and the expressive feeling of our people in general, rich in beautiful traditions."[21] Similar accolades, she proclaimed proudly, had been given the magazine by the Secretary of Public Instruction, J. Manuel Puig Casauranc, Sylvanus Morley of the Carnegie Institution, Franz Blom of Tulane, K. L. Krober [*sic*-A. L. Kroeber] of Berkeley, and Franz Boaz and John Dewey of Columbia.[22]

Toor always steered a path between outright criticism and complete exoneration of the government:

> Everyone knows by this time that the Mexican Revolution of 1920 has brought about a social change. . . . The change got under way with the first of the Revolutionary-Reconstruction Governments, beginning with the incumbency of General Alvaro Obregón in 1920, and has continued down to the present time.

> The change thus far consists chiefly in an attitude. By this I mean that the Revolution has not yet made good in an economic sense all its promises to the people. It has been perhaps unnecessarily slow in its reconstruction work, and the Indian is still poor and illiterate. But at least he has been recognized as a human being.[23]

Toor's editorializing merely reflected the mixture of radical rhetoric and caution which occasionally proceeded from the highest levels of the government itself. In a report on a visit by the Secretary of Education, Ezequiel Padilla, and the President of the Republic, Emilio Portes Gil (a *maximato* puppet put into office after Obregón's assassination), to a rural school in Tepecoacuilco, Guerrero, Toor reproduced the speeches of the president himself:

> We wish to socialize the peasant classes, unifying them as much as possible, so that they may form a united, insuperable front against exploiting capital. We are not enemies of capital, but of capitalist systems that have been the most formidable extortionists of our workers, our women, our children. . . . In our proceedings to socialize the workers, we shall not, in connection with the peasants, arbitrarily despoil of property, but only restore within the law the lands formerly wrested from the villages, the legitimate owners, who still need them. . . .[24]

One of the greatest values of *Mexican Folkways* lies in its contemporaneous nature. Toor and her friends were present "at the creation," so to speak, of a remarkable marriage of the artistic and the political. They were also witnesses to the dramatic integration of the Mexican peasant into the fabric of national life, and the subsequent erosion of traditional values in the *campo*. The photos of Indian peasants in their *huaraches* and *calzones* ("traditional" clothing into which they had been forced centuries ago by the Spanish missionaries) are mute testimony to the disappearance of a way of life which had existed since before the colonial period. Also, here and there in the pages of *Mexican Folkways* can be glimpsed newsworthy events in Mexico in the 1920s, including the union of Frida Kahlo and Diego Rivera and the assassination of ex-president Obregón.

A piece on "Mexican Ballads" by Anita Brenner explains how the corrido is a "unique and characteristic product of native mood tragedy, impersonally, and often sardonically recorded; events of casual journalistic category etched upon a background of fatalistic sorrow." A collection of corridos, she writes, is a truer record of Mexico, a truer mirror of its people, than any text yet written.[25] *Mexican Folkways*'s corridos reflected both the mood and the news of the country. On July 17, 1928, ex- and future president Alvaro Obregón was shot at a banquet in a suburb of the capital by a religious fanatic and sympathizer with the Cristero rebels. In the next number of the journal (mysteriously dated April–June 1928 but presumably printed after the cover date), there appeared a

corrido titled "Trágica muerte de General Obregón," which called the assassin
a treacherous cur. The song mourned:

> Oh beloved country of mine
> Look at the condition you're left in!
> They have killed General Obregón
> Your own and favorite son
>
> Who would have foretold
> That after having triumphed
> And having rid himself of enemies
> A traitor was to murder him
>
> Oh country of mine
> At this time you suffer so;
> The unkindness of your sons
> Offers you new grief to mourn
>
> It seems that so much blood spilled
> By others in the past everywhere
> Has not been enough, poor country
> *Nuestra madre, qué más faltará de hacer?*[26]

A few months after an uprising in Sonora in 1929, Toor published a corrido
titled "Occupation of Chihuahua by Federal Forces," which related how on the
third of the month of March, "day of blackest abuse, there broke out a new revolution in Sonora and Veracruz," and how Manzo in Sonora, Aguirre on the
coast, and Escobar in Torreón, betrayed the Revolution. The cause they proclaimed as the pretext for their action, "*fué suponer que Ortiz Rubio fué impuesto
en la Convención.*" The song related at length how Calles crushed the rebellion
and concluded by cynically observing how the defeated generals would fare:

> Well, they'll pass over to the North,
> To buy pleasure with their money.
> Eight millions of pesos
> Was the profit from the job.[27]

And after Felipe Carrillo Puerto, the left-leaning *agrarista* governor of
Yucatán, was murdered by *delahuerista* rebels in 1924, *Mexican Folkways*
printed a corrido (translated by Anita Brenner) titled "The Death of Felipe
Carrillo Puerto, Martyr of Yucatán," which mourned the death of a son of
Yucatán, killed by the Reaction (with a capital "R"), and concluded:

> Mother mine of Guadalupe,
> The blood of that execution;
> Colors for us to remember,
> Red and black of our revolution!
> Felipe Carrillo Puerto,
> Murdered for keeping his faith . . .[28]

Politics aside, *Mexican Folkways* was also instrumental in publicizing the renaissance in Mexican arts spurred largely by the efforts of José Vasconcelos and his successors in the Ministry of Education. From its inception a number of the muralists, including Jean Charlot, Diego Rivera, and José Clemente Orozco, contributed to the magazine in the form of articles, illustrations, and photos of their recent works on government walls. (Tellingly, David Alfaro Siqueiros, the most Stalinist of the muralists, except perhaps for Xavier Guerrero, never had anything to do with "Paco's" crowd.)

Diego Rivera, who was on the masthead of the magazine as art editor, contributed articles on *pulquerías*, *retablos*, and Mexican painting in general. *Mexican Folkways* published an article by painter Ray Boynton in 1926 which openly spoke of a renaissance in art symbolized by Rivera's frescoes, which Boynton compared to the work of Giotto. The magazine further honored him with an *homenaje* in 1930, dedicating a whole "fresco issue" to his work, particularly the Cuernavaca frescoes which had been painted at the behest of Dwight Morrow, ambassador to Mexico and a man determined to redress some of the injuries caused by less progressive and sympathetic American diplomats. Accompanying the photos of the murals was an effusive tribute by William Spratling, which declared that Rivera "has not only fed on the Mexican revolution but been a conscious part of it; in his painting he has given flower and fruit to it."[29] Later on, when Rivera got into trouble for the radical iconography of his Detroit and New York murals (the latter was destroyed by the Rockefellers after Rivera refused to remove Lenin from the Radio City fresco), Toor defended her friend on the grounds that the quality of his art lifted it above pure politics.[30]

But Toor did more than publicize the muralists. She dedicated an issue in 1928 exclusively to the work of José Guadalupe Posada, writing that long before the modern movement in Mexican art found its inspiration in the Mexican people's struggle for a better social order, Posada had had the same conception of art. "He worked alone and unrecognized," wrote Toor, "yet he was the greatest artist produced by the Revolution."[31] His engravings, she declared, crystallize all the stirring events of the first years of the Madero Revolution—the inevitable struggle of the middle class against feudalism and the reaction of the masses to politics, sport, miracles, crime, the parasitic church, and budding imperialism. "His ensemble of proportions reflect his inheritance from the greatest artists of the Americas, the indigenous masses of Mexico."[32]

Other articles trumpeted the talents of Rufino Tamayo and María Izquierdo, the latter lingering in the shadow of the much better known Frida Kahlo in spite of a similar style and subject matter. (She was assigned to do a public mural, but some of *los jóvenes* got wind of it and torpedoed her efforts before she could begin; few women ever joined the exclusive club of *los muralistas*.) Manuel Alvarez Bravo photographed frescoes for *Mexican Folkways*, and Miguel Covarrubias contributed caricatures. Carlos Mérida, a bona fide muralist, wrote of the new modern art gallery founded in the capital in 1929. After Dwight Morrow organized an exposition of Mexican arts, sponsored by the Carnegie Art Corporation at the Metropolitan Museum of Art in New York in 1929, a Mexican Art Association was founded in that city to maintain a permanent exhibition of Mexican applied arts and to sponsor special exhibitions of fine and applied arts of Mexico in the United States.

But *Mexican Folkways* did launch one artist whose talents might never have been discovered if not for the encouragement of Frances Toor. Tina Modotti, the Italian immigrant to San Francisco who acted in minor Hollywood films and hung out with an artsy Los Angeles crowd, came to Mexico as the lover and assistant of a more established artist, Edward Weston, who took temporary leave of his wife in California and, along with son Chandler and lover Tina, set up a home and photographic establishment in Tacubaya. Even given that the population of Mexico City in the early 1920s had a population of about 625,000 persons, it seemed as if within the shortest time everyone met everyone else worth knowing in the capital. Modotti and Weston dined with an American named Robert Turnbull, who had provided photographs for the text of a folk art exhibit written by Katherine Anne Porter, who was having her own love affair with Mexico; they dined at a restaurant owned by the brother of José Clemente Orozoco. Diego Rivera had been supposed to dine with them, but he failed to show up, so Xavier Guerrero (later Tina's lover and a fiercely dedicated member of the Mexican Communist Party) and his wife joined them. Guerrero was a full-blooded *indio* and a member of the Syndicate of Revolutionary Painters, Sculptors, and Technical Workers who had rediscovered lost fresco techniques and had convinced Rivera to abandon the encaustic method for the fresco.

Tina and Edward Weston's home became a new center for Saturday night gatherings in the capital. As one Modotti biographer wrote:

> ... the Modotti-Weston household became the prime venue for the raucous gatherings of Mexico City bohemia. Mexican and foreign artists, writers and folksingers rubbed shoulders with cabinet ministers, Communist militants and Mexican generals, who sometimes bared their anatomies after a few drinks to compare war wounds. There was little attempt at serious discussion—it was the "art" of having a good time that mattered. The eating, drinking, and dancing lasted all night, occasionally deteriorating into pistol shots at dawn as party guests became over-excited.[33]

Edward Weston kept a diary of his Mexican days and recorded his thoughts on one typical gathering:

> To Monna's and Rafael's for chocolate. In Mexico it is 6:00 o'clock chocolate, instead of 5:00 o'clock tea. A Mexican Senator was there, he and his guitar, a tall handsome charro. He had fought in the revolution, two years

with Villa; everyone here seems to have been in the fight. "Villa was the best loved man in Mexico," said the Senator. "He was an outstanding personality and made a gallant fight for the oppressed." And we in the United States, thanks to our controlled press, think only of "the bandit Villa." Lupe and the Senator sang Mexican popular songs all evening—some were in memory and love of Pancho Villa.

Diego was there. I watched him closely. His six shooter and cartridge belt, ready for service, contrasted strangely to his amiable smile. He is called the Lenin of Mexico. The artists here are closely allied with the Communist Movement; it is no parlor politics with them.[34]

Anita Brenner also kept accounts of gatherings for her journal:

. . . our first semi-pretentious affair. Wild success. House full of notables, smoking and talking. All elements, from art to Charleston. Diego, sitting in one corner and explaining Mexico to admiring gringos. . . . Frank Tannen-baum in one corner, paternally blessing our heads. . . . Salvador Novo examining books and offering awkward gallantries. I think he is reforming his preferences and now has more use for females, especially among them Lupe [Marín], beautiful in electric blue with her dark skin and large deep grey eyes and black close cropped hair. . . . Carlos Merida & Mrs. Carlton [Beals], Frances [Toor] . . . Edward [Weston] . . . Tatanacho [Ignacio Fernández Esperoón], lean, sensual, shy; many others, some of whom I don't know and many whom I don't remember.[35]

At another time Weston wrote:

As usual, last evening, the "reunión." At midnight, Frances said to the few lingering ones, "Let us go dance at the Salón Azteca. It's a tough joint; we'll have fun." There were Anita, Frances, Tina, and there were Charlot, Federico, a couple of Americans, and myself who went to the "Gran Salón Azteca." It was as tough as promised. Logically then it was colorful. Since no restraint of style and method were placed upon the dancers, one saw an unrestricted exhibition of expression, desires, passions, lusts, mostly crude unvarnished lusts—though that French cocotte was subtle indeed and beautiful too. One could not but wonder why she was in such a place among cheap and obvious whores.[36]

Still later Weston recorded: "The evening, Frances took us,—which meant Carleton Beals and the Weston-Modotti household—to Teatro Lírico. Too much 'carne'—though I am not moralizing. I was finally bored by all the wiggling arses and wobbling tits." [37]

All was not fun and games, however; Weston was to stretch the boundaries of his art in Mexico, and Modotti to discover her own talents. In the April–May 1926 issue of *Mexican Folkways*, Diego Rivera applauded their collaboration in extravagant terms (although he paid Weston a rather backhanded complement by writing, "Any day that Weston may wish or any day that some outside force may break through the modesty and indifference that are characteristic of him, he will astonish . . . the poor intellectual bourgeoisie of Mexico with his work."). Of Tina, he wrote, "Tina Modotti, his pupil, has done marvels in sensibility on a plane, perhaps, more abstract, more aerial, even more intellectual, as is natural for an Italian temperament. Her work flowers perfectly in Mexico and harmonizes exactly with our passion."[38]

Weston and Tina traveled throughout Mexico with Anita Brenner taking the photographs that would ultimately illustrate Brenner's groundbreaking work *Idols Behind Altars*. But they grew apart; Weston missed his wife and family in Los Angeles and could never share Tina's growing radicalism, which flowered dramatically in the fertile soil of Mexican communism and anti-imperialism. After he departed for the States, Tina moved into the same apartment building in which Frances Toor lived and edited her magazine, and Toor gave her commissions and put her on the masthead of *Mexican Folkways* as a contributing editor. In 1929 Toor wrote an article on an exhibition of Modotti's photographs in the Library of the National University. She praised Tina for making art with a social conscience: "Her recent work has a very definite place within the Mexican modern art movement. In subject matter and emotional content it is comparable to that of the best revolutionary artists. She, too, has caught and expressed the social unrest of the Mexico of today."[39]

Modotti followed that piece with her own, "Sobre la fotografía." Although she had had little formal schooling, and throughout her life always felt at a disadvantage socializing with people better educated than herself, her intimate association with artists over the years had given her an appropriate esthetic vocabulary. This vocabulary, coupled with her commitment to social justice, led her to criticize what she termed "dishonest" work, photography that strove to impress with distortions, manipulations, and other "artistic" effects (in this regard she seems to have been particularly attacking the avant-garde photography of the Europeans, especially the Dadaists—she referred to superimposing "effects and falsifications that can only please those of perverted taste.") Modotti's objectives were to register objective life in all its aspects; from this, she declared, comes its documentary aspects: "Creo que el resultado es algo digno de ocupar un puesto en la producción social, a la cual todos debemos contribuir."[40]

Tina Modotti's path away from photography and into Stalinist politics has been well documented in a number of biographies.[41] After her split from Weston, she had a brief fling with Diego Rivera, a more serious affair with Xavier Guerrero, and then the most intense relationship of her life, with Cuban exile and anti-Machado Communist Julio Antonio Mella. The night that Mella was shot in a Mexico City street while walking with Tina (almost certainly by a *machadista* gunmen), it was Frances Toor, Diego Rivera, and Carlton Beals who waited with Tina in the San Jerónimo hospital; when Mella died, Tina collapsed weeping into Frances Toor's arms.

Toor's efforts, although almost universally applauded, were not rewarded with commensurate commercial success. *Mexican Folkways* staggered along in a financially perilous state, published with lessening frequency as the new decade of the 1930s began. A bibliography of Latin American folklore by Ralph Steele Boggs commented of *Mexican Folkways*, "Most of the numerous contributions to Mexican folklore of the editor, Frances Toor, appear here. I have encouraged her to continue this very vivid record of Mexican folk life, but she believes its support is insufficient."[42] Perhaps *Mexican Folkways* could not find a sufficient "niche" from which it could appeal to both the serious anthropologist and the sympathetic North American; it could not help that at the same time another English-language journal calculated to appeal to *gringos, Mexican Life,* was also being published.[43]

A review of the magazine appeared in the April–June 1927 issue of *Journal of American Folk-Lore*. The reviewer, a professor at Barnard College, called *Mexican Folkways* a small bright periodical, its aim to record the customs of the Mexicans "which are slowly dying out through the superimposition of white culture and its attendant assimilation." Professor Reichard noted with approval that there was no limit to the type of material that subsequent numbers of the paper had treated, citing pieces on archaeology, history, witchcraft, ceremonials, animal stories, legends of Holy Saints, poetry, song, and drama. Besides contributions to the imaginative arts, one of the main purposes of the journal, she wrote, is to call attention to achievements and trends in the graphic arts. "This periodical," she went on, "because of its interest in all things Mexican, should appeal to all who have even the slightest interest in Mexican affairs."[44]

> For some time the Mexican government has hoped that by recognizing and making a conscious effort to assimilate the ancient primitive customs a happier adjustment of peoples might be made. Most nations proceed on the policy that to govern is to crush all that is indigenous. For this reason the Mexican government is being watched by those who believe that every primitive society has some rights to the culture it has developed.

The reviewer concluded, "The publication, by its quaintness and sympathy with the Mexican natives does much to obliterate the rancid smell of oil which has lately accompanied our notions of Mexico gained from our own periodicals which treat of political matters." [45]

In 1929 William Spratling published a piece on the Mexico City scene in *Scribner's Magazine* titled "Figures in a Mexican Renaissance, Being Various Encounters Among the Intelligentsia Mexicana." After praising the work of Rivera, Orozco, Moisés Sáenz, and Dr. Atl, Spratling termed Frances Toor "the one American . . . who has consistently devoted herself toward preserving what is traditionally and indigenously Mexican in art, and not only this, but to the cause of the artists as well. Hers is almost entirely a work of co-ordination and research, and at the same time she is thoroughly in touch with all the various movements and maintains a certain relationship between the departments of the government and the intelligentsia. The newspapers in Mexico like to refer to her as 'la editora fecunda y sapiente,' an appellation which both she and I found vastly amusing."[46] This *editora,* he reported, was close to the Indian. "She has traveled alone through many remote regions in Mexico for her material, and the results of these trips have occasionally formed priceless chapters in folkloric research."[47]

But Toor's energy and enthusiasm could not make up for the lack of a secure financial base for her magazine. In several editor's notes she alludes to the difficulty of finding funds to continue publishing. At the end of 1932, she wrote, "As nearly always at the end of the year, I find myself without any assurance of being able to continue publication. But Mexico is a land of miracles. Seven have already been conceded me in my seven volumes of Mexican Folkways. Perhaps there will be an eighth!" In "El Milagro . . . !!" in January 1933, she rejoiced at her salvation, in the form of a Mr. and Mrs. William Carr of New York, who had bought some bound volumes of *Mexican Folkways* and who had been disappointed at being told that publication had been suspended because of lack of funds. They were put into contact with Toor and proposed subsidizing the magazine's continued existence.[48]

Mexican Folkways managed to stagger along for another three years; one of the last issues to appear is dated August 1935, a special number devoted to Mexican popular arts. In her editor's note, she restated both the dilemma that modernization presented the indigenous people of Mexico and the systems of belief that had kept her in Mexico for more than a decade on her labor of love:

> This, like all other special numbers of Mexican Folkways, is an attempt to present the subject in a general way, with as many specific examples and details as space will permit. It is not a plea nor a wish that the Indian continue forever making objects for the delight of our esthetic taste, if it means poverty and a low standard of living.
>
> Anyway, no opinions or wishes are going to stop the march of history. Economic forces are at work in Mexico as everywhere else in the world. It is certain that to the extent that the Indian becomes incorporated into modern life, his desire for modern things will increase. He will have to look for higher wages than the handicrafts can yield and will abandon them. And with them will go his time for festivals, and, perhaps, also his capacity for the enjoyment, of leisure and beauty.
>
> There are two classes of North Americans to whom this realization is appalling. First, the sentimental unthinking ones, who at all costs to the Indian, would like to see him remain picturesque and producing lovely handmade things for their delight, without wishing to pay for their value. Second, those who think and feel but have before them the terrible

example of a highly industrialized and mechanized civilization in their own country.

. . . the important question concerning the future of the Mexican Indian is: What will the inevitable change bring him? Will he sell his heritage for the miserable life of the mechanized laborer? Or, will his natural wisdom help him to salvage his intense and virile love of life and beauty?[49]

Two years later, in July 1937, Toor produced one last issue of *Mexican Folkways,* a special number on Yaqui customs, music, and dance. The magazine went out still proudly listing on its masthead its contributing editors: Pablo González Casanova, José de J. Núñez y Domínguez, Elsie Clew Parsons, Robert Redfield, Miguel O. de Mendizábal, Moisés Sáenz, Carlton Beals, Carlos Mérida, Manuel Alvarez Bravo, Enrique Juan Palacios, Miguel Covarrubias, and Rufino Tamayo. Its art editor remained Diego Rivera.

Frances Toor continued to live and work in the capital after her magazine folded. She continued to write books dedicated to folklore and to acquainting her countrymen with Mexico and its arts. She published several guidebooks to Mexico, a Spanish language and vocabulary book for Americans traveling in Latin America, and from the Frances Toor Workshops, a series of monographs on Mexican artists and muralists. In 1947 her masterpiece, *A Treasury of Mexican Folkways: The Customs, Myths, Folklore, Traditions, Beliefs, Fiestas, Dances, and Songs of the Mexican People*, appeared, illustrated with over a hundred drawings by Carlos Mérida. Like Anita Brenner, she was awarded the Order of the Aztec Eagle for her lifetime achievements on behalf of her adopted *patria*; but unlike Brenner, she did not decline the honor, as she was born and remained a *gringa* her whole life. She died in New York in 1956 at the age of 66. Her obituary in the *New York Times* neatly summed up a lifetime in pursuit of *la indígena y el auténtico*:

She went to Mexico for a brief visit, fell in love with the land, and stayed on to become better acquainted with its folkways. On foot, horse, and mule, on bus, auto, train, and plane, Miss Toor wandered up and down the countryside collecting treasures of folklore. Although she was a popular writer, her works on Mexican Folkways became source books for anthropologists. She was especially interested in the fiestas, which she followed round the calendar of Mexican days. She joined in pilgrimages to shrines, feigned illness to be cured by healers and witches, questioned local inhabitants and aged storytellers, rummaged through the literature of padres and conquistadors, and published her own magazine. . . . [50]

Frances Toor, the *gringa folklorista*, made a lifetime pilgrimage, leaving as her legacy a visual record of an era of transition in Mexico for the Indian, between tradition and modernity, as well as a body of socially conscious work as testament to an idealistic, if ephemeral, union between art and politics.

NOTES

1. Patricia Albers, *Shadows, Fire, Snow: The Life of Tina Modotti* (New York: Clarkson Potter, 1999), p.115.

2. Frances Toor, *Mexican Popular Arts* (Mexico City: Frances Toor Studios, 1939), pp. 10–11.

3. "Mexican Folkways," *Mexican Folkways* [hereafter *MF*], v. 7, no. 4 (October–December, 1932), pp. 207–208.

4. See Susannah Joel Glusker, *Anita Brenner: A Mind of Her Own* (Austin: University of Texas Press, 1998), pp. 21–33.

5. Toor, "Mexican Folkways," p. 208.

6. Ibid., p. 208.

7. Frances Toor, "Editor's Foreword," *MF*, v. 1, no. 1 (June–July, 1925), p. 3.

8. Ibid., p. 4.

9. Frances Toor, "Mexico Through Frightened Eyes," *MF*, v. 2, no. 3 (August–September, 1926), pp. 45–47.

10. Isabel Quiñónez, "Popular Narrative and Poetics," in *Encyclopedia of Mexico: History, Society, and Culture,* edited by Michael S. Werner. 2 vols. (Chicago: Fitzroy Dearborn Publishers, 1997), v. 2, p. 1139.

11. Moisés Sáenz, "Las escuelas rurales y el progreso del indio," *MF*, v. 4, no. 1 (January–March, 1928), pp. 73–74.

12. Ibid., pp. 74–75.

13. Moisés Sáenz, "Nuestras escuelas rurales/Our Rural Schools," *MF*, v. 3, no. 1 (February–March, 1927), pp. 46–47.

14. *John Dewey's Impressions of Soviet Russia and the Revolutionary World: Mexico-China-Turkey, 1929,* introduction and notes by William W. Brickman (New York: Bureau of Publications, Teachers College, Columbia University, 1964), pp. 124–126.

15. Sáenz, "Nuestras escuelas rurales," p. 50.

16. James Rockwell Sheffield to William Howard Taft, February 9, 1927, Sheffield Papers; Sheffield to Secretary of State, December 11, 1926, 812.20211/45, Records of the Department of State Relating to Political Relations Between the United States and Mexico. Cited in Helen Delpar, *The Enormous Vogue of Things Mexican: Cultural Relations Between the United States and Mexico, 1920–1935 (*Tuscaloosa: University of Alabama Press, 1992), p. 51.

17. Martinez *[sic]*, "This Will Be Proletarian Revolution," *MF*, v. 5, no. 4 (October–December, 1929), p. 164.

18. C. Gutiérrez Cruz, "El 30-30," *MF*, v. 3, no. 4 (August–September, 1927), pp. 188–190.

19. "Editor's note," ibid., p. 188.

20. See Bertram Wolfe, *A Life in Two Centuries* (New York: Stein and Day, 1981), pp. 353–356.

21. "Nuestro aniversario," *MF*, no. 7 (June–July, 1926), p. 4.

22. Ibid.

23. Toor, "Mexican Folkways," pp. 205–206.

24. Frances Toor, "Noticias de los pueblos/News from the Villages," *MF*, v. 4, no. 4 (October–December, 1928), pp. 232–233.

25. Anita Brenner, "Mexican Ballads," *MF*, v. 1, no. 5 (February–March, 1926), pp. 11.

26. Enrique Munguía, "Trágica muerte del General Obregón," *MF,* v. 4, no. 2 (April–June, 1928), pp. 116–118.

27. Felipe Flores, "Ocupación de Chihuahua por las fuerzas federales," *MF,* v. 5, no. 1 (January–March, 1929), pp. 2–7.

28. "The Death of Felipe Carrillo Puerto, Martyr of Yucatán," translated by Anita Brenner, *MF,* v. 1, no. 5 (February–March, 1926), p. 15.

29. William P. Spratling, "Diego Rivera," *MF,* v. 6, no. 4 (1930), p. 162.

30. "Diego Rivera," *MF,* v. 8, no. 1 (January–March, 1933), p. 52.

31. Frances Toor, "Guadalupe Posada," *MF,* v. 4, no. 3 (July–September, 1928), p. 140.

32. Ibid., p. 142.

33. Margaret Hooks, *Tina Modotti: Photographer and Revolutionary* (San Francisco: Pandora, 1993), p. 70.

34. *The Daybooks of Edward Weston,* v. I: Mexico, edited by Nancy Newhall (New York: Aperture, 1971), p. 35.

35. Brenner journals, April 17, 1926; cited in Glusker, p. 43.

36. Ibid., p. 80.

37. Ibid., p. 134.

38. Diego Rivera, "Edward Weston and Tina Modotti," *MF,* v. 2, no. 1 (April–May 1926), p. 17.

39. Frances Toor, "Exposición de fotografías de Tina Modotti," *MF,* v. 5, no. 4 (October–December 1929), p. 192.

40. Tina Modotti, "Sobre la fotografía/On Photography," *MF,* v. 5, no. 4 (October–December 1929), p. 198.

41. For the most recent biographies, see Pino Cacucci, *Tina Modotti: A Life,* translated from the Italian by Patricia J. Duncan (New York: St. Martin's Press, 1999); Patricia Albers, *Shadows, Fire, Snow: The Life of Tina Modotti* (New York: Clarkson Potter, 1999).

42. Ralph Steele Boggs, *Bibliography of Latin American Folklore* (Washington, DC: Inter-American Bibliographical and Library Association, 1940), p. 5.

43. See John Brown, "Exuberanica mexicano-norteamericana 1920–1940," *Anglia: Anuario/Estudios angloamericanos* (UNAM, Facultad de Filosofía y Letras), v. 1 (1968), pp. 118–119.

44. Gladys A. Reichard, "Book Review: A Cross Section of Mexican Life," *Journal of American Folk-Lore,* v. 40, no. 156 (April–June, 1927), p. 212.

45. Ibid.

46. William Spratling, "Figures in a Mexican Renaissance, Being Various Encounters Among the Intelligentsia Mexicana," *Scribner's Magazine,* v. 85 (January–June, 1929), p. 21.

47. Ibid.

48. Frances Toor, "El Milagro. . . !! / The Miracle," *MF,* v. 8, no. 1 (January–March, 1933), p. 2.

49. Frances Toor, "Nota sobre este Número," *MF* (August 1935), p. 4.

50. Obituary, *New York Times,* June 18, 1956, p. 25.

19. Escritoras cubanas en el exilio

Lesbia Orta Varona

Si abundante es la bibliografía sobre los escritores cubanos exiliados, sus temas, tópicos y aún generalizaciones y sistemas que ya comienzan a trazar líneas caracterológicas, no ocurre lo mismo con la obra de las escritoras cubanas por parte de la historiografía literaria en ambas orillas: dentro y fuera de Cuba. A la altura del 2000 los estudios feministas no han sido incorporados aún como complemento vital de una historia de la literatura cubana. A pesar de la evidencia de su importancia en el cambio de perspectiva que supone este tipo de acercamiento que llena no pocos vacíos, éstos ocupan con sus autoras el sitio de nadie, pues aunque se encuentren publicados, reseñados y hasta aclamados en diferentes eventos, no son tomados en cuenta a la hora de introducir los cambios necesarios de esta historiografía. Ciertamente, en ésta siguen resonando como nombres capitales los de los hombres y mencionados los de las mujeres en pequeños subgrupos que de por sí dan la idea de una clasificación menor.

Pero si la presencia de la voz femenina en la literatura cubana dista desde el siglo pasado con figuras tan cimeras como Gertrudis Gómez de Avellaneda, Luisa Pérez de Zambrana y Mercedes Matamoros, entre otras, también la marca de esta voz en el exilio se encuentra dentro de una tradición histórica en la que figura, por una parte, José María Heredia, y por la otra, la genial poetisa modernista muerta tempranamente, Juana Borrero, cuyos restos, como una magnífica interrogación y símbolo del olvido a esta voz de mujer, se encuentran aún en Key West. La república, al parecer muy atareada, también olvidó el traslado de su poeta a suelo patrio. El período revolucionario tampoco ha hecho mucho. Aunque el año 1959 trajo una aparente política de liberación femenina, ésta ocurrió mucho más en el campo de la manipulación socio-política que en el rescate, relectura y replanteamiento de los valores de la mujer y de su escritura. Sólo a principios de los noventa sería publicado el primer estudio de enfoque feminista en Cuba, tras la tardía influencia de un feminismo latino-americano, en el que sobresale el intercambio de escritoras mexicanas y cubanas.

Por lo que a nosotros respecta, nos atendremos solamente a un breve muestrario de las escritoras cubanas, teniendo en cuenta únicamente una condición—el exilio—hecho que incide en aspectos de la vida del ser y en específico del escritor y de su oficio, y que, por supuesto, origina nuevos caminos para la comprensión y estudio de la identidad, la cultura y la nación cubanas.

En la década del sesenta comenzaría el éxodo incesante de cubanos hacia diferentes partes del mundo. Éxodo que continúa en las décadas del setenta, ochenta y noventa. Situación histórica que nos hace comprender un marco generacional que se desarrolló en algunos casos, de una manera confluyente con el devenir literario de la Isla, y en otros, de una manera diferente, marcada no sólo por el estar y la distancia, sino también por la esencia de otra identidad que determina la conversión y/o el ser de lo cubanoamericano, dada además por el uso de otra lengua y la aprehensión de otra realidad. Este hecho incide notablemente en la creación de muchos cubanoamericanos que han elegido el inglés como su forma de expresión, aunque continúan dando tratamiento a temas y preocupaciones cubanas. A esta altura, resulta casi imposible una clasificación según el modelo tradicional, el arte impone así sus propias circunstancias y variantes. Un problema no menos importante y conflictivo ha nacido también tras las elecciones de expresarse en otro idioma o de vivir en otro país, aspecto en el que profundizaremos más adelante en este recorrido histórico.

Volviendo al sesenta encontramos cómo a la literatura comprometida con la Revolución cubana, el exilio opone una literatura comprometida con el destierro. A la alabanza de la Isla, los exiliados reaccionan con la protesta y la denuncia de una realidad conocida por ellos en su esencia destructiva, pero celebrada a nivel internacional. El consenso y el aplauso de un "naciente, joven y revolucionario estado" determina, en la mayoría de los casos, el olvido y la ignorancia del discurso del destierro que desde muy pronto ha comprendido la otra cara de la moneda de la Revolución cubana. Esta nueva realidad origina un tipo específico de literatura. Así, confluentemente, a una literatura panfletaria revolucionaria de la Cuba de los sesenta, se opone una no menos panfletaria literatura exiliada, en ambos, en sus exponentes menores.

Ahora bien, si por una parte hallamos este tipo de literatura político-tendenciosa, por la otra, descubrimos un balance magnífico de la producción creativa. El exilio ha sido largo en camino y abundante en sufrimiento. Si el segundo es fuente nutricia para el arte, el primero también ha permitido distancia con el objeto creado, y por ende, un alcance en muchísimos casos de altas calidades estéticas. Del mismo modo, dictadura por un lado y exilio por otro, han contribuido a la necesidad de análisis y, por consiguiente, al desarrollo del género ensayístico en ambas orillas.

Poetas y poetisas, narradores y narradoras, dramaturgos y dramaturgas comienzan a cambiar ciertos rumbos, o mejor dicho, a desandar de una manera más profunda sus problemáticas y carencias. Todo ello ocurre hasta el punto de ampliar sus registros y encontrar en el ensayo una forma donde expresar su angustia vital, un género para analizar la idea de nación y de destierro. Dentro de este novísimo y desatendido panorama cultural cubano se encuentran las mujeres que, como creadoras, encuentran el reto de seguir creando fuera de su realidad y lector naturales, y un compromiso de continuidad de su propia obra, que se expresará con aciertos indiscutidos en las mejores.

En este esfuerzo, la escritura femenina tiene un lugar principal. Entre las voces más importantes que continúan su obra de una manera realista, ética y de altos valores estéticos, encontramos poetas y narradoras perfectamente enraizadas a sus generaciones naturales y entre las que sobresalen en este primer grupo: Lydia Cabrera (1900), a quien debemos trabajos capitales de investigación etnográfica y una no menos importante creación narrativa. Le sigue la crítica teatral Dolores Martí de Cid (1916) y las poetas, ensayistas y profesoras Mercedes García Tudurí (1904), Rosario Rexach (1912) y Anita Arroyo (1914), ésta última destacada también por su obra narrativa y periodística.

En el segundo grupo de creadoras distinguimos a las que comenzaron su carrera literaria en los años inmediatamente anteriores a la revolución castrista, e igualmente enraizadas en sus generaciones, y entre las que destacan: las narradoras Hilda Perera (1926), novelista reconocida internacionalmente y escritora de cuentos infantiles; Concepción T. Alzola (1930), también folklorista; así como las poetas Ana Rosa Núñez (1926), Nivaria Tejera (1930) y Pura del Prado (1931). La primera, Ana Rosa Núñez, ha contribuido notablemente a la poesía cubana con su trabajo poético del haiku, así como con revalorizaciones de la obra de poetas capitales cubanos como Dulce María Loynaz, al tiempo que por su propia obra de innegables valores. Pura del Prado, fallecida recientemente, recibió a fines de la década del cincuenta el Premio Nacional de Poesía en Cuba.

Posiblemente, estos sean los dos primeros grupos más fácilmente discernibles, en los que encontramos una interinfluencia generacional, que se traduce en la participación de muchas de estas escritoras en las primeras manifestaciones disidentes que se producen en Cuba alrededor de las ediciones "El Puente", grupo en el que hallamos del mismo modo a las poetas Lilliam Moro, Mercedes Cortázar, Ana María Simó (1943) y María Josefa Ramírez, quienes junto a las antes citadas también formaron parte del exilio casi de inmediato. Un poco más adelante en esta década de los setenta sobresale Belkis Cuza Malé (1942), quien se incorporaría al exilio en 1979, a raíz de los sucesos del "Caso Padilla" y que funda en 1982 la revista literaria *Linden Lane Magazine*. De su labor investigativa nació una biografía sobre Juana Borrero.[1]

Para enriquecer y complejizar aún más este proceso, surge el tercer grupo de creadoras que comenzaron su obra en el exilio, a pesar de haber nacido alrededor de los años treinta, entre las que sobresalen, en el género poético: Marta Padilla (1933), a cuya pluma se debe *Mijares, un óleo* (1974), una increíble develación de este gran pintor cubano. Le sigue en nuestra lista poética Gladys Zaldívar; Juana Rosa Pita (1939), ganadora de varios premios internacionales de poesía; la también actriz y directora de teatro Teresa María Rojas (1938); y Lourdes Casal (1938), personalidad polémica que escribió además de poesía y cuento varios estudios sobre los cubanos como minoría en los Estados Unidos. En este mismo grupo encontramos la obra de Florinda

Álzaga (1930), quien a pesar de escribir cuentos es mucho más conocida por su obra ensayística en la que destacan estudios sobre Unamuno y la Avellaneda. No podrían faltar Eloísa Lezama Lima, a quien debemos una paciente labor de rescate de la obra de su hermano, el gran poeta cubano José Lezama Lima; la profesora y conocida crítica literaria Yara González-Montes; así como Georgina Sabat de River, destacada autoridad de la obra de Sor Juana Inés de la Cruz. Mención aparte merece Amelia del Castillo (1925) quien, a pesar de pertenecer a una década anterior, comienza su labor creadora en Miami por estos mismos años finales de la década del sesenta e inicios del setenta.

Dentro de la misma necesidad de escritura al llegar al exilio, encontramos un cuarto grupo, que se distingue a sí mismo por un elemento generacional. Nacidas en la década de los cuarenta, este cuarto grupo de mujeres se diferencia de los anteriores por su corta edad a la llegada de la Revolución, y por ende, por no ser intelectuales formadas a su llegada al exilio. Otro detalle: el nacimiento del pensamiento de éstas tendría lugar dentro de las universidades americanas y extranjeras en la mayoría de los casos.

En el género ensayístico y en crítica tenemos a María Castellanos (1941); en poesía a Luisa María Perdigó (1947); Uva de Aragón (1944); Maya Islas (1947); y Dolores Prida (1943), quien se destaca igualmente en el teatro; mientras que en el cultivo del cuento hallamos a Marta Domínguez de Fariñas (1946). Con estas escritoras comienza a surgir un signo inquietante de pérdida e identidad. A diferencia de las anteriores, jóvenes en verdad, pero intelectualmente formadas, las nacidas en los años cuarenta asisten a un mundo caótico que, en muchas, establece un rechazo y en otras, un intento de participación y comprensión. El segundo intento, traería la permanencia de una joven intelectualidad en la Isla, mientras que la primera reacción trae consigo una ausencia. En ambas, una opción. Para las primeras, la aceptación del amo, pero con patria. En las segundas, "sin patria, pero sin amo". Nuevamente, en ambas, la decepción, la angustia y la pérdida de un pasado y, por ende, de una identidad.

A partir de este cuarto grupo se establece una característica de angustia vital que toca con igual fuerza a las nacidas en los años cincuenta, quienes también marcan otra época o quinto grupo, ya que para ellas la memoria de sus orígenes será aún más vago y en muchas ocasiones casi nulo. Muchas escritoras parten a temprana edad. Otras más tarde. Muchas parten sin opción. Son sus padres los que deciden el exilio. Otras quedan sin opción. Son igualmente los progenitores los que deciden permanecer en la Isla. Ha nacido, sin apenas darnos cuenta la quinta generación sin alternativas, y con este devenir histórico una característica confluyente para los nacidos y nacidas en los sesenta, setenta y aún ochenta.

Volviendo a las nacidas en los años cincuenta encontraremos nombres de poetas que igualmente desarrollan su labor en el exilio y que alternan su producción creativa con el ensayo, entre ellas: el revelador estudio de "Tierra sin nosotras" de Lourdes Gil (1951); los acercamientos sobre cultura cubana de

Ruth Behar (1956); y Carolina Hospital (1957). Igualmente en su desentrañamiento poético sobresalen: Alina Galliano (1950), Magali Alabau y Carlota Caulfield (1953); mientras que en narrativa se destaca: Mayra Montero (1952), quien recibiera el premio "La Sonrisa Vertical". Todas ellas, a pesar de llegar al exilio muy jóvenes, utilizan el español como su lengua de expresión literaria.

Pertenecientes también a este grupo las narradoras Cristina García (1958) con su archiconocido *Dreaming in Cuban;* Achy Obejas (1956) con sus novelas *Memory mambo* y *We Came All the Way from Cuba So You Could Dress Like This?;* Carolina García Aguilera crea en sus novelas el personaje detectivesco femenino "Lupe Serrano", de nacionalidad cubana y todas ellas se desarrollan en Miami; y la destacada periodista Ana Veciana Suárez de *The Miami Herald,* convertida en los últimos años en novelista. Todas ellas han elegido el inglés como su lengua para la creación literaria, asunto éste que nos sitúa ante otro conflicto.

En las bibliotecas de Estados Unidos, por ejemplo, se han comenzado a clasificar a los escritores cubanoamericanos de acuerdo con la lengua en que escriben. De este modo, Cristina García, Carolina García Aguilera, Achy Obejas y Ana Veciana Suárez son clasificadas como escritoras norteamericanas por el solo hecho de escribir en inglés. Lo mismo ocurre cuando sólo se considera el lugar de residencia de la escritora, de manera que la creadora cubana termina por ser para nuestras bibliotecas y lectores una escritora norteamericana, francesa, alemana o, incluso, española.

En el caso de la literatura cubana escrita en inglés u otro idioma que no sea español, este problema se agrava, ya que generalmente géneros literarios como novela, poesía, cuento, teatro y ensayo no llevan epígrafes en la mayoría de los casos que determinen la nacionalidad del escritor; lo que hace que estos escritores sean asimilados a una literatura a la que no pertenecen, aunque sus temas sean netamente cubanos en la mayoría de los casos. A esta confusión contribuyen del mismo modo las editoriales, que en muchas ocasiones no hacen constar la nacionalidad del escritor en ninguna de las partes del libro.

A los grupos ya mencionados se une una incesante llegada de la diáspora cubana. Tal es el caso de las narradoras de gran resonancia internacional en estos momentos Zoé Valdés (1959) y Daína Chaviano (1957), con libros que con suma distancia de la Isla abordan el fenómeno de lo cubano. Del mismo modo encontramos a la poeta y narradora Rita Martin (1963), una de las pocas escritoras de la nueva hornada que ya figura en la antología narrativa más completa de la diáspora, *Narrativa y libertad, cuentos cubanos de la diáspora* (1996) de Julio Hernández Miyares; así como en *Bridges to Cuba,* realizada por Ruth Behar y Juan León.

Los años pasan y el exilio permanece. Miami, París, Madrid, Toronto o Australia. Tal la naturaleza de la diáspora. Con ella, el dolor y la necesidad y la urgencia de expresar lo cubano, de preservarlo. En esta labor sobresale la labor de las escritoras cubanas del exilio. En cada ensayo y en cada ficción, un reto a la memoria y al olvido.

NOTA

1. Algo distanciadas de los objetivos y calibres estéticos de estas creadoras, se encuentran Caridad Bravo Adams, Delia Fiallo, Inés Rodena y Mercedes Antón, quienes son mencionadas en nuestra reseña por la resonancia internacional que alcanzan sus telenovelas a la manera exitosa de las series de Corín Tellado.

REFERENCIAS BIBLIOGRÁFICAS

Alba-Buffill, Elio. *Conciencia y quimera*. New York: Senda Nueva de Ediciones, 1985.

Alvarez-Borland, Isabel. *Cuban-American Literature of Exile: From Person to Persona*. Charlottesville: University Press of Virginia, 1998.

Anales Literarios. Matías Montes-Huidobro y Yara González Montes, eds. Honolulu, Hawaii: Matías and Yara Foundation, 1995–1996.

Bejel, Emilio. *Literatura de nuestra América: estudios de literatura cubana e hispanoamericana*. Xalapa, Veracruz, México: Centro de Investigaciones Lingüístico-Literarias, Instituto de Investigaciones Humanísticas, Universidad Veracruzana, 1983.

Davies, Catherine. *A Place in the Sun?: Women Writers in Twentieth-Century Cuba*. London; New Jersey: Zed Books, 1997.

Fernández, José B. *Indice bibliográfico de autores cubanos (diáspora, 1959–1979) Literatura; Bibliographical Index of Cuban Authors (Diaspora, 1959–1979) Literature*. Miami, FL: Ediciones Universal, 1983.

Foster, David William. *Cuban Literature: A Research Guide*. New York: Garland Pub., 1985.

Horno-Delgado, Asunción, ed. *Breaking Boundaries: Latina Writing and Critical Readings*. Amherst: University of Massachusetts Press, 1989.

Kanellos, Nicolás. *Biographical Dictionary of Hispanic Literature in the United States: The Literature of Puerto Ricans, Cuban Americans, and Other Hispanic Writers*. New York: Greenwood Press, 1989.

McCracken, Ellen. *New Latina Narrative: The Feminine Space of Postmodern Ethnicity*. Tucson: University of Arizona Press, 1999.

Maratos, Danie C. y Marnesba D. Hill. *Escritores de la diáspora cubana: manual biobibliográfico; Cuban Exile Writers: A Biobibliographic Handbook*. Metuchen, NJ: Scarecrow Press, 1986.

Martínez, Julio A., ed. *Dictionary of Twentieth-Century Cuban Literature*. New York: Greenwood Press, 1990.

Mateo Palmer, Margarita. *Ella escribía postcrítica*. Ciudad de La Habana: Casa Editora Abril, 1995.

Miranda, Julio E. *Nueva literatura cubana*. Madrid: Taurus, 1971.

Monge Rafuls, Pedro R., ed. *Lo que no se ha dicho*. Jackson Heights, NY: Ollantay Center for the Arts, 1994.

Montes Huidobro, Matías y Yara González. *Bibliografía crítica de la poesía culbana; exilio: 1959–1971.* New York: Plaza Mayor, 1972.

Peñas Germejo, Francisco J., ed. *Poetas cubanos marginados.* Ferrol, Spain: Sociedad de Cultura Valle-Inclán, 1998.

Sánchez-Boudy, José. *Historia de la literatura cubana en el exilio.* Miami, FL: Ediciones Universal, 1975.

West, Alan. *Tropics of History: Cuba Imagined.* Westport, CT: Bergin & Garvey, 1997.

IV. Society

20. Cultural Amnesia: Systematically Erasing the History of Brazilian Industrialization

Marshall C. Eakin

It is something of a truism to say that archives and libraries in Latin America are less developed than their counterparts in the United States and Europe. When one moves outside of the national capitals, the underdevelopment of regional and local archives is even more pronounced. Archives and libraries lack basic reference tools, information about collections is not widely or readily available, and in the age of the Internet, Latin American archives and libraries have been slow to computerize. Once again, these problems are even more acute when one works outside the national capitals.

For a historian, especially a historian of the twentieth century, even more distressing than the underdevelopment of archives and reference tools is the failure to collect documents systematically. Moreover, documentary evidence that is not collected is often systematically erased. The problem, in some ways, is worse now that it was in the past. As governments have become larger and more complex, they generate enormous amounts of paper, causing enormous problems for archivists in the United States, a very rich nation with a long tradition of the systematic collection of government documents. In Latin America, where such a tradition often does not exist—or is weak—the enormity of the problem is magnified. This paper addresses the problem with specific reference to Brazil, the Latin American nation I know best, but I suspect the case may be similar elsewhere in the region.

At the outset, an autobiographical note will help in understanding my analysis. I am a historian of nineteenth- and twentieth-century Brazil, and for the past twenty years much of my work has focused on Brazilian industrialization, particularly in the state of Minas Gerais. Although I have worked in libraries and archives in Rio de Janeiro and São Paulo, I have spent the vast majority of my research time in the libraries and archives of Minas Gerais, especially in Greater Belo Horizonte, the state capital. Although Minas Gerais and Belo Horizonte do not have the name recognition and allure of Rio de Janeiro and São Paulo, they are powerful and important places. Minas Gerais is the second most populous state in Brazil (after São Paulo) and Belo Horizonte is the third largest city (after São Paulo and Rio). Along with Rio and São

Paulo, Belo Horizonte forms a triangle in southeastern Brazil that contains some 40 percent of the nation's population and produces 60 percent of the nation's manufactured goods.[1] Throughout much of the last two centuries, Minas Gerais and São Paulo have arguably been the two most important states in Brazilian national politics.

Since 1987 I have been working on a book about the industrialization of Belo Horizonte.[2] Created in the 1890s as a planned city, Greater Belo Horizonte now has a population approaching four million, and it has surpassed Rio de Janeiro to become the second largest industrial center in Brazil. The study examines how Belo Horizonte industrialized so rapidly, especially since 1950. This paper discusses my research on this topic and the problems I have encountered along the way. It is a cautionary tale for historians, archivists, and librarians.

Desperately Seeking Archives

I first went to Brazil in 1979–1980 to do fieldwork for my dissertation. Most of that time I lived and worked in Belo Horizonte and its metropolitan area. I returned again from May to August 1985 to do follow-up research to turn the dissertation into a book.[3] I spent several months in the Arquivo Público Mineiro (APM) in Belo Horizonte, as well as in the company archives of the old British-owned St. John d'el Rey Mining Company in Nova Lima, a suburb of Greater Belo Horizonte.[4] The company archive (nearly entirely in English), one of the richest of its kind in Latin America, contains 130 years of correspondence between the superintendent of the mine and the board in London, as well as hundreds of thousands of documents on all aspects of the company's operations. Fortunately, the current owners of the mine were enlightened enough to hire professional archivists and historians to organize and catalog the archive and to digitize a small portion of it.[5]

The APM is a fairly well organized and managed archive. Created in the 1890s by the new republican government of the state, the APM was housed in the old building of the *prefeitura* of Belo Horizonte from the 1930s until the construction of a modern facility alongside the old quarters in the mid-1970s. From its early years under the guidance of the venerable politician and historian Augusto de Lima, the APM followed a very traditional approach to collection focusing on the colonial period, especially the administrative documents of the various colonial *comarcas* in the captaincy of Minas Gerais from the early eighteenth century to independence in 1822. The APM is also very strong on the documents generated by the provincial governments under the empire (1822–1889). As one moves into the republican era (post-1889) the documentation is increasingly published reports and less and less the day-to-day paperwork of the bureaucracy. The APM has long published a series that makes available guides and documents from the collections.[6] (The public archive of the Casa dos Contos in Ouro Preto is another fine repository in Minas Gerais that focuses on the history of the eighteenth century.)[7]

When I returned to Belo Horizonte in 1987–1988 to begin my fieldwork on the industrialization of the city, I fully expected to spend a great deal of time in nontraditional collections.[8] In particular, I knew that I would be seeking out business archives, the libraries and archives of business associations, and government agencies. I also planned on doing interviews with businessmen and government officials. In addition, I anticipated spending a great deal of time in the APM going through post-1930 government documents as well as the archive's extensive newspaper collection.

Shortly after arriving in Belo Horizonte in August 1987, I began my work in the APM. Previously, I had primarily relied on eighteenth- and nineteenth-century documents. Much to my dismay, I quickly discovered that the collection of government documents in the APM basically ended in the early 1930s. As I asked a long line of archive officials why this was so, the only reason I was given had been passed down through oral tradition. Supposedly, space in the archive was limited in the 1930s, and the director had decided that the APM could not take on new documents! If this is true, it surely must reflect a notion that contemporary events are not history, and that the mission of the archive was to preserve colonial and imperial documents. I also suspect that it may have something to do with the political sensitivities of government officials during the turbulent 1930s which saw full-scale civil war in 1930 and the imposition of a corporatist dictatorship in 1937.[9]

One saving grace of the archive was its systematic and thorough collecting of the official government daily, *Minas Gerais,* as well as other local newspapers. *Minas Gerais* is something of the official record of the state government, which also includes some reporting of local events in politics and economics. Throughout the twentieth century, it has published the annual financial statements of all corporations (public and private) in the state. However brief and guarded, these accounts do allow the historian a glimpse of company directors, assets, and operating expenses for companies in the region.[10]

After my dismaying discovery in the APM I set off in search of government archives. I naively assumed that government agencies that had not forwarded materials to the state archive must have stored them in their own locations. Thus began my trek over months from secretariat to secretariat in search of archives. I began with the oldest secretariats—Agriculture and Public Works—assuming that they would most likely have the continuity and collecting traditions. What I discovered—again, to my great dismay—was that the secretariats and other government agencies systematically tossed out their documents. When I did encounter a large archive in the basement of the Secretariat of Agriculture (a building dating back to the early twentieth century), it turned out to be the personnel records of the secretariat.[11] And these records were a disaster piled up and spilling across a huge basement with no clear organization and no professional archivist. It was, as the Brazilians would say, a *bagunça*.

I reached the end of my rope on the day I made my way to the Secretariat of Culture, the newest of *mineiro* secretariats, created in the 1980s. Nearly everyone who did not have an archive had suggested that maybe the documents and collections had been sent to the Secretariat of Culture, an idea that did have a certain logic to it. After trying (for what seemed like the hundredth time) to explain to officials in the secretariat that I was searching for archives, and drawing blank looks, I turned to the secretary who was typing a letter. "Did she keep a copy of that letter," I inquired? "Yes, of course," she replied. "So where do you put that copy?" I asked. "In that file cabinet behind you," she said pointing to it. Relentlessly pursuing my line of reasoning, I then asked, "So what do you do when the file cabinet is full?" Now I would discover the location of their archive, I thought. "I don't know," she shot back. "We have only been here two years, and we haven't filled them up yet."

Refusing to give up, in desperation I did the most Brazilian thing I could think of—I called on the most influential friends I knew in the government! Amilcar and Roberto Martins are old friends from graduate school days. Roberto earned his doctorate in economic history at Vanderbilt University (1980) and Amilcar in history at the University of Illinois under the guidance of Joseph Love.[12] From an old and very well connected *mineiro* family, Roberto had become a major official in the Partido Social Democrático Brasileiro, and Amilcar had been elected to the city council. Amilcar eventually became the right-hand man of the governor *(secretario do governo)* who just happened to be his brother-in-law! When I gained access to the governor's office and its personnel I discovered that it also had no archive or collecting system. As Amilcar, a trained historian, put it to me, when one administration goes out of office, it cleans the shelves, and the next administration begins to generate new documents only to repeat the process when it leaves office. Government officials, especially the more powerful, regard the documents they generate as their personal archives, and they do not leave them behind.

Even more unfortunate, in Brazil there is almost no tradition equivalent to that in the United States or Europe of public officials donating their personal archives to public collections.[13] In effect, this double problem—cleaning the shelves when leaving office and failing to preserve and make public personal archives—produces the systematic erasure of the historical memory of Minas Gerais. If documents are not published, they disappear into a historical void. Minas Gerais, and to a large extent, Brazil, engages in collective amnesia about the nation's past, especially the history of the twentieth century.

Alternative Strategies and Lessons

When I went to Belo Horizonte in 1987 to begin work on industrialization I had planned on using a wide variety of sources other than the traditional government documents found in state archives. After months of fruitless searching for government archives, the alternative sources had become even more important for my work. I now had to write the history of industrialization from a truly "decentered" approach. My research over the past twelve years has certainly been decentralized and the archives and libraries dispersed. The research has been more difficult than mining a centralized state archive, but it has been much more interesting and rewarding.

Despite the dearth of materials at the APM, some government documents have survived in other locations. The Prefeitura Municipal de Belo Horizonte has a small library that has the annual reports of the *prefeitos,* as well as some unpublished statistical materials. The Câmara Municipal does have an archive, although it is another tale of tragedy. The Câmara moved from its location in the heart of downtown in the early 1990s to a new facility in one of the suburbs (as part of an effort to "decentralize" metropolitan government). Shortly after arriving in Belo Horizonte in 1987, I opened the newspaper one morning to a story about the destruction of much of the Câmara's archive. It seems that a city official had decided that all this "old paper" was taking up too much room and sold much of it off for recycling before he was stopped.[14] The erasure of historical memory continues.

The most important archives and libraries for my study are those of local business interest groups and associations—most prominently the Associação Comercial de Minas (ACM), founded in 1901, the Federação de Indústrias do Estado de Minas Gerais (FIEMG), and the Junta Comercial do Estado de Minas Gerais (JUCEMG). The ACM is the oldest business association in the state, and until the 1950s it consisted almost entirely of business people from Belo Horizonte, despite its name. The ACM has its own building and offices in the center of Belo Horizonte, with a nice library, professional librarian, and an archive that contains the minutes of meetings and elections dating back to the beginning of the century.[15] The Federação also has its own building and offices on the main avenue in downtown, with a similar library, professional library staff, and a small archive.

Perhaps the greatest treasure trove I came across in my pursuit of archives is the JUCEMG. An autonomous state agency, the Junta is the official repository for all company registrations in the state. Any time a company is organized it must register with the Junta and file documents stating the names of company directors and the amount of stock and capitalization. This is an invaluable source for tracking company ownership, business networks, and corporate takeovers. The records are kept in an enormous card filing system that is continually updated. Over the last few years, the Junta has been converting to a computerized data storage system, something that will eventually make it a historian's dream. As always, I could not get access to this rich archive until I came up with the proverbial Brazilian *jeitinho.* I called my friend Amilcar, who then called his friend, the president of the Junta, who then instructed his underlings to give me full access to the records. Although I constantly criticize these pervasive patronage networks in my writing, for once I was very happy to exploit my own connections.

My frustrating and enlightening experience in Belo Horizonte has convinced me of the importance of and urgent need for a cultural policy for the collection of government documents in Minas Gerais (and probably in much of the rest of Brazil as well). I must admit, however, that I am not optimistic that such a policy will be developed any time soon. With the Martins brothers in positions of power at the highest levels in the state government in the mid-1990s, very little seems to have changed. They did manage to attract major private donations (from the Companhia Vale do Rio Doce) for the renovation of the old section of the APM (the old Prefeitura building). And they did begin a preliminary program to canvas and collect government documents. As far as I can tell, this policy does not seem to have produced much collecting, and it is unclear whether it will survive, now that a change has taken place in the state government with the election of Itamar Franco as governor.

One bright spot in this sad tale has been the creation (again largely through the efforts of the Martins brothers) of the Arquivo da Prefeitura de Belo Horizonte—the official repository of the city. Again, however, scarce funds and very little space have made it difficult for the Arquivo to do much systematic collection of recent documents. Much of the collection consists of photographs and volumes that survived in the Prefeitura building downtown.

What historians badly need in Belo Horizonte is more attention to the systematic collection of documents by the state and city archives. The systematic collection of oral histories would also be a great help. Historians and archivists need to urge more prominent politicians, government officials, business people, labor leaders, and other key figures to donate their private archives. In addition, key businesses, especially those that have operated in Minas for decades, could follow the example of the Companhia Cedro e Cachoeira (a prominent textile firm) and Mineração Morro Velho who have created fine business archives open to the public.[16]

Unfortunately, much of the history of *mineiro* industrialization has simply been erased or lost. Ironically, in Minas we can not only bemoan the absence of documents about the *masses (o povo),* but also about the elites who led the process of industrialization. Only with the hard work of historians, librarians, and archivists—in Brazil and abroad—will we avoid the erasure of even more of the history of Brazilian industrialization, and even greater cultural amnesia.

NOTES

1. Marshall C. Eakin, *Brazil: The Once and Future Country* (New York: St. Martin's Press, 1997), p. 75.

2. *Tropical Capitalism: The Industrialization of Belo Horizonte, Brazil, 1897–1997* (forthcoming, St. Martin's Press).

3. The dissertation, "Nova Lima: Life, Labor, and Technology in an Anglo-Brazilian Mining Community" (University of California, Los Angeles, 1981), eventually became *British Enterprise in Brazil: The St. John d'el Rey Mining Company Limited and the Morro Velho Gold Mine, 1830–1960* (Durham, NC: Duke University Press, 1989). Research was financed by a Fulbright-Hays Dissertation Fellowship and the Vanderbilt University Research Council.

4. The gold mine in Nova Lima continues to operate today under the control of the world's largest gold-mining company, the Anglo American Corporation of South Africa. Currently the company in Brazil is known as Mineração Morro Velho S.A.

5. Douglas Cole Libby et al., *Guia do arquivo permanente da Mina de Morro Velho/Guide to the Archives of the Morro Velho Mine* (Belo Horizonte: Centro de Estudos Mineiros, Universidade Federal de Minas Gerais, 1998).

6. *Revista do Arquivo Público Mineiro* (Belo Horizonte), 1896– . Ano XXVIII, April 1977, contains the most complete guide to the manuscript collections of the APM.

7. Herculano Gomes Mathias, *A coleção da Casa dos Contos de Ouro Prêto; documentos avulsos* (Rio de Janeiro: Arquivo Nacional, Publicações, v. 58, 1966). Over the past thirty years the Casa dos Contos has amassed an enormous microfilm collection of eighteenth-century documents from Minas Gerais. Consult http://www.esaf.fazenda.gov.br/casadoscontos/.

8. My research during 1987–1988 was funded by a Tinker Foundation Postdoctoral Fellowship.

9. Eakin, *Brazil,* pp. 41-43; Thomas E. Skidmore, *Brazil: Five Centuries of Change* (New York: Oxford University Press, 1999), pp. 113–120.

10. Recently, the new director of the APM, Norma de Góes Monteiro, decided to move all newspaper collections out of the archive. Until very recently, readers in the archive handled the original volumes of the newspapers, not microfilm copies. (Microfilm readers are few and very often do not function.)

11. With the creation of social security and labor legislation in the 1930s, all employers were required to maintain personnel records for their employees. See, for example, Eakin, *British Enterprise in Brazil,* pp. 99–101.

12. Roberto Borges Martins, "Growing in Silence: The Slave Economy of Nineteenth-Century Minas Gerais, Brazil," Ph.D. dissertation, Vanderbilt University, 1980; Amilcar Vianna Martins Filho, "The White Collar Republic: Patronage and Interest Representation in Minas Gerais, Brazil, 1889–1930," Ph.D. dissertation, University of Illinois, Urbana-Champaign, 1987.

13. An important exception is the Centro de Pesquisa e Documentação de História Contemporânea do Brasil, a first-rate archive attached to the Fundação Getúlio Vargas in Rio de Janeiro. The Centro has attracted the archives of a number of prominent politicians, and it has pursued a longstanding oral history project.

14. *Estado de Minas,* March 11, 1987, p. 7.

15. Consult www.acminas.com.br.

16. For the Morro Velho archive, see Libby. The Cedro e Cachoeira archive is located in Caetanópolis near Belo Horizonte.

21. Documenting Maya Resurgence: Trends in Maya Scholarship and Publishing

Edward F. Fischer

This paper looks at contemporary Maya activism in Guatemala and the sorts of documentary resources being produced by this and other Latin American ethnic movements. I begin by reviewing my own work on the pan-Maya movement in Guatemala. The second half of the paper focuses on the burgeoning business of Maya publishing, fueled by the work of Maya scholars and activists whose writings are at once learned scholarly analysis and primary data for students of identity politics.

The Macro Context

I am an anthropologist, but my theoretical background is in political economy and my work has focused on documenting linkages between particular localities and larger, even global systems. Globalization is, of course, the catchword of the times. One can hardly pick up a newspaper or tune into a news broadcast without hearing about how new technologies are making the world a smaller place. Undeniably, time/space distances are being virtually collapsed: e-mails, faxes, and overnight delivery have made almost instantaneous communication ubiquitous, and even the relatively antiquated technologies of voice telephony and air travel have fallen within the reach of most people, at least in the developed world and increasingly in the underdeveloped world as well. Such advances are not restricted to personal communication and travel as global media outlets have emerged and flourished on the back of satellite transmission: HBO Olé, the Cartoon Channel, CNN—the list goes on—are consumed with equal passion in Des Moines, Iowa, and in rural Guatemala. I work in a small Kaqchikel Maya town, and there, as in other communities, local bootleg cable operations have emerged, requiring no more than a satellite dish and a bale of cable.

These changes are all linked inextricably to a fundamental reorganization in the global political economy. Politically, they can be traced to the advent of post–Cold War political alliances; in the case of Guatemala, the United States is simply no longer willing to financially and ideologically underwrite a war against perceived communist subversion, and flows of foreign aid are increasingly directed toward Eastern Europe. Economically, this is an age of neoliberalism, rising international trade, and the outsourcing of production to less developed areas; in the case of Guatemala, the rise of neoliberal hegemony has forced a number of sweeping structural reforms in the economy including large privatizations and the opening up of internal markets. And it is in this context that the pan-Maya ethnic revitalization movement has emerged and flourished, promoting the resurgence of their ethnic identity long submerged by the bipolarization of Cold War hostilities.

Guatemala

Guatemala is perhaps best known for the period of violence that racked the country in the late 1970s and early 1980s. The U.S. popular press often speaks of Guatemala's 36-year civil war, and it must be a catchy phrase because the *New York Times* has been using it at least since 1990. Actually, this 36-year war is made up of two wars carried out in different places at different times. The first took place in the mid-1960s in the mostly *ladino* (non-Indian)-populated highland area east of Guatemala City. It was started by disenfranchised ladino academics and leftists from Guatemala City and funded in part by Cuba. This revolutionary movement was decidedly defeated by the military in 1967–1968. The second war, called in Guatemala simply *la violencia*, began in the late 1970s after another guerrilla movement (led by some of the veterans of the 1960s campaigns) emerged in the Indian-populated western highlands of Guatemala. In this war ladino elites' cold war–inspired anxiety of communist revolutionaries converged with long-smoldering fears of an Indian uprising, creating an ideological justification for ethnocidal campaigns directed by the military. Ostensibly the military effort aimed to stamp out Marxist revolutionaries, though it targeted not only active subversives but also potential subversives, a category often understood to include all Indians. During the height of the violence (1978–1984) thousands were kidnapped and tortured, tens of thousands were killed, and hundreds of thousands displaced. Recent revelations by the U.N.-sponsored Historical Clarification Commission (popularly known as the Truth Commission) and the National Security Archives are bringing to light for the first time details of the systematic atrocities carried out by security forces (with the complicity of the CIA), confirming survivor reports of mass graves, secret prisons, and vicious torture regimes.

In 1986 nominal civil rule was reestablished in Guatemala with the army's blessing, and in 1996 the government signed a peace accord with rebel forces formally ending the conflict. Yet Guatemalan politics remain turbulent: in 1993, then president José Serrano conducted a short-lived auto-coup, former dictator Efraín Ríos Montt subsequently reemerged as a populist congressional leader with presidential aspirations, and disappearances continue at an alarming pace. At times the press reports from Guatemala have an air of violent surrealism. In 1995 when then U.N. Secretary General Boutros Boutros-Ghali made a brief stop in Guatemala to show his support for the peace process, military air traffic controllers misdirected his official jet and had it land at an abandoned airfield about 30 miles outside of Guatemala City; during dinner that evening with the Guatemalan president a car bomb exploded outside the presidential palace. In 1998, two days after his office issued a scathing report indicting the Guatemalan military in the violence, Bishop Juan Gerardi, the Catholic Church's Ombudsman for Human Rights, was brutally beaten to death in the garage of his home. Declining offers of assistance from the FBI, Guatemalan investigators quickly concluded the case, determining that Bishop Gerardi had happened upon his assistant *en flagrante* with a homosexual lover and the scared priest, fearing for his career, bludgeoned the bishop to death.

Such news events in Guatemala are notoriously difficult to monitor and interpret. Obtaining the news is getting a bit easier with the penetration of the Internet into countries such as Guatemala. All of the major Guatemalan daily newspapers now have fairly extensive World Wide Web sites, and the best of these (*Prensa Libre* at http://www.prensalibre.com/ and *Siglo XXI* at http://www.sigloxxi.com) maintain searchable news archives. Organizations such as the Guatemalan Scholars Network maintain updated Web compilations of breaking news from disparate sources. The availability of primary socio-economic data is also improving, with organizations such as the Inter-American Development Bank (http://www.iadb.org/) and the United Nations Development Programme (http://www.pnud.org.gt/) allowing Internet access to portions of their databases. Notably, the U.N. Truth Commission report is available in its entirety on the Web (http://hrdata.aaas.org/ceh) as are relevant reports from the National Security Archives (http://www.seas.gwu.edu/nsarchive).

Pan-Mayanism

Pan-Mayanism, an ethnic revival movement based on a philosophy of Indian pride and self-determination, amazingly emerged from the ashes of Guatemala's holocaust (see Fischer and Brown 1996 for more detail). Pan-Mayanism is not easy to define. For security as well as ideological reasons, it is a nebulous, decentralized network of Mayan individuals, formal organizations, and informal groups who share a broadly similar philosophy. The movement is led by a young and active group of Maya intellectuals—the first generation of Maya Mayanists—who are relatively well educated and affluent. Pan-Mayanism seeks a culture-based solution to Guatemala's many ills. The approach is two-pronged: first, to work for the conservation and resurrection of elements of Maya culture; and second, to promote legal reform within the framework of the current (1985) Guatemalan constitution and, where that proves insufficient, international law.

Pan-Mayanism is as much an academic movement as it is a political one, and it confounds these two categories in ways that many North American academics find disconcerting. The initial efforts of the Mayan movement have concentrated on reappropriating (from Western academia) and reinterpreting (from an indigenous perspective) research on the ancient and modern Maya.

Mayan leaders are using the information they gather to develop an ideology that emphasizes self-determination, cultural pride, and pan-Maya unity. They believe that a rejuvenated Mayan culture can peacefully lead Guatemala to cultural pluralism and thus allow the indigenous peoples greater access to economic and political institutions. In seeking a model for the future, Mayan scholars tend to idealize pre-contact Mayan culture, describing it as unified, pluralistic, and largely peaceful. By contrasting their view of the past with present conditions, these historical reinterpretations are meant to be relevant: the pluralism of the ancient Maya is a vision of a future Guatemala.

Pan-Mayanist leaders stress that they are primarily working to preserve Mayan languages and culture. Because of this strategic emphasis on cultural issues, their demands fall outside of the historical political confrontations between the Guatemalan left and right, and they are not inherently antagonistic to either side. Segments of the elite sector are ready and willing to grant demands for cultural and linguistic rights, an approach that allows them to demonstrate their progressiveness to the rest of the world in this period of increasing concern over indigenous rights. Such concessions are also timely, given that foreign assistance is tied closely to Guatemala's human rights record.

Pan-Mayanist leaders in Guatemala are in the awkward position of having several constituencies, often with competing interests, to which they are beholden. Their primary obligation is to the country's Maya population, the vast majority of whom live in remote rural areas. Thus initial efforts have focused on raising the cultural consciousness of the masses, demonstrating and reinforcing the value of Maya culture, arguing for its role in the modern world, and recognizing it as a basis for concerted political action. Second, pan-Mayanist leaders must appeal to the powers that be in Guatemala—challenging racist opinions and lobbying for legal changes, certainly, but also portraying the pan-Mayanist agenda as primarily cultural rather than political (and thus nonthreatening and undeserving of violent reprisal). Finally, pan-Mayanists must court the attention and favor of international academics and policy makers. Playing on the recent global valuation of all things indigenous, the recognition of indigenous rights as a subset of fundamental human rights, and the ideological commitment of many academics to support the empowerment of marginalized peoples, pan-Mayanists have been very successful at gaining material support for the movement from international organizations (including the United Nations, the European Union, the U.S. Agency for International Development, and numerous private foundations).

Communication the Message of Pan-Mayanism

Pan-Mayanists have produced a wealth of scholarship and political analyses and have simultaneously had to develop new outlets for disseminating their work. The greatest barrier to effective Maya mass communication is an extremely high illiteracy rate among Maya peoples in Guatemala and the lack of technological infrastructure. For these and other social reasons, Maya culture places a high value on oral skill and dexterity; indeed local political systems are traditionally based on a consensus model, which favors persuasive orators. Building on this cultural bias, early pan-Maya activists distributed teachings and lectures about the value of Maya culture on audio cassette tapes; families and small groups would listen to these and pass them along informal social networks within and between communities throughout Guatemala. And as televisions and video recorders have become more common, these same sorts of materials are being distributed on videotape. One Maya group has bought time on several regional radio stations and broadcasts a weekly radio program, *Mayab' Winäq*. Airing on Sundays from 4:30 A.M. until 7:30 A.M., *Mayab' Winäq* combines music, political commentary, public service announcements, and short radio plays, all with a pan-Mayanist message. As intoned by the deep booming voice of the program's host, Jolom B'alam,

> *Mayab' Winäq* brings together the roots of Maya culture: identity, music, and history. It is the voice of the people, of Maya sentiment and expression. It is the pure and sincere song of a people that holds dear the hope of future peace, equality, brotherhood, and justice for all. It is the musical expression of these words that carries our message of fraternity. It is the thought transmitted from our ancestral parents Xpiapok and Ixmukane.

Ironically, *Mayab' Winäq* seems to have captured perfectly the style of popular Spanish radio programs, down to the richly inflected voice of the announcers and the catchy self-promotional jingles:

> "Mayab' Winäq—el raíz de todo el país."

> "Es la hora de venir a la cita y retornar el camino perdido."

> "Mayab' Winäq es la expresión de un pueblo que solamente pide una oportunidad para vivir."

> "Mayab' Winäq es de nuestras milenarias raíces mayas."

Each episode opens with a dramatic reading from the opening lines of the Popol Wuj: "ha llegado el tiempo de amanecer, de que se terminan la obra . . . se unicaron, llegaron y celebraron consejo en la obscuridad de la noche, discaron y discutieron, reflexionaron y pensaron de esta manera salieron al luz claramente sus decisiones." There are ongoing series that offer mnemonic devices to remember Maya day names and that outline the constitutional rights of Maya peoples. *Mayab' Winäq* has arguably been the most successful effort by Maya leaders to reach out to the rural Maya masses.

Although less widely received, several pan-Mayanist organizations have begun to produce newspapers, magazines, and other printed materials for the Maya public. Notable among these are the Centro Maya Saqb'e's newsletter *Rutzijol*, which includes stories about Maya cultural activities and weekly price reports of basic crops in regional markets. Saqb'e also issues a children's newspaper, *Kukuy* (for "the boys and girls of corn, the future of the Maya people"), and a very useful bimonthly that publishes stories in the Guatemalan national press about Maya peoples.

Pan-Mayanists have also made use of traditional media outlets to communicate their message of cultural pluralism and non-aggressiveness to Guatemala's non-Indian elites. Two of the leading daily newspapers, *Prensa Libre* and *Siglo XXI,* now have full-time Maya editorialists. *Prensa Libre*'s editorialist, Enrique Sam Colop, is a lawyer who also holds a Ph.D. in anthropology from the State University of New York (SUNY), Buffalo. *Siglo XXI* runs a column by journalist Estuardo Zapeta, who is presently completing his doctorate at SUNY, Albany. This is a common pattern for pan-Mayanist leaders: they generally come from relatively affluent families and many have received graduate training abroad. Tellingly, many report that their pan-Mayanist political activism was born of their experiences in the United States or Europe.

As academics, pan-Mayanist leaders self-consciously seek to produce scholarly analyses that promote their political agenda. This work began with a focus on Mayan linguistics and ethnohistory. There has been a long historical association between Maya scholarship and linguistics, and many Maya leaders received their university training in linguistics. Maya scholars argue that speaking a Mayan language is fundamental to understanding and perpetuating a Maya worldview, and their efforts have thus focused on language conservation and revival. A number of excellent grammars, dictionaries, and most recently manuals of style have been produced by Maya linguists (see Oxlajuuj Keej Maya' Ajtz'iib' 1993 and Pakal B'alam 1994). Maya scholars also believe that they must regain control over the production of their own history and have thus produced reinterpretations of Maya life during Spanish colonization. For example, Enrique Sam Colop, in his 1991 *Jub'aqtun omay kuchum kaslemal: Cinco siglos de encubrimiento*, deconstructs the history of contact espoused within the Western tradition in general and by ladino academics in particular. For example, a famous passage from the sixteenth-century Kaqchikel text, the *Anales de los Kaqchikeles*, as translated by a number of scholars into both Spanish and English, reads: "Truly [the Spaniards] inspired fear when they arrived, we did not know their faces, and the lords took them for gods." Sam Colop argues, however, that the Kaqchikel word *kab'owil*, translated above as "gods," is more accurately translated "idol" or "image," belying the claim that the Maya worship the Spaniards or were duped into believing that they were gods.

Recent Maya scholarship has turned toward more overt political analyses. Best known of this category are the works of Demetrio Cojtí Cuxil, a Kaqchikel Maya man who earned a Ph.D. in communications from a Belgian university and is now a consultant for UNICEF. Cojtí has written extensively on issues of Maya identity politics: *Políticas para la reivindicación de los mayas de hoy (fundamento de los derechos específicos del pueblo maya)* (1994) and *Ri Maya moloj pa Iximulew; El movimiento maya (en Guatemala)* (1997). Cojtí calls for, among other things, the establishment of semi-autonomous Maya provinces in Guatemala and the use of affirmative action preferences to enfranchise Maya people in the political process.

Maya Publishing

Because established editorial houses in Guatemala have not been receptive to publishing the work of Maya scholars, several Maya organizations have set up publishing operations. Notable among these is the non-profit Maya editorial and publishing house Cholsamaj, established in the late 1980s. Cholsamaj, a pioneer in the computerization of publishing in Guatemala, has from its earliest days utilized desktop publishing applications. For example, Cholsamaj has developed proprietary software for quickly and easily setting Maya hieroglyphs, and has recently branched out into multimedia with the production of a series of computer-animated Maya folktales. Cholsamaj relies on grants from international organizations and, increasingly, publishing contracts from these groups. Recognizing the vulnerability brought about by this reliance, Cholsamaj created a for-profit subsidiary press, Maya Wuj; the non-profit Cholsamaj owns 51 percent of Maya Wuj and employees of the press own the other 49 percent. Maya Wuj does a lively trade in private printing jobs, including books, diplomas, posters, and wedding announcements. Its best-selling item is an annual date book (Cholb'al Q'ij/Agenda Maya) which combines the hieroglyphic symbols for traditional Maya day names with Gregorian calendar dates and short essays about Maya cultural values and political demands. The 1999 print run produced 10,000 copies, and plans for the 2000 edition include an executive model with a leather case.

The widespread use of Maya hieroglyphs in Maya publications is significant. For Maya scholars, hieroglyphs act as powerful symbols of the splendor and literacy of that culture. For several years, epigrapher Linda Schele offered hieroglyphic workshops for Maya groups. The materials she produced are widely circulated among Maya activists who use them to learn Classic Maya numeration, the calendrical system, and the basic Maya glyphic syllabary. Cholsamaj's policy is to use Maya bar-and-dot numeration for page numbers and to date their publications using the Classic Maya long count notation. The glyphic syllabary was developed to record Classic-era lowland Mayan languages, and current Maya activists speak one of the modern highland Mayan languages. Because of the centuries of divergence between these languages (as well as the incomplete decipherment of the glyphs), glyphic syllabaries are incomplete in their ability to record modern highland languages. Pan-Mayanists have created new glyphic elements to represent the uvular stops /q/, /q'/ and the liquid consonant /r/, sounds that were not present in the Classic period lowland languages.

Implications for Bibliographers

Publications by Maya scholars have become important sources of information for foreign academics but they remain hard to obtain outside Guatemala. Distribution channels are not well developed, and even the success of book-buying trips still depends on serendipity. The annual book fairs in Guatemala City (usually in late May) and Antigua are growing and remain the best single sources of titles published in Guatemala. As Internet access spreads we may also expect more direct and efficient access to Maya publications. A move is already under way in this direction, led by the Los Angeles-based group Yaxte' Press and its founder Fernando Peñalosa. Conducting most of its business over the Internet (http://www.yaxte.org/), Yaxte' is the distributor for several Maya publishers (including Cholsamaj) and also publishes original material and translations of older works.

REFERENCES

B'alam, Pakal (José Obispo Rodríguez Guaján). 1994. *Kojtz'ib'an pa Kaqchi'*. Guatemala: Cholsamaj.

Cojtí Cuxil, Demetrio. 1991. *Configuración del pensamiento político del pueblo maya*. Quetzaltenango, Guatemala: Asociación de Escritores Mayances de Guatemala.

———. 1994. *Políticas para la reivindicación de los Mayas de hoy (fundamento de los derechos específicos del pueblo maya)*. Guatemala: Cholsamaj.

———. 1997. *Ri Maya moloj pa Iximulew; El movimiento maya (en Guatemala)*. Guatemala: Cholsamaj.

COMG (Consejo de Organizaciones Mayas de Guatemala). 1991. *Rujunamil Ri Mayab' Amaq': Derechos específicos del pueblo maya*. Guatemala City: COMG.

Fischer, Edward F., and R. McKenna Brown, eds. 1996. *Maya Cultural Activism in Guatemala*. Austin: University of Texas Press.

Oxlajuuj Keej Maya' Ajtz'iib'. 1993. *Maya' Chii': Los idiomas Mayas de Guatemala*. Guatemala: Cholsamaj.

Sam Colop, Enrique. 1991. *Jub'aqtun omay kuchum kaslemal: Cinco siglos de encubrimiento*. Seminario Permanente de Estudios Mayas, Cuaderno No. 1. Guatemala City: Cholsamaj.

22. Military Power and Privilege in Contemporary Latin America: Suggestions on Sources

Wendy Hunter

Eighteen years have passed since the transition to democracy in Peru, followed by transitions in Argentina, Uruguay, Brazil, Chile, and elsewhere in Latin America. Democratization in the region has given rise to a host of scholarly works on Latin American militaries and their relations with important domestic state and societal actors, as well as foreign parties. Yet important gaps remain in our knowledge about Latin American militaries, gaps that bibliographers of Latin American studies could make a large and important contribution toward filling.

This paper addresses the issue of knowledge accumulation in the literature on civil-military relations in post-authoritarian Latin America. Its purpose is twofold: first, to suggest that how analysts view the military—its political strength, identity, role definition, and attitudes toward civilian authority—is shaped in no small measure by the indicators and sources of documentation they utilize; and second, to identify sources of documentation that I have found useful and interesting in my study of the Brazilian military (Hunter 1997).

Has the military's influence eroded and civilian supremacy been strengthened in the region's new democracies? Have officers' attitudes shifted in a direction more compatible with sustained civilian rule? Have they begun to socialize cadets in ways that cultivate respect for the rule of law? A brief glance at the literature on Latin American militaries and civil-military affairs suggests wide divergences of opinion on these and related questions. For example, while Patrice McSherry (1997) regards Argentina as a "guardian democracy" and criticizes the country's two post-authoritarian presidents for failing to further reduce military power and influence, David Pion-Berlin (1997) and Robert Potash (1996) see a marked strengthening of democracy in Argentina and cite a number of positive developments within military as well as civilian sectors. Similarly, whereas Juan Linz and Alfred Stepan (1996) and Jorge Zaverucha (1994) emphasize the steadfast nature of military influence in post-authoritarian Brazil, Wendy Hunter (1997) contends that military influence in Brazil has eroded in a pronounced fashion since 1985. On Peru, Enrique Obando (1996) asserts that the president has kept, and in some instances even tightened, his control over the officer corps. Philip Mauceri (1995) takes an opposing view.

What accounts for the divergent viewpoints represented by these examples? Sometimes it is simply a matter of emphasis, that is, whether an author chooses to present the glass as half empty or half full. Some authors are naturally more positive and optimistic, stressing the progress achieved and the promise the future holds. Others tend toward pessimism and underscore what remains to be done. Other times, conceptual distinctions account for the different views among analysts. For example, if the yardstick for measuring progress is to compare Latin American militaries with their counterparts in advanced Western democracies, the assessment of Latin American militaries' willingness to accept civilian authority tends to be fairly pessimistic. If the analyst judges progress by looking at how far the military has come compared with where it was on the eve of the transition to civilian rule, a view that focuses on the decline of military power and accommodation to the new rules of the game is more likely to emerge.

But beyond this, much of what shapes analysts' views are the specific empirical factors taken into account, which in turn are partly determined by the sources that inform their scholarship. The empirical indicators of military power that an author chooses to examine greatly influence the conclusions reached about whether the military remains a weighty political actor or not. One of the more common ways of evaluating military power and privilege is to look at formal institutional prerogatives. Some examples of prerogatives that politically interventionist militaries possess include the right to intervene in events that threaten "law and order" and to command troops that act in the capacity of police, to participate in the cabinet, to play an active role in civilian intelligence, to head state enterprises, and to coordinate the defense sector with limited civilian input. The institutional prerogatives approach is exemplified in the work of Alfred Stepan (1988), Jorge Zaverucha (1993, 1994), and Felipe Agüero (1995). The premise that guides such works is that laws constitute an important basis of military conduct and that the focus of civilian reforms should be to remove the military's legal prerogatives. In extreme form, a focus on formal prerogatives implies that because officers enjoy given prerogatives, they actually use them. But just as the existence of laws calling for military subordination to civilians does not guarantee such a stance, the presence of formal prerogatives does not necessarily lead the military to intervene politically.

Conducting research for the approach that focuses on formal institutional prerogatives is not overly difficult. It entails looking at constitutions and other legal provisions, which are generally fairly accessible. Certainly, these are important factors that influence the power and reach of the military. Even if legal preconditions do not translate automatically into related conduct, they make more probable certain military behaviors by legitimizing them. At the same time, this is not the full story. If Latin America's armed forces frequently used all of their legal rights, the civil-military balance would look quite different. An exclusive focus on formal prerogatives tends to overstate the real strength of most Latin America's militaries and the changes that have taken place within them since democratization. A more refined view demands attention to additional indicators. This entails gathering material that is less easy to locate but not entirely out of reach even for those unable to undertake field research and interviews. In any case, bibliographers can certainly help direct researchers in the additional directions suggested below.

Militaries do not always employ the ample (in many cases) formal rights they have. In the aftermath of authoritarian rule, officers in some Latin American militaries seek a return to more strictly professional activities. Their concern is that the armed forces' ability to carry out traditional defense missions suffered during the period when officers were occupied with the responsibilities of government and many troops were oriented toward quelling domestic strife. Furthermore, some leaders fear that the military's reputation among the public would be unduly tarnished if the organization continued to emphasize issues of domestic content. The officer corps could indeed "overplay their cards" by saber rattling and constant intervention in matters outside their own corporate sphere, possibly resulting in a diminution of their political and economic resources.

Hence, it is necessary to look at actual military conduct in addition to formal provisions. Ideally, such an examination would include conduct across a broad array of issue areas. Military belligerence vis-à-vis civilian decision making on explicitly political, social, or economic issues is doubtless more detrimental to democracy than military domination in the defense sector, narrowly defined. What kind of sources detail military behavior, especially in interaction with the civilian world?

For me, major daily newspapers (such as the *Jornal do Brasil* and the *Folha de São Paulo)* have been vital sources because they report a broad range of military behavior, for example, military lobbying in Congress on matters ranging from labor laws to defense expenditures. Very few journal articles or books cast as wide a net as daily newspapers in this respect. Dailies frequently publish useful play-by-play accounts of political processes and negotiations. For example, when major legislation is under consideration in the Congress, newspaper reports often name the political actors who are trying to influence the process, provide details about their goals and tactics, and assess their degree of success. In comparing the legislation as initially proposed with the eventual law, many such accounts identify the turning points in the legislative process and the factors that led to certain amendments. These kinds of reports provide an indispensable entry into many significant arenas of military conduct, even if interviews need to be conducted in order to fill in remaining gaps.

Both the Brazilian Chamber and Senate have clipping archives organized by topic. This is a gold mine for researchers fortunate enough to go to the field.

The less fortunate would find convenient access to microfilm versions of major Latin American dailies enormously helpful. A full sequence of dates is often necessary to understand a complex political issue or process. In this connection, Brazil's major dailies sometimes present detailed accounts, accompanied by graphic presentations, of the various stages of complicated negotiations. The microfilming of major daily Latin American newspapers is one of the most important projects U.S. librarians could undertake in support of political science research.

Another item of tremendous use in understanding military lobbying, especially vis-à-vis the defense sector, are the complete public transcripts of open hearings before congressional committees involving senior military officers. During these hearings, officers provide justification and rationale for the budgets they request and the legislation they support. I imagine it would be difficult to obtain copies of these transcripts without actually going to the Congress. Nevertheless, it is worth trying to obtain them for those researchers interested in civil-military interactions, especially in matters pertaining to legislation.

To gather information about military actions regarding specific issue areas, especially when they do not relate directly to defense or where military interference is somewhat questionable politically, I have found it extraordinarily helpful to visit individual NGOs that specialize in the particular issue area. On such matters, going to military sources seldom yields the wealth or quality of information that results from direct contact with NGOs. For example, the Centro Ecumênico de Documentação e Informação (CEDI) in São Paulo specializes in indigenous peoples in the Amazon. The CEDI archives contain an enormous amount of important information about military activities in the Amazon, an area of vital strategic importance to the organization historically. CEDI also publishes magazines, such as *Tempo e Presença,* that frequently include coverage of the military. Similarly, the Comissão Pastoral da Terra (CPT) is an NGO that specializes in labor issues, primarily in the rural sector but also to some extent in the urban sphere. For my research, I was able to locate invaluable information about the military's attempt to influence peasant and worker movements during the dictatorship and beyond.

Using these kinds of sources to examine the military's outward behavior tends to reveal the pragmatic face of the institution and its ability to adapt to changing domestic and international circumstances, namely, the emergence of a climate in both spheres that is less accepting of authoritarian solutions to problems, such as military force, than in the past. Whereas an exclusive look at formal prerogatives suggests a high degree of continuity with the past, indicators and sources that provide an eye into the institution's conduct reveal considerable change.

Another topic of interest to scholars is the military's identity and role definition. How do officers regard the military institution and profession? What status and place in society and in the state do they accord themselves? What do they see as the proper mission(s) of their institution? For the sake of democracy and civilian rule, the identity that the officer corps embrace and the missions they seek to carry out should revolve largely around issues as strictly related to external defense as possible. Especially given the pervasiveness of the military's political intervention in Latin America's past, identities and tasks that enmesh military personnel in non-military policy arenas bode less well for creating a less politically autonomous military or increasing its subordination to civilian authority.

To some extent, the armed forces' identity and the roles they regard as appropriate or even honorable can be gleaned through their public actions. Yet, fuller insight can be gained by examining military writings and oral presentations that speak directly to these issues. Military journals, while varying considerably in quality, can reveal important information about how the officer corps view themselves and their institution. Examples of such journals for Brazil include an army publication, *A Defesa Nacional,* and *Segurança e Desenvolvimento,* published by the Escola Superior da Guerra. Both journals feature articles on issues related strictly to defense (e.g., weapons systems, foreign threats, military techniques and training, etc.) as well as others on the values and goals of officers, how they regard their contribution to society and the state, and what they see as the limits of their competence and legitimate reach. A content analysis would show what issues the forces choose to write about, reflecting their evolving role over time.

Another document of interest to analysts of the military are the proceedings of the Conference of Latin American Militaries, a meeting held every few years in a different Latin American location and attended by representatives of most militaries in the region. The conference has devoted considerable attention to such topics as military missions, the nature of military involvement in drug interdiction, threats to regional security, and human rights and the military's association with human rights abuses.

Military Web sites, authored by the military's public relations organ, also provide important insight into the content of the identity and role definition of the three branches. These sites sometimes function in the recruitment of cadets and soldiers. For example, the Brazilian army's Web site emphasizes the institution's historical role in delivering health services to rural populations.[1] The site also underscores the contemporary role of the army in the provision of basic vaccines, preventing and controlling epidemics, and in AIDS prevention and treatment. This coverage suggests that the army continues to view civic action as an important contribution to the Brazilian public. The army's appeal to citizens as well as to potential recruits is based in no small part on such grounds. Web sites of other militaries (e.g., the Peruvian and Bolivian) also feature health services and other aspects of civic action and national building, such as the construction of roads and other infrastructure. What we can infer is that the militaries in these countries do not intend to confine themselves to a purely external defense role but rather to aspire to act in the domestic sphere, as they have done historically.

Another aspect of military identity is the ethnic or racial image that the institution tries to project, evident in the public relations material displayed in military Web sites. Officers and soldiers of color are frequently featured, reflecting the institution's historic claim to be one of the few institutions that truly represent "the nation" as a whole. Discrimination based on color and class, a pervasive phenomenon in Latin America, is something most militaries—at least rhetorically—claim exception from. Indeed, the military has traditionally been one of the few avenues of social mobility for young men without financial means. While in most Latin American countries an officership no longer holds the social prestige it once did, for poor youth, often of indigenous or African origin, the military remains a worthy career, especially in rural areas.

While the military's public relations messages are designed partly to gain new recruits, they are also formulated to win support from the broader public. Here as well, the theme of identification and solidarity with ethnic diversity and a broad range of social classes—especially popular sectors—emerges. Several military Web sites feature poor people, often of color, as the recipients of the military's largesse. Strategies that the organization uses to gain and keep support in the interior include the provision of literacy and health services, as well as infrastructure construction projects related to sanitation and enhanced access to markets. This support is sometimes aspired to in an effort to decrease the attraction of competitors to the military's monopoly of force, such as guerrilla organizations operating in the countryside. In short, the nation-building, nation-including aspects of military identity appear to have persisted strongly into the contemporary period.

Yet some aspects of military identity have undergone change. To shed light on how the Brazilian military's identity and composition have changed over time, a source published by the Fundação Getúlio Vargas (1984), titled *Dicionário Histórico-Biográfico,* is informative. It contains short biographies of major public figures in Brazil since 1930. One interesting detail I discovered while examining the biographies concerns the individual's progressive confinement to the military sphere. Whereas many leading officers in the first sixty or so years of this century alternated between holding political office (e.g., governor or member of Congress) and military positions (e.g., commander), they now show more exclusive dedication to the military profession. This shift has had important consequences for military identity and how the organization influences civilian politics.

Related to the issue of military identity are the internal norms that have governed the institution. Some of these have important consequences for how the organization behaves toward the external world. Internal norms and socialization practices are arguably the most difficult area in which to gain knowledge without firsthand contact with the institution. Most analysts suspect that this is where Latin American militaries have changed the least. While pragmatism may dictate a moderation in the military's public behavior, what happens on the inside of the institution is far less subject to scrutiny. It is true that the military in many Latin American countries remains a virtual "black box," outside the privy of most researchers. Yet sometimes there are public clues as to what is taking place within. Military speeches are one source of these clues.

For example, as part of a broader effort to reshape the institution in ways more compatible with democracy and the observance of civil liberties and human rights, the contemporary leadership of the Argentine army has tried to resocialize cadets away from the historical norm and practice of carrying out all orders without question. Until recently, military personnel were instructed to obey commanders without condition. Yet under the requirement and/or pretext of "obeying orders," military personnel have committed heinous acts, including violating the human rights of the civilian population. In a series of commencement speeches at the army academy in recent years, army commander Martin Balza has instructed cadets about the importance of reserving some judgement and of carrying out only those orders that fall within "constitutional limits." He has made quite clear that actions that violate the human rights of fellow Argentines fall outside of these limits. While other internal practices more in line with the military's undemocratic past undoubtedly continue, the leadership's admonition to cadets nevertheless represents a significant break with precedent. The major military journals in Argentina along with the Argentine press have covered this new development extensively, often publishing the entire commencement speech.

Finally, a discussion of military attitudes would be incomplete without mention of civilian attitudes toward the military. Key civilian actors throughout the region have accepted and even called for military intervention time and time again, lending greater legitimacy to praetorian actions. A quest for greater social and political stability—especially on the part of the middle and upper classes—has frequently motivated endorsements of expanded military involvement. Public opinion surveys often include questions about the armed forces, lending insight into why officers have the degree of influence they do. One such survey, *Latinobarómetro,* asks respondents to rate their endorsement of the military relative to other institutions and government entities (Congress, the presidency, the church, etc.) and to state whether they want the military to have more (or less) influence.[2] The survey also assesses the relative importance of various goals, including greater "law and order" and crime control. A positive correlation exists between wanting the military to have more power and the priority people place on social quiescence and control. In Brazil, the public consistently rates the military as one of the most trustworthy institutions in society (certainly above the Congress). Greater "law and order" repeatedly emerges as a high priority. These results suggest that the stability and extensiveness of democracy rest not only on reforming the military but also on better civilian governance and other changes on the civilian side as well.

The more varied the empirical focus of the researcher, the more complex, nuanced, and accurate the picture the researcher can present of the military. Taking into account not only legal rights but also actual conduct and attitudes is essential. But to arrive at such a picture, analysts need to move well beyond the usual secondary sources. I have suggested some of the documents that I have found useful in my own research on the Brazilian military. Since space, budgets, and time are finite, bibliographers may not want to order these items for their own libraries. Nevertheless, librarians can still be of great value in informing researchers about these sources and directing them to the archives and places where they are found.

NOTES

1. See http://www.exercito.gov.br/revista and http:/www.eme.eb.mil.br/campanha/saude/aids3.htm.

2. See, for example, *Latinobarómetro 1995.*

BIBLIOGRAPHY

Agüero, Felipe. 1995. *Soldiers, Civilians and Democracy: Post-Franco Spain in Comparative Perspective.* Baltimore: Johns Hopkins University Press.

Fitch, J. Samuel. 1998. *The Armed Forces and Democracy in Latin America: Context, Ideology, and Institutions.* Baltimore: Johns Hopkins University Press.

Fundação Getúlio Vargas. Centro de Pesquisa e Documentação. 1984. *Dicionário Histórico-Biográfico Brasileiro, 1930–1983.* Rio de Janeiro: Editora Forense-Universitária.

Hunter, Wendy. 1997. *Eroding Military Influence: Politicians against Soldiers.* Chapel Hill: University of North Carolina Press.

Latinobarómetro 1995: Datos Preliminares. 1995. Ann Arbor: University of Michigan, Institute for Social Research, Survey Research Center.

Linz, Juan J., and Alfred Stepan. 1996. *Problems of Democratic Transition and Consolidation: Southern Europe, South America, and Post-Communist Europe.* Baltimore: Johns Hopkins University Press.

McSherry, J. Patrice. 1997. *Incomplete Transition: Military Power and Democracy in Argentina.* New York: St. Martin's Press.

Mauceri, Philip. 1995. "State Reform, Coalitions, and the Neoliberal Autogolpe in Peru." *Latin American Research Review* 30 (1), 7–37.

Obando, Enrique. 1996. "Fujimori and the Military." *Report on the Americas* (North American Congress on Latin America, New York) 30 (July–August).

Pion-Berlin, David. 1997. *Through Corridors of Power: Institutions and Civil-Military Relations in Argentina.* College Park: The Pennsylvania State University Press.

Potash, Robert A. 1996. *The Army and Politics in Argentina, 1962–1973: From Frondizi's Fall to the Peronist Restoration.* Stanford: Stanford University Press.

Stepan, Alfred. 1988. *Rethinking Military Politics: Brazil and the Southern Cone.* Princeton: Princeton University Press.

Zaverucha, Jorge. 1993. "The Degree of Military Political Autonomy during the Spanish, Argentine, and Brazilian Transitions." *Journal of Latin American Studies* 25, 283–299.

_____. 1994. *Rumor de Sabres: Tutela Militar ou Controle Civil?* São Paulo: Editora Ática.

23. Searching for Maroons in the Historical Record: New Approaches

Jane Landers

Having completed a regional study on black slaves who ran southward from the Anglo colonies to become *vecinos* in Spanish Florida, I am now working on a new project on maroons who established hidden settlements in the Spanish colonies from the sixteenth through the nineteenth centuries.[1] This research requires examining vast amounts of material to turn up small scraps of evidence that must then be patched together to try to form whole patterns. It is analogous in many ways to restoring a fractured artifact whose scattered shards must be painstakingly excavated, examined, and manipulated repeatedly to determine how they fit together. In some places—for example, Suriname—there are gaps in the documentary record that can never be filled, and reconstructing the early colonial past, especially that of people of color, is made more difficult. But in many areas of the former Spanish empire rich deposits of black history still wait to be mined. It is certainly not true, as was once thought, that because many people of African descent were enslaved and many were illiterate, they had no history.

Spanish bureaucrats created an extensive documentary record of the Africans living throughout their empire, capturing moments of their lives in censuses, military rosters, civil and criminal proceedings, land grants, and correspondence. And while the Catholic Church never attempted a major missionary effort among Africans as it did among Native Americans, it did try to convert those Africans who lived in Spanish towns or in maroon settlements on the fringe of Spanish settlement. In the process the church generated some of the oldest extant records on Africans in the Americas—dating to the mid-sixteenth century.[2] Catholic baptismal, marriage, and burial registers record not only the name, race, and legal status of the individuals presenting themselves but also their African "nations." In rare cases they may also give birthplaces in Africa. As required by Catholic ritual, African couples chose marriage sponsors and parents chose godparents for their baptized children. These practices enable scholars to reconstitute family and fictive kin networks among some populations. Scholars can also use these serial church records to explore a range of important questions, including mortality and fertility rates, miscegenation and naming patterns, and even rates of manumissions.[3]

Spanish records are somewhat more limited on life in the *palenques*, *manieles*, *mocambos*, and *cumbes* as fugitive slave communities were variously called. Contemporary observers did not always appreciate or record what they saw there, but the accounts of priests sent among the *cimarrones*, and even those of military opponents, can offer useful clues about the physical layout, demographics, and civil, religious, and military leadership of the communities, as well as scattered information on subsistence patterns and trade networks with Europeans, Indians, and other Africans, free and enslaved. When unconquerable *palenques* were legitimated, a new level of documentation was generated through town charters, parish registers, militia records, notarial accounts, and many of the same materials available for other Spanish towns. In most cases these rich sources have yet to be worked.[4]

Most important, perhaps, is the fact that both free and enslaved Africans generated their own historical record in Spanish colonies. Depending on their individual histories, Africans were sometimes literate in several languages and, just as indigenous groups did, they quickly learned and adapted to the Spanish legal culture. They wrote petitions and correspondence to royal officials and to the king, made proclamations of fealty, initiated legal suits and property transactions, and left wills. Their verbatim testimonies also come to us through civil and criminal proceedings, which Spanish notaries recorded and read back to the sworn witnesses for verification, alteration, or amendment.[5]

The evidence is there, then, but it requires determination, creativity, and eventually intimate familiarity with the historical communities to unearth it—not to mention inordinate amounts of time. It took me more than a decade to gather the data for my dissertation and transform the data into a monograph on black Florida but the lessons learned in that effort should facilitate the current project. I began my research in 1984 in the premiere archive of Spanish colonial history, the Archivo General de Indias (AGI) in Seville. As those who have worked there know, the AGI guides vary in usefulness, and I came to find that little bibliographic attention has been given in Spain to the issues that most interested me. Most references to Africans were under the general heading *esclavos* or *esclavitud* with an inordinate amount of attention to slave licenses, contractors, and the economy of the slave trade, but little to the slaves themselves. Still, one has to begin somewhere, and so I pursued the obvious clues and began to work the oft-worked slave trade records. At some point I became intrigued by the record group titled Indiferente General and sidetracked from my carefully planned tour through the Papeles Procedentes de Cuba to explore. In this collection of miscellany I lucked upon a *legajo* which contained a varied assortment of protests and petitions directed to the Spanish Crown by diplomats from England, Denmark, Holland, and France—all complaining about Spain's policy of granting religious sanctuary to fugitive slaves from non-Catholic areas. These reports documented slaves from Curaçao escaping to Venezuela, slaves from Jamaica escaping to Puerto Rico, and slaves from the

Anglo colonies of North America escaping to Spanish Florida. This serendipitous find was exciting, but because of the elite nature of the documents, the maroons I wanted to know about were not really much in evidence. The records described the runaway slaves by name, age, and value—with an occasional reference to their manner of escape.

More satisfying for me were the ground-level documents I subsequently worked in the East Florida Papers, the complete archive of the Spanish government in Florida from 1784 to 1821. The East Florida Papers are held in the Library of Congress but microfilm copies are available in Florida and elsewhere. I worked these records and others in the wonderful special collections of the P. K. Yonge Library of Florida History at the University of Florida. Dedicated archivists from that library have been acquiring microfilm copies of historical records from Spanish and Spanish American archives related to Florida and the Caribbean for decades now and have built a truly exceptional collection. Finally, I was able to get closer to the runaways' perspectives and to begin to piece together their life histories. As I completed my book and began to think about my current project, I am guided by the new questions and new approaches of scholars in historical archaeology, African history, and gender studies in particular.

At the University of Florida I had the good fortune to collaborate with archaeologist Kathleen Deagan on the investigation of Gracia Real de Santa Teresa de Mose, an eighteenth-century town established by fugitive slaves whom the Spaniards granted sanctuary in Florida. As the historical researcher for the project, I returned to the AGI to gather information that would guide Deagan's archaeologists during two seasons of excavations at that site. Suddenly, I found I needed to consider much more carefully the material culture of the history I had been studying. Questions Deagan asked me to research included: the physical layout of the settlement, materials used in its construction, trade in and out of the settlement, natural and military catastrophes that may have damaged the site, the demographic profile and ethnicities of the residents of Mose, and more. The AGI collections provided much of this information but the Spanish Florida parish registers, also available on microfilm in many locations, were also critically important. They captured the great ethnic and racial diversity at Mose, which was also true of the Spanish colony in general. Among the African "nations" specifically identified for the original population at Mose were the Mandinga, Fara, and Arará. Subsequent immigrants further diversified the group, incorporating Congo, Carabalí (Calabari), and Mina to the mix. In the larger community of St. Augustine were also found Gambas, Sambas, Gangás, Laras, and some persons identified only as Guineans. Florida's governors and priests complained about the "bad customs" and "spiritual backwardness" of the *bozales* but also left us documented records of cultural and religious practices and languages of newly introduced Africans that are not often available in documents generated in Protestant areas.[6]

My work with archaeologists sent me tracking more *mapas y planos* than I had before and made me pay attention to details I had previously ignored. I am now an archaeology groupie, so to speak, visiting sites as often as possible and consulting on a number of varied historical archaeological projects such as the San Luis de Talimali mission site in Florida and the Henrietta Marie slave ship which went down off the coast of Cuba.

Historical archaeology is offering important new insights into the material life of Africans, which is not frequently treated in the documentary record, however little has been done on Hispanic areas of settlement. The high costs of fieldwork and the level of technical support required mean that most of this work has been conducted in the British Caribbean and in the United States. Given their own lengthy and specialized training, few archaeologists can devote time to instruction in paleography and foreign languages. Working in English-speaking areas obviates that difficulty but most of the archaeology projects have so far focused on enslaved populations, reinforcing unintentionally the popular notion that black history is slave history. Among the most well known archaeological projects are excavations of the slave quarters of the various plantations of presidents Washington, Jefferson, and Jackson in Virginia and Tennessee, a series of projects in low-country South Carolina and Georgia plantations, plantation slave villages and burial grounds in Jamaica and Barbados, and the African burial grounds in New York City. Attempts by archaeologists to locate maroon settlements in the Great Dismal Swamp and in Jamaica have been unsuccessful although some basic archaeological recovery work has been done at Black Seminole sites in north central Florida and in the Dominican Republic at the Maniel José Leta.[7]

Through such material items as pottery, pipes, baskets, and iron implements; architectural features and spatial patterning; plant and faunal remains; skeletal evidence from bones and teeth, some of which are filed or mutilated; grave goods; and items of seemingly socio-religious significance such as beads (63 percent of which are blue), buttons, pierced or broken coins, gaming pieces, and amulets, to name a few, archaeologists attempt to "recover meaning" and posit African origins and American cultural adaptations.[8]

While such finds are exciting, the notable archaeologist of sub-Saharan Africa, Merrick Posnansky, has urged colleagues working on African sites in the Americas, and historians as well, to reject the fallacy of a common African culture and to pay more attention to the regional and temporal developments in African histories while searching for ethnic and cultural connections. While archaeologists have found treasures in the "hidey holes" under slave cabin floors, Posnansky reminds us of the importance of outside activities in many African cultures and urges more attention be paid to courtyards, the spaces adjoining houses, and to craft production areas, where important ideotechnic finds might be made. Finally, Posnansky argues that recycling, functional substitution, innovation, and adaptation are constants in West African material production and that searching for exact duplication of African patterns and techniques in the Americas is a fool's game.[9]

African historians and archaeologists are often frustrated by scholars of the African diaspora who fail to pay sufficient attention to historical developments in Africa and who generalize about African American ethnicity and culture without sufficient background in their African origins. Having no formal training in African history I have devoted myself to trying to remedy my own failings and have been fortunate to have been included in a group of international scholars working on the UNESCO Tracking the Slave Route Project. By following the work of colleagues in that group, including scholars like Paul Lovejoy, Joseph Miller, Robin Law, David Eltis, and David Richardson, I am slowly getting up to speed on issues such as the transformations of the Atlantic slave trade over time, the dynastic wars which destabilized Kongo and Angola and sent the unfortunate losers into the slave trade, the religious jihads which did the same, and a host of interesting cultural issues that affect the study of the Africans I study on this side of the Atlantic.

With this new awareness, for the last several summers I have been searching for maroons in the national archives of Cuba, Ecuador, and Mexico and in church archives of Cuba and the Dominican Republic where maroonage in the Americas began. The earliest Spanish record on maroons in the Americas is found in Governor Nicolás de Ovando's 1503 complaint to the Spanish Crown that slave runaways could not be recovered from Indian hideouts in the mountains of Hispaniola.[10] By 1519 the Taíno Indian chief Enriquillo had transformed acts of individual flight into an organized resistance movement by Indian rebels and escaped slaves. Although Enriquillo eventually accepted Spanish offers of reward and reconciliation, black runaways fought on through the 1540s in what the Spaniards called the "maroon wars."[11] By the mid-sixteenth century an estimated 7,000 maroons inhabited settlements scattered across the island, and at the close of the century the free population of the island, including Europeans, free mestizos, and mulattoes, numbered only 2,000, while the enslaved population stood around 20,000. The same demographic profile characterized other sixteenth-century Spanish settlements.[12]

Spaniards thus faced similar challenges throughout the circum-Caribbean. They complained that *cimarrones* raided Spanish settlements and enticed or stole away other slaves and carried on contraband trade with corsairs and with Spain's enemies. The fugitive communities also challenged Spanish notions of civilized living, as well as the desired racial and social order, but repeated military efforts to eradicate these *palenques* were, more often than not, unsuccessful.[13] If they were repeatedly unsuccessful, Spaniards used church intermediaries to negotiate peace and "reduce" the communities to legitimate towns. The policy of *reducción* was initially used to congregate indigenous populations into "human polity," meaning into Christian settlements modeled after

Spanish towns, "with streets and plazas." The new Christian Indian towns became the model for later free black towns and in my searches through various archives I have learned to look at materials often archived under the heading *indios* or *fundaciones de pueblos*.[14] Because such towns, like Mose, were considered settlements of "new (read dubious) Christians," missionary priests resided among them, and they were often the same priests who had made initial overtures and attempted to reduce the maroons. Stipends and support for such missionary outreach were often recorded in *hacienda* treasury accounts, being charged either against tribute records or government accounts.

Churchmen and military commanders alike pumped up their c.v.'s with accounts of their *méritos y servicios* in reducing maroons and their accounts are invaluable for my work, if unabashedly self-serving. In 1662, after repeated military campaigns against them failed, the Archbishop of Santo Domingo attempted to persuade 600 families still gathered into four *palenques* along the mountainous southern coast to be "reduced." The Baoruco maroons had already ignored a previous offer and rejected this overture as well, commenting that they did not believe the word of Spaniards. The maroons were living a self-sufficient life and apparently felt no pressure to compromise. According to the Archbishop's report, they produced corn in abundance and a variety of crops and were also raising unnamed livestock. The women panned for gold in the rivers, and their economy supported purchases of clothing, drink, and other items in the capital of Santo Domingo, including iron and steel from which the men fabricated arrows and short, broad swords.[15]

Four years after the Archbishop's visit the Spaniards launched a series of near fatal attacks against the Baoruco settlements but scattered maroon communities persisted well into the eighteenth century. Surface collection and shallow excavations at José Leta, an early-eighteenth-century maroon settlement in eastern Hispaniola, confirm some of the Archbishop's observations about economy and life at such camps. Researchers found numerous bones indicating that inhabitants subsisted largely on wild pigs, although it is presumed they also grew garden crops and gathered wild honey. The site also yielded seventeen copper bracelets, metal arrowtips, incised clay pipes, and a variety of iron objects, including tongs and lance points. Iron slag deposits are evidence that the runaways were manufacturing the objects on this site as the Archbishop said they did at Baoruco.[16] In nearby caves explorers have also found metal daggers, clay water jugs, and triton shell trumpets which they identify to be the work of African runaways.[17] Recently, Dominican archaeologist Manuel García Arévalo has assembled an important new collection of pots made by African runaways and retrieved from water-filled caves near the Santo Domingo airport. These rather crude hand-built and low-fired vessels incorporate indigenous elements in decorative patterns and are examples of a specific type of pottery designated colonoware, a pottery spatially defined by being found in areas where blacks and Indians coexisted. The identification of such wares has prompted scholars to revisit collections once identified as purely Indian in search of African production.[18]

In the 1690s a Spanish priest kept a journal of his trek to the *palenque* of Matudere interior from Cartagena and of his efforts to peacefully reduce its inhabitants. As Father Zapata approached the settlement he was met by Matudere's war captain, Pedro Mina, out on patrol with a squad of eight to ten men whose faces were decorated with red and white paints. The priest noted that the Minas controlled the camp's forty-odd guns, while the criollos used lances, bows, and arrows. He thought the distribution indicated the criollos' preference for such weapons, but it might be more reasonable to assume that the settlement's most able warriors merited the best weaponry. At later festivities the priest again stressed the exoticism (read backwardness) of the Minas whom he described celebrating with their "customary dances." In contrast, he referred to the creoles as "domestic" and was impressed that they had built an "adequate" church which contained "paper images" (presumably Christian ones since he stated no objections).[19]

According to Governor Martin de Cevallos, who eventually destroyed Matudere, African shamans (whom he called *brujos* or witches), using "diabolic artifacts and inventions" including "poisoned arrowheads and cords and other demonic ideas," had assured the *cimarrones* they were invincible. This means that Catholicism and some form of African religious practice coexisted in Matudere and residents may have participated in both simultaneously, just as they did in Spanish cities. Later testimony identified Matudere's shaman as Antonio, the escaped slave of Juan Peña. Residents of Matudere apparently regarded Antonio as a holy man, kissed his hand to show their respect, and obeyed him in everything, including his order to kidnap the women from nearby haciendas to be their wives. Antonio had told his followers that they need not fear the Spaniards because he had a cloth full of powder which he would set afire and make the attackers disappear. Emboldened by this supernatural assurance, only a month after Father Zapata's visit, warriors from Matudere ambushed and defeated a Spanish force of some sixty men sent out against them, appropriated their weapons, and sent the commander's testicles wrapped in a cloth back to the governor in Cartagena.[20]

To settle the hysteria, the governor himself led the retaliatory expedition against Matudere. Calling on the patron saint of the Spanish Reconquest, Santiago or James (known variously as Matamoros, Mataindios, or it would seem Matanegros, depending on the enemy), the Spaniards launched a spectacular night raid. As if on cue, a lightning bolt hit the house in which the *cimarrones* had stored their arms and munitions and blew it up. Spaniards and Africans alike may have read that event as a sign of divine intervention and the light of the fires helped the Spaniards track the scattering maroons.[21]

In the debacle Spanish troops finally caught Domingo Padilla or Domingo Criollo and his wife, Juana Padilla, who claimed to have founded Matudere in

1681. Domingo called himself Captain, but Juana had adopted the Spanish title, Virreina. This choice of rank may have made a political statement as only Mexico (New Spain) and Peru then rated Viceroys and Colombia's (New Granada) highest Spanish official was only a governor. It should be noted that although Spaniards described Domingo as *criollo* and *ladino*, his father, Domingo, who also lived at the Matudere, was born in Angola. Other of the *cimarrones* described as *muy viejos* or very old might also have been sources of direct knowledge about African cultures.[22]

Matudere was composed of about 250 members, more than 100 of whom were either African-born or born to African-born parents. Among the Africans identified by nation were twenty-eight Minas, nineteen Ararás, ten Congos, nine Luangos, five Angolas, three Popos, three Yolofes, two Caravalíes, one Bran, one Goyo, and at least one Biafara.[23] Once the governor and his counselors concluded their interrogations and declared the captives guilty, they hung and quartered thirteen of Matudere's defenders, including Domingo Padilla, and posted their mutilated body parts along the country roadsides "as an example and terror to others of this class." The Virreina, Juana, who was then approximately sixty years old, received 200 lashes and exile, as did many others, and the sick, very old, or very young captives received 100 lashes each before their owners were allowed to post bond and recover them. Before finishing with Juana, Governor Martin de Cevallos brought an artist to the jail to paint the Virreina's portrait, "for the novelty," but he caustically remarked that the man had favored her by making her appear more clean and tidy than she really was.[24]

Nearby in Venezuela rich gold deposits led Venezuela's governors repeatedly to attempt a settlement at Nirgua, but Indians fiercely resisted Spanish encroachment and four towns failed. Since Spanish homesteaders seemed unable to do the job, in 1601 Governor Arias Vaca designated blacks and *zambos* (persons of mixed African and Indian heritage) as *conquistadors*, with the accompanying perquisites. When whites began to move into Nirgua in the eighteenth century, the black descendants of its founders appealed directly to the King to uphold their privileges, which he did. [25] The records of Nirgua's town council or *cabildo* members date from 1628 through 1799 and its documentary history also includes correspondence between town leaders and Venezuelan authorities, Venezuelan authorities and the Crown, Royal Cédulas, a Bishop's pastoral visitation, and traveler accounts.[26]

A surviving drawing of an eighteenth-century Venezuelan *palenque* called Ocoyta accompanies the military reports of its destruction and is yet another form of evidence to be tapped. Ocoyta was destroyed shortly after it was formed, but it had already developed central leadership over multiple sites and an administrative hierarchy. The drawing of Ocoyta's layout shows at the center the house of the leader, Guillermo Ribas, of the Mina nation, his wife, and their three sons, one of whom was born at the settlement. Surrounding this house, in a semicircle, were the houses of Guillermo's officials including his executioner, lieutenant, messenger, and aide, also a Mina named Francisco. Only the latter was married, to María Valentina de Rada, a free *zamba* (a person of African and Indian parentage). The outermost semicircle of eleven houses housed the remaining residents, including two other women, one of whom also had three sons.[27]

With rare exceptions, women have remained largely invisible in the literature on maroons.[28] Their virtual absence is due in part to the traditional male bias in history, and in part to the difficulty of the sources for women's history in general—particularly in more remote time periods. The historical neglect of maroon women is also due in great part to the real sexual imbalance in the communities. More men than women became runaways. As other scholars have noted, women were often restrained from flight by maternal or family obligations.[29] When women did run from slavery, they faced the same dangers encountered by their male counterparts. They had to evade surveillance systems and pursuers, navigate unknown terrain, and brave animals and sometimes hostile Indian groups to find a safe refuge in areas remote from European control. Ethnohistorians and archaeologists have begun to explore the important role of Indian women as cultural mediators on the frontier, but few have yet recognized that African and African American women played similar roles.[30]

In conclusion, the Spanish documentary and legal traditions offer us ways to study maroon communities over a broad temporal and geographic range that includes wide swaths of what is today the United States. From the rich Spanish records we can begin to tease out details about the variety of the enslaved experiences of specific historical actors in specific historical contexts, about their forms of resistance, and how they helped restructure African and African American families and networks free of slavery. Employing the new methodologies of historical archaeology, African history, and gender studies will also help scholars advance the study of cultural adaptation and creolization and the formation of distinct African American communities in the Spanish Americas.

NOTES

1. Jane Landers, *Black Society in Spanish Florida* (Urbana: University of Illinois Press, 1999).

2. Because it affected his conversion efforts, the Jesuit Alonso de Sandoval paid particular attention to the bewildering array of ethnicities and languages of the Africans to whom he ministered in seventeenth-century Cartagena, detailing which groups spoke mutually intelligible languages. Alonso de Sandoval, *Un tratado sobre la esclavitud* (Madrid: Alianza Editorial, 1987).

3. For examples of the variety of records and how they can be used, see Landers, *Black Society*. See also Gwendolyn Midlo Hall, *Africans in Colonial Louisiana: The Development of Afro-Creole Culture in the Eighteenth Century* (Baton Rouge: Louisiana State University Press, 1992), and Kimberly S. Hanger, *Bounded Lives, Bounded Places: Free Black Society in Colonial New Orleans, 1769–1803* (Durham: Duke University Press, 1997).

4. Records generated by other European powers on "notorious" African maroons or rebels occasionally add to the historical record of Africans in areas of Spanish settlement. Landers, *Black Society*, chaps. 1–3.

5. Spanish concepts of *buen gobierno* or just government extended access to groups often excluded by other systems, including women and slaves. See Charles Cutter, *The Legal Culture of Northern New Spain, 1700–1810* (Albuquerque: University of New Mexico Press, 1994). On indigenous use of Spanish law, see Susan Kellogg, *Law and the Transformation of Aztec Culture, 1500–1700* (Norman: University of Oklahoma Press, 1995). For examples of African use of Spanish law, see Landers, *Black Society*. If Africans could not speak Spanish, court officials used translators, just as they did for non–Spanish-speaking witnesses of other ethnicities. This may have added new layers of linguistic filters, but was, nonetheless, an effort to understand and record the voice of Africans. Spanish interrogatories even include idiomatic answers to formal questions.

6. In 1744 Father Francisco Xavier Arturo baptized Domingo, a Carabalí slave, on his deathbed, with the comment that his "crudeness" prevented his understanding of Christian doctrine. Two years later, on separate occasions, Father Arturo gave the Congo slave, Miguel, and the Congo slave, Francisco, conditional baptisms because each told the priest he had been baptized by a priest in his homeland and taught to pray in his own language. As Miguel was baptized, he blessed himself in that unidentified language. In 1748 Father Arturo gave the same conditional baptism to Miguel Domingo, also a Congo slave who had been baptized in Africa and continued to pray in his native language. Baptism of Domingo, December 10, 1744, Catholic Parish Records, Diocese of St. Augustine Catholic Center, Jacksonville, Florida (hereafter cited as CPR), on microfilm reel 284 F, P.K. Yonge Library of Florida History, University of Florida, Gainesville, Florida (hereafter cited as PKY); Baptism of Miguel, September 29, 1746, and of Francisco, October 14, 1746, ibid.; Baptism of Miguel Domingo, January 26, 1748, ibid.

7. Many of the U.S. sites are discussed in Theresa A. Singleton, ed., *"I, Too, Am America"*: *Archaeological Studies of African-American Life* (Charlottesville and London: University Press of Virginia, 1999), and in her earlier book, *The Archaeology of Slavery and Plantation Life* (Orlando, FL: Academic Press, 1985). Douglas V. Armstrong, *The Old Village and the Great House: An Archaeological and Historical Examination of Drax Hall Plantation, St. Ann's Bay, Jamaica* (Urbana: University of Illinois Press, 1990); Jerome S. Handler and Frederick W. Lange, *Plantation Slavery in Barbados: An Archaeological and Historical Investigation* (Cambridge: Cambridge University Press, 1978); Jerome S. Handler, "An African-Type Healer/Diviner and His Grave Goods: A Burial from a Plantation Slave Cemetery in Barbados, West Indies," *International Journal of Historical Archaeology* 1 (1997), 89–128; Larry McKee, "Summary Report on the 1991 Hermitage Field Quarter Excavation," *Tennessean Anthropological Association Newsletter* 18 (1993), 1–17. For periodic updates on New York's African burial ground, see Jerome S. Handler, "Updates # 1, 2, 3, and 4," *African-American Archeology* (Spring 1992, Spring 1993, Winter 1993, and Winter 1994), and Spencer P. M. Harrington, "Bones and Bureaucrats: New York's Great Cemetery Imbroglio," *Archaeology* 46 (1993), 28–38.

8. Leland Ferguson, *Uncommon Ground: Archaeology and Early African America, 1650–1800* (Washington, DC: Smithsonian Institute Press, 1992); Linda France Stine, Melanie A. Cabak, and Mark D. Groover, "Blue Beads as African-American Cultural Symbols," *Historical Archaeology* 30 (1996), 49–75; Jerome S. Handler, "Determining African Birth from Skeletal Remains: A Note on Tooth Mutilation," *Historical Archaeology* 28 (1994), 113–119; Ross W. Jamieson, "Material Culture and Social Death: African-American Burial Practices," *Historical Archaeology* 29 (1995), 39–58.

9. Merrick Posnansky, "West Africanist Reflections on African-American Archaeology," in Singleton, *"I, Too, Am America,"* 21–38. Christopher DeCorse, "Culture Contact, Continuity, and Change on the Gold Coast, A.D. 1400–1900," *African Archaeological Review* 10 (1992), 163–196, and "The Danes on the Gold Coast: Culture Change and the European Presence," *African Archaeological Review* 11 (1993), 149–173.

10. Royal Cédula Replying to Governor Nicolás de Ovando, March 29, 1503, Indiferente General, Archivo General de Indias, Seville, Spain (hereafter cited as AGI); Slave Codes, Santo Domingo (hereafter cited as SD), January 6, 1522, Patronato 295, AGI.

11. Carlos Esteban Deive, *Los guerrilleros negros: esclavos fugitivos y cimarrones en Santo Domingo* (Santo Domingo: Fundación Cultural Dominicana, 1989), pp. 31–54; *Santo Domingo en los Manuscritos de Juan Bautista Muñoz*, ed. Roberto Marte (Santo Domingo: Ediciones Fundación García Arévalo, 1981), pp. 359–360, 412–415.

12. In 1553 Viceroy Luis de Velasco estimated New Spain's black population at more than 20,000. Despite Velasco's recommendation to limit slave imports, blacks were estimated to number ten times the white population by the early seventeenth century (David M. Davidson, "Negro Slave Control and Resistance in Colonial Mexico, 1519–1650," *Hispanic American Historical Review* 66 [1966], 235–253). Gonzalo Aguirre Beltrán also noted the preponderance of blacks over whites (Gonzalo Aguirre Beltrán, *La población negra de México, 1519–1810* [Mexico, DF: Ediciones Fuente Cultural, 1946], pp. 208–213).

13. Richard Price, ed., *Maroon Societies: Rebel Slave Communities in the Americas* (Baltimore: Johns Hopkins University Press, 1979).

14. Declaration of Emperor Charles, 1538, cited in Lyle N. McAlister, *Spain and Portugal in the New World, 1492–1700* (Minneapolis: University of Minnesota Press, 1984), p. 172.

15. Carlos Larrazábal Blanco, *Los negros y la esclavitud en Santo Domingo* (Santo Domingo, Dominican Republic: Editorial Postigo, 1975), pp. 151–153. I have discussed the maroons of Hispaniola, Colombia, and Mexico more fully in "African Ethnicity and Culture in the Americas," in Paul E. Lovejoy, ed., *Identifying Enslaved Africans: The "Nigerian" Hinterland and the African Diaspora* (London: Cassell Publishing, forthcoming).

16. In nearby caves explorers have also found metal daggers, clay water jugs, and triton shell trumpets which they identify to be the work of African runaways (José Juan Arrom and Manuel A. García Arévalo, *Cimarrón* [Santo Domingo, Dominican Republic: Fundación García-Arévalo, 1986], pp. 48–55).

17. Ibid.

18. Interview, Manuel García Arévalo, Santo Domingo, August, 1996. Ferguson, *Uncommon Ground*, pp. 18–32, 109–116, and "Looking for the 'Afro' in Colono-Indian Pottery," in Robert L. Schuyler, ed., *Archaeological Perspectives on Ethnicity in America* (Farmingdale, NJ: Baywood, 1979), pp. 14–28. Also see Ferguson, "'The Cross Is a Magic Sign': Marks on Eighteenth-Century Bowls from South Carolina," and Matthew C. Emerson, "African Inspirations in a New World Art and Artifact: Decorated Pipes from the Chesapeake," in Singleton, *"I, Too, Am America,"* 47–74.

19. Father Fernando Zapata to Governor Martín de Cevallos, April 21, 1693, Santa Fe 213, AGI.

20. Report of Governor Martín de Cevallos, May 29, 1693, Santa Fe 213, AGI. Robin Law shows that ritual decapitation and castration of enemies were important features of warfare in contemporary Dahomey until leaders forbade the practices late in the eighteenth century. Robin Law, "'My Head Belongs to the King': On the Political and Ritual Significance of Decapitation in Pre-Colonial Dahomey," *Journal of African History* 30 (1989), 399–415.

21. Report of Martín de Cevallos, May 29, 1693, Santa Fe 213, AGI. The deposed Oyo king Shango allegedly became an *orisha* who used lightning bolts to strike down enemies who angered him. Henry John Drewel, John Pemberton III, and Rowland Abiodun, *Nine Centuries of African Art and Thought* (New York: Center for African Art in Association with Harry N. Abrams, 1989).

22. Ibid. The community was reproducing itself for there were thirty-four children in the camp, including three orphans whom families had adopted.

23. Pedro Mina escaped capture and ruled the Matudere survivors for two more years, but in 1695 Mina too was apprehended at the *palenque* of Norossi. Report of Sancho Ximeno, September 22, 1695, Santa Fe 212, AGI.

24. Cevallos said that he hung the portrait in the governor's mansion. Martín de Cevallos to Antonio Ortiz de Talora, May 29, 1693, Santa Fe 213, AGI.

25. In 1695 and 1696 the Spaniards legitimated four additional towns combining Africans and Indians along the Tocuyo River. Miguel Acosta Saignes, *Vida de los esclavos en Venezuela* (Valencia: Vadell Hermanos Editores, 1984), pp. 260–266; Royal Cédula, March 7, 1704, cited in Richard Konetzke, ed., *Colección de documentos para la historia de la formación social de Hispanoamérica* (Madrid, 1953), p. 94.

26. Irma Marina Mendoza, "El cabildo de Pardos en Nirgua: Siglos XVII y XVIII," *Anuario de Estudios Bolivarianos* 4 (1995), 95–120.

27. Saignes, *Vida de los esclavos*, pp. 297–307.

28. The essays included in Richard Price's classic collection contain only scattered references to the women living in maroon settlements (*Maroon Societies*). Two subsequent works by Barbara Bush and Hilary Beckles discuss maroon women in the British Caribbean but are limited by the nature of their sources or their area of study. Bush contends that "most slaves were individual runaways and did not aspire to join maroon communities," arguing that most tried to pass for free in nearby towns (*Slave Women in Caribbean Society, 1650–1838* [Kingston: Heinman Publishers, 1990], pp. 63–65). Hilary McD. Beckles considers this strategy urban maroonage but has no real frontier experience to discuss for Barbados (*Natural Rebels: A Social History of Enslaved Black Women in Barbados* [New Brunswick: Rutgers University Press, 1989], pp. 164–170).

29. Ibid.

30. Clara Sue Kidwell, "Indian Women as Cultural Mediators," *Ethnohistory* 39:2 (Spring, 1992), 97–107; Kathryn E. Holland Braund, "Guardians of Tradition and Handmaidens to Change: Women's Roles in Creek Economic and Social Life During the Eighteenth Century," *American Indian Quarterly* (Summer 1990), 239–257; Bonnie E. McEwan, "The Archaeology of Women in the Spanish New World," *Historical Archaeology* 25:4 (1991), 33–41. Also see Jane Landers, "Maroon Women in Spanish America," in David Barry Gaspar and Darlene C. Hine, eds., *Free Women of Color in the Slave Societies of the Americas* (Bloomington: Indiana University Press, forthcoming).

24. Unintended Outcomes: William Walker and the Emergence of Nicaraguan Nationalism

Emily Story

The dramatic and complex story of William Walker's short life (he died at the age of thirty-four) sheds light on the contemporary cultural environments of both Central America and the United States. Walker's military excursions into Mexico and Central America were made possible by internal forces that left the newly independent republics vulnerable to outside invasion. At the same time internal conditions in the United States brought about the phenomenon of filibustering which peaked in the mid-nineteenth century. Because filibustering connoted piracy to contemporaries, Walker and his fellow adventurers resented the term since they perceived themselves as honorable patriots. Today the term filibusters refers to the group of men from the United States, mostly Southerners, who in the 1850s mobilized armed troops to invade nations with which their government was at peace. While the U.S. government officially condemned filibustering, it did little to put an end to the practice. Walker was the most famous of the filibusters and for a brief time captured the imagination of his fellow countrymen. The eruption of civil war in the United States brought an end to filibustering and virtually erased it from the popular memory. The story also lost importance since Walker's several dogged (some would say suicidal) attempts to establish himself as president of all of Central America ultimately failed. It is a story that prompts one to explore "what if" scenarios, but little actually changed. Since the histories of Central America and the United States could have set off on a new course but did not, the filibuster movement has received only a smattering of attention from scholars.

While doing research for a paper on the impact of the Walker episode on Nicaragua's social and political development, I made several trips to the Tennessee State Library and Archives to explore Walker's personal background. Unfortunately, there is little information about his early life. He was born in Nashville in 1824 to James, his Scottish father, and his wife, Mary. The State Archives did not yield much information not already included in published biographies. I did discover that in the Davidson County marriage record Mary's maiden name is spelled slightly differently than in the biographies. I have not determined which version is correct.[1] Records were not systematically kept during Walker's time in Nashville. The city became the state capital in 1826 and its population in 1823, the year before Walker's birth, was a mere 3,463.[2] Walker's father was a merchant and the family lived in the city. He had ample opportunities for education and traveled extensively. Unlike most of Middle Tennessee's population, the family did not work in agriculture, but the Walkers owned at least one slave. From an early age, however, Walker apparently disapproved of slavery and thought it was morally wrong. Walker graduated from the University of Nashville at the age of fourteen. The State Archives now hold the university's records on microfilm. While there is little information about Walker's time at the university, beside his name on the list of the class of 1838 is penciled the notation "The celebrated Filibuster *(sic)* of Nicaragua. Killed in . . ." what appears to read, incorrectly, "Managua."[3] At the University of Nashville students received classical education with a heavy emphasis on morality. The university inculcated in the future leaders of Nashville and the surrounding area a sense of duty to extend and protect liberty and democracy.

Walker's parents wanted the small introspective boy to enter the ministry, but he chose medicine instead. In Nashville he worked for a local doctor, then went to the University of Pennsylvania where he received an M.D. degree in 1843. A medical school classmate and fellow Tennessean, John Berrien Lindsley, kept a scrapbook (now held at the State Archives on microfilm) which includes U.S. newspaper clippings. Several other Middle Tennesseans' personal papers mention Walker and are included in the Archives collection. Former governor (1849–1851) and ambassador to Brazil (1853–1857) William Trousdale collected clippings and mentioned Walker in his personal correspondence. John Sumner Russwurm of Murfreesboro also collected newspaper clippings chronicling Walker's activities. After Walker graduated from medical school his parents funded a two-year stay in Europe for further medical training and travel. Although Walker supposedly spoke a number of European languages, he never mastered Spanish. Upon his return to Nashville, he decided to study law and then moved to New Orleans to set up a practice which soon failed. Unsatisfied with both the medical and legal professions, Walker decided to try his hand at journalism. In 1848 he edited the New Orleans *Crescent*. New Orleans was a major point of departure for filibustering campaigns, and it was there that Walker came into contact with the adventurous southern youths who were undertaking armed excursions to Cuba. Though he would become the most famous of the group, Walker wrote a number of articles condemning the practice of filibustering. He also argued passionately for the abolition of slavery.[4] His youthful stance on slavery leads one to question why President Walker would later issue a decree that reinstituted slavery in Nicaragua. The probable answer is that he reinstituted slavery only after it became clear that he needed soldiers from the U.S. South to fight on his behalf against the united Central American army.[5]

In New Orleans Walker apparently fell madly in love with a deaf-mute named Helen Martin. When Martin died of yellow fever or cholera in 1849, Walker left New Orleans to join the flood of adventurous young men converging on California in search of gold. In San Francisco Walker continued to work as a journalist, editing the *Daily Herald* and stirring up controversy by writing a scathing criticism of a powerful local judge. When the judge jailed Walker for contempt thousands of people protested in front of the courthouse, giving Walker his first taste of fame and public adulation. After a brief stint as a lawyer Walker began making acquaintances with men involved in filibustering. The boy described as gentle began showing an interest in fighting: Walker fought two duels in San Francisco which demonstrated his poor skills with firearms.[6] In leading filibustering excursions Walker found his true passion and his restlessness came to an end. For the last decade of his life he single-mindedly pursued his dream of creating and ruling a new country.

The richest local source of information about Walker's activities in Central America are the papers of newspaper editor John P. Heiss, who served as Walker's informal ambassador to the United States during his brief presidency. In addition to clippings from U.S. papers, the collection includes clippings from Nicaraguan papers which he acquired during several visits there.[7] The U.S. papers document how the national debate over filibustering varied geographically. The *Tennessee Historical Magazine* published a number of excerpts from the Heiss papers in its 1916 issue.[8] During an apparent surge in interest in Walker, William Scroggs's authoritative biography *Filibusters and Financiers* was published (1916). In 1915 the *Tennessee Historical Magazine* published Heiss's diplomatic correspondence as well as an interview with Elleanore Callaghan Ratterman who traveled to Nicaragua with several members of her family and slaves during Walker's war with the intention of settling there.[9]

Why did filibustering attract the support of many Americans? Why did Walker change his position on slavery so radically? To answer such questions one must consider the U.S. context. Filibustering came about as a result of cultural and political forces at work in the United States in the mid-nineteenth century. Several factors led many young men to advocate the expansion of the borders of the United States. In the 1840s and 1850s, the Young America movement instilled in young men a nationalistic zeal to extend the superior U.S. institutions to "backward" neighboring regions.[10] Since its inception, the nation had been continuously extending its territory. Upon reaching the Pacific Ocean, proponents of further expansion looked southward to the newly independent Latin American republics which, as the Mexican-American War demonstrated, were vulnerable to outside intervention. Many Americans resented European activity in the hemisphere and believed it was their "Manifest Destiny" to introduce the superior institutions of the United States to the less civilized peoples of former (or, in the case of Cuba, current) Spanish colonies. Proponents of expansion used the Monroe Doctrine to assert the right of the United States to actively involve itself in the affairs of other American states.

In 1837, the year before Walker's graduation, a man by the name of Philip Lindsley addressed the student body. His speech illustrates the tone of instruction at the University of Nashville which helped shape William Walker's views. Lindsley emphasized the importance of education as a defender of justice and liberty. Referring to Latin America, which he perceived as a less educated region, Lindsley said, "Spanish America had become independent—but the people are not free."[11] Walker took such statements to heart. There is evidence of this type of thinking in Walker's *The War in Nicaragua* and in descriptions of him by contemporaries and scholars. Walker firmly believed that he had the right, indeed the duty, to bring the blessings of U.S. institutions to Latin America.

Walker appears to have been motivated by a genuine belief that his filibustering expeditions would ultimately benefit the people of Latin America. Undoubtedly, Walker was driven by the desire for personal power. He believed strongly that it was his destiny to create a new republic in Central America. Those who followed him to Nicaragua to fight on his behalf had different motivations and probably did not know the details of his plans. While support for filibustering could be found throughout the United States, it held more appeal in the South. The opposing points of view are illustrated by the newspaper clippings in the State Archives. Because of the potential for additional slave states, Northern papers tended to take a more negative view of filibustering than their Southern counterparts. The bulk of Walker's troops came from the South. Many were veterans of the Mexican-American War who sought adventure and glory in battle. In the 1850s the South was a highly traditional society: duels were commonplace and many held a romantic view of the honor which could be achieved through bravery in battle. Walker lured soldiers with promises of land grants in exchange for their services. Land ownership conferred a great deal of prestige in the South, and for many young men fighting in Central America provided the best chance to acquire personal wealth and respectability. Walker's need to attract new troops likely led to his decision to reinstitute slavery, which had been abolished in 1824. In the United States internal tensions surrounding slavery had been mounting for some time. To counter the addition of non-slave states to the union many Southerners advocated annexing regions in Latin America as slave states. Walker's about-face on slavery, therefore, was a desperate political move intended to drum up support for his cause.

While some useful archival material can be found in Nashville, there are other repositories of material on the Walker episode. Tulane University's Fassoux Collection and the University of California, Riverside hold the most extensive archives documenting William Walker's activities. The University of Tennessee at Knoxville's General Lee Christmas and President William Walker Collection reportedly contains a number of personal papers and clippings. The story of William Walker has attracted the attention of amateur collectors who have acquired and, in a number of cases, published important materials such as *El Nicaragüense*, Walker's English-language newspaper.

NOTES

1. Davidson County, Tennessee, Marriage Record Book I, January 2, 1789, to December 13, 1837.

2. *Catalogue of the Officers and Graduates of the University of Nashville* (Nashville: A. Nelson, 1850).

3. University of Nashville records, Tennessee State Library and Archives, microfilm.

4. William O. Scroggs, *Filibusters and Financiers: The Story of William Walker and His Associates* (New York: Macmillan, 1916), pp. 15–17.

5. Robert E. May, *The Southern Dream of a Caribbean Empire: 1854–1864* (Baton Rouge, 1973), p. 4.

6. John M. Bass, *William Walker* (Nashville: Tennessee Historical Society, 1898), p. 2.

7. John P. Heiss papers, Tennessee State Library and Archives, microfilm.

8. Tennessee Historical Society, *Tennessee Historical Magazine* II (1), 1916.

9. Tennessee Historical Society, *Tennessee Historical Magazine* I (1), 1915.

10. May, *Southern Dream*, p. 20.

11. Philip Lindsley, *Speech on Behalf of the University of Nashville Delivered on the Day of the Anniversary Commencement* (Nashville: S. Nye and Co., 1837).

25. Dual Identities? The Andean Gentry in Peru and Alto Peru, 1533–1826

Rafael E. Tarragó

The Andean Gentry under the Hapsburgs (1533–1700)

Contrary to popular wisdom, the indigenous ruling class in the areas of the Americas conquered and settled by the Spaniards was not destroyed at the time of the Spanish Conquest of America. The "señores naturales," as the native rulers were called, survived throughout the three hundred years that the Spanish Crown ruled in continental Spanish America as subordinate elites who acted as intermediaries between Crown and people.[1] In many ways their position within the Spanish monarchy was analogous to that of Cossak and Tartar hetmen in the Polish Commonwealth during the seventeenth century. It is not unimportant that the kings of Spain saw themselves in America as the successors of the vanquished native rulers. This was particularly the case in the territories under the Inca at the time of the Spanish Conquest.[2] Under the Spanish Hapsburgs, the immense territory comprising modern-day Peru, Bolivia, Ecuador, and northern Chile was known as the Kingdoms of Peru. By styling themselves "Hispaniorum et Indianorum Rex," the monarchs of that dynasty acknowledged the separate identity of the many peoples under their rule. The discussion in this paper is limited to the core areas of the vanquished Inca Empire—present-day Peru and Bolivia—which the Spaniards called Peru and Alto Peru.

Although the Andean gentry accepted the sovereignty of the Spanish Crown after the execution of Túpac Amaru I in 1572, they did not base their claims on Spanish law, but on their rights under the Inca.[3] They may have accepted the fact of the Spanish Conquest, but in their eyes the political realities did not deprive them of their identity as members of an Andean nation. In this respect, their position was similar to that of the contemporary Milanese patriciate who saw no conflict between their acceptance of a Spanish (or French) ruler and their identity as Italians. The Andean chieftains, known as *kurakas,* saw themselves as natural rulers born with rights and responsibilities to the people under their rule. Although the elevation of pliable upstarts to chieftaincies by local Spanish authorities (here it is appropriate to recall that in the terminology of the times, Spanish meant white and not necessarily born in Spain), and the self-serving behavior of many kurakas themselves, weakened

270

the bond between chieftains and commoners in the Andean region, they represented a group of power contenders within the Universal Monarchy of the Spanish Hapsburgs.

The Kurakas and the Catholic Church

The Christianization of the New World was one way that the Spanish monarchy justified its rule in the Americas, and it is undeniable that the Spanish monarchs promoted and supported the activities of Catholic missionaries in the Kingdoms of the Indies (as they called their American realms).[4] Christianization required that missionaries learn the languages of the indigenous peoples and that indigenous catechists be trained. For some time in the sixteenth century, the missionaries in Spanish America even contemplated the creation of a native clergy. Educational institutions for the training of sons of Andean kurakas were established with that purpose in mind. Although an indigenous clergy never materialized (partly because of the discovery that the conversions of many prominent indigenous people were not what the European missionaries would consider sincere), colleges for the sons of the indigenous gentry were founded, in accordance with Law II, title 23, of the Laws of the Indies, which stipulated the royal will of their foundation in the major cities of the Kingdoms of the Indies.[5]

Although the late 1500s saw a revival of pre-Christian religions in the Andes, followed by a repressive campaign to extirpate idolatry, the seventeenth century saw the development of a sort of Andean Catholicism. Perhaps syncretic, it was nonetheless recognizable as Catholic to the religious and political authorities. Catholic missionaries set great store on the conversion of kurakas, just like their forebears in Europe had with respect to the conversion of pagan kings like the Frank Clovis and the Hungarian Geza (Saint Stephen).[6] One of the Christian kurakas, don Juan de Santa Cruz Pachacuti, wrote a history of the Inca Empire where he made claims of a pre-Hispanic evangelization of the Andean peoples by Saint Thomas the Apostle.[7]

The Andean Gentry and Andean Culture under the Spanish Monarchy

Although colleges for sons of kurakas may have been Hispanizing institutions, they nonetheless fostered an educated indigenous gentry that rose above the indigenous masses. Some members of the Andean gentry wrote histories of their people and their own versions of the Spanish Conquest. Others wrote or gave patronage to poetry and drama in their native languages, using the Latin alphabet introduced in the Americas by the Spanish conquerors.

The best known of the Andean gentry's chroniclers is the mestizo Garcilaso de la Vega Inca, son of a Spanish conqueror and a royal Inca princess and the only one of them to see his work published. His *Comentarios reales de los*

Incas (an idealized history of the Inca Empire) was published at Lisbon in 1609, and his *Historia general del Perú* (a history of the Spanish Conquest) was published at Córdoba in 1617. In 1908 Richard Pietschman discovered the manuscript of don Felipe Guamán Poma de Ayala's *El primer nueva corónica y buen gobierno* at the Royal Library of Copenhagen, and since then it has attracted the attention of scholars and ideologues. But Garcilaso and Guamán Poma were only two of several Andean indigenous and mestizo chroniclers. The history of the Inca Empire by don Juan de Santa Cruz Pachacuti was mentioned above. Titu Cusi Yupanqui, reigning Inca in exile in Vilcabamba, dictated in Quechua a *Relación de la conquista del Perú*.[8] In her essay, *La apropiación del signo* (Tempe, 1985), Raquel Chang-Rodríguez analyzes the manipulation of the written word by these Andean chroniclers. According to Chang-Rodríguez, the manipulation of the past was a tradition in the Inca Empire, which explains the open and disarming omission or exaltation of facts by the indigenous and mestizo chroniclers of Peru.[9]

After the Spanish Conquest, some indigenous peoples in Spanish America wrote the myths of their ancestors and transliterated hymns and narratives using the Latin alphabet introduced by their conquerors. In sixteenth-century Peru, the informers of Viceroy Francisco de Toledo (1515–1582) compiled the *Ritos y tradiciones de Huarochiri*, and Cristóbal de Molina wrote recorded short speeches in Quechua *(Relación de las fábulas y ritos de los Incas)*. The pre-Hispanic oral literature of the Quechua was intrinsically religious and linked to the songs and dances of pre-Christian rites, which were proscribed after the Spanish Conquest, but much of it survived with the name of God, the Virgin Mary, or some saint substituted for the name of the being involved. By the early seventeenth century, a religious Quechua Christian poetry appeared in Peru, praising the Virgin as Supreme Protectress of Humankind and embracing the themes of human guilt and the littleness of humans before God.[10] In Alto Peru, new poetical forms in Quechua, like the *yaravi* and the *wayñu*, developed after the Conquest.[11]

Plays had been part of Quechua religious life under the Inca and at his court (where noblemen played histrionic roles like Louis XIV of France would do centuries later). After the Spanish Conquest, religious pagan plays were forbidden by the Spanish conquerors, but Christian plays in Quechua were written and promoted by Catholic missionaries. The Andean gentry that became integrated in the hierarchies of the Kingdoms of Peru cultivated poetry in Quechua and patronized a post-Conquest Quechua drama. In the introduction to his anthology of Quechua plays of the seventeenth century, the critic Teodoro Meneses says that the Quechua plays of the seventeenth century were the best dramatic literature produced in Peru during that century.[12] Most pieces of Quechua drama, like *Atau Walpaj P'uchukakuyninpa Wankan* (a play about the capture and execution of Atahualpa by Francisco Pizarro, with an unhistorical finale where Pizarro is humbled by the King of Spain for killing a king and then dies in a fit of rage), are transliterations of plays that originated in a post-Conquest oral tradition. But many plays were written in Quechua, like *Uscar Paucar* (1644/1645), by don Vasco de Contreras y Valverde; *El pobre más rico* (1645–1685), by Dr. Gabriel Centeno de Osma; and *El hijo pródigo* (1643) and *El rapto de Proserpina* (1644), by don Juan Espinosa Medrano.

Don Juan Espinosa Medrano (1629–1688) was the son of a Spaniard and an indigenous woman but was adopted when he was seven years old by a priest surnamed Espinosa Medrano, who sent him to school and who took him to Cuzco in 1637. In Cuzco the young mestizo entered the seminary of Saint Anthony the Abbot, benefiting from one of the scholarships for indigenous men funded by Bishop Antonio de la Raya, and he received holy orders in 1650. Espinosa Medrano wrote sacramental plays *(autos sacramentales)* in Quechua to be performed in public squares during religious festivities (particularly the feast of Corpus Christi). However, it was not as a playwright that he was admired by his contemporaries, but as a preacher. His contemporaries called him "Doctor Sublime," "Fénix Criollo," "Demóstenes Indiano," and "Tertuliano de América." An anthology of his sermons was published in Spain by Dr. Agustín Cortez de la Cruz, who titled it *Novena Maravilla* because he considered Espinosa Medrano's oratorial gifts one of the marvels of the world (after the seven of the Ancient World and the palace of El Escorial in Spain).[13] Today Espinosa Medrano is best known for his *Apologético en favor de don Luis de Góngora* (Lima, 1662), a defense of the poetic style and the literary greatness of that Spanish author.

In his *Apologético*, Espinosa Medrano quotes 130 authors, from Homer to Cervantes, thus revealing his erudition in Western culture. It is said that he could read French, Portuguese, Hebrew, Greek, and Latin and that he translated Virgil into Quechua.[14] He embraced Spanish culturalism in his sermons and his writing, and he became a thomistic philosopher. An Andean mestizo from Cuzco, he was fascinated by ideas and languages that originated in Europe and Asia, but he was not ashamed of his Andean origin. An anecdote, mentioned by D. A. Brading in his book *The First America* (Cambridge, 1991), has him pausing in the midst of a sermon in the Cathedral of Cuzco to exclaim, "Ladies, make way for that poor Indian woman: she is my mother."[15] In the preface to his *Philosophia Thomistica*, published at Rome in 1688, Espinosa Medrano claims to be proud of Peru, his fatherland.[16]

European artistic media and styles were introduced in the Andean region during the sixteenth century, and the cities of Potosí and Cuzco produced accomplished artists in all the fine arts. Ironically, it was in oil painting—a medium completely unknown in the region before the Spanish Conquest—that Andeans proved themselves most accomplished. There were many indigenous artists in Alto Peru, including Titu Yupanqui—sculptor of the statue of the Virgin Mary known as Our Lady of Copacabana—and the celebrated painter Luis Niño.[17] In Cuzco, the roster of indigenous artists is a long one. Notable indigenous Cuzco painters of the seventeenth century were Diego Kusiwaman, Diego Walpa, Fernando Inca, Juan Tupa, and the celebrated Diego Quispe Tito. Among the indigenous Cuzco painters of the eighteenth century were Juan Manco Mayta, Simón Inca, and Alfonso Nina.[18] In Bartolome Arzáns de Orsúa's chronicle of Potosí, Cuzco's indigenous painter Tomás Sairi Tupac is mentioned with praise, and Potosí's Luis Niño is called a "Second Apelles."[19]

The indigenous artists of Cuzco divorced themselves from European models by accentuating symbolic design over naturalistic image. This is most evident in the various depictions of the Virgin Mary, where her bell-shaped gown takes a mountain form, perhaps to meet the needs of Andean devotions. Spanish sources state repeatedly that Andeans worshiped the Earth as their mother, and, indeed, worship of the earth was the most persistent of Andean rituals. The best known of those "mountain" representations of the Virgin Mary is "The Virgin Mary of the Mountain Potosiama," an eighteenth-century anonymous painting where the face and hands of the Virgin are actually within the conical shape of the mountain of Potosí. In front of this Virgin/Mountain there is a globe painted with an image of Potosí flanked by a pope and a cardinal on one side and by the king-emperor Charles I and a member of the Andean gentry on the other.[20] In Cuzco, members of the Andean gentry commissioned portraits of themselves and of the Inca emperors, as well as religious paintings for their parish churches and for private devotion.[21]

The Andean Gentry under the Bourbons (1700–1826): Change, Revolt, and Dissolution

In 1700 Charles II Hapsburg died without issue, leaving the Crown of Spain and the Kingdoms of the Indies to his grandnephew, Philip of Anjou, grandson of the French king Louis XIV. The accession of the House of Bourbon to the Hispanic realm was momentous because that dynasty brought a French centralist mind set, as well as a well-known reformist zeal. In Spanish America, reforms were needed, particularly in the Andean kingdoms, where most of the indigenous population suffered from corruption and venality. The situation undermined the position of the Andean gentry, who lost face before their people when they could not act as protectors.

Vicente Morachimo, kuraka of the Chimo y Chica, near the city of Lambayeque, wrote a protest against abuses by local corregidores and parish priests which was read by the king in 1732, and Fray Calixto Tupac Inca presented a Representación to the king at Madrid in 1750.[22] But the Crown was slow to correct abuses against the indigenous population at a time when it was more concerned about political and economic reforms. Actually, it was royal attempts to raise revenue that sparked rebellion in the Andes in 1780.

Over a hundred times from 1720 to 1790, the native Andean peoples of Peru and Alto Peru rose up in violence. As early as 1742, a self-proclaimed Inca descendant, Juan Santos, led disaffected jungle peoples and highlander migrants. But none of those movements compared to the major civil war that engulfed southern Peru and Bolivia from 1780 to 1782, led by the wealthy member of the Andean gentry don José Gabriel Condorcanqui and his associates Tomás Katari and Julián Apasa. Don José Gabriel took the name of Túpac Amaru, the last reigning Inca (indeed, he descended from the Inca Túpac Amaru I), and attempted to restore the ancient dynasty.[23] Revolts broke out in the core of the central sierra and swept south. By December of 1780, the combined insurrectionary forces led by Tomás Katari and Túpac Amaru II transformed the political landscape of southern Peru and Alto Peru.[24]

The Túpac Amaru rebellion began as a protest against the exactions of corregidores and new taxes prompted by the desire of the Bourbon monarchs to turn the Kingdoms of the Indies into profitable colonies. The loyalty manifested by the rebels for Church and Crown was remarkable. Their loyalty to the Church was even greater than their loyalty to the Crown, perhaps because it was among the curates that the rebels found their closest sympathizers in Creole circles. The fact that the Creole bishop of Cuzco was accused of encouraging the rebellion of Túpac Amaru suggests that the attitude of the Church was not strongly damnatory of it, and, indeed, Túpac Amaru himself insisted that he did not intend to damage the Church.[25] The movement lost Creole support, however, as it became a struggle to restore native Andean glory, and its excesses had the unintended effect of hardening the social fears of whites and fostering a strong Creole tendency toward royalism in Peru and Alto Peru. Túpac Amaru II and his followers were defeated. The leaders of the rebellion were executed in the main square of Cuzco with terror-inspiring cruelty, just like in the Place Royale of Paris, where a man who had tried to kill King Louis XV of France was executed before the avid eyes of the crowd in that enlightened European city.

It is commonly known that after the rebellion of Túpac Amaru II, royal authorities confiscated copies of Garcilaso de la Vega Inca's *Comentarios reales*, destroyed portraits of the Inca emperors, forbade kurakas and other members of the Andean gentry to use insignia reminiscent of the Inca, and deauthorized the concession by royal officers in Peru of nobility titles to Andean gentry. But it is not so well known that in 1784, the Spanish monarchy passed reformist legislation that it implemented in response to the Túpac Amaru II rebellion.[26] Plans for social reform in the Andean kingdoms had been on the drawing boards at Madrid since the scientists Antonio de Ulloa and Jorge Juan visited them in 1735 and wrote *Noticias secretas* in 1749 for the King of Spain.[27] It was a pity that the Spanish Bourbons gave precedence to their revenue-enhancing and centralizing reforms. Furthermore, despite real royal efforts, the implementation of the reforms of 1784 was not a great success because government officers charged with the task were paid ridiculously low salaries which forced them to make ends meet by doing favors at the cost of not doing justice or implementing good government. In 1814 there was another rebellion in Peru led by a member of the Andean gentry, the kuraka Pumacahua.

Given the persistence of grievances against the Spanish monarchy and the rebellion of the kuraka Pumacahua as late as 1814, it is puzzling that at the time of the Bolivarian invasions in the 1820, most indigenous peoples and the Andean gentry of Peru and Alto Peru stood by the royalist cause. It is true that the Cortes of 1812, which counted with the participation of Peruvian deputies, including don Dionisio Inca Yupanqui, passed legislation favorable to the indigenous peoples of the Kingdoms of the Indies, but perhaps they had come to realize that the failure of royal legislation at the local level was due to the uncontrolled greed of American-born Spaniards, who failed to obey and implement it, and who were those who controlled economic and social life in the Kingdoms of Peru.[28] An indigenous royalist movement under General Antonio Huachaca and other Andean chiefs did not accept the end of monarchy and the legitimacy of the Republic of Peru until 1839, when they signed a peace treaty at Yanallay with the republican government.[29]

NOTES

1. Roberto S. Chamberlain, "The Concept of the Señor Natural. . . ," *Hispanic American Historical Review* 19 (May 1939), 130–137.

2. John Rowe, "El movimiento nacional Inca del siglo XVIII," *Sociedad colonial y sublevaciones populares. Túpac Amaru-1780* (Lima: Instituto Nacional de Investigación y Desarrollo de la Educación "Augusto Salazar Bondy," 1976), p. 21.

3. Ibid., p. 22.

4. Claudio Esteva Fabregat, *La Corona española y el indio americano* (Valencia: Asociación Francisco López de Gómara, 1989), vol. 2, p. 158.

5. Fernando Ocaranza, *El Imperial Colegio de Indios de la Santa Cruz de Tlatelolco* (Mexico, 1934), p. 14. For the persistence of non-Catholic beliefs in the Andean region, see Kenneth Mills, *Idolatry and Its Enemies: Colonial Andean Religion and Extirpation, 1640–1750* (Princeton: Princeton University Press, 1997).

6. Richard Fletcher, *The Barbarian Conversion: From Paganism to Christianity* (New York: Henry Holt, 1998), pp. 102–106, 432–433.

7. See Juan de Santa Cruz Pachacuti, *Relación de antigüedades deste reyno de Pirú*, Pierre Duviols and César Itier, eds. (Cuzco: Centro de Estudios Regionales, 1993).

8. *Cronistas indios y mestizos,* Francisco Carrillo, ed. (Lima: Editorial Horizonte, 1991), vol. 1, p. 9.

9. Raquel Chang-Rodríguez, *La apropiación del signo: tres cronistas indígenas del Perú* (Tempe: Center for Latin American Studies, Arizona State University, 1985), p. 24.

10. Edmundo Bendezu Aybar, *Literatura quechua* (Caracas: Biblioteca Ayacucho, 1980), p. xxv.

11. Edgar Avila Echazu, *Historia y antología de la literatura boliviana* (La Paz: Universidad Boliviana, 1978), p. 80.

12. *Teatro quechua colonial, antología,* Teodoro Meneses, ed. (Lima: Ediciones Edubanco, 1983), p. 8.

13. Antonio Centeno Zela, *Lo autóctono y lo hispano en Espinosa Medrano* (Lima, 1988), p. 87.

14. Ibid., p. 75. Although Espinosa Medrano's erudition was extraordinary, it was not rare for kurakas and men of the Andean gentry to write and read and to own books; see the description of the library of a kuraka in Teodoro Hampe Martínez, *Bibliotecas privadas del mundo colonial* (Madrid: Iberoamericana, 1996), pp. 182–184.

15. D. A. Brading, *The First America* (Cambridge: Cambridge University Press, 1991), p. 341.

16. Juan Espinosa Medrano, *Apologético* (Caracas: Biblioteca Ayacucho, 1982), pp. 325–329.

17. See Marcelo Arduz Ruiz, *Tito Yupanqui, el venerable Inca modelador de la imagen de Copacabana* (La Paz: Imprenta Don Bosco, 1996); Mario Chacón Torres, *Arte virreinal en Potosí* (Seville: Escuela de Estudios Hispanoamericanos de Sevilla, 1973), pp. 124–130.

18. Teófilo Benavente Velarde, *Pintores cusqueños de la colonia* (Cuzco: Municipalidad de Cusco, 1995), pp. 17–19.

19. José Mesa and Teresa Gisbert, "Noticias de arte en la obra de Bartolomé Arzáns de Orsúa y Vela," in Bartolomé Arzáns de Orsúa y Vela, *Historia de la Villa Imperial de Potosí*, Lewis Hanke, ed. (Providence, RI: Brown University Press, 1965), vol. 3, pp. 459–460.

20. Carol Damian, *The Virgin of the Andes: Art and Ritual in Colonial Cuzco* (Miami Beach: Granfield Press, 1995), pp. 51–53.

21. See John Howland Rowe, "Colonial Portraits of Inca Nobles," in *The Civilization of Ancient America. Selected Papers of the XXI International Congress of Americanists*, Sol Tax, ed. (Chicago: The University of Chicago Press, 1951), pp. 258–268.

22. Joyce Statton, "The Influence of Sixteenth-Century Missionary Thought on Eighteenth-Century Indian Reformists in Peru," in *University of British Columbia Hispanic Studies* (London: Tamesis Books Limited, 1974), p. 33.

23. There is a genealogy of descendants of the Inca under the Spanish monarchy in John Hemming, *The Conquest of the Incas* (New York: Harcourt Brace Jovanovich, 1974), p. 507.

24. See Steven J. Stern, "The Age of Andean Insurrection, 1742–1782: A Reappraisal," in *Resistance, Rebellion and Consciousness in the Andes Peasant World, Eighteenth to Twentieth Centuries*, Steven J. Stern, ed. (Madison: University of Wisconsin, 1987), pp. 34–93.

25. George Kubler, [selections from] "The Quechua in the Colonial World," in George Kubler, *Studies in Ancient American and European Art: The Collected Essays of George Kubler*, Thomas F. Reese, ed. (New Haven: Yale University Press, 1985), p. 47. See *Túpac Amaru y la Iglesia-Antología* (Lima: Banco de los Andes, 1983).

26. See John Fisher, "La rebelión de Túpac Amaru y el programa de la reforma imperial de Carlos III," *Anuario de Estudios Americanos* 28 (1971), 405–421.

27. See Kenneth J. Andrien, "The Noticias Secretas de América and the Construction of a Governing Ideology for the Spanish Empire," *Colonial Latin American Review* 7:2 (December 1998), 175–192.

28. See Cesáreo de Armellada, *La causa indígena americana en las Cortes de Cádiz* (Caracas: Universidad Católica Andrés Bello, Instituto de Investigaciones Históricas, 1979); Fisher, "La rebelión de Túpac Amaru," p. 421.

29. Patrick Husson, *De la guerra a la rebelión, Huanta, siglo XIX* (Cuzco; Lima: Centro de Estudios Regionales Bartolomé de Las Casas; Instituto Francés de Estudios Andinos, 1992), p. 88.

SELECT ANNOTATED BIBLIOGRAPHY

Specialized Bibliographies and Guides

Hilton, Sylvia L., and Ignacio González Casanovas. *Fuentes manuscritas para la historia de Ibero-América. Guía de instrumentos de investigación.* Madrid: Fundación MAPFRE América; Instituto Histórico Tavera, 1995. 617p.

Excellent guide to guides with a lengthy section on Peru.

The Indians of South America: A Bibliography. Thomas L. Welch, comp. Washington, DC: Columbus Memorial Library, Organization of American States, 1987. 599p.

This bibliography has an extensive section on the indigenous peoples of Peru and present-day Bolivia.

Research Guide to Andean History. Bolivia, Chile, Ecuador and Peru. John J. TePaske, coord. ed. Durham, NC: Duke University Press, 1981. 346p.

Guide to archives in Andean countries. Contains a section on Peru and Bolivia.

Primary Sources

Chronicles, Accounts, and Documents

Colección de documentos para la historia de la formación social de Hispanoamérica, 1493–1810. Richard Konetzke, ed. 3 vols. Madrid: Consejo Superior de Investigaciones Científicas, 1953–1962.

This collection, in five tomes, contains hundreds of petitions, decisions, and *cédulas* related to social issues in Spanish America, including material related to the kurakas under the term *caciques*.

Cronistas indio y mestizos. Francisco Carrillo, ed. 3 vols. Lima: Editorial Horizonte, 1991–1996.

Compilation of fragments from chronicles written by indigenous and mestizo authors, including Guamán Poma and Garcilaso de la Vega Inca.

Guamán Poma de Ayala, Felipe. *El primer nueva corónica y buen gobierno.* John V. Murra and Rolena Adorno, eds. 3 vols. Mexico: Siglo XXI Editores, S.A., 1980.

Definite edition of Guamán Poma's account and proposal to King Philip III. A paper edition of this work was published in 1987 in the series *Historia* 16.

Juan, Jorge, and Antonio de Ulloa. *Noticias secretas de América.* Luis J. Ramos Gómez, ed. Madrid: *Historia* 16, 1991. 778p.

Annotated edition of this account written in 1749 by two Spanish scientists who had traveled in the Kingdoms of Peru for several years in the 1730s. Contains an important section on the conditions of the indigenous peoples, including the indigenous gentry.

Pachacuti Yamqui, Juan de Santa Cruz. *Relación de antigüedades deste reyno del Pirú.* Pierre Duviols and Cesar Itier, eds. Cuzco: Centro de Estudios Regionales Andinos Bartolomé de las Casas, 1993. 276p.

Annotated edition of this account of the history of the Inca monarchy written by a member of the Andean gentry. Includes a facsimile of the original manuscript at the Biblioteca Nacional in Madrid, first published in *Tres relaciones de antigüedades peruanas* (Madrid: Imprenta y Fundicion de M. Tello, 1879).

Ramírez de Aguila, Pedro. *Noticias políticas de Indias y relación descriptiva de la Ciudad de La Plata.* . . . Jaime Urioste Arán, transcriptor. Sucre: Imprenta Universitaria, 1978. 109p.

Chronicle written in the city of La Plata, in present-day Bolivia, in 1639. Has a section on the indigenous people of the area and its gentry.

Toledo, Francisco de. *Disposiciones gubernamentativas para el virreinato de Perú, 1569–1580.* María Justina Sarabia Viejo, transcriptor. 2 vols. Seville: Escuela de Estudios Hispanoamericanos; Consejo Superior de Investigaciones Científicas; Monte de Piedad y Caja de Ahorros de Sevilla, 1986–1989.

Annotated compilation of the laws for the Kingdoms of Peru established under the rule of Viceroy Toledo (1569–1580), preceded by an introduction by Guillermo Lohman Villena.

Túpak Inka, Fray Calixto. *Documentos originales y, en su mayoría, totalmente desconocidos, auténticos, de este apóstol indio.* Francisco A. Loayza, ed. Lima: Los Pequeños Grandes Libros de Historia Americana, 1948. 145p.

Collection of works by an Andean gentleman in the Franciscan Order who, in 1750, wrote petitions on behalf of the indigenous people of Peru, whom he represented at the Court in Madrid.

Vega Inca, Garcilaso de la. *Comentarios reales de los Incas.* César Pacheco Vélez, ed. Lima: Banco de Crédito del Peru, 1985. 518p.

Critical edition of Garcilaso de la Vega Inca's account of ancient Peru under his Inca maternal ancestors. This work was first published in 1609, and again in 1723. A popular modern edition was published in Caracas (Biblioteca Ayacucho, 1976).

————. *Historia general del Perú.* Angel Rosenblat, ed. 3 vols. Buenos Aires: Emecé Editores, 1944.

Critical edition of Garcilaso de la Vega Inca's account of the conquest of Peru by the Spaniards. The first edition of this work was published in Córdoba in 1617.

Yupanqui, Diego de Castro Tito Cusi Inca. *Relación de la conquista del Perú.* Horacio H. Urteaga, ed. Lima: Imprenta y Librería Sanmarti y Cia., 1916. 151p.

Account of the Spanish Conquest by a reigning Inca at the neo-Inca state of Vilcabamba.

Sources Related to Túpac Amaru II

Colección documental del Bicentenario de la revolución emancipadora de Túpac Amaru. Luis Durand Florez, ed. 5 vols. Lima: Comisión Nacional de Bicentenario de la Rebelión de Túpac Amaru, 1980–1982.

Exhaustive annotated compilation of documents related to the rebellion of Túpac Amaru II.

Condorcanqui, José Gabriel. *Genealogía de Túpac Amaru.* Francisco A. Loayza, ed. Lima: Los Pequeños Grandes Libros de Historia Americana, 1946. 172p.

Testimonial arguing the descent of the kuraka don José Gabriel Condorcanqui from Túpac Amaru I.

"Relación histórica de los sucesos de la rebelión de José Gabriel Túpac Amaru en las Provincias del Peru el año de 1780." In Pedro de Angelis, comp., *Colección de obras y documentos relativos a la historia antigua y moderna de las Provincias de la Plata,* VII, pp. 181–368. Buenos Aires: Plus Ultra, 1969–1972.

This account includes letters and documents related to the rebellion of Túpac Amaru.

Sahuarauha Titu Atauchi, Rafael José. *Estado del Perú,* Francisco A. Loayza, ed. Lima: Los Pequeños Grandes Libros de Historia Americana, 1944. 229p.

Account written in 1780 with relevant data concerning the rebellion of Túpac Amaru II. Don Rafael José Sahuarauha was a priest, and in this account he defends Cuzco's bishop, don José Manuel Moscoso, from accusations of implication in the Túpac Amaru rebellion.

Túpac Amaru y la Iglesía: antología. Lima: Banco de los Andes; EDUBANCO, 1983. 389p.

Anthology of mostly unpublished primary sources compiled under the auspices of Cuzco's Comité Arquidiocesano del Bicentenario de Túpac Amaru.

La verdad desnuda o Las dos faces de un obispo. Francisco A. Loayza, ed. Lima: Los Pequeños Grandes Libros de Historia Americana, 1943. 277p.

Anonymous tract written in 1780 by a self-proclaimed impartial religious, implicating Cuzco's bishop in the rebellion of Túpac Amaru.

Literary Works by Andeans under the Spanish Monarchy

Espinosa Medrano, Juan de. *Apologético.* Augusto Tamayo Vargas, ed., and Rafael Blanco Varela, trans. Caracas: Biblioteca Ayacucho, 1982. 421p.

Anthology of works by Espinosa Medrano, including the celebrated *Apologético,* a Spanish translation of his Quechua works, and the preface to his *Philosophia Thomistica,* published in Rome in 1688.

Lara, Jesús. *La literatura de los quechuas. Ensayo y antología.* 2d ed. La Paz: Librería y Editorial Juventud, 1969. 323p.

Anthology of Quechua poetry preceded by a learned article. Includes works composed after the Spanish Conquest.

Molina, Cristóbal de. *Nueva traducción de preces o himnos quechuas del cronista Cristóbal de Molina, el Cusqueño.* Teodoro L. Meneses, trans. and ed. Lima: Universidad Nacional Mayor de San Marcos, 1964. 111p.

> Bilingual Spanish-Quechua edition with an introduction by Dr. Meneses.

Ollanta, drama quichua en tres actos. Constantino Carrasco, trans. Lima: Imprenta Liberal de "El Correo del Perú," 1876. 88p.

> Spanish translation of a celebrated drama in Quechua of unknown date and author. Some believe it dates from pre-Hispanic times, but Ricardo Palma, in an introduction to this translation, claims to see in it influences from sixteenth-century Spanish drama.

Ollantay y cantos y narraciones quechuas. José María Arguedas, César Miró, and Sebastián Salazar Bondy, trans. Lima: Ediciones PEISA, 1974. 159p.

> Spanish adaptation based on the translations by Gabino Pacheco Zegarra and José María Arguedas.

Poesía y prosa quechua, Francisco Carrillo, comp. Lima: Ediciones de la Biblioteca Universitaria, 1967. 135p.

> This anthology is preceded by a prologue written by José María Arguedas. It includes transcriptions of ancient hymns as well as works originating after the Spanish Conquest.

Ritos y tradiciones de Huarochiri. Gerald Taylor, ed. Lima: Instituto de Estudios Peruanos, 1987. 616p.

> Spanish translation of the seventeenth-century Quechua manuscript describing rites and legends under the Inca.

Teatro quechua colonial: antología. Teodoro L. Meneses, ed. Lima: Ediciones Edubanco, 1983. 593p.

> Anthology of Quechua drama after the Spanish Conquest, including the *autos sacramentales* of Espinosa Medrano and "Tragedia del fin de Atahualpa."

Tragedia del fin de Atawalpa. Jesús Lara, trans. and ed. Cochabamba: Los Amigos del Libro, 1989. 149p.

> Bilingual edition of this dramatization of the Spanish Conquest in Quechua. Includes an introductory essay by the editor.

Secondary Sources

The Andean Gentry under the Spanish Monarchy

Altuve-Febres Lores, Fernán. *Los reinos del Peru. Apuntes sobre la Monarquía Peruana.* Lima, 1996. 231p.

> Important study of the political organization of the Kingdoms of Peru, including the claims of continuity of the Spanish Crown and the position of the Andean gentry as an intermediate hierarchy between the Crown and the people.

Choque Canqui, Roberto. "Las haciendas de los caciques Guarachi en el Alto Peru, 1673–1734." *América Indígena* 39:4 (October–December 1979), 733–748.

Analysis of the holdings of the Guarachi family, a powerful line of kurakas in Alto Peru.

Cock C., Guillermo. "Los kurakas de los collaguas: poder político y poder económico." *Historia y Cultura* 10 (1976–1977), 95–118.

Ethnohistorical study of the political and economic power of the kurakas in Collagua.

Díaz Rementería, Carlos J. *El cacique en el Virreinato del Peru, estudio histórico-jurídico.* Seville: Publicaciones de la Universidad de Sevilla, 1977. 260p.

Important work of analysis on the Andean gentry in Peru under the Spanish monarchy.

Diez Hurtado, Alejandro. *Pueblos y caciques de Piura. Siglos XVI y XVII.* Piura: Centro de Investigación y Promoción de Campesinado, 1988. 64p.

Monograph on the Andean gentry of Piura, in northern Peru.

Hemming, John. *The Conquest of the Incas.* New York: Harcourt Brace Jovanovich, 1970. 641p.

Thorough history of the Spanish conquest of Peru. Includes a genealogy of the descendants of the Inca emperors who lived under the Spanish monarchy in the Kingdoms of Peru and in Europe (pp. 506–513).

Martínez Cereceda, José L. *Autoridades en los Andes, los atributos del Señor.* Lima: Pontificia Universidad Católica del Perú, 1995. 256p.

Informative essay on the rituals and the significance of the emblems used by the Andean gentry.

O'Phelan Godoy, Scarlett. *Kurakas sin sucesiones. Del cacique al alcalde de indios (Perú y Bolivia, 1750–1835).* Cuzco: Centro de Estudios Regionales Andinos Bartolomé de Las Casas, 1997. 103p.

Insightful study on the changing status of the Andean gentry from the Kingdoms of Peru to that in the Andean Republics.

Pease G. Y., Franklin. "Curacas coloniales: riqueza y actitudes." *Revista de Indias* 48:182/183 (January–August 1988), 87–107.

Analysis of the position of the kurakas under the Spanish monarchy and comparison with their more independent position in pre-Hispanic times.

Pérez Canto, María Pilar. *El buen gobierno de don Felipe Guamán Poma de Ayala.* Quito: Ediciones Abya-Yala, 1996. 219p.

Analysis of the "buen gobierno" section of Guamán Poma's *Nueva corónica*, where this Andean gentleman gives political advice to King Philip III, as a memorial like those proliferating in Spain during the sixteenth and seventeenth centuries written by "arbitristas."

Ramírez, Susan Elizabeth. *The World Upside Down: Cross-Cultural Contact and Conflict in Sixteenth-Century Peru.* Stanford: Stanford University Press, 1996. 234p.

Ethnohistorical study of Peru during the first century after the Spanish Conquest, including the changing position of the Andean gentry in the Kingdoms of Peru.

Regalado de Hurtado, Liliana. *El Inca Titu Cusi Yupanqui y su tiempo. Los Incas de Vilcabamba y los primeros cuarenta años del dominio español.* Lima: Pontificia Universidad Católica del Perú, 1997. 165p.

Descriptive study of the neo-Inca state founded in Vilcabamba after the Spanish Conquest.

Rostworowski de Diez Canseco, María. *Doña Francisca Pizarro: una ilustre mestiza, 1534–1598.* Lima: Instituto de Estudios Peruanos, 1989. 162p.

Biographical study of the daughter of Francisco Pizarro with Inés Huayllas Yupanqui. Useful work for understanding the interconnection of the Andean gentry with the Spanish conquerors in the first century of the Kingdoms of Peru.

_____. *Curacas y sucesiones. Costa Norte.* Lima: Librería Imprenta Minerva, 1961. 136p.

Analysis of succession custom among the Andean gentry of northern Peru.

Saignes, Thierry. *Caciques, Tribute and Migration in the Southern Andes: Indian Society and the Seventeenth-Century Colonial Order (Audiencia de Charcas).* Paul Garner, trans. London: University of London, Institute of Latin American Studies, 1985. 43p.

Analysis of the relations of the Andean gentry to the administration of the Kingdom of Alto Peru.

Salles-Reese, Verónica. "Yo don Joan de Santacruz Pachacuti Yamqui Salcamayqua … digo." *Revista Iberoamericana* 170/171 (January–June 1993), 107–118.

Analysis of Pachacuti Yupanqui's account of the story of the Inca Empire refuting accusations of collaboration made against the Andean chronicler.

Sempat Assadourian, Carlos. *Transiciones hacia el sistema colonial andino.* Lima: Instituto de Estudios Peruanos, 1994. 304p.

Analytical study of the role of the Andean gentry in the formation of the Kingdoms of Peru and the institutions established there by the Spanish monarchy.

Spaulding, Karen W. "Kurakas and Commerce: A Chapter in the Evolution of Andean Society." *Hispanic American Historical Review* 53:4 (November 1973), 581–599.

This study of the involvement of kurakas in trade concludes that the Andean gentry defended itself from the loss of its estates by adopting European patterns of economic activity.

Stern, Steven. *Peru's Indian Peoples and the Challenge of Spanish Conquest. Huamanga to 1640.* Madison: The University of Wisconsin Press, 1982. 295p.

Seminal work demonstrating the capacity of Andeans, including their gentry, to manipulate their conquerors.

Varón Gabai, Rafael. *Curacas y encomenderos: acomodamiento nativo en Huaraz, siglos XVI y XVII.* Lima: P. L. Villanueva Editor, 1980. 105p.

Analysis of the interactions between the Andean gentry and the Spanish conquerors and their descendants in the region of Huaraz.

The Andean Gentry and the Catholic Church

Armas Medina, Fernando de. *Cristianización de Perú (1532–1600)*. Seville: Publicaciones de la Escuela de Estudios Hispanoamericanos de Sevilla, 1953. 635p.

General history of the Church in Peru during the first century after the Spanish Conquest with informative fragments about the impact of evangelization on the Andean gentry.

Burns, Kathryn. "Nuns, Kurakas, and Credit: The Spiritual Economy of Seventeenth-Century Cuzco." *Colonial Latin American Review* 6:2 (December 1997), 185–203.

Study of the economic connections of Cuzco convents with the kurakas related to indigenous members of the religious orders.

Cangiano, María Cecilia. *Curas, caciques y comunidades en el Alto Perú: Chayanta a fines del siglo XVIII*. Tilcara: Proyecto ECIRA, Sección Antropología Social, 1987. 55p.

Analysis of the interrelations between the Andean gentry and Catholic clergy in present-day Bolivia during the eighteenth century.

Griffiths, Nicholas. *The Cross and the Serpent: Religious Repression and Resurgence in Colonial Peru*. Norman: University of Oklahoma Press, 1995. 355p.

Thorough study of the campaign to extirpate idolatry in the Andean region. The author argues that by the eighteenth century priests occupied a predominant position in Andean communities.

Millones, Luis. "Shamanismo y política en el Peru colonial: los curacas de Ayacucho." *Boletín de Antropología Americana* 15 (July 1987), 93–103.

Study of a conflict between priest and kurakas in an Andean pueblo in the late seventeenth century, interpreted as illustrative of the religious leadership that some kurakas had over the communities under them.

Mills, Kenneth. *Idolatry and Its Enemies: Colonial Andean Religion and Extirpation, 1640–1750*. Princeton: Princeton University Press, 1997. 337p.

This thorough analysis concludes that aspects of Christianity were being embraced voluntarily by some Andean peoples by the seventeenth century.

Regalado de Hurtado, Liliana. *Religión y evangelización en Vilcabamba, 1572–1602*. Lima: Pontificia Universidad Católica del Perú, 1992. 232p.

Descriptive study of the efforts to evangelize the neo-Inca state at Vilcabamba.

El retorno de los huacas: estudios y documentos sobre el Taki Onqoy, siglo XVI. Luis Millones, comp. Lima: Instituto de Estudios Peruanos, 1990. 451p.

Anthology of essays and documents related to the resurgence of pre-Hispanic religions in the Andean region toward the end of the sixteenth century.

Salles-Reese, Verónica. *From Viracocha to the Virgin of Copacabana: Representation of the Sacred at Lake Titicaca*. Austin: University of Texas Press, 1997. 208p.

Thorough study of the Christianization of the Andean region as represented by the substitution of Andean contents for Christian ones.

Staton, Joyce. "The Influence of Sixteenth-Century Missionary Thought on Eighteenth-Century Indian Reforms in Peru." In *University of British Columbia Hispanic Studies*, pp. 33–38. London: Tamesis Books Limited, 1974.

Thorough analysis of the influence of sixteenth-century missionary thought on reformers.

The Andean Gentry and Andean Culture under the Spanish Monarchy

Adorno, Rolena. *Cronista y príncipe: La obra de don Felipe Guamán Poma de Ayala*. Lima: Pontificia Universidad Católica de Perú, 1989. 276p.

Study of the life and work of this well-known member of the Andean gentry.

Anadón, José. *Garcilaso Inca de la Vega, an American Humanist. A Tribute to José Durand*. Notre Dame, IN: University of Notre Dame Press, 1998. 245p.

Compilation of papers on Garcilaso de la Vega Inca delivered at a conference held at the University of Notre Dame, March 31–April 2, 1996. The University of Notre Dame Libraries holds a re-creation of the library of Garcilaso collected by the late Dr. José Durand.

Benavente Velarde, Teófilo. *Historia del arte cusqueño. Pintores cusqueños de la Colonia*. Cuzco: Municipalidad del Qosco, 1995. 224p.

Thorough history of painting in the Cuzco region from the sixteenth to the eighteenth centuries.

Chacón Torres, Mario. *Arte virreinal en Potosí. Fuentes para su historia*. Seville: Escuela de Estudios Hispanoamericanos de Sevilla, 1973. 329p.

Concise history of art in the Potosí region from the sixteenth to the eighteenth centuries, including works by indigenous artists like the painter Luis Niño.

Chang-Rodríguez, Raquel. *La apropiación del signo: tres cronistas indígenas del Perú*. Tempe: Center for Latin American Studies, Arizona State University, 1985. 119p.

Analysis of the chronicles written by Andean gentry don Felipe Guamán Poma, d. Juan de Santa Cruz Pachacuti Yupanqui, and the Inca Titu Cusi Yupanqui.

Chara Zereceda, Oscar, and Viviana Capro Gil. *Iglesias del Cusco. Historia y arquitectura*. Cuzco: Editorial Universitaria, UNSAAC, 1998. 148p.

Illustrated essay describing the churches in Cuzco built between the sixteenth and the eighteenth centuries, including San Pedro and Belén, work of the indigenous master-builder Juan Tomás Tuyrutupa.

Cisneros, Luis Jaime. "Juan de Espinosa Medrano, un intelectual cuzqueño del seiscientos. Nuevos datos biográficos." *Revista de Indias* 48:182/183 (January–August 1988), 327–347.

Biographical study of the Andean humanist, including an exhaustive chronology.

Damian, Carol. *The Virgin of the Andes: Art and Ritual in Colonial Cuzco*. Miami Beach: Grassfield Press, 1995. 110p.

Profusely illustrated essay on the peculiar iconography of the Virgin Mary developed in the Andean region.

Eguiguren, Luis Antonio. *Diccionario histórico cronológico de la Real y Pontificia Universidad de San Marcos y sus colegios.* 3 vols. Lima: Imp. Torres Aguirre, 1940.

A chronological compilation of accounts and documents related to the University of San Marcos in Lima since its founding in 1551. Includes several documents related to the education of kurakas and Andean gentry (vol. 2, pp. 549–603).

Galdo Gutiérrez, Virgilio. *Educación de los curacas.* San Cristóbal de Huamanga: Universidad Nacional de Huamanga, 1982. 83p.

Analysis of the education of the kurakas as a hegemonic project of the Spanish monarchy.

García-Bedoya M., Carlos. "Elites andinas y Renacimiento Inca." *Pretextos* (Lima) 314 (1992), 126–184.

Excellent study of the cultural flourishing that took place in the Andean region under the patronage of the Andean gentry.

Gisbert, Teresa. "Los Incas en la pintura virreinal del siglo XVIII." *América Indígena* 39:4 (October–December 1979), 749–772.

Study of a painting by Alonso de la Cueva representing the genealogy of the Incas.

Mesa, José de, and Teresa Gisbert. *Historia de la pintura cuzqueña.* 2 vols. Lima: Fundación Augusto N. Wiese, Banco Wiese Ltdo., 1982.

Profusely illustrated analysis of Cuzco painting as an intercultural phenomenon.

Montoya, Rodrigo. "¿Existe un tradición quechua en el Peru?" *Hueso Húmero* 31 (December 1994), 53–80.

Survey of the dramatic production in Quechua since the Spanish Conquest. The author concludes that a Quechua literary and dramatic tradition originated in the plays written by members of the Andean gentry in Cuzco.

Porras Barrenechea, Raúl. *Los cronistas de Perú (1528–1630).* Lima: Banco de Crédito de Perú, 1986. 964p.

Anthology of the author's essays about the chronicles of Peru, including those written by indigenous authors like Titu Cusi Yupanqui.

Redmon, Walter. *La lógica en el virreinato del Perú a través de las obras de Juan Espinosa Medrano (1688) e Isidoro de Celis (1787).* Lima; Mexico: Pontificia Universidad Católica del Perú; Fondo de Cultura Económica, 1998. 417p.

This work includes an analysis of the elements of logic in the *Philosophia Thomistica* published by Espinosa Medrano in 1688. The author concludes that philosophy in seventeenth-century Peru reached a high technical level and that criticisms made of it in the past must be reconsidered.

Rowe, John Rowland. "Colonial Portraits of Inca nobles." In *The Civilizations of Ancient America. Selected Papers of the XXIXth International Congress of Americanists*, pp. 258–268. Sol Tax, ed. Chicago: The University of Chicago Press, 1951.

Analysis of five full-length portraits in the Archeological Museum at Cuzco.

Suárez Radillo, Carlos Miguel. *El teatro barroco hispanoamericano.* 3 vols. Madrid: Ediciones Porrúa Turanzas, S.A., 1981.

The second volume of this exhaustive study covers the baroque literature of Peru and present-day Bolivia, including that written in Quechua, the language of most of the Andean gentry.

Transatlantic Encounters: Europeans and Andeans in the 16th Century. Kenneth J. Andrien and Rolena Adorno, eds. Berkeley: University of California Press, 1991. 295p.

Volume of essays concerning cultural interchanges between Europeans and Andeans, including one on the kuraka after the Spanish Conquest.

Valcárcel, Carlos Daniel. *Garcilaso, el Inca humanista.* Lima: Universidad Nacional Mayor de San Marcos, 1995. 244p.

Analysis of the work of Garcilaso de la Vega Inca focusing on the chronicler as a man of two worlds.

Túpac Amaru II and Other Andean Rebels

Busto Duthurburu, José Antonio. *José Gabriel Túpac Amaru antes de su rebelión.* Lima: Pontificia Universidad Católica del Perú, 1981. 134p.

Biographical study of José Gabriel Condorcanqui.

Campbell, León G., Jr. "Rebel or Royalist? Juan Manuel de Moscoso y Peralta and the Túpac Amaru Revolt in Peru, 1780–1784." *Revista de Historia de América* 86 (July–December 1978).

Analysis of the actions of Juan Manuel de Moscoso concluding that the bishop of Cuzco during the Túpac Amaru rebellion was a unique and atypical individual.

Castro Arenas, Mario. *La rebelión de Juan Santos.* Lima: Carlos Milla Batres, 1973. 204p.

Monographic study of the rebellion of Juan Santos in 1742. Includes documentary sources.

Coloquio Internacional Túpac Amaru y Su Tiempo, 11–16 noviembre 1980. Actas. Lima: Comisión Nacional de Bicentenario de la Rebelión Emancipadora de Túpac Amaru, 1982. 693p.

Collected papers presented at an international conference on the Túpac Amaru rebellion.

Durand, José. "Presencia de Garcilaso Inca en Túpac Amaru." *Cuadernos Americanos* 3, Nueva Epoca, no. 18 (November–December 1989), 172–177.

Analysis of the influence of Garcilaso de la Vega Inca's *Comentarios reales de los Incas* on the ideas of Túpac Amaru II.

O'Phelan Godoy, Scarlett. *Rebellions and Revolts in 18th Century Peru and Upper Peru.* Cologne: Böhlau, 1985. 345p.

Analytical study of Andean revolts of the eighteenth century, including those of Juan Santos and Túpac Amaru II. The author argues that the centralist policies of the Spanish Bourbons may have motivated at least in part the rebellion of Túpac Amaru.

Robins, Nicholas A. *El mesianismo y la semiótica indígena en el Alto Perú. La Gran Rebelión de 1780–1781.* Silvia San Martín and Sergio de Río, trans. La Paz: Heisbol, S.R.L., 1998. 219p.

Analysis of the antecedents and the conjunctures that brought about the rebellion of the Catari brothers in Alto Peru.

Sociedad colonial y sublevaciones populares: Túpac Amaru–1780. Alberto Flores Galindo, ed. Lima: Instituto Nacional de Investigación y Desarrollo de la Educación "Augusto Salazar Bondy," 1976. 329p.

Includes articles by eminent scholars such as Scarlett O'Phelan Godoy, John Fisher, and Oscar Comblit.

Stavig, Ward. *The World of Túpac Amaru: Conflict, Community, and Identity in Colonial Peru.* Lincoln: University of Nebraska Press, 1999. 348p.

Attempts to analyze the various elements of the Andean world at the time of the rebellion of Túpac Amaru II. Includes extensive bibliography.

Stern, Steven J. "The Age of Andean Insurrection, 1742–1782: A Reappraisal." *Resistance, Rebellion and Consciousness in the Andean Peasant World, 18th to 20th Centuries.* Steven J. Stern, ed. Madison: University of Wisconsin Press, 1987. Pp. 34–73.

Thorough analysis of the socioeconomic and political conditions in the Andean region leading to revolts of the indigenous peoples against the Spanish monarchy. Includes extensive list of references.

The Andean Gentry from the Bourbon Reforms to the Founding of the Andean Republics

Andrien, Kenneth J. "The *Noticias secretas de América* and the Construction of a Governing Ideology for the Spanish American Empire." *Colonial Latin American Review* 7:2 (December 1998), 175–192.

The author proposes that the *Noticias secretas* incorporated the discourses of protest and reform of various groups (including the Andean gentry) and synthesized them into an official reformist ideology in late-Bourbon Spanish America.

Armellada, Cesáreo. *La causa indígena americana en las Cortes de Cádiz.* Caracas: Universidad Católica Andrés Bello, Instituto de Investigaciones Históricas, 1979. 54p.

The author compares the legislation concerning the American peoples in the Spanish Constitution of 1812 with that of the Spanish American republics established after the break with the Spanish monarchy, and finds many similarities.

Cahill, David P. "Curas and Social Conflict in the Doctrinas of Cuzco, 1780–1814." *Journal of Latin American Studies* 16:2 (November 1984), 241–276.

The author claims that the Bourbon reforms after the rebellion of Túpac Amaru II exacerbated existing social tensions in the Cuzco region.

_____. "Repartos ilícitos y familias principales en el Sur Andino: 1780–1824." *Revista de Indias* 48:182/183 (January–August 1988), 449–473.

Analysis of the economic significance of the *repartimiento* of merchandise in Peru from 1756 to 1780, and of the Criollo power interests that continued it after it was banned following the Túpac Amaru rebellion of 1780.

Cornejo Bouroncle, Jorge. *Pumacahua. La revolución del Cuzco de 1814. Estudio documentado.* Cuzco: Editorial H. G. Rozas, S. A., 1956. 709p.

Scholarly account of the rebellion of 1814 and the kuraka Pumacahua's participation in it.

Husson, Patrick. *De la guerra a la rebelión (Huanta, siglo XIX).* Cuzco: Centro de Estudios Regionales Andinos Bartolomé de Las Casas, 1992. 247p.

Study of two Andean revolts, including an account of the royalist rebellion of the indigenous people in Huanta under the chief General Antonio Huachaca (1828–1839).

Ramos Gómez, Luis Javier. *Epoca, génesis y texto de las "Noticias secretas de América", de Jorge Juan y Antonio de Ulloa.* 2 vols. Madrid: Consejo Superior de Investigaciones Científicas, 1985.

Thorough analysis of this important source, its authors, and its times, in the context of the Bourbon reforms in the Kingdoms of Peru.

Rieu-Millán, Marie-Laure. "Rasgos distintivos de la representación peruana en las Cortes de Cádiz y Madrid (1810–1814)." *Revista de Indias* 48:182/183 (January–August 1988), 475–515.

Analysis of the personality and connections of the Peruvian deputies at Cortes between 1810 and 1814, including don Dionisio Inca Yupanqui.

Sánchez Albornoz, Nicolás. "Tributo abolido, tributo repuesto. Invariantes socioeconómicas en la Bolivia republicana." In *El ocaso del orden colonial en Hispanoamérica,* pp. 159–200. Tulio Halperin-Donghi, comp. Buenos Aires: Editorial Sudamericana, 1978.

Study of the impact in Alto Peru of reforms decreed by the Spanish Cortes of 1812.

Semprún Bullón, José. *Capitanes y virreyes. El esfuerzo bélico realista en la contienda de emancipación hispanoamericana.* Madrid: Ministerio de Defensa, Secretaría General Técnica (Adalid), 1998. 321p.

Military history including information on the royalist activities of the kuraka Pumacahua before he embraced separatism.

Thurner, Marck. *From Two Republics to One Divided.* Durham, NC: Duke University Press, 1997. 203p.

In this monograph about the contradictions of post-colonial nationalism in Peru, the author discusses the disestablishment of the Andean gentry in the Republic of Peru.

26. Old Pitfalls and New Opportunities in Documenting Popular Political Culture in Latin America

Kurt Weyland

The wave of democratization that has swept across Latin America during the last twenty-five years has been preceded and accompanied by an upsurge of popular mobilization. A wide range and vast number of new social movements challenged tottering authoritarian regimes and pressed a host of pent-up demands for urgent social improvements on newly installed democracies. Under the new civilian regimes, sectors of the population that had traditionally participated little in national politics—such as indigenous groups—suddenly mobilized. These newly active groups employed a broad repertoire of tactics for collective action and formed a host of new organizations, social movements, and unions.

This "resurrection [and amplification] of civil society" (O'Donnell and Schmitter 1986:ch.5) has attracted intense and sustained attention from scholars and librarians. There has been an outpouring of academic studies and activist accounts of social movements, unions, and popular parties (e.g., Eckstein 1989; Jaquette 1991; Escobar and Alvarez 1992; Chalmers et al. 1997; Alvarez, Dagnino, and Escobar 1998). These analyses have made crucial contributions by investigating groups that had long been neglected; new types of organizations that enriched the new democracies with their innovative practices; and political actors that seemed to hold the promise of introducing important elements of direct popular participation into elitist civilian regimes.

This essay argues, however, that the actual political significance of new social movements, unions, and popular parties has been overestimated considerably; that fascination with the innovative practices and experiences of these new actors has given rise to serious misunderstandings of popular "culture" and politics; and that scholars and librarians should pay more attention to other expressions of popular culture and politics, which are captured, for instance, by opinion polls.

To provide some empirical support for these deliberately provocative arguments, the first section of this essay provides a brief analysis of the Peruvian case. In the 1980s Peru appeared as a model for the hopes of social movement scholars and activists. A vast number of new social movements, radical unions, and leftist parties were mobilizing and organizing ever wider sectors of the population. Participatory attitudes and "class consciousness"[1] (Stokes 1995) seemed on the rise. Civil society appeared strong and vibrant. But in the 1990s Peruvian civil society has generally been characterized as fragmented and weak (see recently Tanaka 1998). Even more surprisingly, a large proportion of the poor, who appeared as the natural constituency of the left in the 1980s, now supported an autocratic neoliberal, President Alberto Fujimori. Despite his antidemocratic self-coup of 1992 and despite the imposition of brutal, painful adjustment measures, the president won reelection with a striking 64 percent of the vote in 1995. Notably, his backing among the poorest voters was even higher.

What happened? The social movements literature clearly had not anticipated this surprising turn of events. Did the "class consciousness" of the 1980s evaporate and cede to a much more basic, conservative demand for order and stability? The second section of the essay criticizes some important methodological problems of the social movements literature and, especially, of the more general conclusions that these analyses of "best cases" seemed to suggest.

To compensate for these problems, scholars and librarians need to pay more attention to other avenues for ascertaining popular attitudes and culture, such as surveys of representative samples of citizens. While these research instruments have their own deficits and flaws, they constitute a crucially important complement to the social movements literature. Librarians would therefore be well advised to allocate more funds to the published sources that make survey results available to the public. These arguments are developed in the third section of the essay.

A "Best Case" Gone Awry: The Rise and Decline of Popular Activism in Peru

In the course of the 1980s, Peru's new democracy experienced a tremendous upsurge of popular activism that seemed to push the country inexorably toward the left. In the poor neighborhoods of urban areas, a host of social movements emerged and advanced the urgent social needs and demands of long-neglected sectors of the population. A variety of militant trade unions contested business and the state. And a wide range of radical leftist parties vied for political power. Unusually for the Latin American left, many of these groupings joined forces in the United Left coalition (Izquierda Unida–IU) in order to pursue their goal of system transformation with greater prospects for success.

In many ways, this "popular upsurge" was the unintended consequence of the reformist military regime led by General Juan Velasco Alvarado (1968–1975), which had attempted to bring about a comprehensive modernization of Peruvian society in the early 1970s (Stephens 1983). The Velasco regime had pursued a policy of "inclusionary corporatism" (Stepan 1978:chs.

3, 8), seeking to mobilize popular sectors in support of its goals, but also incorporate them in government-controlled unions and other organizations (Palmer and Middlebrook 1976). Yet while successful in its mobilization drive, the Velasco government failed miserably with its control efforts. The successor governments—both the military administration of General Francisco Morales Bermúdez (1975–1980) and the civilian governments of Fernando Belaúnde Terry (1980–1985) and Alan García (1985–1990)—therefore faced a high level of popular activism that was not tempered and controlled by strong national-level organizations.

Peru's new democracy, inaugurated in 1980, saw a mushrooming of social movements and of other innovative forms of popular participation (Stephens 1983). While clientelism retained its hold on a good part of the urban poor, radicalism seemed to be on the advance (Stokes 1995). Analysts found evidence of surprisingly strong and widespread participatory attitudes and "class consciousness" among the popular sectors. This "class consciousness" seemed to be more in tune with the real needs and interests of the poor than clientelist attitudes that led them to identify with unreliable benefactors of higher status or mistakenly cling to aspirations or earlier experiences of social mobility that had long been dashed (Stokes 1995). The expectation that such analyses suggested was that over time "class consciousness" would likely advance further, whereas clientelism would continue to recede. More and more poor people would prefer to advance their needs through collective action with their peers, rather than delegating this task to unrepresentative and unaccountable traditional leaders. At least, "class consciousness" would be unlikely to recede because it had resulted from learning and people's discovery of their true interests. People who had emerged from the fog of clientelist attitudes and had seen the light of collective self-determination had experienced an irreversible conversion and would not return into darkness.

These optimistic expectations, often more implied and suggested than explicitly stated in the scholarly literature, seemed to be confirmed by the political tendencies of the 1980s. After strong tensions inside the populist APRA and the disunity of the left in the 1980 election had allowed center-right populist Fernando Belaúnde to return to power, electoral trends seemed to point unstoppably toward the left. In fact, United Left candidate Alfonso Barrantes won the mayoralty of Lima in the municipal election of 1983 and governed one-third of the national population thereafter. And since the governing center-right was battered by economic problems and the advance of the Shining Path guerrillas, the 1985 presidential election was fought on the left between "social-democratic" populist Alan García and socialist Barrantes. A number of the bold policies of the García government emerged from the fear of a further advance of the left. Since García's "economic populism" soon proved unsuccessful and greatly exacerbated Peru's economic and social crisis in the late 1980s, the left—the only political sector still untainted by glaring failure—

seemed to have excellent chances of winning the presidential election scheduled for 1990.

These expectations, however, were widely off the mark. By 1992 a clear majority of Peruvians—especially among the poor—consistently approved of an autocratic neoliberal president who had interrupted Peruvian democracy, who had systematically undermined and weakened civil society, and who had implemented some of the most brutal, painful, recessionary, orthodox, and dogmatically neoliberal adjustment policies ever enacted in Latin America (Apoyo 1997:6; see also Balbi 1996; Carrión 1998; Panfichi 1997; Cameron and Mauceri 1997; Weyland 1996b:192–197). Indeed, President Alberto Fujimori won an unprecedented reelection victory with a stunning 64.4 percent of the vote in April 1995. Notably, the incumbent often received disproportionately strong backing in opinion polls and elections from the urban and rural poor—the very sectors that social movement scholars and activists had expected to support the left (IMASEN 1992:2–A; IMASEN 1994:13; IMASEN 1995:12–13; IMASEN 1996:8; Goldberg 1998; Weyland 1996a:10–21). Obviously, participatory, democratic, and republican attitudes were weaker and less consistent than expected. Among most of the poor, "class consciousness" was conspicuous by its absence.

The failure of the left resulted in part from persistent internal rivalries and constant bickering that discredited this political force in the eyes of many potential supporters and made it look very similar to established politicians, who concentrate most of their energies on "politicking" rather than representing popular needs and interests (Tanaka 1997:19–23). Furthermore, the democratic left was hampered by competition from the revolutionary left, especially the brutal Shining Path (Roberts 1998:257–264). While most of the United Left leadership clearly distanced itself from the insurgents, the guerrilla movements found varying degrees of "understanding" and support among some of the radicalized militants of the left—which exacerbated the divergences and tensions inside the IU and further discredited it in the eyes of voters.

More basically—and more important for this essay—the failure of the left resulted from the weakness of "class consciousness" in times of severe crisis and the strong majoritarian preference for the "conservative" values of economic stability and political order. As Peru's economic problems kept worsening in the late 1980s and the country seemed to slide to the brink of civil war, collective empowerment and innovative political participation gave way to a strong focus on individual or family survival and on basic safety (Tanaka 1998:235). The grave multifaceted crisis caused social atomization, hindered wide-ranging collective action, and forced many people—especially among the poor—to care first and foremost about immediate concrete needs, not about a structural transformation of politics and society.

Opinion polls clearly reveal popular priorities that diverge strikingly from the picture painted—or suggested—by social movement scholars. When surveyed at the nadir of the crisis in mid-1990 about the three most important problems facing Peru, 81 percent of respondents emphasized inflation, 55 percent terrorism and subversion, and 51 percent unemployment—but only 9 percent mentioned inequality and the differences between rich and poor (Apoyo 1990a:35). Similarly, 37 percent of respondents named inflation as the single most important problem confronting the country in October 1990, 20 percent mentioned unemployment, and 10 percent terrorism and subversion— but a minuscule 1 percent referred to inequality and the differences between rich and poor (Apoyo 1990b:7). Thus, the grave crisis afflicting Peru forced most people to focus on immediate, concrete issues of material well-being and safety and pushed "radical" concerns about social inequality into the background.

Survey respondents also revealed the importance of concrete economic and social issues and of public security in justifying their support for President Fujimori. In July 1993, for instance, 44.6 percent of his supporters mentioned economic improvements, 36 percent enhanced security, and 32 percent social programs (Apoyo 1993:12). And when asked in July 1995 to name the single most important accomplishment of Fujimori's first term, 51 percent of respondents stressed his success in combating guerrilla insurgency and another 30 percent mentioned concrete economic and social improvements (Apoyo 1995:19). Focus groups conducted during the election campaign of 1994/1995 reached similar results (Salcedo 1995:36, 67, 73, 80–81, 95).

Notably, Fujimori's public works and social programs always elicited strongly disproportionate approval from the poorest sectors. In the survey conducted in July 1995, for instance, 19 percent of the poorest respondents, but only 2–3 percent of the better-off categories, classified school construction— the president's principal social/public works program—as the main accomplishment of his first term. Specific surveys conducted among poor urban sectors and intensive field research in urban and rural areas have confirmed these results (Parodi and Twanama 1993:63–65, 79–81, 85–87; Panfichi 1997; Palmer 1998). Thus, the most destitute sectors displayed the least "class consciousness" and the highest appreciation for the paternalistic handouts of the autocratic incumbent. The new social programs instituted by the Fujimori government found tremendous receptivity among the poorest sectors and provided the government with broad political support, for instance in the election of 1995 (Balbi 1996; Graham and Kane 1998; Roberts and Arce 1998; Weyland 1998:557–559). In fact, there is considerable evidence that these social programs gave rise to new patterns of clientelist links between state agencies and many popular sector groupings (Palmer 1998; Tanaka 1998).

While the disproportionately low endorsement of poorer sectors for the government's painful neoliberal economic policies is in line with the "class consciousness" argument (Stokes 1996:557–559), it makes those sectors' strong support for the president who imposed these brutal, costly measures even more puzzling. After all, the category of "class consciousness" implies that people's assessment of economic and social policies drives their evaluation of the initiator of those policies. Yet this was manifestly not the case in Peru during the early 1990s.

Finally, Fujimori's antidemocratic self-coup of April 1992 received endorsement from 70 to 80 percent of all Peruvians (Carrión 1994; Conaghan 1995). It was precisely this autocratic interruption of Peru's fragile democracy that catapulted the president to a much higher level of approval during the next few years (Apoyo 1997:6). Thus, the commitment of the populace to democratic principles also proved much less strong—or at least consistent (see Carrión 1994)—than the social movements literature that focused on the 1980s had suggested.

Because of the rapid evaporation of "class consciousness" under the pressures of a grave economic crisis and of large-scale terrorism, social movements displayed little activism and—especially—radicalism during the early 1990s. Instead, civil society in Peru was largely atomized and fragmented (Roberts 1998:ch. 8; Tanaka 1998). Rather than participating in social and political mobilization, most poor people had to concentrate their energies on ensuring the survival of their families. Therefore, the brutal adjustment policies imposed by the Fujimori government, which included price increases of basic necessities by up to 3,000 percent, triggered surprisingly little contestation and protest.

Political parties have not fared any better than social movements.[2] Like the rest of Peru's established parties, the now dis-United Left has received such meager electoral support that its organizational survival itself is endangered. Even on the municipal level, where leftist parties in Latin America have often done well in the last twenty years, the Peruvian left has achieved disappointing results. In the 1993 contest, for instance, only 6.2 percent of voters in metropolitan Lima opted for the left, whereas a stunning 80.9 percent chose "independent" candidates (Tuesta Soldevilla 1996:107; see also Dietz 1998: 214–215). Since the absence of party organization makes it exceedingly difficult to hold such personalistic politicians accountable, the commitment of large numbers of common citizens to democratic, republican principles seems to be rather weak.

In sum, the picture painted by analysts of Peru's flourishing social movements and the vibrant popular activism of the 1980s suggested expectations of future developments that clearly did not come true in subsequent years. Instead of a further advance of "class consciousness" and political radicalism, the 1990s saw widespread popular support for an autocratic neoliberal neopopulist, who decreed drastic recessionary measures, weakened democracy, and disarticulated civil society. What are the methodological and theoretical reasons for the misleading expectations suggested by social movement studies? And what additional sources do scholars need to consult—and librarians need to collect—in order to paint a more balanced, realistic picture of popular culture in

Latin America? The following two sections, respectively, seek to answer these important questions.

Methodological and Theoretical Limitations of the Social Movements Literature

Why did the expectations suggested by the social movements literature that focused on Peru in the 1980s not come true? This line of scholarship has a number of inherent methodological limitations that—if not carefully kept in mind—tempt "progressive" scholars and activists to hold overly optimistic assessments of current trends and future developments. Above all, social movement scholars like to focus on exceptionally advanced experiences of popular activism—that is, on "best cases" that are unrepresentative of most of the population. With this skewed strategy of case selection, many of these scholars give an unrealistic impression of the level of mobilization and politicization of the populace (similar Haber 1996:172–173, 186–187; for some recent exceptions, see Roberts 1997; Schönwälder 1998).

In most instances, politicized social movements constitute a small fraction of the population. The radicalized attitudes and innovative participatory practices displayed by the members, activists, and leaders of social movements are the features of a clear minority of the population. Furthermore, this minority is self-selected and therefore particularly unrepresentative. Driven in part by "progressive" hopes for social and political transformation, social movement scholars systematically tend to select "best cases." For instance, most analysts of Brazil's urban labor movement focus on Greater São Paulo, where unions are particularly strong and where the leftist "new unionism" emerged in the late 1970s. Similarly, analysts of Brazil's rural unions have a predilection to study the case of Pernambuco, where rural mobilization has had a particularly long tradition (e.g., Pereira 1997).

Why do so many scholars and activists focus on these unrepresentative minority experiences? The underlying theoretical justification for this "best case" selection seems to be a "sprouting bulb" assumption about popular mobilization. Many scholars seem to assume—and hope—that popular participation will soon spread and increase considerably. They therefore see the social movements that have already emerged as the front-runners of a broader trend toward popular activism. Like the first bulbs that pop up in early spring, they signal the appearance of many other flowers that are ready to break through the surface and bloom soon. The currently existing movements are thus regarded as similar to and representative of the many other, still latent movements that will—it is hoped—appear shortly.

Furthermore, many social movement scholars seem to believe that advances in popular consciousness and activism are difficult to reverse. The very notion of "class consciousness" suggests that people who have emerged from ideological hegemony and acquired a clear view of their own interests and needs will not fall prey again to obfuscation. While for tactical reasons, radicalized sectors may temporarily moderate their militant actions, the attitudes that underlie this militancy are unlikely to fall significantly below the most advanced level they have reached. This irreversibility assumption, which is inspired by the very notion of consciousness-raising, justifies a focus on the most advanced episodes of popular activism that occur during the periods of particularly high politicization, such as the mid-1980s in Peru.

This tendency to select unrepresentative "best cases" does not make the resulting case studies per se invalid. Undoubtedly, there have been examples of innovative, ambitious, radical popular participation in Latin America. While the political goals and hopes of social movement activists may sometimes embellish these analyses, many of the experiences described by social movement scholars have a solid factual basis. But it is essential to keep in mind the methodological limitations of the social movements literature when using these case studies to draw broader inferences about popular culture as a whole. Although academic experts may warn against generalizing too much from their case studies, the social movements literature as a whole suggests a skewed, distorted picture of popular politics. The very fact that there are many more studies about the few experiences of mobilization and radicalism than about the many instances of quiescence and apathy creates a misleading impression. The unbalanced treatment in the social movements literature suggests a much higher level of popular activism than actually exists.

First of all, even in the "best cases" of exceptional activism, many people—usually, a clear majority—do not participate in activities of collective empowerment and radical demand-making. Activists and their followers are most often in the minority. Since social movements are recruited by self-selection, leaders who claim to speak for the people usually do not have a mandate from the people, but at best from movement members (Tanaka 1998:231). Thus, self-proclaimed representatives are often not representative of nor accountable to the popular masses. For these reasons, the activities of social movements do not provide a valid gauge for the attitudes of most people and for popular culture as a whole.

Furthermore, the expectations and hopes of spreading popular activism—i.e., the "sprouting bulbs" assumption—may suffer from a fallacy of composition: if additional social movements do spring up, they may not necessarily strengthen the overall pressure for sociopolitical transformation, but may indeed subtract from it. If social movement activists manage to mobilize more people, the membership gets more heterogeneous, and divergences among movements may increase. Successful activism can produce new tensions and conflicts that may over time cause disillusionment and turn off members and activists. Therefore, increases in mobilization do not necessarily have linear effects on popular activism, but may create new tensions and cleavages. After an initial phase of widespread enthusiasm, these problems can soon corrode popular participation, thus helping to account for the frequently rapid decline of popular mobilization and activism.

In fact, even those people who participate in social movements often do not do so for a long time. Contrary to the above-mentioned irreversibility assumption, social movement activity commonly has a cyclical pattern (Tarrow 1994:ch. 9): it declines almost as fast as it arises (although it usually does not disappear completely). This cyclical pattern affects not only political activities, but also the attitudes underlying it. In general, most people do not permanently focus on public issues and political concerns, but have "shifting involvements" (Hirschman 1982): after episodes of high politicization, they tend to withdraw into private life again. In particular, broader political issues of social redistribution and democratic political participation may quickly lose relative importance and salience when a grave and intensifying crisis pushes basic needs of survival to the top of most people's personal agenda. Focusing on the high tide of the occasional episodes of mass mobilization thus creates a misleading impression of popular culture as a whole.

For all of these reasons, the social movements literature does not paint a valid, representative picture of popular culture in Latin America. In particular, its implicit suggestions about future developments are systematically overoptimistic and unrealistic. Scholars need to exercise great caution when using the case studies elaborated by students of social movements to draw broader inferences about popular politics in Latin America. Librarians should keep these problems in mind and adjust their programs of acquisitions accordingly.

The Promise and Limitations of Public Opinion Surveys

Since most extant studies of social movements—especially the common "best case" analyses—provide only partial insights into popular culture, they need to be complemented with other instruments for ascertaining the attitudes of common citizens. The most promising of these instruments are surveys of representative samples of citizens. These polls can gauge people's attitudes at different levels of depth, which range from specific, concrete questions ("Do you approve of the way President XYZ is conducting the business of government?") to abstract questions about underlying values ("In general, what do you consider more important: political liberty or social equality?"). By carefully sampling a representative cross section of the population, surveys minimize the main problem that plagues the social movements literature, namely its focus on an unrepresentative, self-selected minority.

The diffusion of technology, the training of experts in U.S. centers of survey research, the advance of democracy in Latin America, and the decline of party loyalties and the resulting increase in the "independent," fluid electorate have prompted a drastic increase in the number, frequency, and quality of surveys conducted in Latin American countries during the last fifteen to twenty years. Many nations now have well-respected polling institutes that run regular surveys with consistent questions. Special events—such as election campaigns—are covered by additional opinion polls. These surveys ascertain people's attitudes on a vast range of topics that go far beyond politics and include attitudes on social issues, leisure activities, and cultural tastes. Surveys thus provide a wealth of information on a broad cross section of the population. They have become an indispensable instrument for gauging popular culture.

Many surveys conducted in Latin America have problems and limitations, however.[3] First of all, resource constraints often limit the size and quality of the samples. For instance, sample sizes of 4–500 people, which imply high margins of error, are common. Furthermore, samples often overrepresent large urban centers and neglect rural regions. For instance, in several countries—even in prosperous, advanced Argentina—surveys often cover only the metropolitan area of the capital. Thus, many of the polls that have been conducted in Latin America are less than perfectly representative. But even these imperfect surveys rank vastly higher on the scale of representativeness than the "best case" studies of the social movements literature.

A more important and less tractable problem of surveys is that the preference for simple, easily codable and quantifiable answers makes it difficult to ascertain underlying "deep" attitudes in a valid way. For instance, people find it hard to summarize complicated trade-offs among different important values in the clear-cut one-dimensional—if not binary—way that questionnaires often demand. Since value commitments are often complex and context-dependent, not absolute and categorical, they are difficult to fit in the simplified response options offered by pollsters. Therefore, people's commitment to abstract political principles and moral values is hard to gauge through opinion polls. Some of these problems can be avoided by using other instruments, such as focus groups, but at the cost of representativeness.[4]

The root cause of this problem is not the survey instrument itself, however, but the fact that most people simply lack clear, crystallized, easily expressible commitments to abstract principles and values. Cognitive psychology has shown that in their choices, people do not simply act out a consistent, transitively ordered set of well-defined preferences. Rather, complicated choices induce people to clarify—if not discover—their real preferences. For example, only when one spouse of an academic couple receives an attractive job offer in a faraway city do the two partners have to decide on the relative importance of family life versus career goals. People therefore find it difficult to state in general terms whether they prefer, for instance, liberty over equality—and what this preference implies for any specific issue. Instead, "die Qual der Wahl" (the torturous experience of having to make a choice) arises precisely from the common value trade-offs that complicate people's "utility function" and that they do not have to face head-on until they have to make a specific decision—or answer a survey question.

The difficulty of ascertaining people's commitment to abstract principles and values therefore plagues not only surveys (Zaller 1992), but also the social movements literature. It is precisely the fluidity of conflicting considerations that underlies the rapid rise and decline of radicalism and politicization and the resulting cycle of protest activity. And since the social movements literature tends to focus on "best cases"—such as occasional episodes of high politicization—and pays much less attention to the phase of decline, it tends to create a more distorted impression than surveys, which are more often conducted at regular intervals and thus have a better chance of picking up the phases of decline as well.

Thus, despite their undeniable limitations, surveys can make important contributions to gauging and documenting popular culture. In particular, they can serve as an indispensable corrective to the social movements literature.

Conclusion: A Recommendation to Librarians

The preceding assessment of the promise and limitations of different ways to assess popular culture in Latin America suggests that there is not one "true path to virtue." Since none of the available instruments is perfect, a pragmatic combination of different approaches seems most reasonable. Given the skewed nature of the current scholarly literature, which results from the excessive attention paid to unrepresentative experiences of high mobilization, this call for balance implies the need to strengthen survey research. Also, social movements scholars should make more efforts to analyze "less-than-best cases" that provide a more realistic impression of popular culture.

My call for more balanced attention to different types of sources has important implications for librarians. So far, the book market has clearly overrepresented the social movements approach. For instance, there are many more volumes that analyze "progressive" social movements than books about "conservative" actors that command much greater political influence, such as private business or right-wing parties. Exacerbating the imbalance prevailing in the book market, libraries have begun to buy collections of documents produced by social movements. By contrast, the results of survey research are much less easily available. In my view, this imbalance urgently needs to be rectified. Certainly, it makes little sense for libraries to buy original data sets, which are expensive and are of interest only to a few specialists. It is a better use of scarce resources to continue the current practice of having a few established centers of survey research, such as the Roper Center at the University of Connecticut–Storrs and the Institute for Social Research at the University of Michigan, buy these data sets and make them available to other university libraries for a subscription fee.

But many polling institutes in Latin America make their core findings available in monthly newsletters or occasional working papers. These publications present a wealth of useful information on a wide range of political, social, economic, and cultural topics. They thus constitute a gold mine for scholars, students, and other audiences interested in Latin America. But most of these important publications are not held by any U.S. university library at this moment. A WorldCat search found that no U.S. library has the following highly informative publications, for instance: Apoyo (Lima), Informe de Opinión (monthly); IMASEN (Lima), IMASEN Confidencial (monthly); Mora y Araujo, Noguera y Asociados (Buenos Aires), Análisis Socio-Político de la Coyuntura Argentina (published several times per year); Consultores 21 (Caracas), Estudio de Temas Económicos (quarterly).[5] In my view, librarians should make a concerted effort to make these extremely valuable sources of information available to their users. These publications provide crucial insights into popular culture in Latin America and therefore constitute an indispensable complement to other types of library holdings.

NOTES

1. "Class consciousness" is a questionable concept to apply to Latin America's urban poor, given the vast heterogeneity of productive capacities and activities among these sectors. These sectors are more similar in terms of consumption and social prestige and may thus qualify as a status group, but not a class (Weber 1976:177–180).

2. On the political weakness of trade unions in the 1990s, see Balbi (1997).

3. I am grateful to Professor Friedrich Welsch of Simon Bolívar University in Caracas for important insights on the limitations of surveys conducted in Latin America. The best discussion of the political usage of polls in Latin America is Conaghan (1995).

4. For an early effort, see Salcedo (1995). Respected polling institutes such as Instituto Apoyo (Lima) have conducted focus groups for specific clients but cannot make their results available (Guillermo Loli of Instituto Apoyo, personal communication, July 26, 1998).

5. Similarly, *Estudio Nacional de Opinión Pública*, conducted occasionally by Centro de Estudios Públicos (Santiago de Chile), is held by only one or two libraries in the United States; issues through 1995 are held by the University of Wisconsin–Madison, more recent issues by Harvard University.

REFERENCES

Alvarez, Sonia, Evelina Dagnino, and Arturo Escobar, eds. 1998. *Cultures of Politics/Politics of Cultures.* Boulder: Westview.

Apoyo. 1990a. Informe de Opinión (June). Lima: Apoyo.

_____. 1990b. Informe de Opinión (October). Lima: Apoyo.

_____. 1993. Informe de Opinión (July). Lima: Apoyo.

_____. 1995. Informe de Opinión (July). Lima: Apoyo.

_____. 1997. Informe de Opinión (September). Lima: Apoyo.

Balbi, Carmen Rosa. 1996. "El Fujimorismo: delegación vigilada y ciudadanía." *Pretextos* (Lima) 9 (November), 187–223.

_____. 1997. "Politics and Trade Unions in Peru." In Maxwell Cameron and Philip Mauceri, eds., *The Peruvian Labyrinth,* 134–151. University Park: Pennsylvania State University Press.

Cameron, Maxwell, and Philip Mauceri, eds. 1997. *The Peruvian Labyrinth*. University Park: Pennsylvania State University Press.

Carrión, Julio. 1994. "The 'Support Gap' for Democracy in Peru." Paper for XVIII LASA Congress. Atlanta, March 10–12.

_____. 1998. "Partisan Decline and Presidential Popularity." In Kurt von Mettenheim and James Malloy, eds., *Deepening Democracy*, 55–70. Pittsburgh: University of Pittsburgh Press.

Chalmers, Douglass, et al., eds. 1997. *The New Politics of Inequality in Latin America*. New York: Oxford University Press.

Conaghan, Catherine. 1995. "Polls, Political Discourse, and the Public Sphere." In Peter Smith, ed., *Latin America in Comparative Perspective*, 227–255. Boulder: Westview.

Dietz, Henry. 1998. "Urban Elections in Peru, 1980–1995." In Henry Dietz and Gil Shidlo, eds., *Urban Elections in Democratic Latin America*, 199–224. Wilmington, DE: Scholarly Resources.

Eckstein, Susan, ed. 1989. *Power and Popular Protest*. Berkeley: University of California Press.

Escobar, Arturo, and Sonia Alvarez, eds. 1992. *The Making of Social Movements in Latin America*. Boulder: Westview.

Goldberg, David. 1998. "Unlocking the Puzzle: Explaining Informal Sector Support for Alberto Fujimori." Paper for 56th Annual Meeting, Midwest Political Science Association. Chicago, April 23–25.

Graham, Carol, and Cheikh Kane. 1998. "Opportunistic Government or Sustaining Reform?" *Latin American Research Review* 33(1), 67–104.

Haber, Paul. 1996. "Identity and Political Process." *Latin American Research Review* 31(1), 171–188.

Hirschman, Albert. 1982. *Shifting Involvements: Private Interest and Public Action*. Princeton: Princeton University Press.

IMASEN. 1992. IMASEN – Sondeo de Opinión Pública, Gran Lima (August). Lima: IMASEN.

_____. 1994. IMASEN Confidencial (February). Lima: IMASEN.

_____. 1995. IMASEN Confidencial (February). Lima: IMASEN.

_____. 1996. IMASEN Confidencial (May). Lima: IMASEN

Jaquette, Jane, ed. 1991. *The Women's Movement in Latin America*. Boulder: Westview.

O'Donnell, Guillermo, and Philippe Schmitter. 1986. *Transitions from Authoritarian Rule: Tentative Conclusions about Uncertain Democracies*. Baltimore: Johns Hopkins University Press.

Palmer, David Scott. 1998. "La política informal en el Perú: respuestas locales en Ayacucho." Paper for XXI LASA Congress. Chicago, September 24–26.

Palmer, David Scott, and Kevin Middlebrook. 1976. "Corporatist Participation under Military Rule in Peru." In David Chaplin, ed., *Peruvian Nationalism: A Corporatist Revolution*, 428–453. New Brunswick, NJ: Transaction Books.

Panfichi, Aldo. 1997. "The Authoritarian Alternative: 'Anti-Politics' in the Popular Sectors of Lima." In Douglass Chalmers et al., eds., *The New Politics of Inequality in Latin America*, 217–236. New York: Oxford University Press.

Parodi, Jorge, and Walter Twanama. 1993. "Los pobladores, la ciudad y la política." In Jorge Parodi, ed., *Los pobres, la ciudad y la política*, 19–89. Lima: CEDYS.

Pereira, Anthony. 1997. *The End of the Peasantry*. Pittsburgh: University of Pittsburgh Press.

Roberts, Kenneth. 1997. "Beyond Romanticism: Social Movements and the Study of Political Change in Latin America." *Latin American Research Review* 32(2), 137–151.

_____. 1998. *Deepening Democracy? The Modern Left and Social Movements in Chile and Peru*. Stanford: Stanford University Press.

Roberts, Kenneth, and Moisés Arce. 1998. "Neoliberalism and Lower-Class Voting Behavior in Peru." *Comparative Political Studies* 31:2 (April), 217–246.

Salcedo, José María. 1995. *Terremoto: ¿Por qué ganó Fujimori?* Lima: Editorial BRASA.

Schönwälder, Gerd. 1998. "Local Politics and the Peruvian Left." *Latin American Research Review* 33(2), 73–102.

Stepan, Alfred. 1978. *The State and Society*. Princeton: Princeton University Press.

Stephens, Evelyne Huber. 1983. "The Peruvian Military Government, Labor Mobilization, and the Political Strength of the Left." *Latin American Research Review* 18(2), 57–93.

Stokes, Susan. 1995. *Cultures in Conflict*. Berkeley: University of California Press.

_____. 1996. "Economic Reform and Public Opinion in Peru, 1990–1995." *Comparative Political Studies* 29:5 (October), 544–565.

Tanaka, Martín. 1997. "Los espejos y espejismos de la democracia y el colapso de un sistema de partidos: Perú, 1980–1995, en perspectiva comparada." Paper for XX LASA Congress. Guadalajara, April 17–19.

_____. 1998. "From Movimientismo to Media Politics." In John Crabtree and Jim Thomas, eds., *Fujimori's Peru*, 229–242. London: Institute of Latin American Studies, University of London.

Tarrow, Sidney. 1994. *Power in Movement*. Cambridge: Cambridge University Press.

Tuesta Soldevilla, Fernando. 1996. *Sistema de partidos políticos en el Perú, 1978–1995*. Lima: Fundación Friedrich Ebert.

Weber, Max. 1976. *Wirtschaft und Gesellschaft*. 5th ed. Tübingen: J.C.B. Mohr (Paul Siebeck).

Weyland, Kurt. 1996a. "Neopopulism and Neoliberalism in Latin America: Unexpected Affinities." *Studies in Comparative International Development* 31:3 (Fall), 3–31.

_____. 1996b. "Risk-Taking in Latin American Economic Restructuring." *International Studies Quarterly* 40:2 (June), 185–207.

_____. 1998. "Swallowing the Bitter Pill: Sources of Popular Support for Neoliberal Reform in Latin America." *Comparative Political Studies* 31:5 (October), 539–568.

Zaller, John. 1992. *The Nature and Origins of Mass Opinion*. Cambridge: Cambridge University Press.

Contributors

CLAIRE-LISE BÉNAUD, University of New Mexico General Library

ENID BROWN, University of the West Indies, Mona

SIMON COLLIER, Vanderbilt University

SARAY CÓRDOBA G., Universidad de Costa Rica

MARSHALL C. EAKIN, Vanderbilt University

EDWARD F. FISCHER, Vanderbilt University

LEONARD FOLGARAIT, Vanderbilt University

NELLY S. GONZÁLEZ, University of Illinois

MARIAN GOSLINGA, Florida International University

MINA JANE GROTHEY, University of New Mexico

MARK L. GROVER, Brigham Young University

DAN HAZEN, Harvard College

KATHLEEN HELENESE-PAUL, University of the West Indies, St. Augustine

WENDY HUNTER, Vanderbilt University

JENNIFER JOSEPH, University of the West Indies, St. Augustine

JANE LANDERS, Vanderbilt University

ELMELINDA LARA, University of the West Indies, St. Augustine

J. FÉLIX MARTÍNEZ BARRIENTOS, Universidad Nacional Autónoma de México

MARGARET ROUSE-JONES, University of the West Indies, St. Augustine

PETER STERN, University of Massachusetts, Amherst

EMILY F. STORY, Vanderbilt University

RAFAEL E. TARRAGÓ, University of Minnesota

VÍCTOR TORRES, Universidad de Puerto Rico

COLLEEN H. TRUJILLO, University of California, Los Angeles

LESBIA VARONA, University of Miami

KURT WEYLAND, Vanderbilt University

JOHN B. WRIGHT, Brigham Young University

Conference Program

Sunday, May 30, 1999

8:00 A.M. – 4:00 P.M.	Committee Meetings
4:00 – 5:00 P.M.	Vanderbilt University Library Open House
5:30 – 7:30 P.M.	Vanderbilt University Host Reception

Monday, May 31, 1999

8:00 A.M. – 5:00 P.M.	Committee Meetings
6:00 – 8:00 P.M.	Book Dealer Reception, Country Music Hall of Fame

Tuesday, June 1, 1999

9:00 – 10:00 A.M.   **Conference Opening Session**

Richard Phillips, SALALM President, University of Florida

Paula Covington, Chair, Local Arrangements, Vanderbilt University

Paul Gherman, Vanderbilt University Librarian

Russell Hamilton, Dean, Vanderbilt University Graduate School

James Lang, Director, Vanderbilt University Center for Latin American Studies

José Toribio Medina Award   *Barbara A. Tenenbaum,* Library of Congress

Keynote Address   *Margaret Rouse-Jones,* University of the West Indies, St. Augustine, Trinidad, "Preserving a Nation's Culture: Libraries Yesterday, Today, and Tomorrow"
Rapporteur: *Darlene Waller,* University of Connecticut

10:45 A.M. – 12:00 P.M.   **Theme Panel I: Art, Music, and Identity**
Moderator: *William Luis,* Vanderbilt University
Rapporteur: *Peter S. Bushnell,* University of Florida

Simon Collier, Vanderbilt University
"The Tango and the Urban Identity of Buenos Aires,
1900–1950"

Leonard Folgarait, Vanderbilt University
"The Body as Vehicle of Political Identity in the Art of
José Clemente Orozco"

1:30 – 2:50 P.M.   **Theme Panel II: Ethnicity and Resistance**
Moderator: *Jeremy Stahl,* Middle Tennessee State
University
Rapporteur: *Eileen Oliver,* Kent State University

Murdo MacLeod, University of Florida
"Mexican Inquisition and Witchcraft: A Search for Sources"

Jane Landers, Vanderbilt University
"Searching for African Maroons in the Historical Record:
New Approaches"

Rafael Tarragó, University of Minnesota
"Dual Identities: Printed Sources for Research on the
Andean Gentry in the Kingdoms of Peru, 1537–1826"

**Theme Panel III: Famous Folk and Folk of the Fringe:
Documenting Latin American Popular Culture through
Folklore**
Moderator: *John B. Wright,* Brigham Young University
Rapporteur: *Marianne Siegmund,* Brigham Young
University

Colleen Trujillo, University of California, Los Angeles
"In Their Own Words: Folk Literature of South American
Indians"

Peter A. Stern, University of Massachusetts, Amherst
"Gringa Folklorista: Frances Toor and the Mexican Cultural
Renaissance"

John B. Wright, Brigham Young University
"Yo vivo de lo que escribo: Antonio Paredes-Candia,
Bolivian Folklorist"

Theme Panel IV: Cultural Themes
Moderator: *Russell Hamilton,* Vanderbilt University
Rapporteur: *Pamela Howard-Reguindin,* Library of
Congress, Rio de Janeiro Office

Larry Crook, University of Florida
"Maracatu: Music of Recife"

Elizabeth Ginway, University of Florida
"Researching Brazilian Science Fiction, 1909–1989"

Earl Fitz, Vanderbilt University
"Latin American Identity in an Inter-American
Context: The View from Literature"

Christopher Maurer, Vanderbilt University
"García Lorca CD-ROM Project"

3:00 – 5:30 P.M.   Tours of Andrew Jackson Mansion and Bellemeade
                     Plantation

7:30 – 9:30 P.M.   **Session I: The Withering of Latin American Newspaper
                     Microfilm Collections**
                     Moderator: *Scott Van Jacob,* Notre Dame University
                     Rapporteur: *Paul Bary,* Tulane University

                     Edmundo Flores, Library of Congress

                     Alfredo Montalvo, Editorial Inca

                     Scott Van Jacob, Notre Dame University

                     **Session II: Access and Preservation of Caribbean and
                     Latin American Film Resources**
                     Moderator: *Víctor Torres,* Universidad de Puerto Rico
                     Rapporteur: *Marian Goslinga,* Florida International
                     University

                     Film Showing

                     Víctor Torres, Universidad de Puerto Rico
                     "Los esfuerzos por recuperar y preservar el cine
                     puertorriqueño"

                     Gayle Williams, University of Georgia
                     "Latin American Screenplays in Print: A Bibliography and
                     Archival Record"

Wednesday, June 2, 1999

8:30 – 10:15 A.M.   **Workshop: Improving Research Skills: A Critique of Strategies**
Moderator: *Peter T. Johnson,* Princeton University
Rapporteur: *Ramon Abad,* Instituto Cervantes

Hortensia Calvo, Duke University
Norma Corral, University of California, Los Angeles
Harold Colson, University of California, San Diego
Paula A. Covington, Vanderbilt University
Pamela Graham, Columbia University
Peter T. Johnson, Princeton University

Theme Panel V: Oral History as a Source for Documenting Popular Culture
Moderator: *Mark Grover,* Brigham Young University
Rapporteur: *Bartley A. Burk,* Notre Dame University

Margaret Rouse-Jones, University of the West Indies, St. Augustine, and *Enid Brown,* University of the West Indies, Jamaica
"Documenting Cultural Heritage: Focusing on the Oral History Collections at the University of the West Indies"

Mark Grover, Brigham Young University
"Menchú, Stoll and Ideology: Oral History as a Document"

Jennifer Joseph, University of the West Indies, St. Augustine
"Preserving Our Heritage: The Work of Al Ramsawak, Folklorist of Trinidad and Tobago"

Theme Panel VI: The Forgotten Minority: Women in Latin America and the Caribbean
Moderator: *Marian Goslinga,* Florida International University
Rapporteur: *Laura Shedenhelm,* University of Georgia

Marian Goslinga, Florida International University
"The Search for Identity: Caribbean Women Writers Today"

Mina Jane Grothey, University of New Mexico
"The Urban Woman in the Electronic Age: A Survey"

Lesbia Varona, University of Miami
"Escritoras cubanas en los Estados Unidos"

Nelly González, University of Illinois
"A Bolivian Literary Minority: Women Writers"

10:30 A.M. – 12:00 P.M.

Theme Panel VII: Interpreting Sources for Contemporary History and Politics
Moderator: *William Canak*
Rapporteur: *Joseph C. Holub*, University of Pennsylvania

Marshall Eakin, Vanderbilt University
"Cultural Amnesia: Systematically Erasing the History of Brazilian Industrialization"

Wendy Hunter, Vanderbilt University
"Assessing Military Power and Privilege in Present-Day Latin America"

Kurt Weyland, Vanderbilt University
"Old Pitfalls and New Opportunities in Documenting Popular Political Culture in Latin America"

James Lang, Vanderbilt University
"The Potato's Path through the Library: The Untold Story"

Theme Panel VIII: On and Off the Margins: Visual Documentation of Popular Culture and Movements in Latin America
Moderator: *Beverly Karno,* Howard Karno Books, Inc.
Rapporteur: *Nancy Hallock,* Harvard University

Russ Davidson, University of New Mexico
"Art in the Service of the Nation: Populism, National Identity, and Mexico's Taller de Gráfica Popular, 1937–1977"

Sam Slick, University of Southern Mississippi
"The Poster in Latin American Politics and Society, 1975–2000"

Beverly Karno, Howard Karno Books, Inc.
"Perverts, Jailbirds, Nude Ladies, and Mean Kids: The Art of the Comic (Book)"

1:30 – 3:15 P.M.

Workshop on Electronic Resources: Mining Lexis-Nexis Academic Universe for Latin American Topics
Moderator: *Harold Colson,* University of California, San Diego
Rapporteur: *Sara M. Sánchez,* University of Miami

Harold Colson, University of California, San Diego
Mina Jane Grothey, University of New Mexico
Eudora Loh, University of California, Los Angeles
Orchid Mazurkiewicz, Arizona State University
Beth P. Bigman, CIS / LEXIS-NEXIS

Theme Panel IX: Shifting Frontiers, Permeable Borders, and Migrating Records: Documenting Change
Moderator: *Myra Appel,* University of California, Riverside
Rapporteur: *Benita Weber Vasallo,* Inter-American Development Bank

Myra Appel, University of California, Riverside
"Preserving the Cultural Record: COPAR and Latin American Sources"

Adecelia X. López Roblero, Colegio de la Frontera Sur
"La Colección Frontera Sur (FROSUR): una herramienta para repensar la realidad"

Alfonso J. Vijil, Libros Latinos / Libros Centroamericanos
"Five or None: William Walker in Nicaragua"

Emily Story, Vanderbilt University
"Unintended Outcomes: William Walker and the Emergence of Nicaraguan Nationalism"

3:45 – 5:45 P.M.

Theme Panel X: Indigenous Identity and Politics
Moderator: *Wendy Hunter,* Vanderbilt University
Rapporteur: *Orchid Mazurkiewicz,* Arizona State University

Edward F. Fischer, Vanderbilt University
"Articulating Local Concerns in a Global Context: Recent Mayan Scholarship and Research on Identity Politics"

Beth Conklin, Vanderbilt University
"Identity Politics and the Changing Face of Indian-State Relations in Latin America"

Annabeth Headrick, Vanderbilt University
"Ancestral Identities at Teotihuacan"

Theme Panel XI: Documenting Identity
Moderator: *Cecilia Puerto,* San Diego State University
Rapporteur: *Pamela Graham,* Columbia University

J. Félix Martínez Barrientos, Universidad Nacional Autónoma de México
"Centros de documentación y bases de datos sobre asuntos de la mujer y género en América Latina"

Saray Córdoba González, Universidad de Costa Rica
"El papel de la información en la construcción de la identidad cultural"

Clara Chu, University of California, Los Angeles
"Documenting the Chinese in Mexicali: A View from Within and Without"

Gloria Sánchez, Publicaciones Aztecas
"The Present Situation of Indigenous Groups in Chiapas"

6:00 – 7:00 P.M.   **SALALM Authors Workshop**
Barbara Valk, University of California, Los Angeles
Colleen Trujillo, University of California, Los Angeles

Thursday, June 3, 1999

9:00 – 10:30 A.M.   **Session I: Issues in the Organization of Information**
Rapporteur: *Elizabeth Steinhagen,* University of New Mexico

Claire-Lise Bénaud, University of New Mexico
"Considerations for Outsourcing Cataloging"

Cecilia Sercan, Cornell University
"New (and Hot) Issues in Cataloging"

Session II: Overcrowding in the Northeast: Off-Site Storage, Weeding, and Collection Development
Moderator: *Denise Hibay,* New York Public Library
Rapporteur: *Orchid Mazurkiewicz,* Arizona State University

César Rodríguez, Yale University
"Off-Site Library Facilities: Selling the Idea to Library Patrons"

David Block, Cornell University
"Remote Storage: How Did It Come to This?"

Dan Hazen, Harvard University
"The Harvard Depository: Remote Storage as a Way of Life"

Theme Panel XII: The English-Speaking Caribbean: Documenting Aspects of Popular Music and Cultural Traditions
Moderator: *Richard Phillips,* University of Florida
Rapporteur: *Sharon Moynahan,* University of New Mexico

Kathleen Helenese-Paul, University of the West Indies, St. Augustine
"Pan, Parang and Chutney: Music and Popular Cultural Forms in Trinidad and Tobago"

Elmelinda Lara, University of the West Indies,
St. Augustine
"The Way We Live: Fetes and Festivals of the Caribbean"

11:00 A.M. – 12:00 P.M.   **Town Hall**
Moderator: *Richard Phillips,* University of Florida
Rapporteur: *John Wright,* Brigham Young University

2:00 – 4:00 P.M.   **Conference Closing Session and Final Executive Board Meeting**